Elbląg

Olsztyn

WARMIA, MAZURIA AND BIAŁYSTOK REGION

Białystok

Płock

Warsaw

Łódź

MAZOVIA AND THE LUBLIN REGION

Radom

Lublin

Częstochowa

Zamość

MAŁOPOLSKA (LESSER POLAND)

Krakow

Rzeszów

Gdańsk
Pages 236–255

Warmia, Mazuria and Białystok Region
Pages 280–295

0 km   50

0 miles   50

Mazovia and the Lublin Region
Pages 114–131

Warsaw
Pages 62–109

DK EYEWITNESS TRAVEL

Poland

Main Contributors **Teresa Czerniewicz-Umer**
Małgorzata Omilanowska, Jerzy S. Majewski

DK Penguin Random House

Produced By Wydawnictwo Wiedza i Życie, Warsaw

Contributors Małgorzata Omilanowska, Jerzy S. Majewski

Illustrators Andrzej Wielgosz, Bohdan Wróblewski, Piotr Zubrzycki, Paweł Mistewicz

Photographers Krzysztof Chojnacki; Wojciech Czerniewicz, Stanisława Jabłońska, Piotr Jamski, Euzebiusz Niemiec

Cartographers Ewa i Jan Pachniewiczowie, Maria Wojciechowska, Dariusz Osuch (D. Osuch i spółka)

Editor Teresa Czerniewicz-Umer

Dtp Designers Paweł Kamiński, Paweł Pasternak

Proofreader Bożena Leszkowicz

Technical Editor Anna Kożurno-Królikowska

Designer Ewa Roguska i zespół

Cover Design Paweł Kamiński

Translators Mark Cole, Marian Dragon, Teresa Levitt, Joanna Pillans, Vera Rich

Edited and typeset by Book Creation Services Ltd, London

Printed in Malaysia

First American Edition, 2001

18 19 20 21 10 9 8 7 6 5 4 3 2 1

Published in the United States by DK Publishing, 345 Hudson Street, New York, New York 10014

Reprinted with revisions 2004, 2007, 2010, 2013, 2015, 2018

Copyright © 2001, 2018 Dorling Kindersley Limited, London

A Penguin Random House Company

Published in the UK by Dorling Kindersley Limited.

A catalog record for this book is available from the Library of Congress.

ISSN 1542-1554

ISBN 978-1-46546-902-1

Throughout this book, floors are numbered in accordance with local Polish usage; ie. the "first" floor is the floor above ground level.

MIX
Paper from responsible sources
FSC™ C018179
www.fsc.org

Introducing Poland

Warsaw Area By Area

Summer in the mountains of the Tatra National Park

The information in this DK Eyewitness Travel Guide is checked regularly.

Every effort has been made to ensure that this book is as up-to-date as possible at the time of going to press. Some details, however, such as telephone numbers, opening hours, prices, gallery hanging arrangements and travel information are liable to change. The publishers cannot accept responsibility for any consequences arising from the use of this book, nor for any material on third party websites, and cannot guarantee that any website address in this book will be a suitable source of travel information. We value the views and suggestions of our readers very highly. Please write to: Publisher, DK Eyewitness Travel Guides, Dorling Kindersley, 80 Strand, London, WC2R 0RL, UK, or email: travelguides@dk.com.

◀ **Title page** Solina Lake in the Bieszczady Mountains   **Front cover image** A street in Warsaw's Old Town leading to the Royal Castle
Back cover image Wooden mountain huts in the Gąsienicowa Valley, Tatra National Park

Contents

Colourful town houses surrounding the market square in Kalisz

Statues of the apostles on the railings of the Church of Saints Peter and Paul, Kraków

Cathedral of St John, Warsaw

HOW TO USE THIS GUIDE

The detailed information and tips given in this guide will help you to get the most out of your visit to Poland. *Introducing Poland* maps the country and sets it in its historical and cultural context. First is an area-by-area chapter on Warsaw, followed by eight regional chapters, including Krakow and Gdańsk. Main sights are described using maps, photographs and illustrations. Restaurant and hotel recommendations can be found in the *Travellers' Needs* section, together with information about shopping and entertainment. The *Survival Guide* has tips on everything from transport to making a phone call, as well as other practical matters.

Poland Area by Area

Poland has been divided into six main areas, each one identified by its own colour code; the cities of Warsaw, Krakow and Gdańsk also have their own chapters and colour codes. On the inside front cover is a general map of the country showing these areas. All the most interesting places to visit are located on the Regional Map in each chapter.

Each area can be easily identified by its colour-coded thumb tab.

1 Introduction
This section describes the character and history of each area, highlighting its development over the centuries and what it has to offer the visitor today.

2 Regional Map
This shows the road network and provides an illustrated overview of the whole region. The most interesting places to visit are numbered, and there are useful tips on getting around the region by car and public transport.

3 Detailed Information
All the important towns and other places to visit are described individually. They are listed in order and follow the numbering shown on the Regional Map. Detailed information is given about the most important sights.

The Visitors' Checklist provides practical information about transport, opening times, events and the closing dates of places of particular interest.

4 Main Towns
All the main towns have an individual section where the museums, monuments and other places of interest are listed. All the sights of major interest are located on the town map

The town map shows the main roads, stations and tourist offices.

5 Street-by-Street Map
This gives a bird's-eye view of the key areas of interest in the main towns and cities with photographs and captions describing the sights.

Stars indicate the sights that no visitor should miss.

A suggested route for a walk covers the more interesting streets in the area.

6 Major Sights
These are given two full pages. There are cutaways or reconstructions of historic buildings, maps of national parks with information about trails and facilities available, and there are floorplans of the major museums. Photographs highlight the most interesting features.

Stars highlight the details that no visitor should miss.

INTRODUCING POLAND

DISCOVERING POLAND

The following itineraries have been designed to take in as many of Poland's highlights as possible, while keeping long-distance travel manageable. First come three two-day tours: the first covers the capital Warsaw, a boisterous modern metropolis, while the others take in romantic, monument-studded Krakow and the evocative, history-soaked port city of Gdańsk. Next comes a two-week tour of the whole country that includes

everything from vibrant modern cities like Poznań and Wrocław to quaint medieval Toruń and magical Lublin, plus stunning natural landscapes and the snow-capped Tatra Mountains of the far south. Ideas for extending your stay include the tranquil, unspoilt Mazurian Lakes and the hauntingly bare Bieszczady Mountains. Pick, combine and follow your favourite tours, or simply dip in and out and be inspired.

Tatra National Park
Zakopane, seen here from the top of Mount Gubałówka, in the Tatra National Park, is Poland's foremost winter resort. However, it has much to offer all year round, with great walking trails and magnificent scenery.

Two-Week Grand Tour of Poland

- Spend a day exploring the imposing riverside **fortress of Malbork**, former capital of the Teutonic Knights.

- Stroll the streets of charming **Toruń**, a laid-back university town packed with an engaging jumble of medieval, Renaissance and Baroque buildings.

- Study the face of contemporary Poland in **Wrocław**, an arresting historic city that is the commercial and cultural capital of the southwest.

- Experience exhilarating mountain scenery and a rich choice of outdoor activities with a visit to the **Tatra National Park**.

- Spend an evening enjoying the alfresco cafés on the main square in **Zamość** – Poland at its most Italianate.

- Immerse yourself in the magical Old Town atmosphere of **Lublin**, eastern Poland's most evocative city.

◀ A 19th-century depiction of Plac Zamkowy in Warsaw, dominated by Zygmunt's Column

Old Town in Toruń
The university town of Toruń boasts the delightful Old Market Square, which is a popular meeting place for locals and visitors. Among the notable buildings on this pedestrianized plaza is the Town Hall, parts of which date back to the 14th century.

Key

━━ Two-Week Grand
Tour of Poland

Wrocław Cathedral
The Cathedral of St John the Baptist, with its distinctive spires, was erected over several centuries, damaged in World War II and subsequently rebuilt.

Two Days in Warsaw

Poland's vibrant capital is a fast-changing city with a wealth of compelling sights. The centre is easily walkable, and there are also good metro and tram services.

- **Arriving** Warsaw has two airports: one at Okęcie, accessed by fast suburban train; the other at Modlin. The latter, mainly used by budget airlines, is linked to the city by bus. Warsaw is also served by a good train network.

Day 1
Morning Begin with a tour of the **Royal Castle** (see pp70–71), whose opulent interiors recall the glories of the Polish past. From here, dive into the beautifully restored alleys and squares of the Old Town, calling in at the **Cathedral of St John** (see p72) before entering the **Old Town Square** (see p73). Follow this with a visit to **The Barbican and City Walls** (see p73).

Afternoon Head south along **Krakowskie Przedmieście** (see pp80–81), the elegant avenue that runs past the University and the **Church of St Anne** (see p81). Detour west from here to visit either **Zachęta** (see p94), housing Poland's finest contemporary art gallery, or the **Ethnographical Museum** (see p95), with its colourful folk costumes. Unwind with a stroll through the **Saxon Gardens** (see p94), or spend the evening in the restaurants and bars of **Nowy Świat** (see p84).

Day 2
Morning Start the day at the iconic **Palace of Culture and Science** (see p95), a Stalinist-era building that contains a viewing platform and several cafés. Admire the extensive collections of the **National Museum** (see pp86–7) before taking a breather at one of the cafés on **Plac Trzech Krzyży** (see p85).

Afternoon Head south on foot or by bus along **Aleje Ujazdowskie** (see p85) to

Łazienki Palace (see pp100–101), which features a beautiful outdoor space filled with ornamental gardens and lakes. Continue southwards by bus along Aleje Ujazdowskie to **Wilanów Palace** (see pp102–3), which is packed to the gills with fine art.

To extend your trip...
Get to grips with Poland's World War II history by visiting the commemorative sites west of the centre. Start at the **POLIN Museum of the History of Polish Jews** (see p97), then follow the **Trail of Jewish Martyrdom and Struggle** (see p97) to the **Umschlagplatz Monument** (see pp96–7). Finish up with a visit to the superb **Warsaw Uprising Museum** (see p98).

Two Days in Krakow

The former royal capital of Poland boasts a vast array of memorable sights, from the Main Market Square to the Wawel Castle palace complex.

- **Arriving** John Paul II Airport, at Balice, is linked by train to Krakow's main railway station, which is also served by trains from Warsaw, Gdańsk and various European cities.

Day 1
Morning Start with a circuit of the **Main Market Square** (see pp136–7) before exploring

The spendid interior of the Church of St Mary, Krakow

the covered stalls of the Renaissance **Cloth Hall** (see p137). Visit the innovative **Rynek Underground** museum (see p137), then head to the sumptuously decorated **Church of St Mary** (see pp138–9); try to be there by 11:50am sharp to observe the ritual unveiling of Veit Stoss's altar.

Afternoon Stroll north along **Ulica Floriańska** (see p140) in the direction of the **Barbican** (see p139), before heading west through leafy Planty Park towards **Plac Szczepański** (see p140). Delve into inspirational international art exhibitions with a visit to the **Szołaysky House** (see p141). Walk south through the atmospheric University Quarter to the **Collegium Maius** (see p141) and the splendid Baroque **Church of St Anne** (see p141). Finish up at the **Franciscan Church** (see p142), famous for its beautiful Art Nouveau frescoes by Stanisław Wyspiański.

The manicured gardens of Wilanów Palace, on the outskirts of Warsaw

Day 2

Morning Walk south from the Main Market Square along **Ulica Grodzka** (see p142) to **The Wawel** (see pp144–5). View the royal tombs at the **Cathedral** (see pp148–9) and climb the bell tower before taking a tour of the **Wawel Royal Castle** (see pp146–7). Admire the stunning views of the Vistula river from the ramparts of the citadel.

Afternoon A short walk south of the Wawel is the bohemian Kazimierz Quarter, offering plenty of restaurants and cafés that are ideal for lunch. Explore the multicultural past of this historic quarter with a visit to the **Old Synagogue** (see p150), now a museum of Jewish life; next, admire the Gothic **Church of Corpus Christi** (see p150). For the evening, stick around in Kazimierz to enjoy the numerous bars and clubs of this buzzing district.

To extend your trip…
A 90-minute bus journey from the city of Krakow is the **Auschwitz-Birkenau Memorial and Museum** (see p164–7), which was established as a memorial site by former inmates of this notorious camp. Allow time for a three-hour tour of Auschwitz led by expert guides before exploring the vast, numbing expanse of Birkenau, a short way away.

The Cathedral at The Wawel, in Krakow, with its distinctive clock tower

Some of the buildings of Gdańsk's Polish Maritime Museum, on the River Motława

Two Days in Gdańsk

With its canals, historic mansions and Gothic warehouses, the Baltic port of Gdańsk is an evocative city. Also worth a visit are the neighbouring cities of Sopot, with its famous beach, and Gdynia, with its maritime attractions.

- **Arriving** Gdańsk's airport at Rębiechowo is linked to the city centre by bus. Trains from Warsaw arrive at Gdańsk main railway station, a 15-minute walk from the Old Town.

Day 1

Morning Enter the Old Town via the **Highland** or **Golden Gates** (see p248), the traditional starting points of the processional route known as the Royal Way. This route leads past a sequence of fabulously restored merchants' houses, the most famous of which is the **Uphagen House** (see p249), which boasts splendid Baroque interiors. Further down the street, the monumental **Church of St Mary** (see pp244–5) is the largest brick-built medieval church in Europe; nearby **Artus Court** (see p250) is a 15th-century club for aristocratic merchants.

Afternoon Cross the Green Bridge to **Spichlerze Island** (see p252), an atmospheric area of riverside warehouses. Return to the west bank of the Motława and follow the river north to the **Gdańsk Crane** (see p243), nowadays part of the multimedia **National Maritime Museum** (see p251). From here it's a short stroll to the **Raduna Canal** area (see pp240–41), a leafy district of churches and mills. Those who are interested in recent history should visit the **Monument to the Shipyard Workers** (see p241), commemorating the brutally repressed strikes of 1970. Nearby, the **European Solidarity Centre** (see p241) is a museum exploring the history of Solidarity, the Polish trade union and civil resistance movement.

Day 2

Morning Take a boat or bus trip (30 mins) to **Westerplatte** (see p255), a fortress at the mouth of the Vistula river where the first shots of World War II were fired. If time allows, visit the nearby 16th-century **Wisłoujście Fortress** (see p255). After returning to central Gdańsk, take a suburban train (20 mins) to **Sopot** (see p269), a prosperous seaside town famous for its long sandy beach. Full of cafés and restaurants, Sopot is a good place to pause for lunch.

Afternoon Stroll along Sopot's 512-m (1,680-ft) pier before deciding between an afternoon on the nearby beach or a trip to **Gdynia** (another 20 minutes by suburban train; see p269), where the northern pier plays host to two floating museum-ships and a popular aquarium.

The famous Proserpine Fountain in the Old Market Square, Poznań

Two-Week Grand Tour of Poland

- **Airports** The best way to enjoy this tour is to arrive at and depart from Warsaw. Bear in mind, however, that you can also arrive at and depart from Gdańsk, Poznań, Wrocław or Krakow airports, and pick up the circuit described below from a different starting point.

- **Transport** Public transport is time-consuming in Poland, and although this itinerary can be tackled using inter-city trains, travel is much quicker by car.

Days 1 and 2: Warsaw
Follow the two-day city itinerary on page 12.

Day 3: Gdańsk
Travel north from Warsaw across the green plains of northern Poland to the port city of **Gdańsk** *(see pp236–55)*. Spend the afternoon and evening exploring Gdańsk's historic heart by following part of the first day of the two-day city itinerary on page 13.

Day 4: Malbork
Take a day trip from Gdańsk to the town of **Malbork** *(see pp270–71)*, site of Poland's most complete medieval fortress complex. Built in the 13th century by the Teutonic Knights, it served as the capital of their independent state. The Grand Master's Palace, Cathedral and Castle Museum all lie within the walled precinct. With a son-et-lumière show lighting up the fortress in the evening, there's plenty here to fill a day.

> **To extend your trip…**
> Spend a day or two in the resort of **Mikołajki**, 250 km (155 miles) east of Gdańsk, at the heart of the **Great Mazurian Lakes** *(see pp290–91)*. You can take a steamboat trip on Lake Śniardwy, hike to the wild swan reserve at Łuknajno, or simply stroll beside the chic yachting marina or relax in a lakeside café.

Day 5: Toruń
From Gdańsk, travel south along the Vistula river to the partly walled university town of **Toruń** *(see pp276–9)*. Spend the afternoon strolling around the centre, which is packed with medieval churches and Baroque townhouses, taking time to visit the house museum devoted to Toruń's most famous son, the astronomer Nicolaus Copernicus. Be sure to stock up on *piernik*, the local gingerbread, at one of the town's bakeries.

Day 6: Poznań
Travel from Toruń to the vibrant commercial and cultural city of **Poznań** *(see pp220–25)*. Begin an afternoon's sightseeing on the famously well-preserved market square, which is edged by brightly coloured merchants' houses and features an ebullient, Italianate town hall. Have your picture taken in front of the Proserpine Fountain before proceeding to the National Museum, which contains what is arguably Poland's finest art collection outside Warsaw and Krakow. If time allows, stroll round the riverside quarter of Ostrów Tumski, home to Poznań's twin-towered cathedral as well as numerous smaller churches.

Day 7: Wrocław
Drive south from Poznań to **Wrocław** *(see pp194–203)*, the fast-developing capital of Lower Silesia. Wrocław's market square, Poland's second largest, focuses on an arresting Gothic town hall. Visit the extraordinary **Panorama of Racławice** *(see p195)*, a huge circular painting celebrating an 18th-century battle, then head to the quaint Ostrów Tumski cathedral quarter, which is accessed by a landmark cast-iron bridge.

Day 8: Auschwitz-Birkenau Memorial and Museum
From Wrocław, travel east, towards Krakow. Stop off en route at the town of Oświęcim, site of the **Auschwitz-Birkenau Memorial and Museum** *(see p164–7)*. This notorious former World War II concentration camp is on the eastern outskirts of Oświęcim; the much larger Birkenau, where the Nazis committed mass murder on an industrial scale, is a further 3 km (2 miles) to the east. Allow several hours to get the most from your visit, and book tickets in advance.

The rocky shore of Lake Śniardwy, one of the Great Mazurian Lakes

Stairs leading to the Wieliczka Salt Mine, a UNESCO World Heritage Site

Day 9: Krakow
Spend a day in Krakow, choosing one of the itineraries from the Two Days in Krakow tour on pages 12–13.

> **To extend your trip...**
> Spend an extra day in Krakow to visit the remarkable man-made caverns of the **Wieliczka Salt Mine** *(see p168)*, a short suburban train ride to the southeast of the city. The remaining half-day in Krakow can be spent admiring the extensive art and history collections of the **National Museum** *(see p142)*. Do not miss the modern paintings on the top floor.

Day 10: Zakopane
From Krakow, travel through increasingly imposing hills to mountain-ringed **Zakopane** *(see pp170–71)*, gateway to the Tatra National Park. Take a walk along ul. Krupówki, the animated pedestrianized street that runs through the heart of this mountain resort, and admire the many examples of traditional timber architecture in the adjoining lanes and alleys.

Day 11: Tatra National Park
Spend the day in and around Zakopane, enjoying the impressive scenery of the **Tatra National Park** *(see pp170–71)*. You can either take the cable car to Kasprowy Wierch and follow one of the popular high-altitude hiking trails, or travel by funi-

cular up Gubałówka Hill, famous for its sweeping views of the park's highest peaks. An alternative way to spend the day is by floating in leisurely fashion between wooded hills on a log-built craft as part of the **Dunajec Raft Ride** *(see pp172–3)*.

Day 12: Zamość
The long journey from Zakopane to **Zamość** *(see pp130–31)* takes you through varied and unspoilt rural countryside. The compact Renaissance town of Zamość is easy to explore, and a late afternoon or early evening stroll around the main square conveys a strong historical flavour. If you have time for one additional attraction, visit the Polish Army Museum, in the former arsenal, which contains a stirring account of Poland's military history.

> **To extend your trip...**
> It will take two days or more to do justice to the beauty of the **Bieszczady Mountains** *(see pp174–5)*, in Poland's far southeastern corner. Topped by bare grassy ridges, these are among the most haunting highland landscapes that Poland has to offer. The village of Wetlina is a good base from which to tackle the peaks.

Day 13: Lublin
It takes only a couple of hours to travel from Zamość to **Lublin** *(see pp126–7)*, allowing you almost a full day of sightseeing in the main city of eastern Poland. Huddled on a hill,

Lublin's gated Old Town is a fascinating warren of alleys, churches and piazzas. Be sure to visit the castle, with its Holy Trinity Chapel decorated with early 15th-century frescoes. Afterwards, take a stroll along the elegant 19th-century boulevard of Krakowskie Przedmieście, or head to the **Majdanek State Museum** *(see p127)*, one of Poland's most harrowing Holocaust memorial sites.

Day 14: Kazimierz Dolny
Return to Warsaw via some of eastern Poland's most intriguing small-town sights. Stop first at **Kozłówka** *(see p128)*, northwest of Lublin, where a museum of Socialist Realist art recalls the absurdities of Communist Poland. Next, travel east to **Puławy** *(see p125)*, where the former palace of the Czartoryski family is surrounded by a beautiful landscaped park. Reserve the most time for **Kazimierz Dolny** *(see p125)*, a beautifully preserved 15th-century trading town beneath a semi-ruined castle.

> **To extend your trip...**
> Take a couple of days to travel to and from the **Białowieża National Park** *(see p295)*, where a large stretch of dense virgin forest is home to one of Europe's last remaining bison populations. There are numerous hiking trails to follow, and the opportunity for a horse-and-cart trip through the forest.

A hiking trail in the Bieszczady Mountains

Putting Poland on the Map

Poland covers an area of 312,685 sq km (120,696 sq miles) and is located in the centre of Europe. It borders Lithuania, Belarus and Ukraine to the east, Slovakia and the Czech Republic to the south, and Germany to the west. In the north, Poland's coastline stretches for 528 km (330 miles) on the Baltic Sea and borders Kaliningrad, an enclave of Russia. Poland has a population of 38.5 million, making it the eighth most populated country in Europe. The capital, Warsaw, has over 1.7 million inhabitants.

Baltic Sea

Władysławowo

Gdynia
Gdańsk
Lech Wałęsa
Gdańsk

Słupsk

Tczew

Koszalin
Bytów
POMORSKIE
Starogard
Gdański

Bobolice
Biały Bór
Czersk

ZACHODNIO POMORSKIE
Człuchów
Grudziąd

Solidarity
Szczecin-
Goleniów

Szczecin
Złotów

Bydgoszcz

Piła
Bydgoszcz
Toruń

Schwedt/
Oder
Dobiegniew
Człopa
KUJAWSKO-POMORSKIE

Wittstock

Rogoźno
Inowrocław

Oranienburg
Gorzów
Wielkopolski
Oborniki
Gniezno

Berlin
Frankfurt
(Oder)
Łagów
Poznań-Ławica
Poznań

Potsdam
Wolsztyn
WIELKOPOLSKIE
Konin

Luckenwalde
Zielona Góra
Leszno
Jarocin

Coswig
Cottbus
LUBUSKIE
Kalisz

GERMANY
Żagań
Głogów
Ostrów
Wielkopolski

Lubin
Wieruszów

Leipzig
Görlitz
Legnica
Oleśnica

Dresden
Wrocław-Copernicus
Wrocław

Jelenia Góra
DOLNOŚLĄSKIE
Kluczbork

Liberec
Wałbrzych
OPOLSKIE
Opole
Lublin

Hradec
Králové
Kędzierzyn
Koźle

Świtavy
Rybnik

CZECH REPUBLIC
Ostrava

Olomouc

Brno

Piestany

Warta
Odra

Europe

North Sea
NORWAY
SWEDEN
ESTONIA
LATVIA
LITHUANIA
DENMARK
UNITED KINGDOM
NETHERLANDS
POLAND
BELARUS
BELGIUM
GERMANY
CZECH REPUBLIC
UKRAINE
FRANCE
SWITZ.
SLOVAKIA
AUSTRIA
HUNGARY
SLOV.
CROATIA
ROMANIA
BOSNIA HERZ.
SERBIA
ITALY
MONTEN.
BULGARIA
KOS.
MAC.
ALBANIA
GREECE
TURKEY
Atlantic Ocean
SPAIN

For keys to symbols *see back flap*

A PORTRAIT OF POLAND

For over a thousand years, Poland has ranked among the major civilizations of Europe, with a record of historical and cultural achievement that can match any on the continent. The country has a constellation of vibrant cities, including progressive Warsaw and the former royal capital, Krakow. It offers diverse landscapes that encompass beautiful lakelands, dramatic mountains and a wealth of well-preserved folk architecture in villages and towns across the country.

Although it is centred in the plains of Central Europe, Poland has a varied landscape. Alpine scenery predominates in the Tatra Mountains along the country's southern border, while the north is dominated by lakelands, which contrast with the landscape of the Baltic coast. For those who like unspoiled natural scenery, there are areas of primeval forests in Białowieża and extensive marshlands along the banks of the River Biebrza which are a haven for many rare bird and plant species. About 30 per cent of the area of Poland is woodland, including a number of vast forests covering more than 1,000 sq km (390 sq miles). Most of these consist of coniferous trees and mixed woodland, but there are also many forests of deciduous trees, mainly oak and hornbeam, or beech.

Many areas of great natural beauty are protected as national parks or reserves.

Mountain lovers can make use of the well-developed infrastructure of hostels and other shelters, such as those found in the Beskid Sądecki or the Tatra Mountains; the more adventurous can explore the unfrequented and almost inaccessible Beskid Niski or Bieszczady mountain ranges. All areas have clearly marked hiking trails and well-equipped shelters *(schroniska)*. The countless lakes of Warmia and Mazuria, areas known as the Land of a Thousand Lakes *(Kraina Tysiąca Jezior)* are a haven for watersports enthusiasts, as are the waters of Pomerania and Wielkopolska. The lakes are popular with canoeists and in summer are dotted with rowing and sailing boats.

The Bzura, one of Poland's many unspoilt rivers

◄ A wooden chapel in the Beskid Niski mountains of Małopolska

A summer's day on a sandy Baltic beach

Population and Religion

Poland's inhabitants, who number just over 37 million, all but constitute a single ethnic group, with minorities accounting for less than 4 per cent of the population. The largest minorities are Germans, Belarussians and Ukrainians. Many Silesians (in the southwest) and Kashubians (in the north) identify themselves as belonging to a separate nation, although they are generally regarded as Poles by their fellow citizens.

Lacemaker from Koniakowo

The vast majority of Poles are Catholic, but large regions of the country, such as Cieszyn Silesia, have a substantial Protestant population, and followers of other denominations are also widely dispersed. In the east of the country there are many Orthodox Christians; here, religious denomination does not necessarily coincide with ethnic identity, although Belarussians tend to be Orthodox while Ukrainians belong to the Greek Catholic (Uniate) Church. In the Białystok region there are villages where Catholics, Orthodox Christians and Muslims – the descendants of Tatar settlers – live side by side. As in Spain and Ireland, the fact that the majority of the population is Catholic continues to exert a major influence on the moral values of the country, as well as on its political life. An example of this is the many debates in the Sejm (the lower house of the Polish parliament) that have alternately limited and liberalized the right to abortion. For over a decade, Polish politics have been dominated by right-wing and centre-right political movements, with the former emphasizing patriotism, social and cultural conservatism, as well as a certain amount of anti-European Union sentiment. Meanwhile, the centre-right movements take a more liberal approach to domestic and foreign affairs.

Religious belief is outwardly expressed by a deep reverence for religious symbols and rituals. Wayside crosses and shrines

Visitors strolling from the pump room at the spa of Polanica-Zdrój

to the saints or the Virgin Mary, to whom miraculous powers have been ascribed, add charm to the Polish countryside. The main religious festivals – Christmas, Easter, Corpus Christi and Assumption, as well as All Saints' Day, when almost everyone in Poland, regardless of their religious denomination, visits the graves of relatives – are solemnly observed. An unusual cult surrounds the Virgin. For centuries, believers from all over Poland and further afield have made the pilgrimage to the image of the Black Madonna in Częstochowa *(see pp160–1)*. Another famous pilgrimage is made by Orthodox Christians to the holy mountain of Grabarka *(see p295)*.

Although most of the country's Jewish citizens were murdered in the death camps established by the Nazi German occupiers during World War II, Poland remains a major historic centre of Jewish culture to this day.

Young men in white and red robes lead a Corpus Christi procession

Cultural Variety and Shifting Borders

Magnificent buildings can be seen throughout Poland. Not all of them, however, belong to Polish culture, since the country's frontiers have changed many times over the centuries. A particularly important change came at the end of World War II, when the Allies approved a westward shift of Poland's borders. As a result, the inhabitants of the eastern areas were resettled, and many were sent to the western regions, formerly inhabited by Germans – who were in turn displaced.

Restored market square of the Old Town, Wrocław

A poster by Maria Pałasińska dedicated to Solidarity

The legacy of more than 100 years of partition rule is still visible in Poland's cultural landscape today *(see p54)*. Russian, Prussian and Austrian administrations left their mark not only on rural and urban architecture but also on the customs and mentality of the Polish people.

Democratic Change and Economic Development

The fall of Communism in Poland came about largely thanks to the efforts of the trade union Solidarity (Solidarność), which was founded in 1980 but forced to go underground after the imposition of martial law. When the democratic opposition won the elections to the Sejm and the Senate in 1989, Poland again became a country with a parliamentary democracy and a market economy. This was important enough in itself, but it had wider implications too: by tackling its inefficient, crisis-ridden socialist economy, Poland had set the standard for economic reform in Central and Eastern Europe as a whole. Many Polish industries were privatized, and the drastic reforms that were carried through over a number of years accelerated Poland's GDP to make it the fastest-growing economy in Europe. However, such economic shock treatment did not come without serious

Logo of the Polish stock exchange

consequences. It became difficult for the majority of Poland's key industries to cope in the global free-market economy. Heavy industry and shipbuilding, along with the previously flourishing textile industry, were particularly badly hit. An ongoing systematic programme of coal-mine closure forced former mineworkers to look for work elsewhere. Not surprisingly, this brought considerable social and economic problems in its wake.

The archaic farming system is another candidate for restructuring. Polish farming is still based on traditional family smallholdings consisting of no more than a few acres of land. It is seriously under-mechanized and requires a disproportionate amount of manpower.

Session of the Sejm, the lower house of the Polish parliament

The Pazim, the second-tallest building in Szczecin

A fundamental part of the reform process was Poland's drive to join Western military and economic structures. In 1999, Poland became a member of NATO, and then, in 2004, it joined the European Union. This required harmonization of the Polish legal and economic systems with those of the EU countries, providing a further powerful incentive to change. Unemployment and lack of opportunities were keenly felt in former industrial towns and large swathes of the Polish countryside. Emigration provided an outlet for these frustrations, with somewhere between two and three million Poles living and working in other European countries by the dawn of the 21st century. However, Poland's economy fared better than most others following the financial crisis of 2008. Its cities saw dynamic growth, encouraging some migrants to return.

Political and economic changes have had their impact on Poland's towns and cities. Old buildings are being renovated, attention is being paid to the environment, new shops have appeared, and large out-of-town supermarkets and modern petrol (gas) stations have sprung up. New buildings – though not always architecturally distinctive – are going up everywhere. Market squares and main streets in many Polish towns have been pedestrianized. In many of the old towns that suffered damage during World War II – including Szczecin, Kołobrzeg, Głogów and Elbląg – buildings are now being reconstructed. Smaller towns, too – swelled by sprawling apartment housing after the war – are now acquiring more traditional buildings. Nonetheless, the vast concrete housing developments typical of the Communist era still dominate many Polish townscapes.

Many modern public buildings – mainly office blocks – are being built, too. Much of the new development is centred on the capital, Warsaw, although commercial investment is a major factor in other cities, among them Krakow, Katowice, the Baltic conurbation of Gdańsk, Sopot and Gdynia, and Wrocław, Poznań and Łódź as well.

These developments, as well as monuments attesting to Poland's stormy history, demonstrate how far the country has come from its war-ravaged state. Poland once again plays a role on the global stage of sport, culture and politics. Despite these Western developments, the population's sense of community and hospitality remains rooted in Eastern values, making a trip to the country a fascinating experience.

The privatized Grupa Kęty SA metalworks

The Landscape of Poland

Poland's landscape is spectacularly varied. The south of the country is bounded by mountain ranges which, the further north you travel, gradually turn into areas punctuated by hills and low-lying ancient forests. Northern Poland, an area of great natural beauty, has been shaped by a succession of glaciers that moved southwards from Scandinavia. National parks and reserves have been established in many areas. The central regions of the country, consisting of lowlands, merge into picturesque lakelands and coastal plains.

Fauna of Poland

The most typical Polish wildlife – including wild boar, deer and hare – is to be found in mixed and deciduous forests. Some species, such as bison and capercaillie, are found almost nowhere else in Europe. In the Carpathian and Sudety mountains, bears and lynxes may be seen.

European Bison

Mountains

Nutcracker

The Tatra Mountains *(see pp170–71)* are the highest in Central Europe. Though covering a small area, they provide breathtaking alpine scenery. The High Tatras *(Tatry Wysokie)* are mainly granite, with jagged, rocky peaks. At 2,499 m (8,200 ft) above sea level, Rysy is the highest peak in Poland. The Western Tatras *(Tatry Zachodnie)*, consisting of sedimentary rock and crystalline shale, are inhabited by such rare animals as brown bears, marmots and chamois.

Lakeland Scenery

The lakelands that cover much of northern Poland consist of picturesque moraine woodland and thousands of lakes. The largest and most scenic are the Great Mazurian Lakes, in a district known as the Land of a Thousand Lakes *(Kraina Tysiąca Jezior)*. Abounding in forests, marshes and peat bogs, they are a haven for many bird species: the largest concentration of storks in Europe, swans, grebes, cranes and cormorants.

Crane

The crocus *(Crocus satinus)* blooms in early spring in mountain valleys and alpine meadows, mainly in the Tatras and Babia Góra ranges.

Bog arum *(Calla palustra)* is a poisonous perennial plant with a characteristic white leaf below a globular flower. It grows in peat bogs.

The silver thistle *(Carlina acaulis)* is a protected plant. Its leaves form a rosette containing a basket-like flower with a covering of dry, silvery leaves.

The great sundew *(Drosera anglica)*, an insect-eating plant found in peat bogs, is a protected species in Poland.

Deer, which live in herds, are a relatively common sight in Poland's deciduous and mixed forests. They are hunted as game animals.

Marmots, rodents of the beaver family, live in the Tatra National Park. They "whistle" when disturbed.

Wild boar, widespread in Poland, are the ancestors of the domestic pig. Deciduous and mixed forests are their principal habitat.

Moose live in large forests, marshes and peat bogs, even near large cities. Large populations of them can be seen in Kampinoski National Park and in the Białystok region.

The Lowlands

The apparent monotony of the lowlands is broken by elevations, meandering rivers, marshes and peat bogs. Most of the land is under cultivation, but there are also extensive forests. Białowieża National Park (see p295) shelters bison. Moose can be seen in the marshes and storks in the lakes.

Hoopoe

The Coast

The sandy beaches of Poland's Baltic coast are among the finest in Europe. They are situated by sand dunes or cliffs, and were it not for river estuaries, it would be possible to walk along them for the entire length of the coast. Narrow sandy spits formed by the coastal currents and known as *mierzeje* are a characteristic feature of the shoreline.

Seagull

The corn poppy (*Papaver rhoeas*) is becoming increasingly rare as it is weeded out from cereal crops.

Lyme grass (*Elymus arenarius*) grows on the sand dunes. It has pointed leaves and its roots bind the sandy subsoil.

Toadflax (*Linaria vulgaris*) has narrow leaves and yellow-orange flowers with a characteristic spur. It grows in ditches and on wasteland.

Marram grass (*Ammophila arenarea*) has narrow grey-green leaves, and flowers between June and August. Like lyme grass, it helps to bind the sand dunes where it grows.

Early Polish Architecture

Over the centuries, and particularly during World War II, Poland lost a great deal of its architectural heritage. However, major efforts on the part of both private individuals and the government have meant that many important buildings have been restored, and in some cases completely rebuilt. Royal and aristocratic palaces, churches, castles and entire streets of old towns can thus be admired today. Traditional wooden buildings are another interesting feature of Polish architecture.

Renaissance courtyard at Wawel Royal Castle

Romanesque Architecture

The Romanesque style of architecture seen in Polish cathedrals, palace chapels and monasteries flourished largely as a result of the country's conversion to Christianity in the 10th century. Unfortunately, few Romanesque buildings have survived intact. Among those that have are the collegiate church at Tum near Łęczyca *(see p235)* and the monastery at Czerwińsk on the Vistula *(see p120)*, both of which are decorated with stone carvings. The Romanesque style reached its apogee during the 12th century.

Semicircular presbytery

Triforium with decorative columns

Narrow windows that also served defensive purposes

The collegiate church at Tum near Łęczyca, dating from the mid-12th century, is Poland's largest surviving Romanesque religious building.

This 12th-century Romanesque doorway is from the Cathedral of St Mary Magdalene *(see p196)*.

Gothic Architecture

Gothic elements began to appear in late Romanesque architecture in the early 13th century; this transitional style can be seen in the abbeys at Wąchock, Sulejów and Koprzywnica. By the end of the century, the Gothic style was prevalent throughout Polish architecture. Many fortified castles were built at this time, more than 80 being founded by Kazimierz the Great. Notable examples are those at Będzin, Ogrodzieniec and Bobolice *(see pp162–3)*. Gothic churches and monasteries were also built throughout the country, fine examples surviving in Krakow and Wrocław. The oldest surviving wooden churches, such as that at Dębno, date from the same period. In Polish provincial architecture, the Gothic style persisted until the early 17th century.

The 15th-century church at Dębno Podhalańskie *(see p171)* is one of the oldest surviving wooden churches in Poland.

The doorway of the early 15th-century Church of St Catherine in Krakow has an ornamental stepped frame.

The Renaissance and Mannerism

Renaissance architecture was introduced to Poland in the early 16th century by the Italian architect Bartolomeo Berrecci, who designed Wawel Royal Castle and the Zygmunt Chapel in Krakow. Many of the churches in Mazovia (as at Pułtusk and Płock) were influenced by the Italian Renaissance, as were the town halls in Poznań and Sandomierz. From the mid-16th century onwards, buildings in Pomerania were designed in the northern Mannerist style.

The Zygmunt Chapel *(see p149)* is one of the finest examples of Renaissance architecture in Poland.

Decorative ceilings such as those in the churches of Lubelszczyzna and Kalisz illustrate provincial interpretations of Renaissance and Mannerist forms.

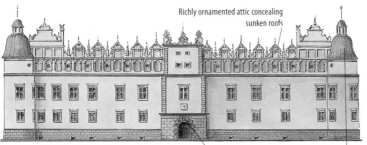

Richly ornamented attic concealing sunken roofs

Leszczyński Castle in Baranów Sandomierski *(see p159)* is one of the few surviving late Renaissance buildings in Poland.

Central gateways leading to a courtyard surrounded by cloisters

Corner lookout turret

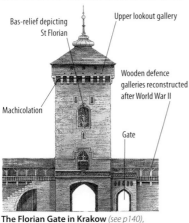

Bas-relief depicting St Florian

Upper lookout gallery

Wooden defence galleries reconstructed after World War II

Machicolation

Gate

The Florian Gate in Krakow *(see p140)*, a surviving city watchtower with Gothic fortifications, dates from the 13th to 15th centuries.

Architecture of the Age of the Teutonic Knights

The Teutonic Knights, who ruled Eastern Pomerania and Prussia in the 13th and 14th centuries, left impressive brick-built Gothic buildings. The knights built defensive castles (such as those at Malbork, Gniew and Bytów) and city walls (as at Chełmno and Toruń), and founded numerous churches.

The imposing bulk of the Upper Castle, part of the Malbork Castle complex

Later Polish Architecture

Buildings dating from the Baroque era are quite a common sight in Polish towns and cities. Many distinctive 19th-century residences and architectural ensembles are also noteworthy, as in Łódź. Around 1900, at a period coinciding with that of Art Nouveau, attempts to build in a Polish national style produced particularly felicitous results. Folk architecture is another area of great interest, and the best way to explore it is to visit the *skansens* (open-air museums) which exist in each region of the country.

Baroque cartouche with the emblem of Poland

Baroque Architecture

In the first half of the 17th century, architects of Italian descent started to introduce the early Baroque style to Poland. Nobles built imposing residences, chief among them Krzyżtopór Castle in Ujazd *(see pp50–51 and p158)*, in the Mannerist style, and the fortified early Baroque palace in Łańcut *(see pp178–9)*. Italian architects were also commissioned to design the Royal Palace in Warsaw, the country's new capital. The destruction wrought during the Polish-Swedish war was followed by a period of building in the late Baroque style. In Warsaw, the renowned Dutch architect Tylman van Gameren designed a large number of buildings, alongside Italian architects. During the rule of the Saxon kings in Poland, architects from Dresden designed many new buildings in Warsaw, as well as palaces like the one at Białystok *(see p294)*.

High gable framed by volutes

Pediment decorated with coat of arms

Edena House in Gdańsk is a fine example of the Mannerist style.

Kodeń Church, with its broken façade, is typical of the late Baroque period.

Steep broken roof

Bay window with a decorative gable

This country house in Koszuty *(see p217)* is a typical example of an aristocrat's country seat in the Baroque style.

Porch in front of main entrance

Corner turrets

Neo-Classicism

Neo-Classicism appeared in Poland during the rule of Stanisław August Poniatowski, the country's last king. The Royal Palace and Łazienki Palace in Warsaw were built in the Neo-Classical style, as were many others including those at Lubostroń and Śmiełów. Features included landscaped gardens in the English manner.

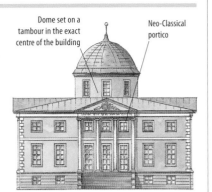

Dome set on a tambour in the exact centre of the building

Neo-Classical portico

The town hall in Łowicz is an example of small-town public buildings in the Neo-Classical style of the early 19th century.

Lubostroń Palace *(see p227)* is a fine example of Palladianism, a refined Neo-Classical style imitating the work of the Italian Renaissance architect Andrea Palladio – in this case, his Villa Rotonda at Vicenza.

Historicism and Modernism

The second half of the 19th century saw a proliferation of Neo-Gothic, Neo-Renaissance and Neo-Baroque buildings. In the 1880s there was a movement towards creating an architecture in the Polish national style, which gave rise to some very picturesque structures. Art Nouveau was short-lived in Poland, although it did leave a number of attractive buildings, primarily in Łódź.

The wooden chapel at Jaszczurówka is an example of a building in the Polish national style.

The Warsaw School of Economics combines modern features and traditional elements.

Traditional Architecture

Fine examples of wooden architecture can be found today at most *skansens*. Log cabins, often with thatched roofs, can still be seen in many villages in Poland.

Painted interior of a peasant dwelling in Zalipie

Beehive in human form

Windmill at the *skansen* (open-air museum) in Wdzydze Kiszewskie

The Literature of Poland

Polish literature has always been inextricably linked to the historical development of the country, as the political situation, particularly over the last two centuries, has not always favoured freedom of speech. Many writers were forced to emigrate, while those who remained were often obliged to publish their works in other countries. Poland boasts four winners of the Nobel Prize for Literature: Henryk Sienkiewicz, Władysław S. Reymont, Czesław Miłosz and Wisława Szymborska.

The Middle Ages

Polish writing originates in the 11th century. The earliest works were in Latin, often written by people from other regions who copied hagiographies and holy chronicles. The oldest Polish chronicle, by the Benedictine monk Gall Anonim, dates from the beginning of the 12th century. Native Polish writers soon appeared, and Polish literature expanded into all the literary forms known in Europe at the time. The first work in the Polish language was written in the second half of the 13th century. The earliest religious song in Polish, *The Mother of God (Bogurodzica)*, was probably written at the end of the 13th century, although it is not found in manuscript until the 15th century. The Polish *Holy Cross Sermons (Kazania świętokrzyskie)* date from around 1450.

Jan Kochanowski writing *Treny*, a lament for his daughter's death

Renaissance and Baroque

The Renaissance is regarded as the Golden Age of Polish literature, when both prose and poetry flourished. Mikołaj Rej (1505–69), the first significant writer in the Polish language, is generally regarded as the father of Polish literature.

The most prominent poet of the time was Jan Kochanowski (1530–84), who wrote the first Polish tragedy, entitled *The Dismissal of the Greek Envoys (Odprawa posłów greckich)*. He was also the author of the humorous *Trifles (Fraszki)* and the sorrowful *Laments (Treny)*, a lament in the form of a cycle of 19 poems. Other notable figures among Poland's early poets are Mikołaj Sęp Szarzyński (1550–81) and Szymon Szymonowic (1558–1629).

The greatest works of the Baroque period are by Jan Chryzostom Pasek (1636–1701), who wrote highly colourful accounts both of great historical events and of the everyday life of the Polish nobility in the reign of Jan III Sobieski.

Romantic poet Adam Mickiewicz by Walenty Wańkowicz

The Enlightenment and the 19th Century

The Enlightenment, and particularly the reign of the last king of Poland, Stanisław August Poniatowski, was an important period in the development of Polish literature. The first Polish novel, *The Adventures of Mikołaj Doświadczyński (Mikołaja Doświadczyńskiego przypadki)*, was written by Bishop Ignacy Krasicki (1735–1801), a moralist and satirical poet. Polish Romantic poetry played an important role in keeping

Polish Cinema

The first Polish feature film was made as early as 1902, but it was not until after World War II that Polish film-makers achieved international renown. The best-known Polish film directors include Andrzej Wajda, whose *Man of Iron* won the Palme d'Or at the 1981 Cannes Film Festival, Krzysztof Zanussi, Krzysztof Kieślowski *(Decalogue, Three Colours – Blue/White/Red)* and Roman Polański *(Chinatown)*, who has spent

many years making films in the USA and France. In 2015 Pawel Pawlikowski's drama *Ida* won the Oscar for Best Foreign Film.

Scene from Jerzy Hoffman's film *Colonel Wolodyjowski*

nationalist sentiment alive. The outstanding writers of that time, Adam Mickiewicz, Juliusz Słowacki and Zygmunt Krasiński, wrote outside Poland. To this day, their work forms the canon of patriotic literature, whose jewel in the crown is Mickiewicz's *Pan Tadeusz*, which is both a nostalgic evocation of the vanishing traditions of the nobility and a vision of the emergence of more modern social attitudes. Also notable at this time was the comedy writer Aleksander Fredro, whose works include *Revenge (Zemsta)* and *Husband and Wife (Mąż i Żona)*. Another writer who holds a prominent place in the history of Polish Romantic literature is Cyprian Kamil Norwid, regarded as the precursor of Modernism. Eliza Orzeszkowa (1840–1910) and Bolesław Prus (1847–1912) are the principal figures in the next phase of the development of the Polish novel. Another major writer of this time was Henryk Sienkiewicz (1846–1916), best known in Poland for his trilogy of historical novels describing events in 17th-century Poland, and *The Teutonic Knights (Krzyżacy)*, which is devoted to the late 14th and early 15th centuries. Outside Poland, Sienkiewicz is better known for *Quo Vadis?*, which deals with the beginnings of Christianity and for which he was awarded the Nobel Prize for Literature in 1905.

20th- and 21st-Century Literature

From 1900 onwards, Young Poland *(Młoda Polska)*, a modern trend in Polish literature particularly

associated with the artistic community of Krakow, began to emerge. A key role in this was played by Stanisław Wyspiański (1869–1907), author of the Symbolist play *The Wedding (Wesele)*, which was made into a film by Andrzej Wajda 70 years later. Also influential in Young Poland was a Bohemian group surrounding Stanisław Przybyszewski, a friend of Henrik Ibsen and Edvard Munch.

Another Nobel laureate was Władysław Reymont (1865–1925), who wrote society novels. He was awarded the Nobel Prize in 1924 for *The Peasants (Chłopi)*, which describes the lives of the inhabitants of a village near Łowicz. Between the wars, avant-garde writers such as Stanisław Ignacy Witkiewicz (called Witkacy, 1885–1939), Bruno Schulz (1893–1942) and Witold Gombrowicz (1904–69) came to prominence.

Polish literature after World War II spawned many famous writers, several of whom wrote

Monument to Aleksander Fredro in Wrocław

Wisława Szymborska receiving the Nobel Prize for Literature

from abroad for political reasons. Stanisław Lem (1921–2006) wrote philosophical science fiction, which has been translated into many languages. His *Solaris* was made into a film twice – in 1972 by Andrei Tarkovsky and in 2002 by Steven Soderbergh. Tadeusz Różewicz (1921–2014), also well known as a poet, and Sławomir Mrożek (1930–2013) were prominent playwrights. Hanna Krall (b.1935) and Ryszard Kapuściński (1932–2007) are known for their documentary writing. Andrzej Szczypiorski, who wrote *A Mass for Arras (Msza za miasto Arras)* and *The Beginning (Początek)*, has also achieved international recognition.

Poetry has a special place in modern Polish literature. Apart from Tadeusz Różewicz, its main exponents are Zbigniew Herbert, and Nobel laureates Czesław Miłosz (1911–2004) Wisława Szymborska (1923–2012). Contemporary novelists with a strong international following include Olga Tokarczuk, Paweł Huelle, and the masters of Polish urban noir fiction Zygmunt Miłoszewski and Marek Krajewski.

Critically acclaimed author Olga Tokarczuk

The Music of Poland

Poland has made a major contribution to the international music scene, as much through the works of great composers as through its renowned jazz musicians and colourful folk music. Polish classical composers such as Fryderyk Chopin (1810–49), Stanisław Moniuszko (1819–72), Karol Szymanowski (1882–1937) and Wojciech Kilar (1932–2013) have often been inspired by folk music, as have modern jazz and rock musicians. Poland has also given the world such outstanding musical performers as the tenor Jan Kiepura and the pianists Artur Rubinstein and Witold Małcużyński.

Fryderyk Chopin in a portrait by Eugène Delacroix

Early Music

Although they are not widely known, there is much of interest in the works of early Polish composers. Mikołaj z Radomia, a composer of the first half of the 15th century, produced both religious and secular works. In the Renaissance, composers such as Wacław of Szamotuły and Mikołaj Gomółka brought Polish music into the European mainstream. The first Polish opera stage was set up in the 17th century at the court of Władysław IV. Court and religious music flourished at that time, and the works of such composers as Adam Jarzębski, Stanisław S. Szarzyński and Marcin Mielczewski are still widely performed by Polish musicians today.

The 19th and 20th Centuries

The most prominent Polish composer of the Romantic era was undoubtedly Fryderyk Chopin, who composed almost exclusively for the piano. Chopin contributed to the establishment of a Polish national style in music, and exerted a great influence on the development of European piano music. During his short life he composed a large number of preludes, mazurkas, polonaises, waltzes, études and other pieces. Many of Chopin's works contain elements of folk music. The Chopin Piano Competition, held in Warsaw, has been a regular event since 1927, and award-winners have gone on to become world-famous pianists.

Stanisław Moniuszko is regarded as the father of the Polish national opera. His most famous operas are *Halka*, inspired by highland folklore, and *The Haunted House (Straszny dwór)*, which evokes the traditions of the Polish nobility.

In the second half of the 19th century, the violinist Henryk Wieniawski and the pianist Ignacy Paderewski achieved world renown. The latter was also prominent in politics, serving for a time as Prime Minister of Poland.

Before World War I, the town of Zakopane was a major centre of Polish culture. It drew not only artists but also composers who sought inspiration from the landscape of the Tatra Mountains and the colourful folklore of the highland dwellers. Among composers associated with Zakopane is Mieczysław Karłowicz (1876–1909), noted especially for his symphonies. Karłowicz perished tragically in an avalanche in the Tatras at the young age of 33. Another frequent visitor to Zakopane was Karol Szymanowski, whose fascination with the folk music of the region inspired him to compose a number of works, including the ballet *Harnasie*. One of the best-known modern composers is Krzysztof Penderecki (b. 1933), whose oeuvre includes epic symphonies, oratorios and operas. His opera *The Devils of Loudun (Diabły z Loudun)* has been

Jan Kiepura (1902–1966)

Jan Kiepura achieved international renown as an opera singer. He performed on the world's greatest stages, and from 1938 was with the Metropolitan Opera of New York. He gained popularity through his appearances in operettas and musicals, where he performed together with his wife, Marta Eggerth.

Stanisław Moniuszko

performed all over the world. Other prominent composers of international standing are Andrzej Panufnik (1914–91), Witold Lutosławski (1913–94) and Henryk Górecki (1933–2010), whose works include the outstanding Symphony No. 3, which has topped the classical music charts for years. Wojciech Kilar (1932–2013) and Zbigniew Preisner (b. 1955), are widely known for their film music. While Kilar is famous as the music director of *The Promised Land* and *Bram Stoker's Dracula*, Preisner is known for the music in Kieślowski's *Three Colours* trilogy.

Folk band outside the Cloth Hall (Sukiennica) in Krakow

The composer and conductor Krzysztof Penderecki

Jazz

Jazz traditions in Poland go back to the inter-war years After World War II, jazz was deemed by the authorities to be "alien to the working class", and it was not until 1956 that jazz could be performed in public. An important jazz musician of that time was the pianist and composer Krzysztof Komeda (1931–69), who wrote the haunting lullaby for Roman Polański's film, *Rosemary's Baby*.

During the 1960s, other jazz musicians came to prominence, including Adam Makowicz, Tomasz Stańko and Michał Urbaniak. Jazz clubs opened throughout the country, and the Warsaw Jazz Jamboree, first held in 1958, became the world's biggest jazz festival. Another renowned festival is Jazz on the Oder, which is held in Wrocław.

Among the musicians achieving public recognition in the 1970s and 1980s, were the pianist and saxophonist Włodzimierz Nahorny, the saxophonists Zbigniew Namysłowski and Janusz Muniak, and the pianist Sławomir Kulpowicz. Today, popular musicians include pianist and composer Leszek Możdżer, and jazz-rock bassist Tymon Tymański.

Folk Music

Polish folk music is unusually colourful. Every region has its own specific tradition, and the music of the Tatra Mountains is unique. Folk bands play quite a basic range of instruments, the main one being the fiddle, and sometimes bagpipes or drums and basses. Depending on the region these instruments are supplemented by clarinets, horns, accordions and occasionally dulcimers.

The best way of getting to know and enjoy Polish folk music is to attend some of the concerts traditionally held during the summer months, such as the Kazimierz or Zakopane festivals. Here there is a chance to listen to live music being played and to watch the dance groups that perform in colourful folk costumes.

Polish vocal and dance groups have brought world-wide popularity to Polish folk music. The Mazowsze group, for example, gives stage performances that are inspired by the folk traditions of various regions.

The Warsaw Jazz Jamboree

The Traditional Nobility

The tradition of the Polish nobility was dominated by the idea of Sarmatism, which was based on the myth that the Polish aristocracy were descended from an ancient warrior people called the Sarmatians. Sarmatism was influential in shaping the ideology of the ruling class, as well as its customs and lifestyle. A Sarmatian embraced the old order, was patriotic and Catholic, and at the same time valued freedom and privilege, lived life as a landowner and upheld family traditions. Sarmatism played an important part in art and literature, particularly memoirs.

A kulawka was a special toasting goblet for drinking "bottoms up", as it could only be set down on its rim.

Noblemen's houses were typically single-storey buildings fronted by an imposing colonnade. Rooms flanked the central entrance hall.

A Traditional Beverage

Mead was a favourite drink of the Polish aristocracy. It is made by fermenting wort, a solution of honey and water that has been flavoured with herbs. The most popular type of mead is *trójniak*, in which honey makes up one-third of the total wort. The rarest is *półtorak*, with two parts honey and one part water. Although mead is no longer widely drunk, it is still produced today.

Stolnik mead

Turban

Headpiece with heron feathers

Kontusz in the style worn by ladies

Wyloty – slit sleeves rolled back and over the shoulder

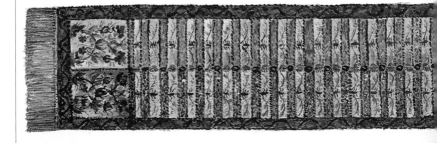

A PORTRAIT OF POLAND | **3 5**

An election gathering, at which the nobility elected the king, is portrayed here. This was one of the greatest privileges exercised by the gentry.

Coats of Arms

The coats of arms of aristocratic families in Poland number no more than about 200. They were held in common by members of clans with different names. Aristocratic titles were not used at the time of the Republic (with the exception of the titles of Lithuanian princes), while magnate families looked to foreign rulers for titles. Polish heraldic symbols usually had their origins in individual symbols; they were therefore relatively simple and differed from those of Western Europe.

Cielątkowa

Łodzia

Szreniawa

Polish National Dress

Required attire of the nobility in the Baroque era, its main elements were the żupan (a kind of shirt) and the kontusz (an outer garment tied with a waistband). Headgear took the form of either a kołpak (fur hat) or a square-bottomed rogatywka. Men wore their hair short and sported a moustache, and sometimes a beard.

Kołpak

Żupan

Wyloty

Kontusz sash

The kontusz was an outer garment with cutout sleeves, which were thrown over the shoulders.

The karabela was a traditional sword that had a single-sided blade and a highly ornamented handle, often with inlaid precious stones.

Coffin portraits of the deceased were painted in oils on metal plates cut to the shape of the cross-section of a coffin, to which they were attached during funerals.

Silk sashes known as *kontusze* were an indispensable part of a nobleman's attire. Several yards in length, they were worn wrapped around the waist and tied in a decorative knot, allowing the tassels to hang downwards.

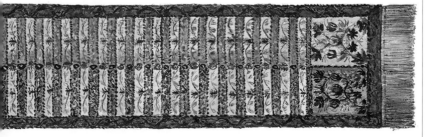

The Different Religions of Poland

Although the majority of the Polish population today is Roman Catholic, in the course of the country's history its inhabitants have adhered to a variety of faiths. Besides Roman Catholics, there have been Orthodox Christians, Uniates and Jews (most of whom were murdered by the Nazis in World War II), and, since the 16th century, Lutheran and Calvinist Protestants. Eastern Poland has always included significant minorities of Uniate Ukrainians and Orthodox Belarusians, as well as a small pocket of Muslim Tatars. The westward shift of Poland's borders after World War II brought in many German Protestant churches. The wide variety of Poland's ecclesiastical architecture bears witness to the many cultures and religions that have existed there.

Convent of the Old Believers at Wojnowo is one of the few places where this Orthodox religious group can still be found.

Orthodox Christians today are found mainly in the eastern parts of the country, where many of their historic churches still stand.

The Evangelical Reform Church in Warsaw was built after the Reformation and used by the small group of Calvinist believers in Poland.

The Basilica of the Holy Cross and the Birth of the Holy Mother (*Bazylika Krzyża Świętego i Narodzenia Matki Boskiej*) has the second-tallest church tower in Poland.

The cemetery at Kruszyniany, one of the few Muslim burial grounds in Poland, is used by people of Tatar descent.

The "Church of Peace" (Kościół Pokoju) at Świdnica was one of three churches to be built specifically for Silesian Protestants after the Thirty Years' War, which ended in 1648.

Other Denominations

Some of Poland's historic churches have changed denomination over the years – for instance, when Polish Catholics took over disused Protestant churches. Although the original interiors have generally not survived, the exteriors have often been carefully conserved. Some religious denominations no longer have followers in Poland, although their places of worship remain. An example is the Mennonite chapel in Gdańsk.

Old Mennonite chapel in Gdańsk

Open-air altar

Pauline monastery

Judaic artifacts in museums are poignant vestiges of the synagogues that were once so numerous in Poland. As a result of the Holocaust and the ensuing Communist era, there are few Jews in Poland today.

Częstochowa Pilgrimage

The Monastery of Jasna Góra in Częstochowa is the most important Catholic shrine in Poland – and one of the greatest in the Christian world. The image of Our Lady of Częstochowa, also known as the Black Madonna, draws pilgrims all year round. The main pilgrimage, which attracts hundreds of thousands of believers from Poland and beyond, is held in the meadows at the foot of the monastery on 15 August each year.

The picturesque wooden churches of the Ukrainian Uniates, or Greek Catholics, built for the Lemk and the Boyk minorities, survive in the Carpathian Mountains. Their congregations were resettled in other areas during Operation Vistula after World War II.

POLAND THROUGH THE YEAR

As the majority of Poles are Catholics, traditional Catholic feast days are the most important holidays. Although many visitors choose to visit Poland during the highlights of the Christian calendar (Christmas, Easter and Corpus Christi), the country draws visitors throughout the year. Tourists tend to visit Poland in the summer, between June and September. During that period, the most popular tourist spots are crowded, and a variety of open-air events, from street theatre festivals to re-enactments of medieval tournaments, take place throughout the country. The main music and drama festivals are held in spring and autumn. The best way of spending winter in Poland is skiing in the mountains.

Spring

The official beginning of spring, 21 March, is an unofficial day of truancy among young people in Poland. However, this chaos ushers in warm and pleasant days.

March

Topienie Marzanny (23 Mar). This is the day when, in many areas of the country, children throw small dolls – symbolizing winter – into rivers.

The International Poster Biennial (even-numbered years), Warsaw. International graphic and poster artists.

Festival of Stage Songs, Wrocław. Polish and international performers take part in this festival celebrating cabaret, singer-songwriters and musicals.

April

Palm Sunday (the Sunday before Easter) is the day when "palms" are blessed in the churches. The most colourful celebrations take place in villages in Kurpie and Małopolska – in particular Rabka, Lipnica Murowana and Tokarnia. During Holy Week (the week leading up to Easter), mystery plays are performed in churches around the country. The oldest and best-known spectacle is *Chwalebne Misterium Pańskie*, a passion play which has been performed in Kalwaria Zebrzydowska (see p167) since the 17th century.

Holy Saturday, is when Easter food is taken to church in baskets and blessed. Visits are also made to symbolic sepulchres in churches.

Easter Sunday is the most important Catholic holiday, when the grandest mass is held to mark the Resurrection.

Easter Monday (*Śmigus-dyngus*) is marked by the custom of people throwing water over one another.

Warsaw Theatre Meetings (*late April*). The best performances from theatres around Poland.

Jazz on the Oder, Wrocław. Renowned jazz festival.

Blessing baskets of food on Holy Saturday in a church in Lublin

May

International Labour Day (1 May).

3 May The most important public holiday, marking the adoption of the first Polish constitution of 1791 (see p53).

Łańcut Music Festival (first 2 weeks in May), Łańcut. This is an international event attracting world-class chamber and orchestral music.

International Book Fair (last 2 weeks in May), Warsaw. One of the largest events of its kind in Europe.

Kontakt Theatre Festival (last 2 weeks in May), Toruń. International festival of ground-breaking theatre, held every two years.

Festival of Theatre Schools, Łódź. Performances are held in the town's major theatres, and there are also panel discussions and workshops.

Kraków Film Festival, Krakow. The oldest film festival in the country.

Passion play, *Chwalebne Misterium Pańskie*, in Kalwaria Zebrzydowska

Average Daily Hours of Sunshine

Sunny days
The period from May to August has the greatest number of days of sunshine. April and September are often also sunny, while December has the least sunshine.

Summer

From the end of June to the beginning of September, open-air events really take off, with a plethora of al fresco folk, rock and film festivals. Most tourist resorts organize a season of cultural events, while the theatre and concert programmes of big cities take a summer break.

June

Festival of Polish Song *(early Jun)*, Opole. Polish stars of popular music perform.
Corpus Christi *(variable)*. Solemn processions are held throughout the country.
Jarmark Jagiellonski *(mid-Jun)* Lublin. Street festival featuring craft stalls, and recreations of medieval life.
Orange Warsaw *(mid-Jun)* Warsaw. International rock/pop festival featuring big names
Midsummer's Night *(23 Jun)*. Wreathes known as wianki are thrown into the Vistula in Warsaw and Krakow.
Fishermen's Sea Pilgrimage *(29 Jun)*. Decorated fishing boats sail into the port of Puck across the bay.
Mozart Festival *(late Jun–early Jul)*, Warsaw. Chamber music and opera.
Malta International Theatre Festival *(late Jun)*, Poznań. International drama and alternative music.
Summer Film Festival *(late Jun)*, Łagów. Feature films from Poland and Central and Eastern Europe.
Festival of Folk Bands and Singers *(late Jun)*, Kazimierz Dolny. Traditional music from Poland and beyond.

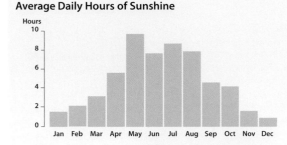

Corpus Christi procession in Spicimierz

Jewish Culture Festival *(Jun/Jul)*, Krakow. Klezmer music, theatre and film.
Open'er *(Jun/Jul)*, Gdynia. Big outdoor rock festival with a mostly international bill.

July

Viking Festival, Wolin. Viking battles. Most of the boats arrive from Scandinavia.
Tauron New Music *(mid-Jul)* Katowice. Cutting-edge electronic dance music.
Different Sounds Art and Music Festival *(mid-Jul)* Lublin.

Outdoor rock and world-music festival with an alternative flavour.
Piknik Country *(end of Jul)*, Mrągowo. International country music festival.

August

Dominican Fair *(first 2 weeks in Aug)*, Gdańsk. Street theatre, music and outdoor markets.
Chopin Festival *(second week in Aug)*, Duszniki Zdrój. Piano recitals featuring top performers
OFF Festival *(early/mid-Aug)* Katowice. Indie and alternative rock with an international pedigree.
Kraków Live *(mid-Aug)* Krakow. Big international pop and alt-rock stars perform in fields behind the Aviation Museum.
Feast of the Assumption *(15 Aug)*. This is a religious holiday, but it is also the day on which Poles commemorate their victory over the Bolsheviks in 1920.
International Song Festival *(late Aug)*, Sopot. Polish pop stars performing in an open-air arena.

Fishermen's sea pilgrimage in the bay of Puck

Average Precipitation

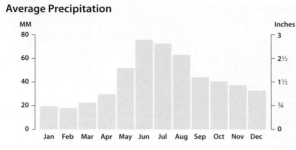

Rainfall and snow
Although autumn showers are the most unpleasant, the heaviest rainfall occurs in summer. Heavy snow is usual in winter.

Autumn

Fine weather continues in Poland to the end of October. Autumn comes soonest in Pomerania, Warmia and Mazuria, as well as Suwalszczyna. The transition from September to October – when fallen leaves create a riot of colour – is known as the "golden Polish autumn". It is also a time when major cultural events take place, as well as the beginning of the new academic year.

Inauguration of the academic year

September
Wratislavia Cantans (early Sep), Wrocław. Oratorio and cantata festival.
Warsaw Autumn (mid-Sep), Warsaw. Contemporary classical music.
Sacrum Profanum (mid-Sep) Krakow. Contemporary classical and experimental electronic music.
Polish Feature Film Festival, Gdynia. The best Polish films of the year.

October
Unsound (early-Oct) Krakow. Offbeat electronica and experimental rock.
Konfrontacje Theatre Festival, Lublin. Experimental theatre and music.
Warsaw Film Festival, Warsaw. International features and red-carpet guests.
Festival of Early Music (late Oct). An international festival with venues in Warsaw, Krakow and other cities.

November
All Saints' Day (1 Nov). People visit the graves of their relatives and light candles there.
All Souls Jazz Festival, Krakow.
"Etiuda" International Film Festival (early Nov), Krakow. Shorts by young filmmakers.
Wrocław International Guitar Festival, Wrocław. Classical, jazz, rock and flamenco.
Independence Day (11 Nov). The biggest ceremonies in honour of Polish independence in 1918 take place in Warsaw.
St Martin's Day (11 Nov). In Wielkopolska and Eastern Pomerania people cook a goose and bake pretzels and

Celebration of Polish Independence Day in Warsaw

croissants. There are major ceremonies in Poznań, where St Martin is the patron saint.
Camerimage (mid-Nov), Bydgoszcz. International film festival with emphasis on camerawork

Winter

The first snow can fall as early as November, although snowless winters are becoming more common. Subzero temperatures and hard frosts are not unusual.

Candles lit at a cemetery on All Saints' Day

Average Monthly Temperature

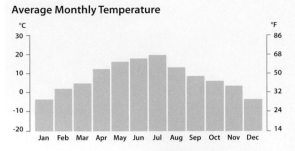

Temperatures
Temperatures are highest in the summer, when they can exceed 30° C (86° F). In winter, temperatures can fall below zero (32° F), although this is usually short-lived.

The coldest part of the country is Suwalszczyna, in the northeast corner.

December
Barbórka *(4 Dec)*. The day of Saint Barbara, traditionally the patron saint of miners, is widely celebrated in the mining regions of Poland (Silesia and Lesser Poland). Parades by the miners' orchestras are followed by parties, concerts and balls.

Christmas Crib Competitions *(first week in Dec)*, Krakow. The market square is invaded by children and adults presenting their handmade cribs.

Christmas Eve *(24 Dec)*. The beginning of Christmas is marked with a meat-free dinner and midnight mass.

Christmas *(25 and 26 Dec)*. Public holidays, with masses held in all churches.

New Year's Eve *(31 Dec)*. Throughout Poland, people see in the New Year at balls and parties, and at various celebrations in the main squares of most towns.

Cribs being brought to Krakow's Christmas Crib Competitions

January
New Year *(1 Jan)*. Public holiday. The first day of the year marks the beginning of a carnival and the opening of a season of balls.

Epiphany *(6 Jan)*. Colourful parades and Nativity plays take place on the streets of numerous Polish cities. The biggest event is held in the capital, Warsaw.

February
Feast of St Mary Gromniczna *(2 Feb)*. Wax candles known as *gromnice* are lit in churches.

End of Carnival The last Thursday before Lent is marked by eating doughnuts or other fried delicacies known as *faworki*. Splendid balls, concerts and shows are put on throughout the country to mark the last Saturday of the carnival.

Public Holidays
New Year's Day (1 Jan)
Epiphany (6 Jan)
Easter Monday (variable)
May Day (1 May)
Constitution Day (3 May)
Corpus Christi (variable)
Feast of the Assumption (15 Aug)
All Saints' Day (1 Nov)
Independence Day (11 Nov)
Christmas (25 and 26 Dec)

Winter in Gdańsk

THE HISTORY OF POLAND

Polish history remains a dramatic narrative and an important source of pride, as well as inspiration to the present generation. The origins of the Polish nation go back to the 10th century, when Slav tribes living in the area of Gniezno united together under the Piast dynasty, which then ruled Poland until 1370.

Mieszko I, the first historic prince of this line, converted to Christianity in 966, bringing his kingdom into Christian Europe. After the Piast dynasty died out, the Lithuanian prince Jagiełło took the Polish throne and founded a new dynasty. The treaty with Lithuania signed at Krewo in 1385 initiated the long process of consolidation between these nations, culminating in 1569 with the Union of Lublin. The resulting Republic of Two Nations (Rzeczpospolita Obojga Narodów) was one of the largest and most powerful states in Europe. After the Jagiellonian dynasty died out in 1572, the authorities introduced elective kings, with the nobility having the right to vote. As a result, the country became weaker. Poland's political and military fragility led to its partitioning by Russia, Prussia and Austria. In 1795 Poland was wiped off the map of Europe for more than 100 years.

Attempts to wrest independence by insurrection were unsuccessful, and Poland did not regain its sovereignty until 1918. The arduous process of rebuilding and uniting the nation was still incomplete when, at the outbreak of World War II, a six-year period of German and Soviet occupation began. The price that Poland paid was extremely high: millions were murdered, including virtually its entire Jewish population. The country suffered devastation and there were huge territorial losses, which were only partly compensated by the Allies' decision to move the border westwards. After the war, Poland was subjugated by the Soviet Union and did not become a fully democratic nation until 1989. Poland, however, continues to become more involved in the international political stage as a fully-fledged member of the European Union.

Map of the Republic of Two Nations (Rzeczpospolita Obojga Narodów) in the 17th century

◀ Stanisław August Poniatowski, the last king of Poland

Poland under the Piast Dynasty

During the 6th century AD, Slav tribes began migrating from the east to what is today Polish territory. The Vistulanians (Wiślanie) settled around Krakow, and the Poles (Polanie) around Gniezno. The Polanie united under the rule of the Piast dynasty in the 10th century, and the conversion of Mieszko I (c. 960–92) to Christianity in 966 led to the formation of the Polish state. After Mieszko, Bolesław the Brave (992–1025) acquired significant new territories. Later Piast rulers reigned with variable fortune. On the death of Bolesław the Wry-Mouthed (1107–38), the nation was divided into districts, not to be reunified until the reign of Władysław the Elbow-High (1306–33). The country flourished under the rule of his son, Kazimierz the Great (1333–70).

Poland in the Years 1090–1127

☐ Polish territory

Bishop Stanisław of Szczepanów

Prayer at the grave of St Wojciech
The Czech bishop Wojciech, who was martyred while on a mission to Prussia in 997, was the first Polish saint.

Tomb of Henry IV
The Silesian prince Henry IV, the Good (Henryk IV Probus, 1288–90) tried to unite Poland but died, probably by poisoning. His tomb is a fine example of early 14th-century Gothic sculpture.

Martyrdom of St Stanisław
A 1504 embroidery from the chasuble in Kmita depicts the murder of Bishop Stanisław of Szczepanów in 1079.

997 Martyrdom of Bishop Wojciech while on a mission to Prussia	**1000** Congress at Gniezno; convocation of the Polish church metropolis		**1124–1128** Bolesław the Wry-Mouthed initiates the conversion of Western Pomerania to Christianity
		1025 Coronation of Bolesław the Brave, first king of Poland	
950	**1000**	**1050**	**1100**	1
	966 Adoption of Christianity	**1079** Martyrdom of Bishop Stanisław of Szczepanów	**1138** Beginning of the division of Poland

Coin minted in the reign of Bolesław the Brave

Vistulanian Plate
This Romanesque floor laid with plaster c.1170, preserved in the collegiate church in Wiślica, depicts a scene of adoration.

Kazimierz the Great
This 14th-century sculpture from the collection in the Collegium Maius in Krakow depicts Kazimierz the Great, who "found Poland of wood, and left it in stone".

Vestiges of the Piast Dynasty

The Piast dynasty witnessed the development of Romanesque and early Gothic architecture. Romanesque churches have survived in Tum *(see p235)*, Czerwińsk on the Vistula *(see p120)* and Tyniec *(see p151)*. The abbeys in Sulejów, Wąchock *(see p158)* and Koprzywnica date from the 13th century. Some of the Gothic castles of Kazimierz the Great can be seen in the Jura region – for example at Będzin, Olsztyn and Bobolice *(see pp162–3)*.

The Crypt of St Leonard is a vestige of the Romanesque cathedral at Wawel Royal Castle in Krakow *(see pp146–7)*.

Bolesław the Bold

The castle at Będzin is the best preserved of all the Gothic castles built by Kazimierz the Great *(see p211)*.

Founding Document of the Krakovian Academy
Founded in 1364, the Krakovian Academy was the second university (after Prague) to be established in Central Europe.

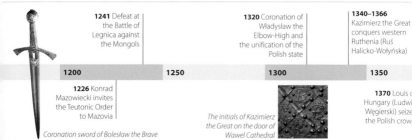

1241 Defeat at the Battle of Legnica against the Mongols

1320 Coronation of Władysław the Elbow-High and the unification of the Polish state

1340–1366 Kazimierz the Great conquers western Ruthenia (Ruś Halicko-Wołyńska)

1200 **1250** **1300** **1350**

1226 Konrad Mazowiecki invites the Teutonic Order to Mazovia

Coronation sword of Bolesław the Brave

The initials of Kazimierz the Great on the door of Wawel Cathedral

1370 Louis of Hungary (Ludwik Węgierski) seizes the Polish crown

Poland under the Jagiellonians

The marriage treaty signed in Krewo in 1385 proved to be a decisive moment in the history of Central Europe. The Grand Duke of Lithuania Władysław Jagiełło received the hand of Jadwiga, the young and beautiful ruler of Poland, and was crowned king of Poland. Jadwiga died in 1399, but the relationship between Poland and Lithuania established by the Union of Krewo was gradually strengthened. Jagiełło founded the Jagiellonian dynasty and, by the reign of Kazimierz the Jagiellonian in the mid-15th century, Poland and Lithuania had come to be the greatest power in Central Europe. At various times, the Jagiellonian kings also ruled the Czech nations and Hungary.

**Poland and Lithuania
in the Years 1386–1434**

☐ Poland   ☐ Lithuania
☐ Feudal territories

**Second Treaty
of Toruń**
Signed in 1466, the treaty concluded the Thirteen Years' War with the Teutonic Knights, who lost nearly half their territory to Poland.

Ulryk von Jungingen,
Grand Master of the
Teutonic Order

Chapel at Lublin Castle
Ruthenian paintings in the Catholic Chapel of the Holy Trinity founded by Władysław Jagiełło reflect the multicultural nature of the Polish-Lithuanian state.

**Plate showing Filippo
Buonaccorsi**
This sculpture commemorating the Italian humanist and educator of the young royals, who died in 1496, is by the eminent late medieval sculptor Veit Stoss.

1399 Death of Queen Jadwiga

1411 First Treaty of Toruń, establishing peace with the Teutonic Knights

1413 Treaty of Horodło, strengthening the bond between Poland and Lithuania

1440 Formation of the Prussian Union, in opposition to the Teutonic Knights

1385   **1400**   **1415**   **1430**

1385 Union of Krewo joins the Polish and Lithuanian royal dynasties in marriage

Queen Jadwiga's sceptre

1410 Battle of Grunwald

1415 At the Council of Constanz, Paweł Włodkowic attacks the Teutonic Order for its wars of conquest in northeastern Europe

Virgin from Krużlowa
This statue, of around 1400, is a masterpiece of late Gothic sculpture.

Gothic Pax
The skill of medieval goldsmiths can be seen in this finely crafted cross.

Gothic Architecture

Many late Gothic buildings have survived in Poland. Among the most important are the Collegium Maius and the Barbican in Krakow *(see p139)*. After the formation of Royal Prussia, many parish churches were built in the towns lying within its territory, the largest being the Church of St Mary in Gdańsk *(see pp244–5)*.

The imposing twin-tower façade of the Church of St Mary reflects Krakow's former status *(see pp138–9)*.

Witold, the Grand Duke of Lithuania

Battle of Grunwald

In one of the greatest medieval battles, on 15 July 1410, Poland and Lithuania, with their Ruthenian allies, routed the armies of the Teutonic Knights, who never regained their former might. The scene is depicted in this painting by Jan Matejko of 1878.

Deposition from Chomranice
This *Deposition of Christ* (c.1450) is held to be the apogee of Polish Gothic art.

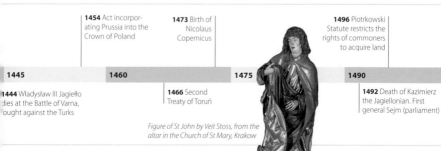

Figure of St John by Veit Stoss, from the altar in the Church of St Mary, Krakow

Poland's Golden Age

The Republic of Two Nations (Rzeczpospolita) was formed by Poland and Lithuania by the Union of Lublin in 1569, thus creating one of the largest powers in Europe. The union, at that time, in terms of language, nationality and religion was considered the most diverse political entity on the continent. In the western territories of the Polish Crown there was peace, relative prosperity and – rare elsewhere – religious tolerance. Under the Jagiellonians, and later under the first elective kings, art, education and the economy flourished. In the political sphere there was a significant movement to improve the Republic and institute reforms.

Republic of Two Nations, Early 16th Century

- Poland
- Lithuania
- Feudal territories

Nicolaus Copernicus (1473–1543)
This Polish astronomer and humanist showed that the Earth revolves around the Sun.

Representatives of the peoples of the East and West

Nobleman who brought the news of the Chancellor's death

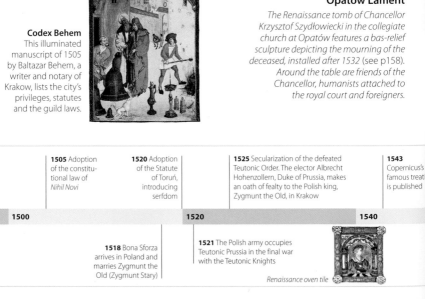

Codex Behem
This illuminated manuscript of 1505 by Baltazar Behem, a writer and notary of Krakow, lists the city's privileges, statutes and the guild laws.

Opatów Lament
The Renaissance tomb of Chancellor Krzysztof Szydłowiecki in the collegiate church at Opatów features a bas-relief sculpture depicting the mourning of the deceased, installed after 1532 (see p158). Around the table are friends of the Chancellor, humanists attached to the royal court and foreigners.

1505 Adoption of the constitutional law of *Nihil Novi*

1520 Adoption of the Statute of Toruń, introducing serfdom

1525 Secularization of the defeated Teutonic Order. The elector Albrecht Hohenzollern, Duke of Prussia, makes an oath of fealty to the Polish king, Zygmunt the Old, in Krakow

1543 Copernicus's famous treati is published

1500

1520

1540

1518 Bona Sforza arrives in Poland and marries Zygmunt the Old (Zygmunt Stary)

1521 The Polish army occupies Teutonic Prussia in the final war with the Teutonic Knights

Renaissance oven tile

Tomb of Stefan Batory
Despite his short reign, Batory was one of the most illustrious of the elective monarchs.

Union of Lublin
The federation of Poland and Lithuania established under the Union of Lublin in 1569 provided for a joint Sejm (parliament), king and foreign policy. However, each country had its own government, army, treasury and judiciary.

Zygmunt the Old

Vice-chancellor Piotr Tomicki

Jan Tarnowski, the deceased's son-in-law

Dogs, symbolizing the loyalty of the dead man's friends

Tapestry with Satyrs
The collection of tapestries at Wawel Royal Castle (see pp146–7) comprises over 160 splendid pieces. They were brought to the castle in the 16th century.

16th-Century Architecture

The first instance of the Renaissance style in Poland dates from 1502. Often imitated but never equalled, the most splendid early Renaissance building was the Zygmunt Chapel in Wawel Cathedral (see p149), completed in 1533.

This castle in Książ Wielki, built by Santi Gucci between 1585 and 1589, is the most splendid example of Italian Mannerism in Poland.

The collegiate church in Pułtusk (see p119), built c.1560 by the architect Gianbattista of Venice, has barrel vaulting.

1557 Outbreak of the war with Russia over Livonia

1563 Split of Polish Calvinists and isolation of the Polish Brethren, an extreme group of Reformationists

1564 Jesuits arrive in Poland

1587 Zygmunt III Vasa is elected king of Poland

Grotesque mask from Baranów Sandomierski

1560

1580

1600

1561 Livonia (Western Latvia) is incorporated into Poland-Lithuania, sparking conflict with both Sweden and Moscow

1569 Union of Lublin

1579 The capture of Połock marks the start of Stefan Batory's victory in the war against Russia

1596 The capital is moved from Krakow to Warsaw

The "Silver" 17th Century

The 17th century was dominated by the wars that the Republic of Two Nations waged against the Swedes, Russia and the Ottoman Empire. An uprising in Ukraine in 1648 marked the beginning of a series of catastrophes. In 1655 the Republic of Two Nations was invaded and largely occupied by the Swedes. Although it was short-lived, the Swedish occupation – known as the Deluge *(Potop)* – wreaked havoc. The final triumph of the Republic of Two Nations was the victory against the Ottomans at the Battle of Vienna in 1683, during the reign of Jan III Sobieski. The country eventually emerged from the wars without major territorial losses, but it was considerably weakened and its dominance was over.

Republic of Two Nations in the Years 1582–1648

▢ Poland ▢ Lithuania
▢ Feudal territories

A rebus on the main gate spells out "Krzyżtopór" with a cross *(Krzyż)* and an axe *(Topór)*.

Siege of Jasna Góra, the Luminous Mountain
The run of Swedish victories ended in 1655 with the heroic Polish defence of the Pauline Monastery in Częstochowa.

Nobleman in a Dance with Death
The figure of a common Polish yeoman in traditional dress decorates the Chapel of the Oleśnicki family in Tarłów.

Moat

Krzyżtopór Castle
In the first half of the 17th century, dazzling residences were built in the Republic of Two Nations. The most splendid was the eccentric castle in Ujazd. Built at great expense, it stood for barely 11 years. It was demolished in 1655 by the Swedes and remains in ruins to this day (see p158).

1601 Outbreak of Polish–Swedish War

1606 Zebrzydowski Rebellion

1629 Truce with Sweden in Altmark

1634 Władysław IV's victory over Russia, and peace in Polanów

1655 Beginning of the Swedish Deluge

1600

1605 Poles put pretender Demetrius on the Moscow throne

Zygmunt III Vasa

1620

1620 Battle against the Ottomans and Tatars at Cecora

1632 Death of Zygmunt III Vasa

1640

1648 Death of Władysław IV, start of the Chmielnicki Uprising in the Ukraine

Baroque Monstrance
This monstrance, at Pelplin Cathedral in Pomerania, dates from 1646.

Shrine of St Stanisław
Relics of the patron saint of Poland are preserved in a shrine that was installed in Wawel Cathedral between 1626 and 1629.

The cloister walls
around the courtyard are painted with real and legendary ancestors of the Ossoliński family.

Bastions

Husaria
Charges by the famous Hussars, the best heavy cavalry in Europe, decided the outcome of many battles. Their greatest victory was against the Ottomans at the Battle of Vienna (1683).

17th-Century Architecture

Many magnificent buildings in the late Mannerist and early Baroque styles were erected in the first half of the 17th century, during the reign of the Vasa dynasty. After the destruction wrought by the Swedish Deluge, there was no further artistic flowering until the reign of Jan III Sobieski. The early Baroque castles – for example, the Royal Castle in Warsaw (see pp70–71) – as well as numerous churches, of which the most impressive are the Jesuit churches in Krakow, Warsaw and Poznań, are all splendid examples of the architecture of this period.

The Bishops' Palace in Kielce
(see p156) is the best-preserved early Baroque residence.

The Royal Chapel (see p245) in Gdańsk, commissioned by Jan III Sobieski, was built by Tylman van Gameren and Andreas Schlüter in the Baroque style.

1658 Polish Brethren exiled from Poland

1660 Peace treaty signed in Oliwa ends the Polish-Swedish War

1660

1667 Ottomans invade the southeastern borderlands

1668 Abdication of Jan Kazimierz

1686 Signing of the Perpetual Peace with Russia

1680

1683 Jan III Sobieski's victory over the Ottomans at the Battle of Vienna

1699 Peace of Karłowice with Ottoman Empire

1700

Pair of cherubs

Mannerist window frame

Poland in the 18th Century

In the first half of the 18th century, Poland was ruled by the Wettin dynasty of Saxony. Polish interests were gradually subordinated to those of neighbouring powers, and the election of Stanisław August Poniatowski as king, supported by the Tsarina Catherine the Great, sealed the nation's fate. Attempts to counteract Russian influence came to an end with the First Partition of Poland in 1772. The efforts of the patriotic faction's Four-Year Sejm changed little to restore the Republic's fortunes. The Second Partition followed in 1793, and when the uprising led by Tadeusz Kościuszko – the final attempt to save the country – was quashed, Poland lost its statehood for over 100 years.

Republic of Two Nations before the Partitions
Poland   Lithuania

Stanisław August Poniatowski

Rococo Statue from Lwów
In southeastern Poland, original altar statues by sculptors of the Lwów School can still be admired.

Rococo Secretaire
This desk incorporates a clock cabinet and is decorated with painted panels depicting mythological scenes.

Portrait of Maria Leszczyńska
After the Polish king Stanisław Leszczyński lost the throne, his daughter Maria settled in Nancy and married Louis XV of France.

1697 Coronation of August II, the Strong

1704 Coronation of Stanisław Leszczyński, supported by the king of Sweden

1717 "Dumb Sejm" – freedom of debate is hampered by Russian pressure

1733 Election of August III

1740 Opening of Collegium Nobilium, Warsaw

1700

1720

1740

1700 Outbreak of Great Northern War

1709 August II, the Strong returns to the throne

1733 Stanisław Leszczyński is re-elected king

1721 End of Great Northern War

Casing of a grenadier's cap

Tadeusz Kościuszko
This man fought in the American War of Independence and led the insurrection against the Russians in 1794.

August III
This Saxon king of the Wettin dynasty was an ardent lover of porcelain. His likeness was reproduced in Meissen.

18th-Century Architecture

During the 18th century – the era of the late Baroque and Rococo – artists and architects from Saxony joined those who had already come to Poland from Italy. Many palaces, including Radziwiłł, were built in Warsaw and the provinces, such as Białystok *(see p294)*. Thanks to the patronage of Stanisław August Poniatowski, many Neo-Classical buildings were created, among them Łazienki in Warsaw.

The Palace on the Water *(see pp100–101)* in Warsaw was the royal summer residence.

Hugo Kołłątaj

Prince Józef Poniatowski

Stanisław Małachowski, Speaker of the Sejm

Constitution of 3 May

The Constitution of 3 May 1791 was a radical experiment in democracy and reform – the first such in Europe. It was, however, soon annulled as a result of conservative opposition and external interference from Russia. Jan Matejko's painting shows members of the Sejm (parliament) marching on Warsaw Cathedral to swear allegiance.

Hugo Kołłątaj
A leading intellectual of the Polish Enlightenment, Kołłątaj collaborated on the Constitution of 3 May.

1764 Coronation of Stanisław August Poniatowski

1773 Convocation of National Education Commission

1794 Insurrection against the Russians

1795 Third Partition of Poland

Coat of arms of Stanisław August Poniatowski

1760

1780

1800

1756 Outbreak of the Seven-Year War

1772 First Partition of Poland

1788–1792 Deliberations of the Four-Year Sejm

1793 Second Partition of Poland

1791 Adoption of the Constitution of 3 May

Poland under the Partitions

Russia, Prussia and Austria deprived Poland of its independence, making it a territory for exploitation. The hopes that Napoleon would liberate the country proved illusory. His Grand Duchy of Warsaw lasted only eight years. The failure of the successive November and January insurrections (1830 and 1863) led to further restrictions by the Tsarist rulers: landed property was confiscated and cultural and educational institutions dissolved. Many Poles fled abroad. The collapse of the partitioning empires in World War I enabled Poland to regain its independence in 1918.

Republic of Two Nations under the Partitions

- Russian partition
- Prussian partition
- Austrian partition

Patrol of Insurgents
This painting by Maksymilian Gierymski of around 1873 shows a scene from the January Insurrection. Several insurgents are patrolling the land.

Beggar waiting for alms

Emperor Franz Josef enjoying the loyalty of his subjects

Henryk Sienkiewicz's House in Oblęgorek
The small palace was given to the Nobel laureate Henryk Sienkiewicz in 1900 to mark the occasion of 25 years of his work as a writer.

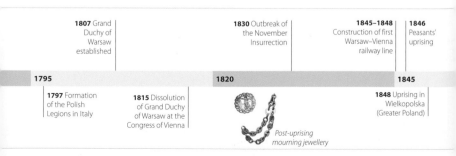

1807 Grand Duchy of Warsaw established

1830 Outbreak of the November Insurrection

1845–1848 Construction of first Warsaw–Vienna railway line

1846 Peasants' uprising

1795

1820

1845

1797 Formation of the Polish Legions in Italy

1815 Dissolution of Grand Duchy of Warsaw at the Congress of Vienna

Post-uprising mourning jewellery

1848 Uprising in Wielkopolska (Greater Poland)

Fryderyk Chopin
This genius of a composer and pianist was born in Żelazowa Wola but left Poland forever in 1830.

Stained-glass Window
The stained-glass windows designed by Stanisław Wyspiański for the Franciscan Church in Krakow are among the most beautiful works of Art Nouveau art in Poland.

The Great Emigration

In the 30 years following the November Insurrection, nearly 20,000 Poles left the country, the majority going to France. An important group of émigrés gathered around Prince Adam Czartoryski in Paris. Famous Poles in exile included the composer Fryderyk Chopin and poets Adam Mickiewicz, Zygmunt Krasiński, Juliusz Słowacki and Cyprian Kamil Norwid.

Prince Adam Czartoryski, an exile in Paris, was considered the uncrowned king of Poland.

The inhabitants of Krakow greet the emperor

Emperor Franz Josef Enters Krakow
Juliusz Kossak produced a series of paintings to commemorate the emperor's visit to Krakow in 1880. The city's inhabitants received him with great enthusiasm.

Prince Józef Poniatowski
Bertel Thorvaldsen designed this monument to Prince Józef Poniatowski, who died in 1813. Poniatowski was considered a Polish national hero.

1861 Founding of the National Sejm in Galicia

1873 Founding of the Academy of Sciences in Krakow

1903 Marie Curie (Maria Skłodowska-Curie) receives the Nobel Prize for Physics

1905 Henryk Sienkiewicz receives the Nobel Prize for Literature

1870

1895

1864 Final abolition of serfdom

1863 Start of the January Insurrection

Art Nouveau wall painting in Krakow's Franciscan Church

1915 Russian troops leave Warsaw

Poland from 1918 to 1945

Poland regained its independence in 1918, but for several years afterwards battles raged over its borders. In 1920, independence was again threatened by the Red Army. Despite domestic conflicts, Poland made considerable economic progress. The territories of the three areas previously held by Russia, Austria and Prussia were consolidated. The country's brief period of independence ended in 1939 with the German and Soviet invasions. Poland was occupied and its population persecuted, terrorized and partially exterminated. About 6 million Poles were killed, including 3 million Jews *(see pp164–7)*. An underground state operated, with the Home Army answering to the government in exile. Polish soldiers, serving with the Allies, fought the Germans on all fronts.

Poland in 1938
☐ Polish territory

Volunteers fighting alongside the soldiers

Gdynia
Although Poland gained access to the sea, it had no port. Work on the construction of a port at Gdynia began in 1922.

Interior of the Silesian Sejm
The industrialized region of Silesia had its own parliament in the interwar years, a sign of its importance.

Miracle on the Vistula
This was the name given to Marshal Józef Piłsudski's victory at the Battle of Warsaw on 13–16 August 1920, which halted the Soviet march westwards and shattered the Bolshevik hope of a proletarian revolution throughout Europe.

1918 Uprising against the Germans in Greater Poland. Warsaw is liberated from German occupation

1920 Miracle on the Vistula. Second Silesian uprising

1921 Germano-Polish plebiscite in Upper Silesia. Third Silesian uprising

1925 Start of the German–Polish trade war

1926 May Coup

1915

1920

1925

1930

1919 Start of the first Silesian uprising

1922 Murder of the president, Gabriel Narutowicz

1924 Złoty introduced to replace German Mark

1929 Start of the Great Depression

Magazine cover featuring the National Universal Exhibition in Poznań

Józef Piłsudski

Józef Piłsudski led the Polish legions which were set up in the Austrian sector before turning his attention to Polish Independence. In 1918 he became the first leader of an independent Poland.

Warsaw Uprising

On 1 August 1944 the underground Home Army (Armia Krajowa) launched an uprising in Warsaw against the occupying Germans. Its aim was to liberate the capital before the arrival of the Red Army. The Soviets were waiting on the left bank of the river, allowing the Germans to suppress the insurgents. The uprising lasted over two months and led to the complete destruction of the city as well as the loss of tens of thousands of lives.

Plaque to the Victims of Execution
One of many plaques in Warsaw marking places of execution during World War II.

In his film *Kanał*, the director Andrzej Wajda showed the insurgents struggling through sewers beneath German-occupied districts of Warsaw.

Father Ignacy Skorupka leads soldiers into attack

Bolshevik soldiers flee the battlefield

Hanka Ordonówna
She was one of the most popular actresses between the wars.

Monument to Those Fallen and Murdered in the East
This monument honours all the Poles who were killed or deported after the Soviet invasion in 1939.

Modern Poland

In 1945 the allies agreed that Poland should be included in the Soviet zone of influence. The Big Three (Britain, the USA and the Soviet Union) also decided to alter Poland's borders. After rigged elections in 1947, the Communists took complete control. Despite successes in rebuilding the country, the socialist economy proved ineffective. The formation of Solidarity (Solidarność) in 1980 accelerated the pace of change, which was completed when Poland regained its freedom after the 1989 elections.

1968 In March, conflicts occur between students and security forces. The authorities provoke incidents of an anti-Semitic and anti-intellectual nature

1966 Celebrations marking the millennium of Christianity in Poland, organized separately by Church and State

1945 After the terrible devastation of the war, the country is hauled out of the ruins by the effort of the whole nation

1947 Communists falsify the results of elections to the Sejm (parliament)

1955 30,000 delegates from 114 countries take part in the World Festival of Youth in Warsaw. This is the first time that the Iron Curtain has been briefly lifted

1945	1950	1955	1960	1965	1970	1975
1945	1950	1955	1960	1965	1970	1975

1953 Height of the persecution of the Catholic Church, trial of priests of the metropolitan curia of Krakow; Cardinal Stefan Wyszyński, Primate of Poland, is arrested

1958 First International Jazz Jamboree in Warsaw

1968 Polish forces take part in the armed intervention in Czechoslovakia

1957 Premiere of *Kanał*, directed by Andrzej Wajda, one of the first films of the Polish School

1946 Rigged referendum on abolishing the Senate, introducing agricultural reforms, nationalizing industry and the western border

1956 In June, a workers' revolt in Poznań is bloodily suppressed. In October, after more demonstrations by students and workers, Soviet intervention is threatened. Władysław Gomułka becomes First Secretary of the Central Committee of the Polish United Workers' Party

1945 End of World War II

1970 Bloody suppression of a strike and workers' demonstrations on the coast. Edward Gierek becomes First Secretary of the Central Committee of the Polish United Workers' Party

1976 Demonstrations against price rises, by workers in Radom and Ursus, are quashed. The opposition forms the Workers' Defence Committee. At the 21st Olympics in Montreal, Irena Kirszenstein-Szewińska wins gold for track and field sports for the third time

1979 First visit of John Paul II, the "Polish Pope", to his homeland. Both a religious and a political event, it rekindles Polish hopes of regaining freedom

2010 A tragic air crash kills 96 people, including President Lech Kaczyński and his wife; Bronisław Komorowski (left) elected president of Poland

80 Agreements signed in ańsk on 31 August end the kes and allow the formation the first Independent tonomous Trades Unions. Lech łęsa becomes their leader

1990 Lech Wałęsa elected president of Poland

2012 Poland and Ukraine host the UEFA Football Championship – Euro 2012

1981 Under the leadership of General Wojciech Jaruzelski, the Communist authorities introduce martial law. Solidarity goes underground

1997 The worst flood in a century devastates large areas of southern Poland

1999 Poland joins NATO

2002 Poland formally invited to join EU in 2004

2005 Death of John Paul II, the "Polish Pope"

2014 Canonization of Pope John Paul II

80	1985	1990	1995	2000	2005	2010	2015

80	1985	1990	1995	2000	2005	2010	2015

1990 Official end of the Polish People's Republic, adoption of Leszek Balcerowicz's radical market reforms

2004 Poland joins the EU

2015 Paweł Pawlikowski's film *Ida* wins the Oscar for Best Foreign Film

1989 At round-table talks, the opposition negotiates with the authorities about legalizing Solidarity and calling an election, in which the "civic society" then wins a landslide victory

2000 Krakow is European City of Culture

2007 Poland joins the Schengen Area

2005 Lech Kaczyński elected president of Poland

1984 Assassination of Father Jerzy Popiełuszko, Solidarity's pastor

1997 On a visit to Warsaw, US president Bill Clinton announces that Poland is to join NATO

The Rulers of Poland

At the time of its formation in 966, the Polish nation was ruled by the Piast dynasty. Bolesław the Brave, son of Mieszko I, was the first king of Poland. During the Period of Disunity from 1138, rulers bore only the title of prince, until the coronation of King Przemysław II in 1290. After the death of Kazimierz the Great, the Polish crown passed to Louis of Hungary of the Angevin dynasty. The marriage of his daughter Jadwiga to the Lithuanian duke Jagiełło in 1384 established the Jagiellonian dynasty. From 1572 the Republic of Two Nations was ruled by elective kings with no hereditary rights. The last king was Stanisław August Poniatowski.

1386–1434
Władysław II
Jagiełło

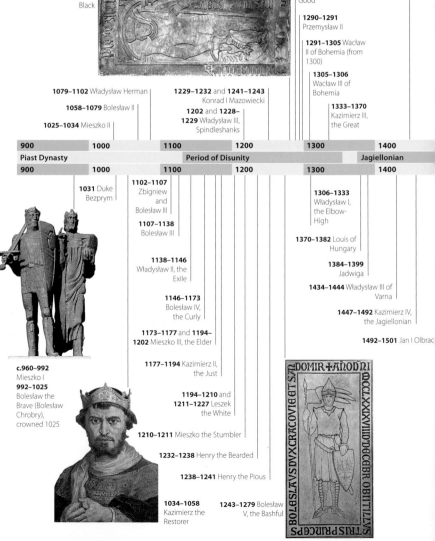

1279–1288
Leszek the
Black

1288–1290 Henry IV, the
Good

1290–1291
Przemysław II

1291–1305 Wacław
II of Bohemia (from
1300)

1305–1306
Wacław III of
Bohemia

1079–1102 Władysław Herman

1058–1079 Bolesław II

1025–1034 Mieszko II

1229–1232 and **1241–1243**
Konrad I Mazowiecki

1202 and **1228–
1229** Władysław III,
Spindleshanks

1333–1370
Kazimierz III,
the Great

900	1000	1100	1200	1300	1400
Piast Dynasty			**Period of Disunity**		**Jagiellonian**
900	1000	1100	1200	1300	1400

1031 Duke
Bezprym

1102–1107
Zbigniew
and
Bolesław III

1107–1138
Bolesław III

1306–1333
Władysław I,
the Elbow-
High

1370–1382 Louis of
Hungary

1138–1146
Władysław II, the
Exile

1384–1399
Jadwiga

1146–1173
Bolesław IV,
the Curly

1434–1444 Władysław III of
Varna

1173–1177 and **1194–
1202** Mieszko III, the Elder

1447–1492 Kazimierz IV,
the Jagiellonian

1177–1194 Kazimierz II,
the Just

1492–1501 Jan I Olbrac

1194–1210 and
1211–1227 Leszek
the White

c.960–992
Mieszko I
992–1025
Bolesław the
Brave (Bolesław
Chrobry),
crowned 1025

1210–1211 Mieszko the Stumbler

1232–1238 Henry the Bearded

1238–1241 Henry the Pious

1034–1058
Kazimierz the
Restorer

1243–1279 Bolesław
V, the Bashful

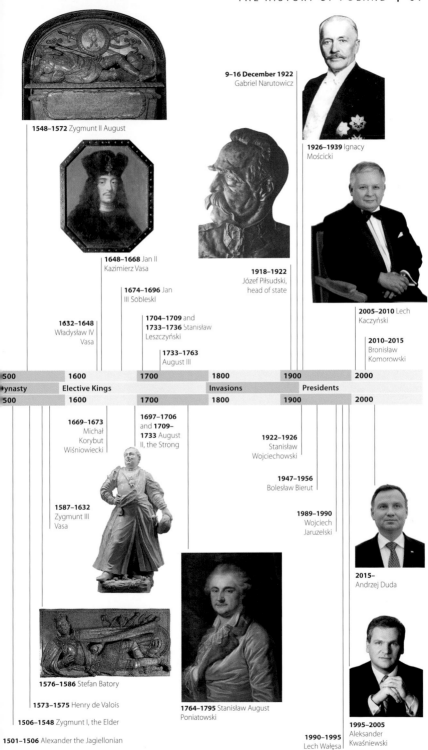

1548–1572 Zygmunt II August

9–16 December 1922 Gabriel Narutowicz

1926–1939 Ignacy Mościcki

1648–1668 Jan II Kazimierz Vasa

1918–1922 Józef Piłsudski, head of state

1674–1696 Jan III Sobieski

2005–2010 Lech Kaczyński

1704–1709 and **1733–1736** Stanisław Leszczyński

1632–1648 Władysław IV Vasa

2010–2015 Bronisław Komorowski

1733–1763 August III

500	1600	1700	1800	1900	2000
Dynasty	Elective Kings		Invasions	Presidents	
500	1600	1700	1800	1900	2000

1669–1673 Michał Korybut Wiśniowiecki

1697–1706 and **1709– 1733** August II, the Strong

1922–1926 Stanisław Wojciechowski

1947–1956 Bolesław Bierut

1989–1990 Wojciech Jaruzelski

1587–1632 Zygmunt III Vasa

2015– Andrzej Duda

1576–1586 Stefan Batory

1573–1575 Henry de Valois

1506–1548 Zygmunt I, the Elder

1501–1506 Alexander the Jagiellonian

1764–1795 Stanisław August Poniatowski

1990–1995 Lech Wałęsa

1995–2005 Aleksander Kwaśniewski

WARSAW AREA BY AREA

Warsaw at a Glance

Most places of interest are located in the centre of Warsaw. This area not only forms the geographical heart of the city, but is also Warsaw's largest municipality. It is made up of seven smaller districts, Śródmieście being the central one. In the pages that follow, however, Warsaw is divided into three parts: the Old and New Towns, the Royal Route and the City Centre. The most interesting historical features of Warsaw are located along the Royal Route (Trakt Królewski), a series of roads linking the Old Town (Stare Miasto) and the Royal Castle (Zamek Królewski) with the Water Palace (Łazienki) and Wilanów, the palace of Jan III Sobieski, which stands just outside the city.

The Old Town Square, surrounded by town houses rebuilt after wartime destruction, is one of the most beautiful features of Warsaw. It teems with tourists and local people throughout the year. A statue of the Mermaid, symbol of Warsaw, is a prominent feature in the centre of the square.

The Palace of Culture is still the tallest building in Warsaw, despite the ongoing construction of skyscrapers in the city. The 30th floor has a viewing terrace as well as a multimedia tourist centre.

The buildings on the north side of Theatre Square now house banks and luxury shops, as well as the little church of St Albert and St Andrzej, which contains important works of art.

◀ The colourful architecture of Castle Square, with Zygmunt's Column, in Warsaw's Old Town

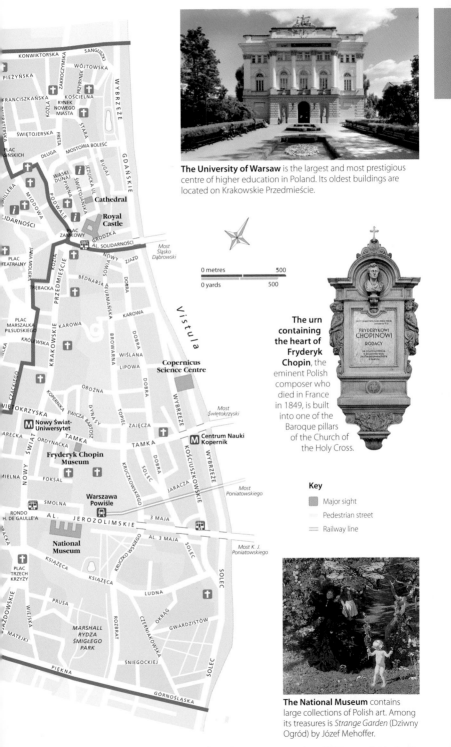

The University of Warsaw is the largest and most prestigious centre of higher education in Poland. Its oldest buildings are located on Krakowskie Przedmieście.

0 metres 500
0 yards 500

The urn containing the heart of Fryderyk Chopin, the eminent Polish composer who died in France in 1849, is built into one of the Baroque pillars of the Church of the Holy Cross.

Key

▮ Major sight

Pedestrian street

═ Railway line

The National Museum contains large collections of Polish art. Among its treasures is *Strange Garden* (Dziwny Ogród) by Józef Mehoffer.

For keys to symbols *see back flap*

THE OLD AND NEW TOWNS

The Old Town (Stare Miasto), partially surrounded by medieval walls, is the oldest district in Warsaw. It was founded at the turn of the 13th and 14th centuries, growing up around the castle of the Mazovian princes. Its medieval urban layout survives to this day. The pride of the Old Town is the market square with its colourful town and the Cathedral of St John. Next to the Old Town is the New Town (Nowe Miasto), which became a separate urban entity in 1408.

The reconstruction of the Old Town and New Town, including the Royal Castle, after both of these areas were almost completely destroyed during the war, was an undertaking on a scale unprecedented in the whole of Europe. Today, after being rebuilt, these two districts are the most popular tourist attractions in Warsaw, particularly the Old Town, which pulsates with life until late evening. There are many interesting little streets and an abundance of cafés, good restaurants and antique shops.

Sights at a Glance

Churches
3 *Cathedral of St John p72*
4 Jesuit Church
5 Church of St Martin
8 Church of the Holy Spirit
11 Church of St Jacek
14 Church of St Kazimierz
15 Church of the Visitation
　　of the Virgin Mary

Historic Streets and Squares
6 Old Town Square
12 Ulica Freta
13 New Town Square

Historic Buildings and Monuments
1 Zygmunt's Column
2 *Royal Castle pp70–71*
7 The Barbican and City Walls
9 Raczyński Palace
10 Monument to the 1944
　　Warsaw Uprising

See also Street Finder, maps 1 & 2

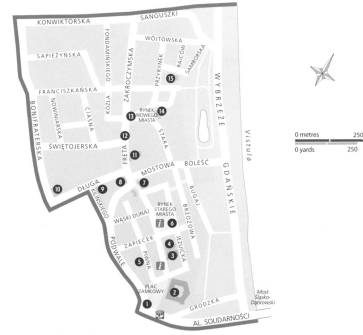

0 metres　　250
0 yards　　250

The Old Town

The Old Town Square (Rynek Starego Miasta) is surrounded on all sides by town houses, rebuilt after World War II with great devotion. Today, it is one of the most attractive places in Warsaw. From spring to autumn it is filled with café tables, and also becomes an open-air gallery of arts and crafts. There are several restaurants and bars squeezed into neighbouring streets, especially in Piwna and Jezuicka. Remains of the former city walls give the ensemble an evocatively medieval feel. The whole of the Old Town is not only a tourist attraction but also a favourite place for local people.

❺ Church of St Martin
This striking modern crucifix incorporates a fragment of a figure of Christ that was burned during the 1944 Warsaw Uprising.

❸ ★ Cathedral of St John
After suffering damage during World War II, the cathedral was rebuilt in the Gothic style.

❹ Jesuit Church
The Baroque-Mannerist sanctuary of Our Lady of Mercy, patron saint of Warsaw, was rebuilt after World War II.

❶ Zygmunt's Column
This is the oldest secular monument in Warsaw.

❷ ★ Royal Castle (Zamek Królewski)
This former royal residence, rebuilt in the 1970s, is today the symbol of Polish independence.

The Palace Under the Tin Roof was the first house in the city of Warsaw to have a tin, rather than tiled, roof.

PODWALE

PIEKARSKA

PIWNA

ŚWIĘTOJAŃSKA

PLAC ZAMKOWY

❼ Barbican and City Walls
These brick bastions once protected the northern approach to the city.

Locator Map
See Street Finder, map 2

The Historical Museum of Warsaw occupies the north side of the market square.

Statue of Zygmunt III Vasa at the top of Zygmunt's Column

❶ Zygmunt's Column

Plac Zamkowy. **Map** 2 D3.
🚌 116, 175, 178, 180, 190, 222, 503.
🚊 20, 23, 26.

Zygmunt's Column, in the centre of Plac Zamkowy, is the oldest secular statue in Warsaw. It was erected in 1644 by Zygmunt III's son Władysław IV. The monument, which stands 22 m (72 ft) high, consists of a Corinthian granite column supported on a tall plinth and topped with a bronze statue of the ruler, who is depicted with a cross in his left hand and a sword in his right. The figure is the work of Clemente Molli, and the whole monument was designed by Augustyn Locci the Elder and Constantino Tencalla, two Italian architects working for the king. This monument, unusual in European terms, glorifies the secular ruler in a manner which had until then been reserved for saints and other religious subjects. Despite repeated damage and repairs, the statue retains its original appearance. The column on which it stands, however, has already been replaced twice. An older, fractured shaft can be seen on the terrace near the south façade of the Palace Under the Tin Roof.

SZEROKI-DUNAJ

NOWOMIEJSKA

KOŁO

KRZYWE

RYNEK STAREGO MIASTA

Statue of the Mermaid

❻ ★ Old Town Square
The square pulsates with life until late in the evening.

0 metres 100
0 yards 100

Key
— Suggested route

❷ Royal Castle

The decision to build the Royal Castle (Zamek Królewski) was made when Zygmunt III Vasa moved the capital from Krakow to Warsaw in 1596. It was built in the early Baroque style by the Italian architects Giovanni Trevano, Giacomo Rodondo and Matteo Castelli between 1598 and 1619, incorporating the earlier castle of the Mazovian princes. Successive rulers remodelled the castle many times. The late Baroque façade overlooking the River Vistula dates from the time of August III, and the splendid interiors from that of Stanisław August. Completely destroyed by the Germans during World War II, the castle was reconstructed from 1971 to 1988.

★ Ballroom
Decorated with 17 pairs of golden columns, the ballroom is one of the castle's most elaborate interiors.

Royal Princes' Rooms
Historical paintings by Jan Matejko are displayed here.

Senators' Room
In this room, the Constitution of 3 May was formally adopted in 1791. The coats of arms of all the administrative regions and territories of the Republic are depicted on the walls. A reconstructed royal throne is also on show.

Main entrance

KEY

① **The Lanckoroński Gallery**
on the ground floor contains two paintings by Rembrandt: *Portrait of a Young Woman* and *Scholar at his Desk*.

Zygmunt Tower
This tower, 60 m (197 ft) high, was built in 1619. It is crowned by a cupola with a spire. It is also known as the Clock Tower (Zegarowa), since a clock was installed in 1622.

★ Marble Room

The interior dates from the time of Władysław IV. The magnificent portraits of Polish rulers by Marcello Bacciarelli are the only later additions.

VISITORS' CHECKLIST

Practical Information

Plac Zamkowy 4. **Map** 2 D3. **Tel** 22 355 51 70. Reservations: 9am–2pm Tue–Fri (institutions only). Fax: 22 355 51 27. **Open** May–Sep: 10am–6pm Mon–Sat (to 8pm Thu), 11am–6pm Sun; Oct–Apr: 10am–4pm Tue–Sat, 11am–4pm Sun. **Closed** Oct–Apr: Mon, 1 Jan, Easter Sat & Sun, 1 May, Corpus Christi, 1 Nov, 24, 25 & 31 Dec. (free on Sun except Royal and Grand Apartments). except Sun. No flash.
w zamek-krolewski.pl

Transport

116, 128, 175, 178, 180, 222, 503, 518. 4, 13, 20, 23, 26.

Knights' Hall

The finest piece in this beautiful interior is the Neo-Classical sculpture of Chronos by le Brun and Monaldi.

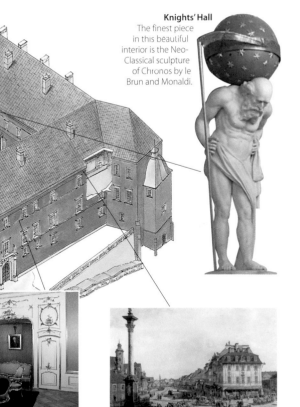

Apartment of Prince Stanisław Poniatowski

The Rococo panelling, thought to be by the French cabinet-maker Juste-Aurèle Meissonier, was taken from the former Tarnowski Palace.

★ Canaletto Room

The walls of this room are decorated with scenes of Warsaw by Canaletto, the famous Venetian painter who was one of the most commercially successful artists of his day.

❸ Cathedral of St John

The Cathedral of St John started life as a parish church at the beginning of the 15th century, only acquiring cathedral status in 1798. Over the years, successive rulers endowed it with new chapels and other elements. Important ceremonies have taken place here, including the coronation of Stanisław August Poniatowski in 1764 and the oath of allegiance to the Constitution of 3 May in 1791. Many famous Poles are buried in the cathedral, among them the Polish primate, Cardinal Stefan Wyszyński. Having been seriously damaged in World War II, the cathedral was rebuilt; its new façade was designed by Jan Zachwatowicz in the spirit of Mazovian Gothic architecture.

VISITORS' CHECKLIST

Practical Information
ul. Świętojańska 8. **Map** 2 D3.
Tel 22 831 02 89. **Open**
10am–5pm Mon–Sat,
3–5pm Sun.

Transport
🚌 116, 128, 175, 178, 160, 180, 190, 222, 503, 518. 🚊 4, 13, 20, 23, 26.

Narutowicz Crypt
Gabriel Narutowicz, first president of the Polish Republic, is interred in the cathedral with other distinguished Poles.

Choir Stalls
The choir stalls are a copy of those donated as a votive offering after Poland's victory in 1683 at the Battle of Vienna.

Main entrance

Baryczkowski Crucifix
This crucifix, famed for its miraculous powers, dates from the start of the 16th century and contains natural human hair.

Małachowski Family Tomb
This monument, carved in white marble, is based on a design by the Danish Neo-Classical sculptor Bertel Thorvaldsen.

❹ Jesuit Church

ul. Świętojańska 10. **Map** 2 D3.
Tel 22 831 16 75. 🚌 116, 128, 175,
178, 160, 180, 190, 222, 503, 518.
🚊 4, 13, 20, 23, 26.

This Mannerist-Baroque church
was built for the Jesuit order
between 1609 and 1629.
Although it had a somewhat
chequered history, it survived
without major changes until
1944, when it was almost completely destroyed. When it was
rebuilt after World War II, the
church's somewhat unusual
architecture was restored on
the basis of the original plans,
which had survived. Located in
a narrow space, it has a unique
layout; especially original is the
way in which the chancel is
flooded by light falling from
the lantern in the elliptical
dome over the apse. The crypt,
which contains a stonecutter's
workshop, is in the space once
occupied by the basements of
the Gothic town houses that
stood on the site.

Jesuit church, dedicated to the Merciful
Mother of God

❺ Church of St Martin

ul. Piwna 9/11. **Map** 2 D3. **Tel** 22 831
02 21. 🚌 116, 128, 175, 178, 160, 180,
190, 222, 503, 518. 🚊 4, 13, 20, 23, 26.

The existing post-Augustan
Church is the result of two
reconstructions in the Baroque
style, carried out in 1631–6 and
in the early 18th century. The
latter phase of rebuilding took
place under the direction of
architect Kaŕrol Bay, who

designed the undulating façade.
The late Baroque decoration of
the interior was destroyed in
1944. Only a partially burned
crucifix survived. After the war,
the interior was restored to a
design by Sister Alma
Skrzydlewska and the crucifix
incorporated into a modern
design. In the 1980s, the church
was a meeting place for the
political opposition to the
Communist government.

❻ Old Town Square

Map 2 D3. 🚌 116, 128, 175, 178, 160,
180, 190, 222, 503, 518. 🚊 4, 13, 20,
23, 26. Museum of Warsaw: **Tel** 22 596
67 00. **Open** 10am–7pm Tue–Sun. 🌐
🅦 muzeumwarszawy.pl

Until the end of the 18th century,
this rectangular market square
was the most important place in
Warsaw. The houses around the
square were built by the most
affluent members of the community. Most of the buildings date
from the 1600s, and it is these
that give the square its period
character. In the centre there was
once a town hall, a weigh house
and stalls, all demolished in 1817.
In their place now stands a
statue of the Mermaid *(Syrenka)*.

Each row of houses bears the
name of one of the people
involved in the Four-Year Sejm.
On the north side is Dekerta –
named after Jan Dekert, mayor
of Warsaw in the 18th century.
All the houses are inter-
connected and now host
the **Museum of Warsaw**,
which reopened in 2017 after
extensive restoration. It has
acquired three million original
items over the years, one of
the largest collection in the
world. This compelling range
of artifacts and personal

memories includes utility items,
artworks and keepsakes of
people and events. These are
displayed innovatively in 21
themed rooms that take visitors
through the history of the city.

The Barbican, standing on the site of the
former outer city gate

❼ The Barbican and City Walls

ul. Nowomiejska. **Map** 2 D2.

Warsaw is one of the few
European capitals where a
large portion of the old city
wall survives. Construction of
the wall began in the first half
of the 14th century and continued in phases up to the
mid-16th century. A double
circumvallation, reinforced with
fortresses and towers, encircled
the town. The earliest part of the
fortifications is the Barbican,
erected around 1548 by
Gianbattista of Venice. It was
built on the site of an earlier
outer gate and was intended
to defend the Nowomiejska
Gate (Brama Nowomiejska).
The northern part of this defensive building, in the form of a
dungeon reinforced by four
semicircular towers, survived
as the external wall of a town
house. After World War II, parts
of the wall were rebuilt and the
Barbican, which had ceased to
exist for a long period,
was restored to its
full scale.

Old Town Square, a favourite place both for local people and tourists

New Town

The New Town took shape at the beginning of the 15th century along the route leading from Old Warsaw to Zakroczym. Of interest here are the Pauline, Franciscan, Dominican and Redemptorist churches and the Church of the Holy Sacrament, which were all rebuilt after World War II, and the colourful reconstructed town houses. Ulica Mostowa, the steepest street in Warsaw, leads up to the fortress that defended one of the longest bridges in 16th-century Europe.

⑬ ★ New Town Square
A town hall once stood in the centre of this irregularly shaped square.

❽ Church of the Holy Spirit
Every year, pilgrims gather at this Baroque church before setting off to Jasna Góra, in Częstochowa.

⑫ Ulica Freta
This is the main thoroughfare in New Town. *Freta* means an uncultivated field or suburb.

⑪ ★ Church of St Jacek
A feature of the unusually elongated interior is the 17th-century mausoleum of the Kotowski family.

⑭ ★ Church of St Kazimierz
This beautiful church is connected to the Convent of the Order of the Holy Sacrament.

The Old Powder Magazine was once the bridge gate.

Locator Map
See Street Finder map 2

0 metres	100
0 yards	100

⓯ **Church of the Visitation of the Virgin Mary**
This is the oldest surviving church in New Town. Princess Anna of Mazovia funded its construction in the early 15th century.

Key
— Suggested route

❽ Church of the Holy Spirit

ul. Długa 3. **Map** 2 D2. **Tel** 22 831 45 75. 🚌 116, 175, 178, 180, 222. **Open** 6–8am, 4–6pm Mon–Sat, 6:30am–2pm, 4–7:30pm Sun. At other times, on request.

The little wooden Church of the Holy Spirit (Kościół św. Ducha) already existed in the 14th century. Repeatedly extended, it was burned down during the Swedish invasion in 1655. As the townspeople could not afford to rebuild the church, King Jan Kazimierz donated the site to the Pauline fathers from Częstochowa, who were renowned for defending their monastery at Jasna Góra *(see pp160–61)*. In return, and at their own expense, the monks built a wall that enclosed the church and the monastery within Warsaw's defences.

The present church was built in 1707–17, based on a design by the architect Józef Piola. The work was directed by Józef Szymon Bellotti and later Karol Ceroni. The interior was completed in 1725.

Rebuilt after war damage, the church is known today – as it has been since 1711 – as the main starting point for pilgrimages to the shrine of the Virgin Mary at Jasna Góra.

In Ulica Długa, a small Neo-Classical house abuts the church. It was built at the beginning of the 19th century on the smallest plot in Warsaw; it occupies only a few square metres and has its own registry number.

Church of the Holy Spirit, facing down Ulica Mostowa

Façade of Raczyński Palace, which today is the Old Records Archive

❾ Raczyński Palace

ul. Długa 7. **Map** 2 D2. **Tel** 22 635 45 32. 🚌 116, 175, 178, 180, 222.

Raczynski Palace (Pałac Raczyńskich), rebuilt in 1786 to a design by the royal architect Jan Christian Kamsetzer, houses the Old Records Archive. The most beautiful feature of this former residence is the early Neo-Classical ballroom – damaged in the war but restored afterwards – which is decorated with stuccowork and allegorical paintings on the theme of Justice.

The subject of the paintings was manifestly at odds with the sentiments of the residence's owner, Kazimierz Raczyński, who held high office in the royal court and was considered a traitor to his country by his contemporaries. In the 19th century, the palace was the seat of the Government Justice Commission, and, in the interwar period, of the Ministry of Justice.

Particularly tragic events occurred here during World War II. Bullet marks in the wall of the building are evidence of the street execution of 50 local inhabitants who were arrested at random on 24 January 1944. But the worst crimes were committed here during the Warsaw Uprising. On 13 August 1944 a tank-trap exploded, killing some 80 insurgents, and on 2 September the Nazi SS killed several hundred injured people in the building, which was being used as a hospital.

Monument to the 1944 Warsaw Uprising

⑩ Monument to the 1944 Warsaw Uprising

pl. Krasińskich. **Map** 1 C2. 🚌 116, 178, 180, 222, 503.

This monument, unveiled in 1989, commemorates the heroes of the historic Warsaw Uprising. It consists of sculptures by Wincenty Kućma placed in an architectural setting by Jacek Budyń. The sculptures represent soldiers – one group defending the barricades, the other going down into the sewers. (The insurgents used the sewer system to move around Warsaw during the uprising.) The entrance to one such sewer is still to be found near the monument.

It was in front of this monu-ment, during the celebrations marking the 50th anniversary of the uprising, that the President of the Federal Republic of Germany, Richard Herzog, apologized to the Polish nation for the unleashing of World War II by the Third Reich and the bloody suppression of the Warsaw Uprising.

⑪ Church of St Jacek

ul. Freta 8/10. **Map** 2 D2. **Tel** 22 635 47 00. 🚌 116, 178, 180, 222, 503.

At the beginning of the 17th century, while the Jesuits were building a Baroque church in the Old Town, the Dominicans started work on a Gothic chancel for the Church of St Jacek (Kościół św. Jacka). They returned to the Gothic style partly because of the conservatism of Mazovian buildings and partly in an attempt to endow the church with the appearance of age, so as to create an illusion of the age-old traditions of the order – which had in fact only been set up in Warsaw in 1603. When work was interrupted by a plague that raged in Warsaw in 1625, the few remaining monks listened to confessions and gave communion through openings drilled in the doors. The work was completed in

Church of St Jacek from Ulica Freta

1639. Next to it was erected the largest monastery in Warsaw.

Interesting features inside the church, rebuilt after World War II, include the beautiful vaulting above the aisles, the Gothic chancel, decorated with stuccowork of the Lublin type, and the 17th-century tomb-stones shattered in 1944. The Baroque tomb of Adam and Małgorzata Kotowski, by the Dutch architect Tylman van Gameren, is also noteworthy. The domed chapel in which it stands is decorated with portraits, painted on tin plate, of the donors, who became prosperous and were ennobled despite their humble origins.

⑫ Ulica Freta

Map 2 D2. 🚌 116, 178, 180, 222, 503. Maria Skłodowska-Curie Museum: **Tel** 22 831 80 92. **Open** 10am–4:30pm Tue–Sun (Jun–Aug: to 7pm). 🅿️ 🚻 🅦 muzeum-msc.pl

The main road in the New Town, Ulica Freta developed along a section of the old route leading from Old Warsaw to Zakroczym. At the end of the 1300s, buildings began to appear along it, and in the 15th century it came within the precincts of New Warsaw (Nowa Warszawa).

Several good antique shops and cafés are on this street. The house at No. 15, where Marie Curie was born, is now a museum dedicated to her. Films about her life and the history of chemistry are presented to groups on request at an extra charge.

Maria Skłodowska-Curie (1867–1934)

Maria Skłodowska (Marie Curie) was 24 years old when she left Warsaw to study in Paris. Within a decade she had become famous as the co-discoverer of radioactivity. Together with her husband, Pierre Curie, she discovered the elements radium and polonium. She was awarded the Nobel Prize twice: the first time in 1903, when she won the prize for physics jointly with her husband – becoming the first woman Nobel laureate – and the second in 1911 for chemistry.

The triangular-shaped New Town Square

⓭ New Town Square

Map 2 D2. 🚌 116, 178, 180, 222, 503.

The heart of the New Town is the market square (Rynek Nowego Miasta). Once rectangular, it acquired its odd triangular shape after reconstruction. When the town hall, which stood in the centre of the square, was demolished in 1818, a splendid view of the Baroque dome which crowns the Church of St Kazimierz was opened up. Destroyed in 1944, the church was rebuilt in a manner reminiscent of the 18th century, though not exactly replicating the original. The façades of many buildings around the square are covered with Socialist Realist murals. A charming 19th-century well is to be found near Ulica Freta.

⓮ Church of St Kazimierz

Rynek Nowego Miasta 2. **Map** 2 D2. **Tel** 22 635 71 13. 🚌 116, 178, 180, 222, 503. Convent: **Closed** Church: open to visitors.

The Church and Convent of the Order of the Holy Sacrament, designed by Tylman van Gameren, was built in 1688–92 by King Jan III Sobieski and Queen Maria Kazimiera. The remarkable domed building is distinguished by its clear Baroque architecture of classic proportions. The interior, which was damaged in the war, has

since been renovated. Previously polychrome, it is now white. The most beautiful reconstructed feature is the tomb of Maria Karolina, Princesse de Bouillon, granddaughter of Jan III Sobieski. It was installed in 1746 by Bishop Andrzej Załuski and Prince Michał Kazimierz Radziwiłł, a well-known reveller who once, unsuccessfully, sought her hand in marriage. The tomb features a fractured shield and a crown falling into an abyss, references to the Sobieski coat of arms and the death of the last member of the royal line. At the rear of the convent, a garden, unchanged since the 17th century, descends in tiers to the River Vistula below.

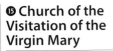

Tomb of Maria Karolina, Princesse de Bouillon

⓯ Church of the Visitation of the Virgin Mary

ul. Przyrynek 2. **Map** 2 D1. **Tel** 22 831 24 73. 🚌 116, 178, 180, 222, 503.

The brick tower of the Church of the Visitation of the Virgin Mary (Kościół Nawiedzenia NMP) rises over the roofs of the houses in New Town. This church is the oldest in the New Town. It was built at the beginning of the 15th century by the Mazovian princess, Anna, wife of Janusz I, the Elder, and is reputed to stand on the site of a sacred pagan spot.

Damaged during World War II, it was subsequently rebuilt in the 15th-century Gothic style. The vaulting above the chancel was completed by medieval methods: that is, it was filled by hand, without the use of prefabricated moulds.

In the cemetery next to the church there stands a modern statue of Walerian Łukasiński (1786–1868), founder of the National Patriotic Society.

An inspiring statue of Nobel Prize-winning scientist Maria Skłodowska Curie, holding a symbol of an atom, can be seen on the terrace next to the Church. The statue was erected in 2014 on the 80th anniversary of the scientist's death. There are also magnificent views of the Vistula valley from this terrace.

Church of the Visitation of the Virgin Mary

THE ROYAL ROUTE

The Royal Route (Trakt Królewski) is so named because of the former royal residences that line it. It stretches from Belvedere Palace (Belweder) up to the Old Town, along Aleje Ujazdowskie, through Nowy Świat and on to Krakowskie Przedmieście. This part of Warsaw has been largely rebuilt after destruction suffered in World War II. On Aleje Ujazdowskie there are beautiful parks and little palaces surrounded by gardens, most of which now house embassies. The Neo-Classical Nowy Świat, its wide pavements decorated with

baskets of flowers in the summer, is lined with cafés and elegant shops. The most impressive buildings are on Krakowskie Przedmieście. This splendid location on the edge of the escarpment inspired powerful citizens to build large houses with gardens. Many churches and monasteries were also located here, as well as the president's residence and university buildings. In the street itself, there are statues of distinguished Poles. In summer, fêtes and bazaars are often organized along the Royal Route.

Sights at a Glance

Churches
1. Church of St Anne
3. Carmelite Church
5. Church of the Visitation
7. Church of the Holy Cross

Historic Buildings and Monuments
2. Statue of Adam Mickiewicz
4. Namiestnikowski Palace
6. University of Warsaw
8. Staszic Palace
16. Parliament

Streets and Squares
11. Nowy Świat
14. Plac Trzech Krzyży
15. Aleje Ujazdowskie

Museums
9. Copernicus Science Centre
10. Fryderyk Chopin Museum
12. National Museum pp86–7
13. Polish Military Museum

See also Street Finder maps 2 & 4

0 metres 500
0 yards 500

◀ A cyclist on the pretty Nowy Świat

For keys to symbols see back flap

Krakowskie Przedmieście

Krakowskie Przedmieście is undoubtedly one of the most beautiful streets in Warsaw. Rebuilt after the war, the magnificent palaces that lie along it now generally house government departments. There are also pleasant restaurants, bars and cafés. The street is lined with trees, green squares and little palaces with courtyards. On weekdays, Krakowskie Przedmieście is one of the liveliest streets in Warsaw, as two great institutions of higher education are situated here: the University of Warsaw and the Academy of Fine Arts.

❺ **Church of the Visitation**
Also known as the Church of St Joseph, this is one of the few churches in Warsaw that was not destroyed during World War II. Its interior features are intact.

❸ **Carmelite Church**
The Church of Our Lady of the Assumption and St Joseph the Bridegroom has a splendid early Neo-Classical façade crowned with a green globe representing the earth.

❹ **Namiestnikowski Palace**
This former palace, rebuilt in the Neo-Classical style for the tsar's governor in the Kingdom of Poland, is now the president's residence.

❷ **Statue of Adam Mickiewicz**
The unveiling of the statue in 1898 was a great manifestation of patriotism.

❶ ★ **Church of St Anne**
The Neo-Classical façade of the church is reminiscent of the style of the 16th-century Italian architect Andrea Palladio.

The Hotel Bristol, which overlooks the Namiestnikowski Palace, is the most luxurious, as well as the most expensive, hotel in Warsaw.

For hotels and restaurants see p302 and pp310–11

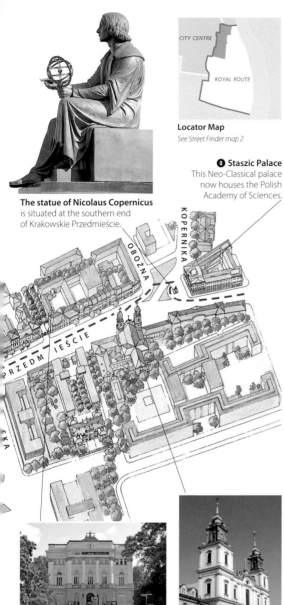

The statue of Nicolaus Copernicus is situated at the southern end of Krakowskie Przedmieście.

Locator Map
See Street Finder map 2

CITY CENTRE

ROYAL ROUTE

❽ **Staszic Palace**
This Neo-Classical palace now houses the Polish Academy of Sciences.

❻ ★ **University of Warsaw**
The University of Warsaw is the largest educational institution in Poland. Only some of the faculties are situated at its main site on Krakowskie Przedmieście.

0 metres	100
0 yards	100

Key

— Suggested route

❼ ★ **Church of the Holy Cross**
Inside this church are urns containing the hearts of Fryderyk Chopin and Władysław Reymont, winner of the Nobel Prize for Literature.

❶ Church of St Anne

ul. Krakowskie Przedmieście 68. **Map** 2 D3. **Tel** 22 826 89 91. **Open** 8am–3pm Mon–Sat, 8am–7pm Sun. **Closed** during the services. 116, 175, 178, 180, 195, 222, 503. 13, 20, 23, 26.

This Gothic church was built for the Bernardine order by Anna, widow of the Mazovian prince Bolesław III, in the second half of the 15th century. It was extended between 1518 and 1533. Destroyed during the Swedish invasion in 1655–60, it was rebuilt in a Baroque style to a design by Józef Szymon Bellotti. The Gothic chancel and the external walls were retained. The Neo-Classical façade, by Chrystian Piotr Aigner and Stanisław Kostka Potocki, is a later addition.

When the monastery was closed in 1864, the church became a religious academic institution, a role that it maintains to the present day. The relics of St Ładysław of Gielniów, one of the patron saints of Warsaw, are preserved in a side chapel. The magnificent interior of the church has polychrome paintings by Walenty Żebrowski and a series of Rococo altars. Inside the monastery, part of which dates from the 16th century, the crystalline vaulting in the cloisters has survived.

Crystalline vaulting in the cloister of the Bernadine monastery

❷ Statue of Adam Mickiewicz

ul. Krakowskie Przedmieście. **Map** 2 D4.

This statue of Poland's most distinguished Romantic poet was unveiled in 1898, on the centenary of his birth. Erecting the statue during the period of intense Russification that followed the January Insurrection of 1863 was a great achievement on the part of the committee in charge of the project, led by Michał Radziwiłł and Henryk Sienkiewicz. The statue was designed by Cyprian Godebski, and the plinth by Józef Pius Dziekoński and Władysław Marconi. It was set up in a square off Krakowskie Przedmieście that was once lined with houses flanked by side streets. The houses were later demolished and the road widened. Only the statue of the Mother of God of Passau, dating from 1683, on the edge of the square, survives. It was made in the workshop of Szymon Belloti to a commission from Jan III Sobieski as an offering in thanks for a Polish victory at the Battle of Vienna and for the protection of the royal family.

The early Neo-Classical façade of the Carmelite Church

Statue of Adam Mickiewicz

❸ Carmelite Church

ul. Krakowskie Przedmieście 52/54. **Map** 2 D4. 🚍 116, 175, 178, 180, 222, 503.

The Baroque Church of Our Lady of the Assumption (Kościół Wniebowzięcia NMP) was built for the order of Discalced Carmelites in 1661–82, probably to a design by Józef Szymon Belloti, although the Neo-Classical façade is considerably later. Designed by Efraim Schroeger, it dates from 1782 and is one of the earliest examples of Neo-Classicism in Poland. Despite suffering war damage, the church, consisting of a nave with interconnecting side chapels and a transept, has

many of its original features. The main altar, with sculptures by Jan Jerzy Plersch, is beautiful. Plersch also carved the sculptural group of the *Visitation of the Virgin*, a very sophisticated and Romantic piece which was transferred from an earlier Dominican church and can now be seen on the altar near the rood arch. Also noteworthy are the Baroque paintings, especially the two small works in the side altars near the chancel, by Szymon Czechowicz.

During the Great Northern War, in 1705, Stanisław Leszczyński held peace negotiations with Charles XII in the church. From 1864, after the closure of the monastery, the monastic buildings housed a seminary.

❹ Namiestnikowski Palace

ul. Krakowskie Przedmieście 46/48. **Map** 2 D4. 🚍 116, 175, 178, 180, 222, 503. **Closed** to the public.

The palace owes its elegant Neo-Classical form to refurbishment carried out by Chrystian Piotr Aigner in 1918–19. However, this work conceals much older walls, as a palace stood on this site as early as the mid-17th century.

Namiestnikowski Palace was home to several prominent familes, among them the Koniecpolskis, the Lubomirskis and, from 1685, the Radziwiłłs. From them the government of the Kingdom of Poland bought the palace in 1818 as the residence of the governor-general of the tsarist government. Among the people who lived here were General Józef Zajączek, viceroy of Tsar Alexander, and the much-hated General Iwan Paskiewicz. The wife of General Zajączek was a very colourful figure; she was a prima ballerina and shocked the town with her love affairs late into old age.

The palace escaped serious damage during World War II. After refurbishment, it was designated the seat of the Council of Ministers and witnessed many important political events: the signing of the Warsaw Pact in 1955, the treaty normalizing relations with Germany in 1970, and the Round Table Talks in 1989. Since 1994 the palace has been the residence of the president of the Republic of Poland.

Namiestnikowski Palace with a statue of Józef Poniatowski

Baroque ebony tabernacle in the Church of the Visitation

❺ Church of the Visitation

ul. Krakowskie Przedmieście 34. **Map** 2 D5. 116, 175, 178, 180, 222, 503.

The Order of the Visitation was brought to Poland by Maria Gonzaga, wife of Jan Kazimierz. Work on the Church of the Visitation (Kościół Wizytek) began in the same year but was interrupted, and not resumed until the 18th century, when the architect Karol Bay took control of the project. The façade, by Efraim Schroeger, was completed in 1763. The church suffered no war damage, so its interior features have survived intact. The most splendid of these are the Rococo pulpit in the form of a ship and the sculptures on the high altar. Many fine paintings have also survived, including *The Visitation* by Tadeusz Kuntze-Konicz, *St Luis Gonzaga* by Daniel Szulc and *St Francis of Sales* by Szymon Czechowicz. The ebony tabernacle, decorated with silver plaques by Herman Pothoff, was commissioned by Ludwika Maria and completed in 1654. Next to the church, the Baroque convent building and garden are still used by the Nuns of the Visitation today.

❻ University of Warsaw

ul. Krakowskie Przedmieście 26/28. **Map** 2 D5. **Tel** 22 552 00 00. 116, 175, 178, 180, 222, 503. Nowy Świat–Uniwersytet.

The nucleus of the University of Warsaw (Uniwersytet Warszawski) grew from a summer palace known as the Villa Regia. In the first half of the 17th century, the palace belonged to the Vasa dynasty. From then on it underwent many phases of refurbishment, and in 1816 was chosen to house what was then the new university. After further alteration, the former palace acquired the late Neo-Classical appearance that it has today – as did the outbuildings to each side (designed by Jakub Kubicki in 1814–16), the main school (Corrazzi, commenced 1841), and the lecture hall and the former Fine Arts Department (both by Michał Kado, 1818–22). After the January Insurrection – when the university was run by the Russian authorities – a library was added (Stefan Szyller and Antoni Jabłoński, 1891–4). The Auditorium Maximum was built when the university passed back into Polish hands after the country regained its independence.

Today, the University of Warsaw is Poland's largest educational establishment. The complex around Kazimierz Palace (Pałac Kazimierzowski), which houses several buildings, is now mainly used as its administrative centre.

❼ Church of the Holy Cross

ul. Krakowskie Przedmieście 3. **Map** 2 D5. **Tel** 22 826 89 10. 116, 175, 178, 180, 222, 503. Nowy Świat–Uniwersytet.

The original Church of the Holy Cross (Kościół św. Krzyża, 1626) was destroyed during the Swedish Deluge of the 1650s. The current Baroque missionaries' church was designed by Giuseppe Simone Bellotti and built between 1679 and 1696. The façade was completed in 1760.

The church is a splendid example of Varsovian church architecture of the late 17th century. During World War II, it suffered major damage and most of its interior was destroyed. The most interesting surviving feature is the altar in the south wing of the transept, designed by Tylman van Gameren. Many important ceremonies have taken place in the church, including the funerals of political thinker Stanisław Staszic (1755–1826), composer Karol Szymanowski (1882–1937) and painter Leon Wyczółkowski (1852–1936). Urns containing the hearts of composer Fryderyk Chopin (1810–49) and novelist Władysław Reymont (1867–1925) are built into a pillar of the nave.

SVRSVM CORDA

Statue of Christ, Church of the Holy Cross

Monument to Nicolaus Copernicus in front of Staszic Palace

❽ Staszic Palace

ul. Nowy Świat 72. **Map** 2 D5. 🚌 111, 116, 125, 175, 180, 222, 503. Ⓜ Nowy Świat–Uniwersytet.

Contrary to what its name suggests, Staszic Palace (Pałac Staszica) never belonged to Stanisław Staszic, nor did he ever live here – although he did fund it. The palace was built by Antonio Corazzi between 1820 and 1823 in the late Neo-Classical style, as the headquarters of the Royal Society of Friends of Science. Since World War II it has housed the Polish Academy of Sciences and the Warsaw Scientific Society. The monument to astronomer Nicolaus Copernicus that stands in front of the building is by Bertel Thorvaldsen and was unveiled in 1830.

❾ Copernicus Science Centre

Wybrzeże Kościuszkowskie 20. **Map** 2 D5. **Tel** 22 596 41 00. 🚌 118, 150, 506. Ⓜ Centrum Nauki Kopernik. **Open** Apr–Jun: 8am–6pm Tue–Fri, 10am–7pm Sat & Sun; Jul & Aug: 9am–7pm Tue–Sun; Sep–Mar: 9am–6pm Tue–Fri, 10am–5pm Sat & Sun. **Closed** Mon & pub hols. 🚾 ♿ 🖥 ✏ 📷 🚾 **kopernik.org.pl**

One of the most visited attractions in Poland, Copernicus Science Centre (Centrum Nauki Kopernik), opened in 2010. The centre is constantly buzzing with school groups, families and individual visitors. More of a hands-on educational park than just a traditional museum, it is filled with games, puzzles and interactive content that will appeal to children of all ages. There are special areas designated for toddlers and young children, as well as sections on biology and technology that keep teenagers and adults entertained. Visitors can enjoy sweeping views of the River Vistula from its roof garden, which is open from May to October.

❿ Fryderyk Chopin Museum

ul. Okólnik 1. **Map** 4 D1. **Tel** 22 441 62 51. 🚌 102, 105, 111, 116, 118, 175, 178, 180, 503. **Open** 11am–8pm Tue–Sun. 🖥 📷 🔊 🎫 🎵 Concerts: 🚾 **chopin.museum/en**

One of Warsaw's most visited Museums, the Fryderyk Chopin Museum (Muzeum Fryderyka Chopina) occupies the splendid Gniński-Ostrogski Palace. Begun in 1681, it is one of Tylman van Gameren's grand masterpieces. The palace was constructed on top of a bastion, making it a fortress. According to legend, a golden duck lived under the palace, guarding its treasures.

Today the museum houses portraits, letters and autograph manuscripts, as well as the grand piano at which Chopin composed during the last two years of his life. It is also the home of the Chopin Society, and regular performances of Chopin's music take place here.

⓫ Nowy Świat

Map 3 C1, 3 C2, 4 D1. 🚌 E-2, 111, 116, 128, 175, 180, 222, 503. 🚋 7, 8, 9, 22, 24, 25. Ⓜ Nowy Świat–Uniwersytet.

The street known as Nowy Świat (New World) is a stretch of the medieval route leading from the castle to Czersk and on to Krakow, and thus forms part of the Royal Route. Buildings started to appear along a section of the road at the end of the 18th century. By the end of the 19th century, Nowy Świat was an elegant street of restaurants, cafés, summer theatres, hotels and shops. After serious damage in World War II, only the Neo-Classical buildings were reconstructed, although later buildings were given pseudo-Neo-Classical features to preserve a uniformity of style.

Today, Nowy Świat is one of the most attractive streets in Warsaw, with wide pedestrian areas and cafés with pavement gardens. At the roundabout on the intersection of Nowy Świat and Aleje Jerozolimskie stands

Nowy Świat, a street of elegant shops and cafés

a palm tree, planted here by artist Joanna Rajkowska in 2002. The tree is intended as a playfully ironic comment on the local street name ("Jerusalem Alley"), and a reference to Poland's historical role as a major centre of Jewish culture.

⑫ National Museum

See pp86–7.

⑬ Polish Military Museum

Aleje Jerozolimskie 3. **Map** 4 D2 and 6 E1. **Tel** 22 629 52 71/2. 🚌 111, 117, 158, 507, 517, 521. 🚋 7, 8, 9, 22, 24, 25. **Open** 10am–5pm Wed, 10am–4pm Thu–Sun. 🐾 (free on Sun). 🌳 Outdoor exhibition: **Open** until dusk, free admission. 📱 📷 🖥 **muzeumwp.pl**

The Polish Military Museum (Muzeum Wojska Polskiego), established in 1920, contains a collection of Polish arms and armour spanning more than 1,000 years. The most interesting aspect of the permanent exhibition is probably the collection of armour, which ranges from the early Middle Ages to the end of the 18th century.

Among the more compelling exhibits are medieval jousting armour and an impressive collection of 17th-century armour of the Husaria, the famous Polish cavalry, with eagle wings, leopardskins and a mounted cavalryman in full regalia. Heavy weapons from the two World Wars and the Cold-War era are displayed in the park outside.

The museum is due to move to a new site at the Citadel, a Tsarist-era fort just north of the New Town, in the near future.

⑭ Plac Trzech Krzyży

Map 3 C2, 3 C3. 🚌 E-2, 108, 116, 118, 166, 171, 180, 222, 503.

Plac Trzech Krzyży (Three Crosses Square) is something of a misno-

mer. Mounted on top of Baroque columns are two gilded crosses, commissioned by August II and made by Joachim Daniel Jauch in 1731, that mark the beginning of Droga Kalwaryjską (Road of Calvary). The third cross is held by St John Nepomuk, whose statue was erected in 1752 by Grand Crown Marshal Franciszek Bieliński to mark the completion of the project to pave the streets of Warsaw. A fourth cross crowns the dome of the 19th-century Church of St Alexander (Kościół św. Aleksandra). The oldest buildings around the square are two 18th-century town houses: No. 1 Nowy Świat, which has an early Neo-Classical façade, and No. 2 Plac Trzech Krzyży, part of the complex of the Institute of the Deaf and Blind, established in 1817.

Statue of St John Nepomuk

⑮ Aleje Ujazdowskie

Map 3 C3, 3 C4, 3 C5. 🚌 116, 118, 138, 166, 180, 182, 187, 188, 502, 503, 514, 520, 523, 525.

Aleje Ujazdowskie is one of the most beautiful streets in Warsaw – a good place for a stroll in the summer. While the east side is bordered by parks, the west is lined with elegant houses originally built for Warsaw's ruling classes but now largely occupied by embassies. No. 17 and No. 19, by architect Stanisław Grochowicz, are especially splendid. No. 17, built in 1903–4, has an eclectic façade.

No. 1, formerly a barracks, houses the offices of the Council of Ministers.

⑯ Parliament

ul. Wiejska 2/4/6. **Map** 4 D3, 4 D4. **Tel** 22 694 25 00. 🚌 E-2, 107, 108, 116, 118, 159, 166, 171, 180, 222, 503. **Open** by prior arrangement.

The parliamentary tradition in Poland dates from 1453, but it was interrupted by the loss of Polish sovereignty in the late 1700s. Only after the restoration of Poland's independence in 1918 was its two-chamber parliament – comprising the Sejm and the Senate – reconvened. Lacking a suitable building, representatives and senators gathered for a time in the former Institute for the Education of Young Ladies.

In 1925–8, a lofty semicircular hall was built, with a debating chamber for the Sejm. It was designed by Kazimierz Skórewicz and decorated with Art Deco bas-reliefs by Jan Szczepkowski. After damage suffered in World War II, the parliamentary buildings were significantly extended in the spirit of the comparatively refined Socialist Realist style, to a design by Bohdan Pniewski.

In 1989, after the first free elections since World War II, the upper parliamentary chamber, abolished under Communist rule, was restored.

In 1999, a monument in honour of the Home Army was unveiled in front of the Sejm.

The semicircular parliament (Sejm) building, with Art Deco bas-reliefs

⑫ National Museum

The National Museum (Muzeum Narodowe) was originally the Museum of Fine Arts, acquiring its present status in 1916. Despite wartime losses, today it has a huge collection of works of art covering all periods from antiquity to modern times. Due to lack of space, not all the exhibits are on permanent display.

★ Virgin and Child
This important painting by Sandro Botticelli is the only work by the artist in Polish collections.

★ St Anne Fresco
This fresco of St Anne is one of the most stunning 10th-century wall paintings discovered by Polish archaeologists in Faras, Sudan.

Battle of Grunwald, a painting by Jan Matejko *(see pp46–7)*, is the most famous in the Gallery of Polish Art.

Greek Vase
Some of the Greek vases displayed in the Gallery of Ancient Art are from a private collection.

Key

- ▨ Ancient Art
- ▨ Faras Collection
- ▨ Medieval Art
- ☐ 19th-century Art
- ▨ 20th- and 21st-century Art
- ☐ 15th- to 18th-century European Paintings
- ☐ 15th- to 19th-century Polish and European Portraits
- ▨ Polish Decorative Art
- ▨ European Decorative Art
- ▨ L. Kronenberg Silver Room
- ▨ Temporary exhibitions
- ☐ Non-exhibition areas

Ground floor

Virgin from Wrocław
This "Beautiful Madonna" is an early 15th-century sculpture that exemplifies the International Gothic style.

The Raising of Lazarus

This painting by Rembrandt pupil Carel Fabritius is one of his finest, and one of the most important exhibits in the Foreign Art Gallery.

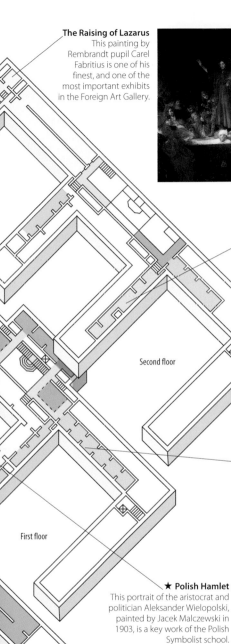

Second floor

First floor

Furniture

This bedroom designed by Karol Tichy in 1909 reflects the utilitarian aspect of 20th-century design. It is on display in the Decorative Arts Gallery.

Banquet

The painter and mathematician Leon Chwistek developed a theory of "zonism", according to which various areas of a painting are dominated by certain shapes and colours, as in this scene.

★ Polish Hamlet

This portrait of the aristocrat and politician Aleksander Wielopolski, painted by Jacek Malczewski in 1903, is a key work of the Polish Symbolist school.

Gallery Guide

The collections are arranged on three floors. On the ground floor are the Galleries of Ancient Art, the Faras Collection and the Gallery of Medieval Art. On the first floor is the collection of Polish art. Foreign paintings can be seen on the first and second floors.

THE CITY CENTRE

From the late 18th to the mid-19th century, the area around Ulica Senatorska and Plac Teatralny was the commercial and cultural centre of Warsaw. Imposing Neo-Classical buildings with impressive colonnades are still to be seen there. The Grand Theatre (Teatr Wielki) on Plac Teatralny is one of the largest buildings of its type in Europe. The Saxon Gardens (Ogród Saski), stretching through the centre of the district, are what remains of a former royal park that adjoined the Saxon king August II's residence. In the second half of the 19th century, the city's commercial centre moved to the area around Ulica Marszałkowska, prompted by the opening in 1845 of Warsaw's first railway station at the junction with Aleje Jerozolimskie. The city centre was completely transformed after the damage inflicted during World War II. Today, its principal landmark is the Palace of Culture and Science (Pałac Kultury i Nauki). The western part of the city centre is dominated by tower blocks. For tourists, the eastern side is of most interest. Here, several historic buildings have survived, dating from the 18th to the early 20th century.

Sights at a Glance

Places of Worship
❸ Capuchin Church
⓬ Evangelical Church of the Augsburg Confession
⓯ Nożyk Synagogue

Buildings and Historic Monuments
❶ Primate's Palace
❷ Branicki Palace
❹ Pac Palace
❺ Krasiński Palace
⓮ Palace of Culture and Science

Monuments and Commemorative Sites
⓱ Umschlagplatz Monument
⓲ Monument to the Heroes of the Ghetto
⓴ Monument to those Fallen and Murdered in the East

Streets and Squares
❽ Plac Bankowy
❾ Plac Teatralny

Parks
❿ Saxon Gardens

Museums and Galleries
❻ Archaelogical Museum
❼ Independence Museum
⓫ Zachęta
⓭ Ethnographical Museum
⓰ Pawiak Prison
⓳ POLIN Museum of the History of Polish Jews

See also Street Finder maps 1, 2 & 3

◀ The Palace of Culture and Science, the tallest building in Poland

For keys to symbols *see back flap*

Ulica Miodowa

Ulica Miodowa lies just outside the much-visited Old Town. Tourists rarely venture here, but it holds many attractions nonetheless. The street has three Baroque churches and several palaces – including the Neo-Classical Primate's Palace and the Rococo Branicki Palace – set behind spacious courtyards. The former Collegium Nobilium, the most famous Polish school for the children of the nobility in the 18th century, now houses the Academy of Dramatic Arts.

The Basilian church is hidden behind the palace façade. Byzantine-Ukrainian masses are celebrated here.

❹ ★ Pac Palace
The 19th-century interiors are decorated in the Gothic, Renaissance, Greek and Moorish styles.

Nike Monument

❸ ★ Capuchin Church
In accordance with the rule of poverty for the Capuchin order, the altars in this church have no gilt or polychrome decoration.

❷ Branicki Palace
Rebuilt after World War II, the palace was crowned with sculptures derived from paintings by Canaletto.

Locator Map
See Street Finder maps 1 & 2

The Primate's Palace, a building in the Neo-Classical style

The Field Cathedral of the Polish Armed Forces was built in the 17th century as a church for the Piarist order.

Key

— Suggested route

0 metres	50
0 yards	50

❶ Primate's Palace

ul. Senatorska 13/15. **Map** 2 D3. Belloto Hotel: **Tel** 22 829 64 44. 🚌 111, 116, 175, 180. **Closed** to the public.

The present-day appearance of the Primate's Palace (Pałac Prymasowski) reflects the refurbishments carried out by Efraim Schroeger in 1777–84 for the Primate of Poland, Antoni Ostrowski. Schroeger's work was then continued by Szymon Zug for the next primate, Michał Poniatowski. The unusual arrangement of the building, with its semicircular wings, is reminiscent of the designs of the most celebrated architect of the Italian Renaissance, Andrea Palladio (1508–80).

The Primate's Palace is generally considered to be the first Neo-Classical palace built in Poland. It was destroyed during World War II, then was rebuilt in 1949–52. Today it houses company offices, conference facilities and the Bellotto hotel.

The superb Great Hall (Sala Wielka) is decorated with Ionic columns and delicate Neo-Classical stuccowork.

❷ Branicki Palace

ul. Miodowa 6. **Map** 2 D3. 🚌 116, 180, 195. **Closed** to the public.

Branicki Palace (Pałac Branickich) was built for Jan Klemens Branicki, adviser to August III. This powerful magnate was known both as a distinguished soldier and a connoisseur of fine art. Work began on the palace in 1740, to a design by Jan Zygmunt Deybel, and was completed by Giacopo Fontana.

Following extensive destruction during World War II, this Rococo palace was rebuilt between 1947 and 1953. The reconstruction was based on historical research and 18th-century paintings.

❸ Capuchin Church

ul. Miodowa 13. **Map** 1 C3. 🚌 116, 174, 175, 180, 503.

The Capuchin Church (kościół Kapucynów), or Church of the Transfiguration, was built by Jan III Sobieski in gratitude for the Polish victory over the Turks at the Battle of Vienna in 1683. Building began in the same year under the direction of Izydor Affaita – probably to designs by Tylman van Gameren and Agostino Locci the Younger – and was completed by Carlo Ceroni in 1692. The modest façade recalls the Capuchin church in Rome. The church houses urns containing the heart of Jan III and the ashes of the Saxon king, August II. In the crypt, there is a nativity scene with emotive figures.

Sarcophagus with the heart of Jan III Sobieski in the Capuchin Church

❹ Pac Palace

ul. Miodowa 15. **Map** 1 C3. **Tel** 22 634 96 00. 🚌 116, 175, 180, 195. **Open** occasionally.

The Baroque Pac Palace (Pałac Paca), formerly the residence of the Radziwiłł family, was designed and built by Tylman van Gameren between 1681 and 1697. One of the palace's 19th- century owners, Ludwik Pac, commissioned the architect Henryk Marconi to redesign it; work was completed in 1828. The interiors were decorated in the Gothic, Renaissance, Greek and Moorish styles, and the façade remodelled in the Palladian manner. The palace gate was modelled on a triumphal arch and decorated with Classical bas-relief sculptures – the work of Ludwik Kaufman, a pupil of the celebrated Neo-Classical sculptor Antonio Canova. Today, the palace houses the Ministry of Health.

Neo-Classical medallion on the façade of Pac Palace

❺ Krasiński Palace

pl. Krasińskich 5. **Map** 1 C2. **Tel** 22 531 02 00. 🚌 116, 178, 180, 222. **Open** during exhibitions.

Krasiński Palace (Pałac Krasińskich), in the Baroque style, is regarded as one of the most beautiful late 17th-century buildings in Warsaw. It was designed by Tylman van Gameren and built between 1687 and 1700 for the mayor of Warsaw, Jan Dobrogost Krasiński.

A triangular pediment features ornamental reliefs depicting the heroic deeds of the Roman patrician Marcus Valerius (known as Corvinus), a legendary ancestor of Jan

Krasiński Palace seen from the palace gardens

Dobrogost Krasiński. The reliefs are the work of Andreas Schlüter, an outstandingly gifted sculptor and architect who later designed the Archaeological Museum and Royal Castle in Berlin. Rebuilt after war damage, the palace now houses a collection of antique prints and manuscripts from the National Library.

❻ Archaeological Museum

ul. Długa 52. **Map** 1 B3. **Tel** 22 831 15 37. 🚌 E-2, 107, 111, 127, 160, 171, 180, 190, 503, 512, 520. 🚊 4, 15, 18, 20, 23, 26, 35. Ⓜ Ratusz. 🌐 **pma.pl** Archaeological Museum: **Open** 9am–4pm Mon–Thu & Sat, 10am–4pm Sun. **Closed** 3rd Sun in the month. 🐾 (free on Sun). 📷

Housed in the former arsenal, the Archaeological Museum was built between 1638 and 1647, in the Baroque style during the reign of Władysław IV Vasa. It was here during World War II that boy scout soldiers of the Grey Ranks (Szare Szeregi) released 21 prisoners from the hands of the Gestapo; this brave action is commemorated by a plaque.

The museum displays exhibits from excavations carried out within both the country's pre-war and present day borders. The exhibition on prehistoric Poland is highly recommended. A highlight of the medieval collections is a replica of the 12th-century door of Płock Cathedral (the original is now in Velikiy Novgorod in Russia), decorated with striking Romanesque reliefs.

❼ Independence Museum

al. Solidarności 62. **Map** 1 C3. **Tel** 22 826 90 91. 🚌 E-2, 107, 111, 160, 171, 190, 503, 512, 527. 🚊 13, 18, 20, 23, 26, 35. Ⓜ Ratusz. Independence Museum (Muzeum Niepodległości): **Open** 10am–5pm Wed–Sun. 🐾 (free on Thu). 📷

Before World War II, this Baroque palace was situated in a narrow shopping street. When the East–West (W-Z) route was constructed (1948–9), it suddenly found itself surrounded by a major traffic artery. The palace, which has the most beautiful mansard roofs in Warsaw and an oval bow-fronted façade, was built in 1728 to a design by Jan Zygmunt Deybel. Since 1990 it has housed the Independence Museum (Muzeum Niepodległości), which features a collection of documents relating Poland's history.

The Baroque Przebendowski-Radziwiłłów Palace, housing the Independence Museum

❽ Plac Bankowy

Map 1 B3 and 1 B4. 🚌 E-2, 107, 111, 127, 171, 180, 190, 512. 🚊 13, 18, 20, 23, 26, 35. Ⓜ Ratusz. John Paul II Collection: pl. Bankowy 1. **Tel** 22 620 27 25. **Open** 9am–6pm Tue–Sun. 📷 W mkjp2.pl

Today Plac Bankowy (Bank Square) is one of the busiest places in Warsaw. Once a quiet little square, it was radically altered after the construction of the East–West route and Ulica Marszałkowska. A statue of Feliks Dzierżyński, the founder of the Soviet security service, was erected here, and the square was renamed in his honour. In 1989, to the joy of local inhabitants, the statue was removed and the square's original name restored. Plac Bankowy was once the site of the largest synagogue in Warsaw. It was demolished after the collapse of the Ghetto Uprising of 1943. A tower block now stands on the site. The most interesting buildings are on the west side of the square. The group of Neo-Classical buildings zealously rebuilt after World War II were designed by Antonio Corazzi. The most impressive is the three-winged palace of the Commission for Revenues and Treasury, which today serves as a town hall. From the junction with Ulica Elektoralna, visitors can admire the fine building of the former Bank of Poland (Bank Polski) and Stock Exchange (Giełda). The building now houses the John Paul II Collection, donated by Janina and Zbigniew Porczyński. It consists of over 450 works by famous artists and is arranged thematically.

Neo-Classical frieze on the façade of the Grand Theatre in Plac Teatralny

❾ Plac Teatralny

Map 1 C4. 🚌 111.

Before 1944, Plac Teatralny (Theatre Square) was the heart of Warsaw. The enormous Neo-Classical Grand Theatre (Teatr Wielki) on the south side was designed by Antonio Corazzi and Ludwik Kozubowski and completed in 1833. The façade is decorated with a Neo-Classical frieze by Paweł Maliński depicting Oedipus and his companions returning from the Olympian Games. The theatre was rebuilt and greatly enlarged after suffering war damage. Two statues stand in front of the building: one depicts Stanisław Moniuszko, the father of Polish opera (*see p32*), and the other Wojciech Bogusławski, who instigated the theatre's construction. Today it is the home of the National Opera and the National Theatre.

In 1848, the Russian composer Mikhail Glinka (1803–57) lived and worked in the house at No. 2 Ulica Niecała, just off Plac Teatralny.

Bogusławski Monument

Opposite the theatre, on the north side of the square, stood the small Church of St Andrew and the enormous, repeatedly extended Jabłonowski Palace, which was refashioned as the town hall in 1817–19. Close by was Blank's Palace, a late Baroque building, which was owned by Piotr Blank, a banker at the time of Stanisław August Poniatowski (1764–95). At the beginning of the Nazi occupation of Poland, the Germans arrested Stefan Starzyński, the heroic mayor of Warsaw, in this building. During the Warsaw Uprising, the poet Krzysztof Kamil Baczyński died amid its ruins. In the years after World War II, only Blank's Palace was rebuilt; Jabłonowski Palace and the church – now the Church of St Brother Albert and St Andrew – were rebuilt at the end of the 20th century. The Nike Monument, which once stood in Plac Teatralny in memory of Warsaw's resistance against the Nazis, was moved to a different site near the East–West route, where it stands on a high plinth.

Municipal government buildings on Plac Bankowy

Tomb of the Unknown Soldier in the Saxon Gardens

⓿ Saxon Gardens

Map 1 B4, 1 C4, 1 C5. 🚌 102, 107, 160, 171, 174. 🚋 4, 15, 18, 35.

The Saxon Gardens (Ogród Saski) were laid out between 1713 and 1733 by August II, the Strong, to a design by Jan Krzysztof Naumann and Mateus Daniel Pöppelmann. Originally the royal gardens adjoining Morsztyn Palace, they became the basis for a Baroque town-planning project in Warsaw known as the Saxon Axis (Osią Saską). In 1727 the Saxon Gardens became the first public park in Poland, and for two centuries they served as an alfresco "summer salon" for Varsovians. At the time of August III, Karol Fryderyk Pöppelmann built a Baroque summer theatre here; this stood until 1772. Between 1816 and 1827, James Savage refashioned the gardens in the English style. In 1870 they were graced by an enormous wooden summer theatre, which was destroyed in September 1939, at the start of World War II. The gardens are now adorned with 21 Baroque sandstone statues made by sculptors including Jan Jerzy Plersch in the 1730s. There were once many more statues here; some were removed to St Petersburg by Marshal Suvorov, who recaptured

Baroque sculpture from the Saxon Gardens

Warsaw during the uprising led by Tadeusz Kościuszko in 1794. Saski Palace, which once stood in the gardens, was destroyed at the end of 1944. All that remains today is the Tomb of the Unknown Soldier, where the body of a soldier who fell in the defence of Lwów (1918–19) was interred on 2 November 1925. Plans are afoot to restore the palace.

⓫ Zachęta

pl. Małachowskiego 3. **Map** 1 C5. **Tel** 22 556 96 00. 🚌 E-2, 102, 174. **Open** noon–8pm Tue–Sun. 🖼 (free on Thu). 🅆 zacheta.art.pl

The Zachęta building – now the National Gallery of Contemporary Art – was built between 1899 and 1903 for the Society for the Promotion of Fine Arts. It was designed by Stefan Szyller, the leading architect of Warsaw's Revival period, a 19th- and early 20th-century architectural movement.

It was conceived as a monumental building in the Neo-Renaissance style, with four wings (only completed in 1995) and a glass-roofed inner courtyard.

In order to promote the work of contemporary Polish artists, the Society organized exhibitions and competitions, and purchased works of art. The Zachęta's permanent collections were transferred to the National Museum, and the building, as before, now serves as a venue for temporary exhibitions of modern art.

It was here in 1922 that Gabriel Narutowicz, the first president of the newly independent Polish Republic, was assassinated by Eligiusz Niewiadomski, a Polish painter, critic and fanatic.

⓬ Evangelical Church of the Augsburg Confession

pl. Małachowskiego 1. **Map** 1 C5. **Tel** 22 556 46 60. 🚌 102, 174. **Open** 11am–5pm Mon–Sat, noon–4pm Sun. 🅆 trojca.waw.pl

The Evangelical Church of the Augsburg Confession (Kościół św. Trójcy) was designed by Szymon Bogumił Zug and built in 1777–81. The Neo-Classical building is crowned by a dome 58 m (189 ft) high. For a long time the church was the highest building in Warsaw, and bore witness to the religious tolerance of the Polish nation and of Stanisław August Poniatowski (1764–95), the last king of Poland. The church is reminiscent of the Pantheon in Rome; however, this ancient

Façade of the Zachęta building (National Gallery of Contemporary Art)

The interior of the Evangelical Church of the Augsburg Confession

model was merely a starting point from which Zug developed a unique design. The interior of the church features a vast barrel-vaulted nave with rectangular transepts. The west front features a massive Doric portico which emphasizes the severity of the façade, regarded as one of the outstanding examples of Neo-Classical architecture in Poland. The interior, with its double tier of galleries supported by columns, has excellent acoustics and is used for choral and other concerts.

⑬ Ethnographical Museum

ul. Kredytowa 1. **Map** 1 C5. **Tel** 22 827 76 41/5. 🚌 102, 105, 107, 174. **Open** 10am–5pm Tue, Thu & Fri, 11am–7pm Wed, 10am–6pm Sat, noon–5pm Sun. **Closed** public hols. 🅿 (free on Thu). 🅶 🚻 📷 🖼 💻 🆆 ethnomuseum.pl

The Ethnographical Museum (Państwowe Muzeum Etnograficzne w Warszawie) is housed in a Neo-Renaissance building on the south side of Plac Małachowski. The former head office of the Land Credit Association, it was built in 1854–8, to a design by Henryk Marconi, an Italian architect who settled in Warsaw. It recalls the Libreria Sansoviniana in Venice, and is one of the city's finest 19th-century buildings. The museum contains a fantastic display of Polish folk costumes, folklore and arts and crafts. An entire section of the

Sacred figure, Ethnographical Museum

museum is dedicated to traditional Polish musical instruments that includes recordings of the sounds the instruments originally produced. There is also a small display on Judaica, as well as collections of ethnic and tribal art from around the world, including Africa, Australia and Latin America. It also mounts occasional temporary exhibitions. In a neighbouring building on Ulica Mazowiecka, behind a gate with bullet marks, is the glass-fronted Artist's House (Dom Artysty), which contains a modern art gallery. Up until the beginning of World War II, Ziemiańska, a very famous café at Mazowiecka 2, was where the cream of society and the artistic community met to exchange ideas and gossip over coffee.

⑭ Palace of Culture and Science

pl. Defilad 1. **Map** 3 A1, 3 B1. **Tel** 22 656 76 00. 🚌 109, 117, 127, 128, 131, 158, 160, 171, 175, 227, 501, 504, 507, 517, 519, 521, 522, 525. 🚊 4, 7, 8, 9, 15, 17, 22, 24, 25, 35. Ⓜ Centre (Centrum). Viewing platform: **Open** 10am–8pm daily (May–Sep: to 11pm). 🚹 🅶 🚻 🆆 pkin.pl

Queen Juliana of the Netherlands is reputed to have described the Palace of Culture and Science (Pałac Kultury i Nauki) as "modest but tasteful". This enormous building – a gift for the people of Warsaw from the nations of the USSR – was built in 1952–5 to the design of a Russian architect, Lev Rudniev. At the time, this monument to "the spirit of invention and social progress" was the second tallest building in Europe. It resembles Moscow's Socialist Realist tower blocks, and although it has only 30 storeys, with its spire it is 230 m 68 cm (750 ft) high. It is said to incorporate many architectural and decorative elements taken from stately homes after World War II. Despite the passage of time, this symbol of Soviet domination still provokes extreme reactions, from admiration to demands for its demolition. Visit the viewing terrace at night, or even for a rooftop concert, for an unforgettable experience.

Palace of Culture and Science, reminiscent of a Socialist Realist tower block

Magnificent interior of Nożyk Synagogue

⑮ Nożyk Synagogue

ul. Twarda 6. **Map** 1 A5. **Tel** 22 620 43 24. 🚌 109, 160, 178. **Open** 9am–8pm Mon–Thu, 9am–2pm Fri, 11am–8pm Sun. 🌐 **warszawa.jewish.org.pl**

Nożyk Synagogue was founded by Zelman and Ryfka Nożyk, who in 1893 donated the land on which it was to be built. Later they left half of their estate to the Orthodox Jewish community. The synagogue was built between 1898 and 1902. The interior has an impressive portico, crowned by a metal dome bearing the Star of David, which contains the Torah Ark. In the centre of the nave is a raised pulpit known as a bema. The nave is surrounded by galleries that were originally intended for female worshippers.

Today, this is the only active synagogue in Warsaw. When it was built, it was hidden away in the heart of a housing estate, amidst high-rise buildings. After the war, few of these were still standing. During the Nazi occupation, the synagogue was closed for worship and the German forces used it as a warehouse. Reopened in 1945, it was eventually restored to its original condition (1977–83).

Of a total population of no more than 1,300,000, there were about 450,000 Jews in Warsaw before World War II; the city had the second largest Jewish population after that of New York. The northern part of Warsaw, which was inhabited predominantly by Jews, was densely built up, with tenement blocks. The languages spoken here were Yiddish and Hebrew, as well as Russian, spoken by Jews who had fled Russia.

Those interested in Jewish history and culture should visit the historic – though overgrown – cemetery on Ulica Okopowa and the POLIN Museum of the History of the Polish Jews.

⑯ Pawiak Prison

ul. Dzielna 24/26. **Map** 1 A2. **Tel** 22 831 13 17. 🚌 107, 111, 180. 🚊 15, 18, 33, 35. **Open** 10am–5pm Wed–Sun. 🚻 ♿ 📷 👫

Pawiak Prison was built in the 1830s by Henryk Marconi. It became notorious during the Nazi occupation, when it was used to imprison Poles and Jews arrested by the Germans. It now serves as a museum and houses photo displays, belongings of the prisoners, and reconstructed cells. In front of the prison stands a long-dead tree, covered with obituary notices for prisoners who died there.

Tree with obituary notices in front of Pawiak Prison

⑰ Umschlagplatz Monument

ul. Stawki. **Map** 1 A1. 🚌 157. 🚊 15, 18, 33.

The Umschlagplatz Monument, unveiled in 1988, marks the site of a former railway siding on Ulica Dzika. The German word *Umschlagplatz* translates as "collection point". It was from this location that some 300,000 Jews from the Warsaw Ghetto and elsewhere were summarily loaded onto cattle trucks and dispatched to almost certain death in the extermination camps. Among them was Janusz Korczak, an educator who despite multiple offers of sanctuary, chose to remain with his group of Jewish orphans. Living conditions in the ghetto were inhumane, and by 1942 more than 100,000 of the inhabitants had died. The monument, on which the architect Hanna Szmalenberg and the sculptor Władysław Klamerus collaborated, is made of blocks of black and white marble resembling an open cattle truck and

Umschlagplatz Monument on the Path of Remembrance

bearing the names of hundreds of Warsaw's Jews.

Between the Monument to the Heroes of the Ghetto and the Umschlagplatz Monument runs the **Trail of Jewish Martyrdom and Struggle**, unveiled in 1988. It is marked by 16 blocks of granite bearing inscriptions in Polish, Hebrew and Yiddish and the date 1940–43. Each block is dedicated to the memory of the 450,000 Jews murdered from the Warsaw Ghetto in the years 1940–43, to the heroes of the Ghetto Uprising in 1943 and to certain key individuals from that momentous time. The site of a bunker, in which the Uprising's commanders blew themselves up, has been specially marked.

⓲ Monument to the Heroes of the Ghetto

ul. Zamenhofa. **Map** 1 B2. 🚌 111, 180, 227.

The Monument to the Heroes of the Ghetto (Pomnik Bohaterów Getta) was erected in 1948, when the city of Warsaw still lay in ruins. Created by the sculptor Natan Rapaport and the architect Marek Suzin, it symbolizes the heroic defiance of the Ghetto Uprising of 1943, which was

Monument to the Heroes of the Ghetto (detail)

planned not as a bid for liberty but as an honourable way to die. It lasted one month.

Reliefs on the monument depict men, women and children struggling to flee the burning ghetto, together with a procession of Jews being driven to death camps under the threat of Nazi bayonets.

In front of this monument, on 7 December 1970, Willy Brandt, Chancellor of West Germany, knelt in homage to the murdered victims. Today, people come here from all over the world to remember the heroes of the Uprising.

⓳ POLIN Museum of the History of Polish Jews

ul. Mordechaja Anielewicza 6. **Map** 1 B2. **Tel** 22 471 03 01. **Open** 10am–6pm Wed–Mon (to 8pm Sat). **Closed** public hols. 🖼️ 🛗 🖊️ 📷 ✂️ 🅦 polin.pl/en

Housed in a breathtaking contemporary building designed by Rainer Mahlamäki, the country's largest Jewish heritage museum takes visitors on a journey through 1,000 years of the history of Polish Jews – from the Middle Ages, when the Jewish community first settled here, until the present day. The fascinating displays illustrate how the country became the centre of the Jewish diaspora and the home of the largest Jewish community in the world. The centrepiece of the collection is the painted ceiling of a 17th-century synagogue that used to stand in Gwozdziec, east of Krakow. Overall this is a spectacular celebration of Jewish life and culture, although the tone becomes understandably more sombre as the exhibition turns to the Holocaust and the mass murder of Poland's Jews by the Nazis.

⓴ Monument to those Fallen and Murdered in the East

ul. Muranowska. **Map** 1 C1. 🚌 116, 157, 178, 503. 🚊 6, 15, 18.

This emotionally stirring monument, designed by Mirosław Biskupski, has the form of a typical railway wagon in which Poles were deported from the country into the depths of the Soviet Union. It is filled with a pile of crosses symbolizing the hundreds of thousands of Poles transported to the East in cattle trucks and murdered in Soviet prison camps.

Ghetto Uprising

The Nazis created the Jewish ghetto on 16 November 1940. The area was carefully isolated with barbed wire fencing, which was later replaced with brick walls. Over 450,000 people were crowded into the ghetto: Jews from Warsaw and other parts of Poland, as well as gypsies. In March 1942, the Germans began to liquidate the ghetto, deporting over 300,000 people to the death camp in Treblinka. The Ghetto Uprising, which began on 19 April 1943 and lasted one month, was organized by the secret Jewish Fighting Organization. Following the suppression of the Uprising, the Nazis razed the whole area to the ground.

Further Afield

There are many places of interest outside the centre of Warsaw. The most important lie along the Royal Route stretching from the Royal Castle in the north to Wilanów Palace in the south, and also on the edges of the escarpment that runs down to the left bank of the River Vistula; here there are country mansions with extensive parks. Most can be reached by a combination of tram, metro or bus.

Grave of Father Jerzy Popiełuszko, Church of St Stanisław Kostka

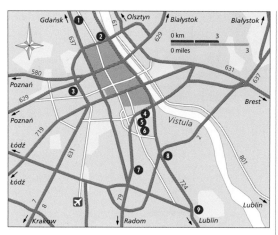

Sights at a Glance

1. Church of St Stanisław Kostka
2. Katyń Museum
3. Warsaw Uprising Museum
4. Centre for Contemporary Art
5. Łazienki Park
6. Belvedere Palace
7. Królikarnia Palace
8. Church of St Anthony
9. Wilanów Palace

Key

■ City centre
▬ Main road
═ Other road

❶ Church of St Stanisław Kostka

ul. Hozjusza 2. **Tel** 22 839 45 72.
🚌 114, 116, 122, 157, 181, 185, 303, 503. 🚋 6, 15. Ⓜ Pl. Wilsona

The Modernist Church of St Stanisław Kostka (Kościół św. Stanisława Kostki), set among the villas of Żoliborz, is the burial place of Father Jerzy Popiełuszko, the pastor of the Solidarity movement who was beatified in 2010. Because of this it is a place of pilgrimage for Poles. Popiełuszko was a national hero, renowned for his courageous sermons in defence of Poland's freedom. He was eventually murdered in 1984 by Communist security agents. His grave is in the church cemetery; it is covered with a stone cross and surrounded by linked rocks arranged in the manner of a rosary. The church itself is distinguished by its openwork twin towers. Inside, there are Baroque paintings by the Silesian artist Michael Willmann.

❷ Katyń Museum

ul. Jana Jeziorańskiego 4.
Map 3 C5. **Tel** 26 187 83 42.
🚌 127, 176. 🚋 1, 6, 16, 18.
Ⓜ Dworzec Gdański
Open 10am–4pm Tue–Sun (to 5pm Wed).

Located in the red-brick battlements of the Citadela, a fortification built by the Russians in the 19th century, the Katyń Museum (Museum Katyńskie) commemorates the 20,000 Polish officers murdered by the Soviet security apparatus in 1940. When Polish army units surrendered to the invading Red Army in September 1939, the officers were separated from the other ranks and interned in camps in Western Russia. The majority of them were shot and buried in mass graves the following spring. The moving, and at times harrowing, exhibition pays tribute to the victims and displays row upon row of personal effects retrieved from the graves.

❸ Warsaw Uprising Museum

ul. Grzybowska 79. **Tel** 22 539 79 05. 🚌 105, 109, 159. 🚋 1, 8, 22, 24. Ⓜ Rondo Daszyńskiego.
Open 8am–6pm Mon, Wed–Fri (to 8pm Thu), 10am–6pm Sat & Sun. 🎟 (free on Sun). 🚻 ♿ 📷
🌐 **1944.pl**

One of the most popular museums in Warsaw opened in 2004 to commemorate the 60th anniversary of the Warsaw Uprising in 1944. A tribute to those who fought and died for Poland's independence, the museum re-creates the atmosphere during those 63 days of military struggle, but it also conveys what everyday life was like under Nazi occupation. The complicated international situation during the post-war years and at the time of the Uprising is portrayed in innovative displays that contain a wealth of photographs, audio recordings and films.

❹ Centre for Contemporary Art

Jazdów 2. **Map** 3 C5. **Tel** 22 628 12 71.
🚌 E-2, 116, 138, 166, 180, 182, 187,
188, 411, 502, 503, 514, 520, 523, 525.
Open noon–7pm Tue–Sun (to 9pm
Thu). 🎨 (free on Thu). 🎫 ♿ 🏛 🅿
〰 📷 🌐 **u-jazdowski.pl**

The Centre for Contemporary Art (Centrum Sztuki Współczesnej) organizes exhibitions of the work of artists from all over the world. The centre is housed in Ujazdowski Castle, an early Baroque fortification built at the beginning of the 17th century for Zygmunt III Vasa and his son Władysław IV. The castle's layout was spacious – it had an internal cloistered courtyard and four towers – but its splendour was destined to be short-lived; the Swedish army sacked it in 1655 and it later changed hands repeatedly, being rebuilt many times. During World War II, Ujazdowski Castle was destroyed by fire and rebuilding of the castle only began in the 1970s.

❺ Łazienki Park

See pp100–101.

❻ Belvedere Palace

ul. Belwederska 52. 🚌 116, 166, 180, 503. **Closed** to the public; access to exhibition with prior reservation – call 022 695 19 53.

The history of Belvedere Palace (Belweder) goes back to the

17th century. Its present appearance, however, dates from 1818, when it was refashioned by Jakub Kubicki for the Russian governor general Prince Constantine (the much hated brother of Tsar Alexander I) and his Polish aristocrat wife. On the night of 29 November 1830, a detachment of cadet officers, together with a number of students, attacked the palace, starting the November Insurrection, which lasted almost a year.

After 1918, Belvedere Palace became the official residence of the presidents of Poland, including Marshal Józef Piłsudski (1867–1935), to whom an exhibition situated in the palace is devoted.

❼ Królikarnia Palace

ul. Puławska 113a. **Tel** 22 843 15 86. 🚌 218. 🚋 4, 10, 14, 31, 35. **Open** 10am–6pm Tue–Sun (to 8pm Thu). 🎨 (free on Thu). 🎫 🚫 no flash. ♿ 🌐 **krolikarnia. mnw.art.pl**

Królikarnia Palace (Pałacyk Królikarnia) owes its name ("rabbit hutch") to the fact that it stands on the site of a rabbit farm that belonged to August II in the 1700s. It is a square building covered with a dome, recalling Andrea Palladio's masterpiece, the Villa Rotonda,

Baroque Church of St Anthony at Czerniaków

near Vicenza in Italy. This exquisite little Neo-Classical palace is set in a garden on the slope of the escarpment in the district of Mokotów. It was designed by Dominik Merlini for Karol de Valery Thomatis, the director of Stanisław August Poniatowski's royal theatres.

Today the palace houses the Xawery Dunikowski Museum, dedicated to this contemporary Polish sculptor.

❽ Church of St Anthony

ul. Czerniakowska 2/4. **Tel** 22 842 03 71. 🚌 131, 159, 162, 180, 185, 187. **Open** by appt only, or during ceremonies.

The Baroque Church of St Anthony (Kościół św. Antoniego), built between 1687 and 1693 by the monks of the Bernardine order, was designed by Tylman van Gameren. The church stands on the site of the former village of Czerniaków, which belonged to Stanisław Herakliusz Lubomirski, the Grand Crown Marshal.

The relatively plain façade of this church belies its ornate interior, which includes trompe l'oeil paintings, stuccowork and altars by the painter Francesco Antonio Giorgiolo and the renowned sculptor Andreas Schlüter, among others. The main theme of the paintings is the life of St Anthony of Padua.

Fatum, a sculpture by Xawery Dunikowski in Królikarnia Park

Façade of the Neo-Classical Belvedere Palace, looking onto the gardens

❺ Łazienki Park

Łazienki Park is part of a great complex of heritage gardens. In the 17th century there was a royal menagerie along the foot of the escarpment. In 1674, Grand Crown Marshal Stanisław Herakliusz Lubomirski acquired the park and, engaging the services of Tylman van Gameren, he altered the southern part of the menagerie, building a hermitage and a bathing pavilion on an island. The pavilion gave the park its name (Łazienki meaning "baths"). In the second half of the 18th century, the park was owned by Stanisław August Poniatowski, who commissioned Karol Ludwik Agricola, Karol Schultz and later Jan Christian Schuch to lay it out as a formal garden. Lubomirski's baths were refashioned into a royal residence, Łazienki Palace, or Palace on the Water, which is now a museum.

Peacocks
Just as in Stanisław August Poniatowski's time, visitors to Łazienki Park can admire the peacocks and take a boat ride on the lake, which is full of carp.

Old Orangery
In 1774–8, Dominik Merlini created the Stanisławowski Theatre in the Old Orangery. It is one of the few remaining 18th-century court theatres in the world.

```
0 metres          100
0 yards           100
```

Monument to Chopin
This Art Nouveau monument was sculpted in 1908 by Wacław Szymanowski but not unveiled until 1926. Positioned at the side of a lake, it depicts Poland's most celebrated composer sitting under a willow tree, seeking inspiration from nature.

Temple of the Sibyl
This Neo-Classical building, based on an ancient Greek temple, dates from the 1820s. It is made of wood.

★ **Palace on the Water**
Stanisław Lubomirski's 17th-century baths were converted (1772–93) into the Palace on the Water, Stanisław August Poniatowski's summer home.

VISITORS' CHECKLIST

Practical Information
Łazienki Królewskie, ul. Agrykola 1.
Map 3 C5. **Tel** 22 506 01 01.
Park: **Open** daily until dusk. Palace on the Water: **Open** 10am–6pm daily. (free on Thu). Myślewicki Palace: **Open** 10am–6pm daily. Old Orangery: **Open** 10am–6pm daily. (free Thu).
lazienki-krolewskie.pl

Transport
108, 116, 138, 166, 180, 187, 503.

Myślewicki Palace
Dominik Merlini designed the early Neo Classical Myślewicki Palace in 1775–84 for Stanisław August Poniatowski's nephew, Prince Józef Poniatowski.

★ **Theatre on the Island**
The stage of the Theatre on the Island has a permanent backdrop imitating the ruins of a temple in the ancient city of Baalbek, Lebanon.

New Orangery
This building in cast iron and glass was designed by Józef Orłowski and Adam Loewe in 1860–61.

Wilanów Palace

Wilanów Palace was built at the end of the 17th century as the summer residence of Jan III Sobieski. This illustrious monarch, who valued family life as much as material splendour, commissioned Augustyn Locci to build a modest country house. Later the palace was extended and adorned by renowned architects and artists, including Andreas Schlüter and Michelangelo Palloni.

The small Chinese Pavilion stands in the English-style garden on the north side of the palace.

Great Crimson Room
Originally a three-room apartment, the Great Crimson Room was reconstructed in 1900 to house the museum's array of foreign paintings.

Main Gateway
Dating from the time of Jan III Sobieski, the Main Gateway is crowned with allegorical figures of War and Peace.

★ **Poster Museum**
A former riding school rebuilt in the 1960s now houses the Poster Museum, the first of its kind in Europe.

For hotels and restaurants see p302 and pp310–11

VISITORS' CHECKLIST

Practical Information
ul. SK Potockiego 10/16. **Tel** 22 544 27 00. Palace: **Open** Apr–mid-Oct: 9:30am–6pm daily; mid-Oct–Mar: 9:30am–4pm Wed–Mon. **Closed** mid-Dec–mid-Jan. (free Thu). Park: **Open** 9am–dusk. **wilanow-palac.pl**

Transport
E-2, 116, 164, 180, 317, 379, 519, 700, 710, 724, 725, 742.

★ Rose Garden
This section of Wilanów's garden, to the south of the palace, was created in the 19th century.

★ Queen's Antechamber
The walls are covered with original Baroque fabric while the ceiling has allegorical paintings.

Rear Façade of the Palace
Open perspectives allow the rear façade of the palace to be seen from across the park, and even from the adjoining fields of Morysin.

King's Bedchamber
The bed canopy is made of fabric brought back by Jan III Sobieski from his victory against the Turks at the Battle of Vienna in 1683.

0 metres 50
0 yards 50

WARSAW STREET FINDER

The coordinates given alongside the names of buildings and attractions in Warsaw refer to the street plan on pages 106–9. Map coordinates are also given alongside information about Warsaw hotels *(see p302)* and restaurants *(see pp310–11)*. The first digit indicates the relevant map number; the letter and following number are grid references. On the plan opposite, Warsaw is divided into four sectors corresponding to the four maps on pages 106–9. The symbols that appear on the maps are explained in the key below. The plan of the city identifies the most important monuments and places of interest.

Key

- Major sight
- Place of interest
- Other building
- Railway station
- Tram stop
- M Metro station
- *i* Tourist information
- Hospital or first aid
- Police station
- Church
- Railway line
- Pedestrianized street

Scale of Maps 1–4

0 metres	250
0 yards	250

Summer café garden in the Old Town

Marathon runners on Krakowskie Przedmieście

Façade of the Neo-Classical Grand Theatre designed by Antonio Corazzi, on Plac Teatralny

Church of the Holy Spirit from Ulica Freta

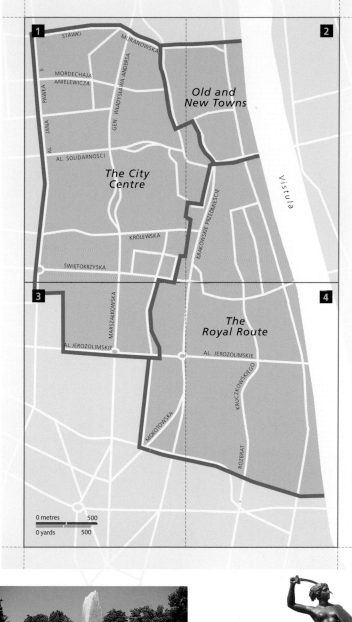

Old and
New Towns

The City
Centre

The
Royal Route

Vistula

STAWKI
MURANOWSKA
MORDECHAJA
ANIELEWICZA
GEN. WŁADYSŁAWA ANDERSA
AL. JANA PAWŁA II
AL. SOLIDARNOŚCI
KRÓLEWSKA
KRAKOWSKIE PRZEDMIEŚCIE
ŚWIĘTOKRZYSKA
MARSZAŁKOWSKA
AL. JEROZOLIMSKIE
AL. JEROZOLIMSKIE
KRUCZKOWSKIEGO
MOKOTOWSKA
ROZBRAT

0 metres 500
0 yards 500

Fountain in Saxon Gardens

Statue of *The Mermaid* in the Old Town

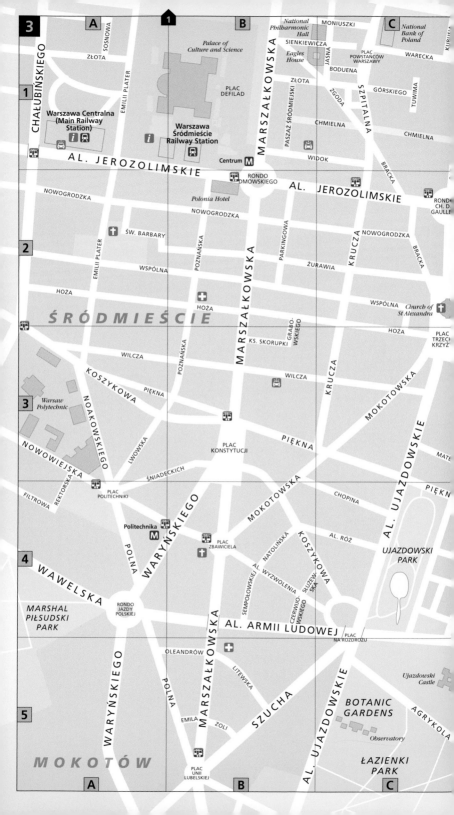

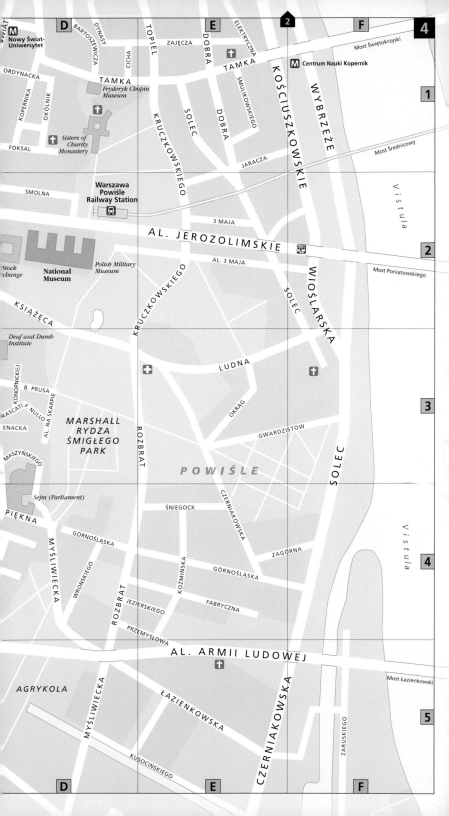

POLAND REGION BY REGION

Poland at a Glance

While southern Poland consists of a band of mountains and uplands, Central Poland is a land of endless plains. In the north, a postglacial scene dominates, and the Baltic coast, though fairly cool, has beautiful sandy beaches. Poland's provinces also offer unblemished natural landscapes. The Tatra Mountains, the highest in the country, are traversed by well-marked footpaths, from which fine views and a pure alpine environment can be enjoyed. Apart from the varied landscape, there is plenty to explore in terms of the historic buildings that have survived in Poland, despite the country's stormy history.

The Gdańsk Crane *(see p243)* is one of the largest European cranes dating from the Middle Ages. Restored after war damage, it stands as a symbol of the city's former commercial might.

Many of the attractive sandy beaches *(see p265)* on the Baltic Sea are backed by cliffs, which are vulnerable to storm damage.

GDAŃSK
(See pp236–55)

Koszalin

Elb

POMERANIA
(See pp256–79)

Szczecin

Piła   Bydgoszcz

Toruń

Gorzów Wielkopolski

Włocławek

Poznań

Zielona Góra   Rogalin

WIELKOPOLSKA (GREATER POLAND
(See pp212–35)

Łódź

SILESIA
(See pp180–211)

Wrocław

Raczyński Palace *(see pp218–19)* at Rogalin is one of the most splendid residences in Greater Poland. The late Baroque palace now houses a museum of interiors and a valuable collection of paintings. It is surrounded by a beautiful park with ancient oaks.

Częstochowa

Opole

Katowice

The town hall in Wrocław *(see p197)* is one of the most interesting late Medieval buildings in Central Europe. It is crowned with unusual finials and fine stone sculptures.

0 kilometres   75

0 miles   75

◀ Aerial view of the Renaissance architecture in the picturesque small town of Kazimierz Dolny

The Great Mazurian Lakes (see pp290–91), known as "The Land of a Thousand Lakes", consists of wilderness, with great forests, extensive woods and marshlands, alongside brick-built houses, Gothic churches and castles. Unspoilt by civilization, it is appreciated by storks and more nest here than anywhere else in Europe.

In Kazimierz Dolny (see p125), under the Renaissance colonnades of the market square, paintings are on display and wicker baskets are for sale. Kazimierz's riverside setting and unique collection of historic architecture makes it Poland's most compelling small town.

Isztyn

Augustów

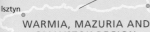
WARMIA, MAZURIA AND BIAŁYSTOK REGION
(See pp280–95)

Białystok

The Cloth Hall in Krakow (see p137), a ravishingly ornate building in the centre of Main Market Square, once contained market stalls. Today it is filled with shops selling souvenirs and local folk art, and popular cafés. On the first floor there is a splendid gallery of 19th-century Polish art.

WARSAW
(See pp62–109)

MAZOVIA AND THE LUBLIN REGION
(See pp114–31)

Radom

Kazimierz
Dolny

Lublin

MAŁOPOLSKA (LESSER POLAND)
(See pp152–79)

Zamość

Rzeszów

RAKOW
e pp132–51)

Krasiczyn

Krasiczyn Castle (see p176), dating from the early 17th century, is defended by sturdy towers. The walls have elaborate parapets.

MAZOVIA AND THE LUBLIN REGION

In the lowland landscape of Mazovia, sandy roads wind through the fields, lines of windswept willows stand in isolation, and meadows stretch to the edge of valleys where swift rivers flow. East of Mazovia, Podlasie was for centuries the borderland between the Poles and the eastern Slavonic peoples.

For centuries, Mazovia was, both culturally and economically, one of the least developed areas of the ethnically Polish lands of the Commonwealth of Two Nations. In the early Middle Ages it was the homeland of the Mazowie tribe. It was united with the state of the Polanie under Prince Mieszko I (963–92). The Principality of Mazovia came into existence in 1138, during the division of Poland, and it preserved its independence for nearly 400 years. Mazovia was incorporated into the Kingdom of Poland in 1526 after the death of the last Mazovian princes, and in 1596, Sigismund III Vasa moved the capital of the Commonwealth of Two Nations from Krakow to Warsaw, in Mazovia.

Mazovia's cultural distinctiveness has been influenced by the presence of a politically active yet conservative gentry.

Even today, in the east of the region and in Podlasie, farmsteads, with their humble cottages built to mimic the style of mansions, can be seen. Apart from Warsaw, the towns of Mazovia have always been modest, and this is evident in more recent buildings and modern urban planning.

The gently-rolling Lublin area differs considerably from Mazovia, in both landscape and culture. The region has many excellent examples of Renaissance and Baroque architecture. Its architectural jewel is the delightful town of Kazimierz Dolny, on the banks of the Vistula.

After the Congress of Vienna (1815), Mazovia and the Lublin region formed part of the Congress Kingdom, under Russian rule. In 1918, the whole area was returned to the reborn country of Poland.

Brightly-coloured blooms in one of Mazovia's orchards

 Detail of a colourful and beautifully decorated building on Zamość's Main Market Square

Exploring Mazovia and the Lublin Region

The Kampinoska Forest (Puszcza Kampinoska), a national park, extends out from the suburbs of Warsaw into Mazovia. There are also large tracts of woodland, with wild animals, in the north and south of the region, as well as ruins of brick-built castles and many country mansions. Żelazowa Wola is Fryderyk Chopin's birthplace and nearby Łowicz is a well-known centre of folklore. Lublin has a more diverse landscape. The gorge of the Vistula, around the town of Kazimierz Dolny, is one of the most pretty sights. Zamość, described as the "pearl of the Renaissance", is also very picturesque, while the rivers and forests of the Roztocze offer an unspoilt natural oasis.

The house of the novelist Stefan Żeromski (1864–1925) in Nałęczów

Sights at a Glance

1 Płock
2 Ciechanów
3 Opinogóra
4 Pułtusk
5 Czerwińsk on the Vistula
6 Żelazowa Wola
7 Łowicz
8 Arkadia
9 Nieborów
10 Treblinka
11 Węgrów
12 Czersk
13 Radom
14 Szydłowiec
15 Iłża
17 Kazimierz Dolny
18 Lublin pp126–7
19 Kozłówka
20 Radzyń Podlaski
21 Chełm
22 Zamość pp130–31

Tours

16 A Tour around
Kazimierz Dolny

Panoramic shot of Old Town, Lublin

For hotels and restaurants see p302 and pp311–12

Key

=== Motorway
━━━ Main road
─── Minor road
─·─ Main railway
─── Minor railway
▬▬ International border
─── Regional border

Detail of the Romanesque portal of the church in Czerwińsk on the Vistula

Getting Around

Warsaw, the chief city of Mazovia, has regular air links to major cities worldwide and to principal towns in Poland. All the larger towns in both regions have rail links. Travelling by express from Warsaw to Lublin takes a little over two hours. All places recommended in this guidebook are accessible by bus. However, many of the smaller ones are more easily reached by car. Highway E30 crosses Mazovia from east to west. From Warsaw, take highway E77 for Radom and highway 17 for Lublin.

Białystok

Ostrów Mazowiecka

10 TREBLINKA

Stara Wieś

11 WĘGRÓW
Liw

Kałuszyn   Łosice

Siedlce

wiecki   Biała Podlaska

Łuków   Międzyrzec Podlaski

wolin   Żelechów   Kobrin

20 RADZYŃ PODLASKI

Kock

LUBELSKIE

olin   Włodawa

A TOUR AROUND
16 KAZIMIERZ DOLNY   Lubartów   Polesian National Park

eń   Puławy   **19** KOZŁÓWKA

owiec   Nałęczów

17 KAZIMIERZ DOLNY   Łęczna

18 LUBLIN   **21** CHEŁM

Kraśnik   Krasnystaw

Wyżyna Lubelska   Hrubieszów

Janów Lubelski   Szczebrzeszyn   **22** ZAMOŚĆ

Frampol

Rzesów   Biłgoraj   *Roztocze*

Taneu   Tomaszów Lubelski

Lviv

0 kilometres   25
0 miles   25

The nave of the Renaissance cathedral in Płock

❶ Płock

Road map D3. 126,500.
ul. Stary Rynek 8 (24 367 19 44).
turystykaplock.eu

This city, beautifully situated on the high Vistula Bluff, is best known today for its large petrochemical plants. Its history, however, goes back many centuries. From 1075, Płock was the seat of the bishopric of Mazovia. Under Władysław I (1079–1102) and his heir Bolesław III Wrymouth (1102– 1138), Płock was the capital of Poland and the favoured royal seat. From 1138 to the end of the 15th century, Płock was the place of residence of the Mazovian and Płock princes. In the 12th century, it was an important centre of political and cultural life in Poland.

The buildings of old Płock are relatively modest, although the small Neo-Classical houses, now restored, make a picturesque ensemble. Particularly noteworthy is the Neo-Classical **town hall,** built in 1824–7 to a design by Jakub Kubicki. Here, on 23 September 1831 during the uprising against Russian rule, the final session of the insurgent Sejm of the Kingdom of Poland was held.

Another notable building is the large Neo-Gothic cathedral (1911–19) of the Mariavite Church of Poland. Also worth seeing are the Baroque church, the Classical toll-gates and the remains of the Gothic city walls.

⬆ Cathedral of Our Lady of Mazovia
ul. Mostowa 2. **Tel** 24 262 34 35.
Open 10am–5pm Mon–Sat, 11am–2pm Sun. **katedraplock.pl**

The most interesting part of Płock is Tum Hill (Wzgórze Tumskie), with its Renaissance **Cathedral of Our Lady of Mazovia** and **castle** remains. The cathedral, built in 1531–5 was the first large Renaissance church in Poland. It was raised by Andrzej Krzycki, Bishop of Płock, later Primate of Poland and a noted scholar and poet. Giovanni Cini and Bernardino Zanobi de Gianotis were the architects, with later rebuilding by Gianbattista of Venice. The interior of the cathedral is full of Renaissance and Baroque tombstones. A marble sarcophagus in the Royal Chapel holds the remains of Władysław I and his son Bolesław III. The grand Neo-Renaissance façade of the cathedral, with its twin towers, was built at the start of the 20th century to a controversial design by Stefan Szyller, who was in charge of the restoration work.

⬛ Diocesan Museum
ul. Tumska 3a. **Tel** 24 262 26 23.
Open 10:30am–2pm Tue–Fri, 10am–6pm Sat.
mdplock.pl

The Diocesan Museum (Muzeum Diecezjalne) contains a rich collection of cathedral treasures. Especially noteworthy are the gold vessels and liturgical textiles, particularly the chasubles, the oldest of which date from the 1400s. The museum also possesses

The Neo-Classical town hall in the Old Market Square in Płock

woven sashes from the old court dress of the nobility *(see pp34–5)*. Sashes were often made into vestments.

⬛ Museum of Mazovia
ul. Tumska 8. **Tel** 24 364 70 71.
Open 1 May–14 Oct: 10am–5pm Tue–Sun; 15 Oct–30 Apr: 10am–4pm Tue–Sun. (free on Thu).
muzeumplock.eu

The Museum of Mazovia (Muzeum Mazowieckie) is located in a former monastery and houses one of the largest collections of Art Nouveau in the world. Exhibits include reconstructions of domestic interiors, with works of art, furniture, textiles and everyday objects of the period.

Environs
There are sports facilities on **Lake Włocławek**, a reservoir on the Vistula, and a stud farm at **Łąck**, 9 km (5 miles) from Płock.

Płock's Tum Hill from the Vistula, with the cathedral and Benedictine abbey

Ruins of the Gothic Castle of the Mazovian princes in Ciechanów

❷ Ciechanów

Road map E3. 🗺 45,900.
🚉 🚌 𝒊 ul. Warszawska 34.
W umciechanow.pl

On the edge of the town stand the Gothic ruins of the red-brick **Castle of the Mazovian princes**, built around 1420–30. After Mazovia was incorporated into the Kingdom of Poland, the widowed Queen Bona often stayed here. Today, the castle accommodates one of the exhibitions of the **Museum of the Mazovian Nobility** (Muzeum Szlachty Mazowieckiej).

In the town itself is the Gothic **Church of the Annunciation**, founded in the first half of the 16th century and rebuilt in the 17th, the parish **Church of the Nativity of the Blessed Virgin Mary**, dating from the 16th century, and the modest Neo-Gothic **town hall**, designed by Henryk Marconi in the mid-19th century. The low-rise apartment blocks with gable roofs near the railway station were built during the Nazi occupation. After the fall of Poland in September 1939 and the annexation of northern Mazovia to the Third Reich, the Nazis planned to settle German colonists in many towns here. Except for the castle and parish church, they intended to demolish the whole of Ciechanów and build it anew.

🏛 Museum of the Mazovian Nobility
ul. Warszawska 61a. **Tel** 23 672 53 46.
Open 8am–4pm Tue–Sun (Jul–Aug: 10am–6pm). 🗺 (free one day a week, usually Sat). W muzeumciechanow.pl

❸ Opinogóra

Road map E3. 🗺 630. 🚉 🚌

Opinogóra is closely associated with Count Zygmunt Krasiński (1812–59), a leading Romantic poet. The tiny Neo-Gothic mansion, situated in a landscaped park, was built as a wedding present for him. According to the locals, it was designed by the French architect Eugène Emmanuel Viollet-le-Duc, although art historians attribute it to Henryk Marconi. Today, the mansion houses the **Museum of Romanticism** (Muzeum Romantyzmu).

The romantic park in which the mansion is set also contains the parish church, with the mausoleum of the Krasiński family where the poet is buried. Noteworthy too is the marble tomb of Count Zygmunt's mother, Maria Krasińska, by Luigi Pampaloni, dating from 1841.

🏛 Museum of Romanticism
ul. Krasińskiego 9. **Tel** 23 671 70 25.
Open 10am–6pm Tue–Sun (Oct–Apr: 8am–4pm). 🗺 🏧 W muzeum romantyzmu.pl

❹ Pułtusk

Road map E3. 🗺 19,200. 🚌
𝒊 Rynek 41, Town Hall Tower (23 692 84 24). W pultusk.pl

Of all the small towns in Mazovia, Pułtusk has the most beautiful setting. Its historic centre, located on an island formed by an arm of the River Narwa, has one of the longest market squares in Europe. The town hall, with its

Gothic brick tower, houses the small **Regional Museum**. Of equal interest is the Gothic-Renaissance **collegiate church**, with barrel vaulting over the nave executed by Gianbattista of Venice in 1551 and 1556.

To the south of the market square rise the walls of the castle of the bishops of Płock. Destroyed and rebuilt a number of times, it incorporates Renaissance, Baroque and Neo-Classical elements. After restoration work in the 1980s the **House of the Polish Diaspora** (Dom Polonii) was set up here. Visitors can stay in the hotel and enjoy tennis, canoeing, rowing, horse riding and winter sledging parties. The old-time Polish kitchen, which serves home-made fruit and berry liqueurs and home-baked sourdough bread, is recommended. Also worth seeing in the old town is the 18th-century Jesuit Church of Saints Peter and Paul.

🏛 Regional Museum
Rynek 43. **Tel** 23 692 51 32.
Open 10am–4pm Tue–Sun & public hols. 🗺 (free on Thu). W muzeum. pultusk.pl

Environs
Near the town, on the right bank of the Narwa, are water meadows and the **White Forest** (Puszcza Biała), which has a rich variety of plants and wildlife, including over 200 species of birds.

The town hall at Pułtusk, in one of Europe's longest market squares

The twin-towered basilica in Czerwińsk on the Vistula

❺ Czerwińsk on the Vistula

Road map E3. 🚗 1,200. 🚌

The church and monastery in Czerwińsk on the Vistula, formerly owned by the Canons Regular and now by the Salesian order, are among the oldest buildings in Mazovia. The monastery was in existence by 1155 and the Romanesque **basilica** was probably built in the time of Bishop Aleksander of Płock in the mid-12th century. In spite of later Gothic and modern alterations, the main body of the building largely retains its original appearance. The basilica's nave and aisles each end in an apse – a characteristic feature of Romanesque churches. In 1410, the massed armies of Małopolska, Lithuania and Ruthenia gathered around the Gothic bell tower on their march to war against the Teutonic Knights.

Environs
A few miles west of Czerwińsk is the poor but nonetheless charming little town of **Wyszogród**, overlooking the Vistula. In the Middle Ages it had a castle (demolished at the end of the 18th century) and was the seat of a castellany. Evidence of the town's past glory survives in the church and partially preserved former Franciscan friary, founded in 1406 and rebuilt several times in the 17th and 18th centuries. There is also a Baroque parish church dating from 1779–89.

❻ Żelazowa Wola

Road map E3. 🚗 60. 🚌

The romantic manor set in a verdant, well-tended park is the birthplace of the composer Fryderyk Chopin (1810–49). At the time of his birth, however, it was no more than a thatched outbuilding in which Chopin's parents, Mikołaj and Justyna Tekla, rented a few rooms. In 1930–31, the building was converted into the **Chopin Museum** (Muzeum – Dom Urodzenia Fryderyka Chopina) and the park around it planted with trees and shrubs donated by horticulturalists from all over Poland. Inside were assembled all kinds of objects associated with the composer. During the German occupation, many of these were looted by the Nazis, the music of Chopin was banned, and all pictures and busts of the composer were destroyed. After World War II, the manor was rebuilt, and in 1948 the museum was finally reopened once more to the public.

Concerts of Chopin's music are given in the house and garden, providing visitors with a unique opportunity to hear the music of the most inspired composer of the Romantic period in the atmosphere of an early 19th-century mansion.

Near Żelazowa Wola lies the village of **Brochów**, on the edge of the Kampinoska Forest (Puszcza Kampinoska). Fryderyk Chopin was christened in the fortified Renaissance church here.

🏛 **Chopin Museum**
Tel 46 863 33 00. **Open** Apr–Sep: 9am–7pm Tue–Sun (Oct–Mar: to 5pm). Concerts: May–Sep: noon Sat & Sun (Sun also 3pm). **Closed** public hols. 📷 (free Wed). 🆆 **chopin.museum**

Woman from Łowicz dressed in regional costume

❼ Łowicz

Road map D3. 🚗 32,200. 🚆 🚌
ℹ Stary Rynek 17 (46 837 34 33). 🆆 **lowiczturystyczny.eu**

The relatively small town of Łowicz, established in the 13th century, was the seat of one of the oldest castellanies in Poland. For several centuries, its castle (which is no longer standing) was the residence of the bishops of Gniezno, primates of Poland. The **collegiate church**, which was founded in the Middle Ages and rebuilt in the 17th century, contains many notable works of art. It also houses a number of tombs, the most illustrious

The manor in Żelazowa Wola, birthplace of Fryderyk Chopin

occupant of which was Primate Jakub Uchański (d. 1581). His tomb's most noteworthy features are a 16th-century alabaster carving by Jan Michałowicz of Urzędów and an early Neo-Classical frame by Ephraim Schroeger, dating from 1782–3.

The magnificent late Baroque high altar was made between 1761 and 1764 by Jan Jerzy Plersch to a design by Schroeger. It is considered by many to be one of the most original altars in Poland. The altar painting, crowned by an aureole and enclosed between the pilasters of a narrow frame, makes a great impression on churchgoers and tourists alike.

Near the collegiate church is the old **Piarist church** (kościół Pijarów) – the Piarists were a Catholic order. Its late Baroque undulating façade, which dates from around 1729, is extremely eye-catching. The interior of the building has Baroque altars by Jan Jerzy Plersch.

On the other side of Old Market Square, in the buildings of a former monastery and seminary for missionaries, is the **Łowicz Regional Museum** (Muzeum Ziemi Łowickiej) devoted to the folklore of the Łowicz area. Its exhibits include characteristic Łowicz costumes of the 19th and early 20th centuries, decorative paper cut-outs and folk embroidery.

In the former chapel, built in 1689–1701 to designs by Tylman van Gameren and decorated with frescoes by Michelangelo Palloni, objects from the prehistoric Sarmatian culture are on display.

Łowicz comes alive at Corpus Christi, when in honour of this celebration local people dress in colourful traditional costumes to take part in a splendid procession that winds its way through the centre of town.

🏛 **Collegiate Church**
Stary Rynek 24. **Tel** 46 837 32 66.

🏛 **Łowicz Regional Museum**
Stary Rynek 5/7. **Tel** 46 837 39 28. **Open** 9am–4pm Tue–Sun. **Closed** Mon & pub hols. 📷 (free on Sat). 🅦 **muzeumlowicz.pl**

Temple of Diana in Arkadia, the landscaped park near Łowicz

❽ Arkadia

Road map D3. 🚗 250. 🚌

Not far from Łowicz, on the road to Nieborów, lies Arkadia, a sentimentally romantic landscaped park. Laid out in 1778 by Princess Helena Radziwiłłowa, Arkadia's attractions include a lake with two islands and a number of romantic pavilions fancifully designed on historical or mythological themes by Szymon Bogumił Zug and Henryk Ittar.

Among ancient trees stand the Temple of Diana, the High Priest's House, the Margrave's Cottage with Greek arch, the Gothic Cottage, the Grotto of the Sybil and the Aqueduct.

On some of the pavilion walls, fragments of decorative carving and stonework salvaged from the destroyed Renaissance bishops' castle in Łowicz are mounted.

❾ Nieborów

Road map E3. 🚗 950. 🚌 Nieborów Palace: **Tel** 46 838 56 35. **Open** May & Jun: 10am–6pm daily; Jul–Apr: 10am–4pm Tue–Sun. 📷 (free May & Jun: Mon; Jul–Apr: Tue). 🅦 **nieborow.art.pl**

The Baroque palace in Nieborów was built by Tylman van Gameren between 1690 and 1696 for Primate Michał S. Radziejowski, Archbishop of Gniezno. Radziejowski was a noted connoisseur of literature, music, art and architecture, and as such was a client worthy of Tylman. A symmetric garden was also laid out. Around 1766, at the wish of a later owner, Prince Michał K. Ogiński, the building's façade was adorned with a Rococo figure portraying a dancing Bacchus, with a bunch of grapes and a garland on his head. Ogiński is also famous for the construction of a canal, which, via the river system, linked the Black Sea to the Baltic.

Between 1774 and 1945, Nieborów Palace was the property of the aristocratic Radziwiłł family. It is famous for its fine furnishings, which include Antoine Pesne's portrait of the famous beauty Anna Orzelska, who was the natural daughter of August II (1697–1733), and the antique head of Niobe, praised in the poetry of Konstanty Ildefons Gałczyński (1905–53). This Roman head, which was carved in white marble after a Greek original of the 4th century BC, was presented to Princess Helena Radziwiłłowa by Catherine the Great.

A grand interior at Nieborów Palace

Monument to the victims of the death camps at Treblinka

❿ Treblinka

Road map F3. 🏔 270. 🚇 🚌

In 1941, the Nazis established a labour camp, Treblinka I, and in 1942 a death camp, Treblinka II. Around 800,000 people, mainly Jews from liquidated ghettos, were murdered here. Those brought to Treblinka II were taken off the trains and herded, without even being registered, to the gas chambers. Up until March 1943, the victims were buried in mass graves. After March 1943, the graves were dug up and the bodies burned. Thereafter all bodies were burned. In November 1943, Treblinka II was closed and the ground ploughed over and seeded. Today, the **Treblinka Museum of Struggle and Martyrdom** stands as a reminder of the past.

In 1964, two monuments were erected on the site of the camp. The monument at Treblinka II spreads over 13 ha (30 acres). It gives an impression of "hundreds of thousands of human beings, coming from nowhere, in a spectral pilgrimage, going to their deaths". It is the work of the architect Adam Haupt and the sculptors Franciszek Duszenko and Franciszek Strynkiewicz.

🏛 **Treblinka Museum of Struggle and Martyrdom**
Kosów Lacki 76. **Tel** 25 781 16 58. **Open** 9am–6:30pm daily (Nov–Mar: to 4pm). 🐾 🎫
🌐 treblinka-muzeum.eu

⓫ Węgrów

Road map F3. 🏔 12,600. 🚌

Węgrów is a small town situated on the historical boundary between Mazovia and Podlasie. Its large, rectangular marketplace is distinguished by the Gothic-Baroque **parish church**, dating from 1703–6. Its interior is decorated with paintings by Michelangelo Palloni and fine Baroque images. The sacristy contains a mirror with a Latin inscription indicating that the legendary Pan Twardowski – the Polish Faust, who reputedly flew to the moon on the back of a cockerel – used it in his practice of the black arts. Nearby stands a somewhat neglected **post-Reformation church**, dating from 1693–1706. Inside is an impressive Baroque monument to the founder, Jan Bonawentura Krasiński, depicting Chronos and a female figure pointing to the spot where Krasiński is buried.

Armour, Museum of Arms, Liw

Environs

At **Liw**, 6 km (4 miles) west of Węgrów, are the remains of a Gothic castle erected in the 15th century. The castle was surrounded by marshes, and the gates could be reached only by a causeway. It was twice stormed by Swedes in the 17th century. In 1782, a small house was erected on the rubble for the county chancellery. Today it houses a **Museum of Arms** (Muzeum Zbrojownia), which besides a display of weaponry contains portraits by the 18th-century Sarmatian School.

In **Stara Wieś** to the north is the palace of the Krasiński-Golicyny family, which has the finest examples in Poland of interiors in the English Gothic style.

🏛 **Museum of Arms**
Liw, ul. Batorego 2. **Tel** 25 792 57 17. **Open** 10am–4pm Tue–Sat, 11am–4pm Sun & public hols (May–Sep: 11am–6pm Sat & Sun). 🐾 🎫

⓬ Czersk

Road map E4. 🏔 400. 🚌

Today, Czersk is no more than a small village; in the distant past it was the capital of Mazovia. By 1413 – most probably due to a change in the course of the Vistula, which had suddenly moved away from Czersk – that role had passed to Warsaw. The spectacular ruins of the princely **castle** tower over the Vistula. The road to the fortress crosses a bridge over the moat. Here, three high towers still stand. In the 12th century, Prince Konrad Mazowiecki used one of its dungeons to imprison the small boy who later became Prince Bolesław the Shy of Krakow, and Prince Henryk the Bearded of Wrocław.

Ruins of the castle at Czersk

Environs

Góra Kalwaria, 3 km (2 miles) north of Czersk, was once an important place of pilgrimage. Interesting features include the **market square**, with the **Church of the Exaltation of the Holy Cross** and the small Neo-Classical trade halls. The present **parish church** once belonged to the Bernardines. Before World War II, many Jews lived in Góra Kalwaria. Today, the Jewish cemetery serves as a memorial to that time.

An exhibit at the Centre for Polish Sculpture in Orońsko

⓭ Radom

Road map E4. 🏔 215,500. 🚌 🚐
ℹ ul. Traugutta 3 (48 360 06 10).
W cit.radom.pl

This comparatively large town was at one time best known for its arms industry, but today it is more readily associated with the workers' protests of 1976, which took place four years before the founding of Solidarity. Although Radom was rebuilt in the 19th century, several of its older buildings can still be viewed. Nothing, however, remains of the old town itself, which until 1819 was surrounded by a wall.

The most interesting feature of Radom is the Gothic **parish church** in Ulica Rwańska, which was built in 1360–70 and later remodelled. Two Baroque buildings – Esterka and Gąska at Nos. 4 and 5 Rynek – house the **Gallery of Contemporary Art**; beside them stands the arcaded **town hall**, by Henryk Marconi. Also worth visiting are the **Bernardine monastery** and **church**, which contain 30 tombs and memorial plaques, the oldest of which dates from the 1500s.

Wooden cottages, windmills and two 18th-century manors are displayed in the *skansen* at **Radom Rural Museum**.

🏛 **Radom Rural Museum**
ul. Szydłowiecka 30. **Tel** 48 332 92 81.
Open 9am–5pm Tue–Fri, 10am–6pm Sat & Sun (winter: to 3pm). **Closed** public hols. 📷 (free on Mon).
W muzeum-radom.pl

Environs

The mansion of **Józef Brandt** (1841–1915), the noted painter of battle scenes, is set in parkland at **Orońsko**, 17 km (11 miles) from Radom. It is open to visitors, for whom a display of objects relating to the artist's life and work has been laid out. Another attraction is the **Centre for Polish Sculpture**, housed in a modern building within the park. International exhibitions and a sculpture biennale are held here.

🏛 **Centre for Polish Sculpture**
ul. Topolowa 1, Orońsko. **Tel** 48 618 45 16. **Open** Apr–Oct: 8am–4pm Tue–Fri, 10am–6pm Sat & Sun; Nov–Mar: 7am–3pm Tue–Fri, 8am–4pm Sat & Sun.
W rzezba-oronsko.pl

⓮ Szydłowiec

Road map E4. 🏔 12,000. 🚐
W szydlowiec.pl

The most significant features of this small town are the late Renaissance **town hall** and the Gothic-Renaissance **castle**, set on an island. The castle was built in 1510–16 and remodelled in the 17th century. Of its rich interior decoration, only traces remain. Of greater interest is the **Museum of Folk Musical**

Late Renaissance town hall in Szydłowiec

Instruments, the only museum of its kind in Poland.

🏛 **Museum of Folk Musical Instruments**
ul. Sowińskiego 2. **Tel** 48 617 17 89. **Open** 9am–4pm Tue–Fri, 10am–5pm Sat & Sun (Oct–Mar: 9am–4pm Tue–Sun). **Closed** public hols. 📷 (free on Sat).

Environs

In **Chlewiska**, 11 km (7 miles) west of Szydłowiec, are the remains of an early 19th-century ironworks. A palace stands nearby.

Tower of the castle of the bishops of Krakow in Iłża

⓯ Iłża

Road map E4. 🏔 5,100. 🚐

Although the castle of the bishops of Krakow has been in ruins since the beginning of the 19th century, its tower still dominates the town. It was built in the 14th century by Bishop Jan Grot. Later owners transformed it into an elegant Renaissance residence. In 1637, Władysław IV came here in disguise. Hiding in the crowd, he wanted to get a secret look at the bride he had married by proxy, Cecilia Renata, daughter of Leopold II of Austria. Dazzled by her beauty, he quickly made his presence known. Unfortunately, the marriage did not prove a happy one.

⑯ A Tour around Kazimierz Dolny

The environs of Kazimierz Dolny are renowned for their picturesque landscapes and rich heritage of historic buildings. Here the Vistula valley is cut by deep ravines, while from the gentle hills magnificent views unfold. It is tempting to linger in Nałęczów, with its popular spa, and in Puławy, where Czartoryski Palace stands in a landscaped park. The journey from Kazimierz Dolny to Janowiec can only be made by ferry; this provides an excellent opportunity for photographing both banks of the Vistula.

⑥ Gołąb
The Mannerist-Baroque church, which dates from 1628–36, has brick walls and fantastic decoration; beside it stands the Lorentine Chapel.

⑦ Sieciechów
The late Baroque Church of the Assumption of the Blessed Virgin towers over the buildings of the former Benedictine abbey. It was built between 1739 and 1769, though the walls contain Romanesque remains. The interior is adorned with Rococo-Neo-Classical-style paintings by Szymon Mankowski.

Map labels: Kock, Kozienice, Dęblin, Wieprz, Vistula, Radom, Zwoleń, Piewka, Lubl, 48, 7, 801, 738, 6, 824, 8, 5, 12, 824, 12, 79, 1, 2, 4, 830

0 kilometres 5
0 miles 5

⑧ Czarnolas
This was the home of Jan Kochanowski (1530–84), the greatest poet of the Polish Renaissance. Little is left of his wooden manor, and the museum devoted to the poet's life and work is housed in the 19th-century mansion.

① Janowiec
The extensive ruins of the castle that was built for the Firlej family in the 16th century now house a museum. It includes a small *skansen* where several wooden buildings, including an 18th-century manor and storehouse, have been re-erected.

Tips for Drivers
Tour length: 150 km (94 miles)
Stopping-off points: Good cafés and restaurants are in Kazimierz Dolny, Nałęczów and Puławy. The ferry from Kazimierz to Janowiec runs from Apr to Nov, every 30 mins.

⑤ Puławy
The former residence of the Czartoryski family is set in a large park, landscaped in the English style. Many small ornamental buildings, such as the Temple of the Sybil and the Gothic House, are to be seen here.

④ Bochotnica
In this hamlet stand the ruins of a 14th-century castle that, according to legend, Kazimierz the Great (1333–70) built for Esterka, the beautiful Jewish girl who became his mistress.

St Christopher, House of Krzysztof Przybyła, Kazimierz Dolny

③ Nałęczów
This health resort also has a spa park, with a pump room and a modern swimming pool. The wooden cottage housing the museum of the novelist Stefan Żeromski (1864–1925) is open to visitors.

② Kazimierz Dolny
One of the most perfectly-preserved Renaissance towns in Poland, Kazimierz Dolny swarms with tourists in summer. The town is well provided with guesthouses, good restaurants and cafés. There are also handicraft stalls and young artists offering their work for sale.

Bystra

③

Lublin

Key
■ Tour route
■ Other road

Czartoryski Palace at Puławy

After the partitions of Poland at the end of the 18th century, the Puławy residence of Princess Izabella and her husband became an important centre of artistic and political life. In the garden pavilions, the princess established the first Polish national museum, called the Shrine of Memory. After the November Insurrection of 1831 failed, Puławy was deserted. The Czartoryskis went into exile abroad and their property was confiscated by the Russians.

Izabella Czartoryska

⑰ Kazimierz Dolny

Road map F4. 🚐 3,570. 🚌 ℹ️ Rynek 27 (81 881 07 09). 🎭 Festival of Folk Bands and Singers (Jun); Two Shores Film Festival (Aug). 🌐 **kazimierz-dolny.pl**

This delightful little town, the favourite holiday resort of poets and painters, was probably founded by Kazimierz the Great. In the 16th and 17th centuries, it grew rich from the grain trade. The ruins of a Gothic **castle** with a high tower dominate the town. At its foot can be seen the Renaissance **Parish Church of Saints John the Baptist and Bartholomew** built in 1610–13, which incorporates the walls of an earlier Gothic church. The interior has provincial stuccowork decoration in the vaulting, and early Baroque chapels.

The most attractive part of town is the **market square**, flanked by several Mannerist houses, with rich ornamental coverings. Particularly attractive are the **House of Mikołaj Przybyła** and **House of Krzysztof Przybyła**, at Nos. 12 and 13, dating from around 1615. There are also some 16th-century houses in Ulica Senatorska, which leads down to the Vistula, including the **Celej House**, which dates from around 1635. While strolling through the town, note the former synagogue, dating from the 18th century, the granaries on the banks of the Vistula, and the pre-war villas.

For hotels and restaurants see p302 and pp311–12

⑱ Lublin

Lublin, the largest city in southeastern Poland, is well-endowed with historic buildings. It is also an important centre of academic life; its best-known seat of learning is the Catholic University of Lublin. Before World War II, the only Jewish college of higher education in Poland was located here. In 1944, after Lublin had been liberated from the Nazis, Poland's first Communist government, convened at Stalin's behest, arrived here on the tanks of the Red Army.

Colourful buildings around the Town Hall in Lublin's Old Town

Exploring Lublin

The most attractive district of Lublin is the **Old Town** (Stare Miasto), situated on the edge of the escarpment. It is reached through **Krakow Gate** (Brama Krakowska), which has become a symbol of the city. This old part of Lublin is a maze of romantic lanes and alleys. The façades of the houses are decorated with Mannerist and Baroque ornamentation and have splendid attics. Many of the buildings have Socialist Realist paintings dating from 1954, when the whole town was renovated to celebrate the tenth anniversary of the establishment of the Communist Lublin Committee *(see p57).* At the centre of the Old Town is the **Market Square**, with Lublin's town hall. Here, the Crown Tribunal

of the Kingdom of Poland once had its seat. In the 18th century, the town hall was rebuilt by Dominik Merlini in the Neo-Classical style. Today its cellars house an exhibition on the history of Lublin and are part of **Lublin's Underground Route**, which runs for 300 m (984 ft) along a series of 16th-century cellars. The most magnificent place of worship in the Old Town is the **Dominican church** (kościół Dominikanów), founded in 1342 and rebuilt in the 17th and 18th centuries. The finest of its 11 chapels is the mid-17th-century Mannerist-Baroque Firlej Chapel. Its ribbed dome is an ambitious confection ascribed to the mason Jan Wolff. The main street in Lublin, Krakowskie Przedmieście, is now a pedestrian

Krakow Gate, one of Lublin's symbols

precinct lined with elegant shops. In Plac Unii Lubelskiej are the **Capuchin church** (kościół Kapucynów) and the **Church of Our Lady Victorious** (Kościół Matki Boskiej Zwycięskiej), founded by Władysław Jagiełło (1386–1434) to commemorate his victory over the Teutonic Knights at the Battle of Grunwald in 1410 *(see pp46–7).*

The Jewish **cemetery** adjoining Ulica Kalinowszczyna, established in 1555, is evidence of the Jewish community that existed in Lublin for many centuries. This community is celebrated in the novels of Nobel laureate Isaac Bashevis Singer (1904–91).

🏛 **Lublin's Underground Route**
Rynek 1. **Tel** 81 534 65 70. **Open** 10am–3pm Mon–Fri; Sat & Sun: tours at noon, 1pm, 2pm & 4pm. 🖼

Interior of the dome of the Firlej Chapel in the Dominican church

⛪ **Cathedral of Saints John the Baptist and John the Evangelist**
pl. Katedralny. **Tel** 81 532 11 96. **Open** 10am–4pm Tue–Sat.
The interior of this former Jesuit church is a triumph of Baroque art. Trompe l'oeil frescoes painted by Joseph Mayer in 1756–7 depict scenes set against a background of illusory architecture. The most beautiful frescoes are those in the cathedral treasury, depicting *Heliodorus Expelled from the Temple.*

Neo-Gothic façade of Lublin Castle

Lublin Castle

pl. Zamkowy 1. **Muzeum Lubelskie Tel** 81 532 50 01. Museum: **Open** 9am–5pm Tue–Sun. Chapel of the Holy Trinity: **Open** 9am–5pm daily.
muzeumlubelskie.pl

Lublin's most important historic building is the **Chapel of the Holy Trinity** (Kaplica Świętej Trójcy). It forms part of Lublin Castle, which was built in the 14th century and remodelled in the Gothic style in 1823–6 for use as a prison. The interior of this Catholic chapel (see p46) is covered with Byzantine frescoes painted in 1418 by Orthodox artists. Among the saints and angels is a portrait of Władysław Jagiełło, the chapel's founder. The chapel is evidence of the cultural diversity of the Kingdom of Poland and the coexistence at this time of the Roman Catholic and Orthodox faiths.

In the museum laid out in the rest of the castle are exhibitions of Polish and foreign paintings, folk art and weaponry.

Majdanek State Museum

Droga Męczenników Majdanka 67. **Tel** 81 710 28 33. **Open** 9am–6pm daily (Nov–Mar: to 4pm). **Closed** public hols. **majdanek.pl**

In 1941, the Nazis established a camp at Majdanek for Soviet prisoners of war, but it later became a death camp, primarily for Jews. Of the 150,000 people who passed through Majdanek, 80,000 were murdered. The camp has been preserved as a museum and memorial to the victims of extermination.

Lublin Rural Museum

Aleja Warszawska 96. **Tel** 81 533 85 13. **Open** Apr–Oct: 9am–6pm daily; Nov–Mar: 9am–3pm Tue–Sun. **skansen.lublin.pl**

Here you can see rural buildings from villages, small towns and manorial estates, together with their furnishings.

Frescoes in the Chapel of the Holy Trinity

Central Lublin

① Capuchin Church
② Church of Our Lady Victorious
③ Krakow Gate
④ Cathedral of Saints John the Baptist and John the Evangelist
⑤ Market Square
⑥ Town hall
⑦ Dominican Church
⑧ Lublin Castle

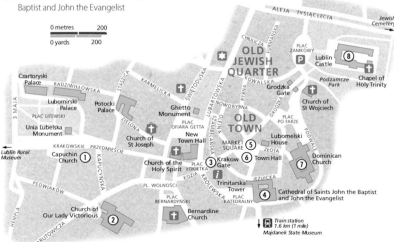

0 metres   200
0 yards   200

For keys to symbols see back flap

⑰ Kozłówka

Road map F4. 800.

The magnificent palace at Kozłówka is one of the best-preserved aristocratic residences in Poland. Built between 1735 and 1742 in the Baroque style by Giuseppe Fontana, its first owner was Michał Bieliński, Palatine of Chełm, who at the wish of August II was married – albeit briefly – to one Aurora Rutkowska, who happened to be the king's illegitimate daughter by a Turkish lady named Fatima.

Kozłówka Palace later passed to the famous Zamoyski family, and was rebuilt in the Empire style and renamed **Zamoyski Palace**. In 1903, Konstanty Zamoyski established what in property law is called an "entail", in order to ensure that the palace would remain the undivided inheritance of the Zamoyski family.

Zamoyski was regarded by contemporaries as a "handsome man, outstanding for his good companionship and sense of humour". He was a great collector, a lover of music and a connoisseur of painting. He was educated in the France of Louis- Napoleon, and the style of the Second Empire is clearly visible in the rich decor of the palace interior, with its Neo-Rococo stuccowork, enormous ceramic stoves, chimneypieces in coloured marble, huge

Picture gallery and White Staircase, Zamoyski Palace, Kozłówka

chandeliers, lambrequins, curtains, and furniture decorated with inlays and bronze – mainly excellent copies in Louis XV and Louis XVI style from the best French workshops.

Today, the palace is a **museum**. Its entire contents have been preserved, making it Poland's finest collection not only of 19th-century art but also of everyday objects. (Do not miss the early 20th-century bathroom, which is most elegantly equipped, or the palace kitchens.)

Most impressive of all the exhibits is the collection of some 1,000 paintings, which almost completely cover the walls. These are not original works but high-quality copies of the masterpieces of European painting – the largest collection in Poland of its kind.

The palace chapel – which was modelled on the Royal Chapel at Versailles – was built between 1904 and 1909 by Jan Heurich junior, the pioneer of modern architecture in Poland. It contains a copy by Lorenzo Bartolini of the tomb of Zofia Zamoyska that is in the church of Santa Croce in Florence.

An annexe of Kozłówka Palace is occupied by a unique gallery housing Socialist Realist art. The building is surrounded by a park that extends over 190,000 sq m (47 acres).

🏛 **Zamoyski Palace and Museum**
Tel 81 852 83 10. **Open** Apr–Nov: 10am–4pm Tue–Sun (to 5pm in summer). 🖼 W **muzeum zamoyskich.pl**

Socialist Realist Art, Kozłówka

Socialist Realism was a doctrinal art style that was developed in the Soviet Union in the Stalinist era. In Poland, it was current after World War II, from about 1949 to 1955. Its theoretical principles were unclear, and in practice what counted were the instructions given to the

Exhibition at Kozłówka Palace

artists. The heroes of Socialist Realist works were party apparatchiks, buxom peasant women and muscular workers. A great number of such works, which were often to be seen on the roofs of public buildings and museum storehouses, can be seen in Kozłówka Palace, where the largest collection in Poland of Socialist Realist art has been assembled.

⑳ Radzyń Podlaski

Road map F4. 🏔 16,000. 🚉 station 8 km (5 miles) from the town. 🚌
ℹ️ ul. Jana Pawła II 2 (83 352 15 60).

In its splendour, **Potocki Palace** rivals Branicki Palace in Białystok, the "Versailles of Podlasie" *(see p294)*. It was built for the ambitious Eustachy Potocki, who later became a general in the Lithuanian artillery. The palace was to be dazzling. It was reconstructed in 1750–58, in the Rococo style, by Giacopo Fontana and his talented team of artists. The painted decoration is by Jan Bogumił Plersch and the carving by Michał Dollinger and Chrystian Redler. The appearance of the palace, like the career of its owner, was calculated to have a great effect. With its elongated wings, it was remarkable not only in form but also in character. Viewed from the courtyard, the unusual monumental wing, with its imposing gate tower (visible even from the town), looks almost like a single-storey outbuilding. Similarly, the main block of the palace, which looks modest from the courtyard, overwhelms with its richness when viewed from the garden.

Dynamic Rococo carvings decorate the palace and adjacent orangery. The most interesting are the four groups of Hercules and the Lion, the Hydra, the Minotaur, and the Dragon. Today, the palace houses various institutions.

In Radzyń Podlaski itself is the **Church of the Holy Trinity** (Kościół Świętej Trójcy), built in 1641 by Jan Wolff, the illustrious mason of the Zamoyski family. The church contains the imposing red marble Renaissance tomb of Mikołaj Mniszech and his wife Zofia, possibly the work of Santi Gucci.

㉑ Chełm

Road map G4. 🏔 65,500. 🚉 🚌
ℹ️ ul. Lubelska 63 (82 565 36 67).
🎭 International Choral Meetings (Apr). 🌐 itchelm.pl

The most interesting aspect of Chełm is its network of underground tunnels, the remains of **chalk mines** (Podziemia). The tunnels are on three levels and descend to a depth of 30 m (100 ft); visitors may walk along them, candle in hand. In the 17th century, as many as 80 houses had an entrance to the workings. Mining ended in the 1800s. Above ground, the town's most impressive building is the **Piarist church**. It was built by Paolo Fontana in 1753–63 and has an undulant façade, elliptic nave and imposing dome. The Baroque interior is decorated with paintings by Joseph Mayer. The best view of Chełm is from Castle Hill (Góra

The highly ornate Baroque interior of the Piarist church in Chełm

Zamkowa), where there are the remains of a 13th-century princely castle. From here, the towers of Roman Catholic churches, the onion domes of a Greek Catholic and an Orthodox **church**, and a fine Baroque **synagogue** can be made out. A Jewish community, one of the earliest in Poland, settled here in the 12th century.

🏛 Chalk Mines
ul. Lubelska 55a. **Tel** 82 565 25 30.
Open visits at 11am, 1pm and 4pm daily. **Closed** public hols. 🎟

Environs
The **Polesian National Park** (Poleski Park Narodowy) lies 40 km (25 miles) northwest of Chełm. It forms part of the Łęczyńsko-Włodarskie Lake District and has many swamps, peat bogs and small lakes.

Rococo carvings on the orangery at Potocki Palace, Radzyń Podlaski

㉒ Zamość

Zamość is one of the best-preserved Renaissance towns in Europe. It was one of the first to be planned and built from scratch according to Italian concepts of the ideal town. The moving force behind this project was Jan Zamoyski (1541–1605), chancellor and commander-in-chief of the Crown, one of the most powerful and enlightened magnates of Poland's Golden Age, and the owner of Zamość. Bernardo Morando was the architect and work began in 1581, continuing for more than ten years. A programme of restoration was carried out in the 1970s, and in 1992 UNESCO declared the town a World Heritage Site. Today, theatrical performances and many other cultural events take place in the Main Square.

★ Town Hall
With its fine ornamental tower and imposing fan staircase, the Town Hall is the focal point of Zamość.

★ Cathedral
The cathedral, designed by Bernardo Morando in 1587, was completed in the 1630s. It was rebuilt in 1824–6. It has an unusual Mannerist façade and distinctively decorated vaulting.

Arsenal
The Arsenal, closely connected with the town's formidable fortifications, is today the Polish Army Museum.

KEY

① **Former Church and Monastery of the Order of St John of God**

② **The Church of St Nicholas,** built for the Greek Catholic Basilian order, is now Roman Catholic, demonstrating the multi-ethnic character of old Zamość.

Franciscan Church
In the 19th century, this large church was turned into a barracks and its Baroque gables pulled down.

VISITORS' CHECKLIST

Practical Information
Road map F5. 🏛 65,200. **ℹ**
Rynek Wielki 13 (84 639 22 92).
Regional Museum: ul. Ormiańska
30. **Tel** 84 638 64 94. **Open** 9am–
4pm Tue–Sun. 🐾 📷 🅿 📸
Jazz on the Borderlands (May);
International Meeting of Jazz
Vocalists (Sep). **W** zci.zamosc.pl

Transport
🚌 🚐

Bastion Fortifications
The fortifications around Zamość allowed the town to resist a Cossack siege as well as the Swedish Deluge of the 1650s.

★ Main Market Square
The Main Market Square (Rynek Wielki) is surrounded on all four sides by arcaded houses two storeys high. Due to the Armenian origin of the merchants who lived here, many of their façades have unusual and elaborate decorations with an Oriental flavour.

Doorway of the Old Rectory
This magnificent rectory, adjoining the cathedral, is one of the oldest houses in Zamość.

KRAKOW

Krakow is one of the most beautiful cities in Europe. Over the centuries, many important artists and architects came to work here, among them Veit Stoss from Germany, Bartolomeo Berrecci and Giovanni Maria Padovano from Italy, and Tylman van Gameren from Holland. Krakow has been spared major destruction, so it preserves the largest assemblage of historic buildings and monuments in Poland.

The earliest mention of Krakow in the historical records dates from the middle of the 10th century; it had certainly been incorporated into the Kingdom of Poland before 992. In 1000, it became a bishopric and around 1038 it assumed the importance of a capital. Wawel Hill became the seat of government, and from 1257, when Bolesław the Chaste gave the city a municipal charter, it began to spread and flourish at the foot of the hill. In 1364 the Krakow Academy was founded, increasing the city's importance on the European stage. During the 14th and 15th centuries, large sums of money were spent on the development of the city, as can be seen from the numerous Gothic churches and secular buildings that survive to this day.

At the beginning of the 16th century, Krakow came under the influence of the Renaissance. The Wawel Royal Castle, the Cloth Hall in the Main Market Square, and many private houses and mansions in the city were rebuilt in the Renaissance style. Krakow gradually lost its significance, and in 1596 the capital was moved to Warsaw, but it was in Wawel Cathedral that successive kings of Poland were crowned and entombed, and the city continued to acquire many magnificent buildings. Under the Partitions of Poland (see pp52–5), Krakow came under Austrian rule, which nevertheless permitted a relatively large degree of local autonomy. Hence it began to assume the role of the spiritual capital of all Poles, both in their native country and abroad. Krakow escaped significant damage during the two World Wars, and in 1978 UNESCO declared it a World Heritage Site.

Memorial to Adam Mickiewicz, Poland's national poet, outside the Cloth Hall in the Main Market Square

◀ A cupola of the Gothic Cathedral on the Wawel

Exploring Krakow

As most places of interest in Krakow are located in its fairly compact historic centre, the city is best seen on foot. A good place to start is Wawel Hill (Wzgórze Wawelskie), with its imposing Wawel Royal Castle and Gothic cathedral, in the crypt of which many kings of Poland are interred. North of Wawel Hill lies the old city of Krakow with its attractive market, the Church of St Mary, the picturesque Cloth Hall and many interesting old houses. To the south of Wawel Hill is the Kazimierz district, with its preserved Jewish quarter. Outlying parts of the city are served by an extensive bus and tram network.

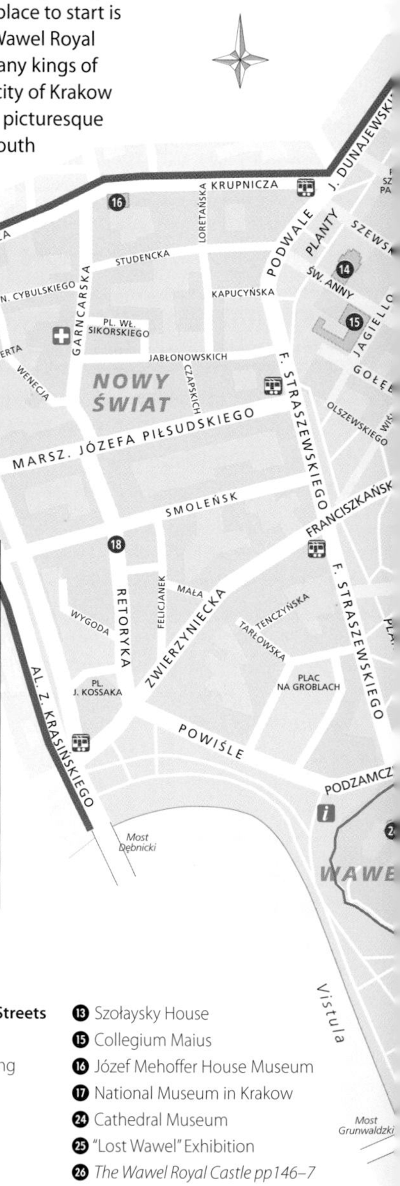

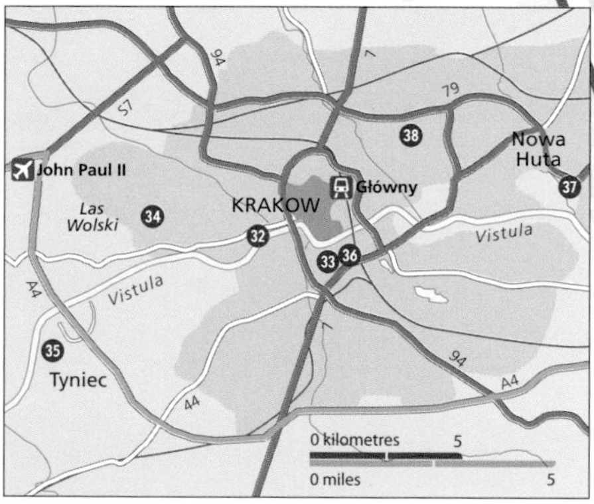

Sights at a Glance

Churches

❸ *Church of St Mary pp138–9*
❺ Dominican Church
⓫ Piarist Church
⓮ Church of St Anne
⓳ Franciscan Church
㉑ Church of Saints Peter and Paul
㉗ *The Cathedral pp148–9*
㉘ Pauline Church on the Rock
㉙ Church of Corpus Christi
㉜ Premonstratensian Church
㉞ Camaldolite Monastery in Bielany
㉟ Benedictine Abbey in Tyniec
㊲ Cistercian Abbey in Mogiła

Buildings, Squares and Streets

❷ City Hall Tower
❻ Medical Society Building
❼ Plac Matejki
❽ Barbican
❾ Ulica Floriańska
⓬ Plac Szczepański
⓲ Ulica Retoryka
⓴ Ulica Grodzka
㉒ Ulica Kanonicza
㉓ Fortifications on the Wawel

Museums and Galleries

❶ Cloth Hall
❹ Rynek Underground
❿ Princes Czartoryski Museum
⓭ Szołaysky House
⓯ Collegium Maius
⓰ Józef Mehoffer House Museum
⓱ National Museum in Krakow
㉔ Cathedral Museum
㉕ "Lost Wawel" Exhibition
㉖ *The Wawel Royal Castle pp146–7*
㉝ Pharmacy under the Eagle
㊱ Schindler's Factory and MOCAK
㊳ Polish Aviation Museum

Synagogues and Cemeteries

㉚ Old Synagogue
㉛ Remuh Cemetery and Synagogue

For hotels and restaurants see pp302–3 and pp312–13

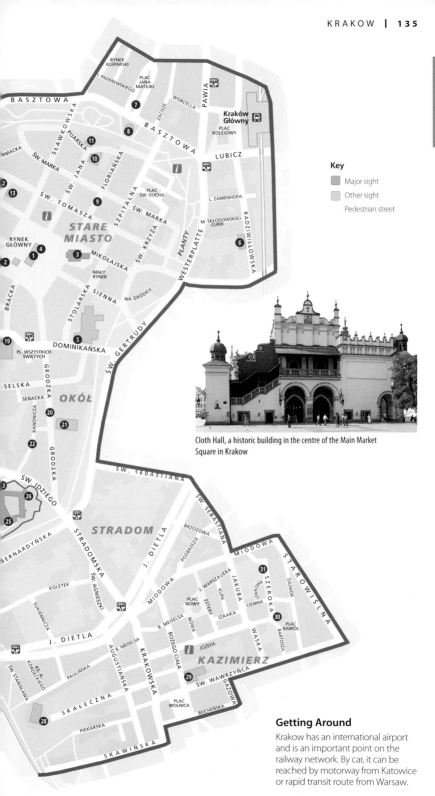

RYNEK
KLEPARSKI

I. PADEREWSKIEGO

PLAC
JANA
MATEJKI

WORCELLA

PAWIA

Kraków
Główny

PLAC
KOLEJOWY

7

ZACISZE

BASZTOWA

BASZTOWA

LUBICZ

SŁAWKOWSKA

PIJARSKA

8

11

RMACKA

ŚW. MARKA

ŚW. JANA

FLORIAŃSKA

10

L. ZAMENHOFA

PLAC
ŚW. DUCHA

M. SKŁODOWSKIEJ-
CURIE

RADZIWIŁŁOWSKA

2

13

ŚW. TOMASZA

SZPITALNA

ŚW. MARKA

9

i

STARE
MIASTO

ŚW. KRZYŻA

PLANTY

6

RYNEK
GŁÓWNY

MIKOŁAJSKA

3

4

WESTERPLATTE

2

1

MAŁY
RYNEK

STOLARSKA

SIENNA

NA GRÓDKU

BRACKA

19

PL. WSZYSTKICH
ŚWIĘTYCH

DOMINIKAŃSKA

5

ŚW. GERTRUDY

SELSKA

SENACKA

GRODZKA

OKÓŁ

KANONICZA

20

21

22

GRODZKA

ŚW. SEBASTIANA

ŚW. IDZIEGO

3

26

BRZOZOWA

25

ŚW. SEBASTIANA

STRADOM

J. DIETLA

MIODOWA

31

STAROWIŚLNA

BERNADYŃSKA

STRADOMSKA

PODBRZEZIE

DAJWÓR

ŚW. AGNIESZKI

J. DIETLA

MIODOWA

J. WARSZAUERA

JAKUBA

KUPA

NOWY

CIEMNA

SZEROKA

30

PLAC
BAWÓŁ

BARTOSZA

KOLETEK

MIODOWA

PLAC
NOWY

ESTERY

IZAAKA

NOWA

WĄSKA

SUKIENNICZA

B. MEISELSA

JÓZEFA

i

J. DIETLA

B. MEISELSA

BOŻEGO CIAŁA

KAZIMIERZ

KS. A.
KORDECKIEGO

AUGUSTIAŃSKA

KRAKOWSKA

29

ŚW. WAWRZYŃCA

GAZOWA

ŚW. STANISŁAWA

PAULIŃSKA

28

SKAŁECZNA

PLAC
WOLNICA

BOCHEŃSKA

PIEKARSKA

SKAWIŃSKA

Cloth Hall, a historic building in the centre of the Main Market
Square in Krakow

Key

Major sight

Other sight

Pedestrian street

Getting Around

Krakow has an international airport
and is an important point on the
railway network. By car, it can be
reached by motorway from Katowice
or rapid transit route from Warsaw.

For keys to symbols see back flap

Main Market Square

This huge market square (Rynek Główny) was laid out when Krakow received its new municipal charter in 1257. One of the largest in Europe, it seethes with life all year round. In summer, pedestrians find themselves negotiating the maze of café tables that surround the square, along with a host of shops, antique dealers, restaurants, bars and clubs. There are also many interesting museums, galleries and historic sights, including some splendid Renaissance and Baroque houses and mansions.

❸ ★ **Church of St Mary**
This main parish church in Krakow is renowned for its asymmetrical twin towers.

❹ **Rynek Underground**

❶ ★ **Cloth Hall**
This beautiful Renaissance building replaced an earlier Gothic market hall. The upper floor houses a gallery that exhibits 19th-century art.

❷ **City Hall Tower**
The Gothic tower is the only remaining part of the former City Hall. A café has been opened in the basement.

St Wojciech is a small but splendid Romanesque church. One of the oldest stone churches in Poland, it pre-dates the planning of this vast square and is all but lost in it.

Key

— Suggested route

Locator Map

The Church of St Barbara, dating from the late 14th century, contains many treasures, including a 15th-century Gothic pietà.

House known as "At the Sign of the Lizards"

ENNA

RODZKA

0 metres 50

0 yards 50

● Cloth Hall

Rynek Główny 1/3. 🚌 124, 152, 304, 502. 🚃 3, 4, 7, 13, 14, 18, 19. Gallery of Polish Painting: **Tel** 12 433 54 00. **Open** 10am–6pm Tue–Sun. 🅿 (free on Sun). 📷 🚫 🔇 ♿ 🏠 **W** mnk.pl

Set in the centre of the Main Market Square, the Cloth Hall (Sukiennice) replaces an earlier Gothic trade hall dating from the second half of the 1300s. Destroyed in a fire, then rebuilt by Giovanni Maria Padovano, it owes something of its present appearance to Tomasz Pryliński's Romantic-style restoration (1875–9). The ground floor has cafés and souvenir shops, while on the upper floor is the Gallery of Polish Painting. Its collection of 19th-century works includes art by Jan Matejko, Marcello Bacciarelli and Piotr Michałowski.

● City Hall Tower

Rynek Główny 1. 🚌 124, 152, 304, 502. 🚃 3, 4, 7, 13, 14, 18, 19. Branch of the Historical Museum of Krakow: **Tel** 12 619 23 35. **Open** Apr–Oct: 10:30am–6pm daily; Nov–Mar: noon–4pm daily. **Closed** public hols. 🅿 🔇 ♿

The Gothic tower, crowned by a Baroque cupola, that dominates the Main Market Square is the only remaining vestige of the City Hall, built in the 14th century and pulled down in the first half of the 19th. The tower houses a branch of the Historical Museum. Aspects of the city's history are also documented in the Museum of the History of the Market, in the crypt of the neighbouring Church of St Wojciech.

● Church of St Mary

See pp138–9.

● Rynek Underground

Rynek Główny 1. **Tel** 12 426 50 60. **Open** Apr–Oct: 10am–10pm daily (to 8pm Mon, to 4pm Tue); Nov–Mar: 10am–8pm daily (to 4pm Tue). **Closed** 1st Tue of month. 🅿 (free on Tue). 🔇 **W** podziemiarynku.com

This high-tech museum, tracing the story of the city, is located under the Main Market Square. The underground vaults contain displays on transportation and trade, as well as archaeological finds such as the remains of an 11th-century cemetery and ancient coins and clothing. The museum cleverly blends modern technology with interactive exhibits and more traditional displays.

● Dominican Church

ul. Stolarska 12. **Tel** 12 423 16 13. 🚃 1, 3, 6, 8, 13, 18. **Open** 6:30am–8pm daily.

The origins of the Dominican Church (Kościół Dominikanów) go back to the second half of the 13th century. Rebuilt a number of times, by the middle of the 1400s it had become the magnificent Gothic building that still stands today. A number of mortuary chapels were also added; many of them are major works of Renaissance and Baroque art in their own right, with rich decorations and furnishings. Of particular note are the Baroque chapel of the Zbaraski family, at the west end of the north aisle, and the Mannerist chapel of the Myszkowski family, in the first bay of the south aisle. The church was badly damaged by a great fire that swept through the city in 1850, destroying most of its wooden furnishings, although it was promptly restored.

Shrine of St Jacek in the Dominican church

❸ Church of St Mary

The imposing Church of St Mary (Kościół Mariacki) was built by the citizens of Krakow to rival the Royal Cathedral on Wawel Hill. Building began in 1355, but work on the vaulting and the chapels continued until the mid-15th century, and the lower tower was not completed until the early 16th century. At this time, sermons were preached in German. This great basilica, with its rows of side chapels, contains an exceptional number of important works of art.

★ Crucifix
The large sandstone crucifix by Veit Stoss is a fine example of 15th-century sculpture.

Hejnał Tower
The famous trumpet call – the Hejnał – is sounded hourly from the tower. The call is unfinished, in memory of a medieval trumpeter, shot while sounding the alarm. The Hejnał is broadcast live by Polish radio daily at noon.

Main entrance

Baroque Porch
This pentagonal porch was built in the mid-18th century to a design by Francesco Placidi.

Ciborium
This large ciborium, in the form of a Renaissance church, was made by Giovanni Maria Padovano in about 1552.

For hotels and restaurants see pp302–3 and pp312–13

Gothic
stained-glass
window made
around 1370

Stained-glass window, Medical
Society Building

❻ Medical Society Building

ul. Radziwiłłowska 4. **Tel** 12 422 75 47.
🚊 3, 10, 20, 24, 52. **Open** 10am–3pm
Mon–Fri (stained glass by appt).
W tlk.cm-uj.krakow.pl

The Medical Society Building
(Gmach Towarzystwa
Lekarskiego) was designed
by Władysław Kaczmarski and
Józef Sowiński and built in
1904. It would hardly merit
mention were it not for its
interior decor, the creation of
Stanisław Wyspiański, one
of the most talented artists of
the Young Poland movement.
He was responsible for the
interior decoration of individual
rooms and furnishings inspired
by folk art, as in the magnificent
stained-glass window *Apollo
and The Solar System.*

❼ Plac Matejki

🚌 124, 152, 304.
🚊 2, 4, 7, 14, 24.

This typical Krakovian
square was laid out at
the end of the 19th
century. The Church
of St Florian (Kościół
św. Floriana),
on the corner of
Ulica Warszawska,
is considerably
older. Its present
appearance is the
result of frequent
rebuilding – in
particular a

Neo-Baroque reconstruction
in the early years of the
20th century. The original
church on this site was built
in the early 13th century. At
the end of the 19th century,
huge monumental public
buildings and splendid private
houses were erected around
the square. The Academy of
Fine Arts, at No. 13, designed
by Maciej Moraczewski and
built between 1879 and 1880,
is particularly impressive.

The Grunwald Monument in
the centre of the square was
unveiled in 1910 to mark the
500th anniversary of the Battle
of Grunwald *(see pp46–7)*, in
which the armies of the Teutonic
Knights were routed. The huge
sculpture of Władysław Jagiełło
is by Antoni Wiwulski.

❽ Barbican

ul. Basztowa. **Tel** 12 422 98 77.
🚌 124, 152, 304, 502. 🚊 2, 4, 7, 14,
24. **Open** Apr–Oct: 10:30am–6pm
daily. 🚻

The Barbican (Barbakan) is one
of the remaining elements of
Krakow's medieval fortifications.
The double ring of walls that
once surrounded the city was
built in stages from 1285 to the
beginning of the 15th century.
Most of the circumvallation
was pulled down in the 19th
century. The Barbican was
built in 1498–9, when the city's
defences were strengthened
in response to advances in
military tactics and equipment.
It protected the Florian Gate,
to which it was connected by
an underground passage. The
latter's route is indicated by
a change in the colour of the
paving stones.

Visitors'
entrance

The 15th-century Barbican, based on Arab designs

★ **Altarpiece of Veit Stoss**
This polyptych – the world's
largest Gothic altarpiece – is
11 m (36 ft) wide and 13 m (42 ft)
high. It was carved by Veit Stoss
in 1477–89.

The Florian Gate, Ulica Floriańska

❾ Ulica Floriańska

🚌 124, 152, 304, 502. 🚋 2, 4, 7, 14, 18, 19, 20, 24. Matejko's House: **Tel** 12 422 59 60. **Open** 10am–6pm Tue–Sat, 10am–4pm Sun. 🖼 (free on Sun). 🗺 👫 🖳 mnk.pl

This charming street in the old town is full of restaurants, cafés and shops. It leads from the Main Market Square to the Florian Gate and was once part of the Royal Route, along which rulers would ride on their way from Warsaw to their coronation in Krakow.

At No. 41, **Matejko's House** (Dom Matejki) is the birthplace of the painter Jan Matejko (1838–93). He spent most of his life here. On display is a collection of his paintings – also his studio, full of artist's materials. A little further on, at No. 45, is **Jama Michalika**, a café that was extremely fashionable in the late 19th to early 20th centuries. The fine Art Nouveau decor by Karol Frycz can still be seen.

The **Florian Gate,** at the end of the street, is one of the few surviving remnants of the city's medieval fortifications, along with a section of the city wall and three towers.

❿ Princes Czartoryski Museum

ul. św. Jana 19. **Tel** 12 370 54 60. 🚌 124, 152, 304, 502. 🚋 2, 4, 7, 14, 18, 19, 24, 30. **Closed** for renovation until 2020. 🖼 ♿ 🗺 👫 🖳 mnk.pl

This relatively small museum has one of the most interesting art collections in Poland. Assembled in Puławy at the end of the 18th century by Izabella Czartoryska (see p125), it was the private collection of the Czartoryski family. The collection was later taken to

Leonardo da Vinci, *Lady with an Ermine*, Princes Czartoryski Museum

Paris and then to Krakow, where it was put on public view. Its most famous artworks include Leonardo da Vinci's *Lady with an Ermine* (c.1485) and Rembrandt's *Landscape with Good Samaritan* (1638).

The museum is closed for long term renovations. However, some of its artworks might be on display at a few buildings belonging to the National Museum.

⓫ Piarist Church

ul. Pijarska 2. **Tel** 12 422 22 55. 🚌 124, 152, 502. 🚋 2, 4, 7, 14, 18, 24. **Open** during services only.

The exceptionally beautiful Rococo façade of the Piarist Church (Kościół Pijarów), which stands at the top of Ulica św Jana, was built to the design of Francesco Placidi between 1759 and 1761. It conceals the façade of the older Baroque church of 1718–28 designed by Kacper Bażanka. The interior has stuccowork by Chrystian Bol and paintings by Franz Eckstein.

⓬ Plac Szczepański

🚌 124, 152, 304, 502. 🚋 2, 4, 8, 13, 14, 18, 24. Fine Arts Society Building: **Tel** 12 422 66 16. **Open** 8:15am–6pm Mon–Fri, 10am–6pm Sat & Sun. 🖼 The Bunker of Arts: **Tel** 12 422 10 52. **Open** 11am–7pm Tue–Sun. 🖼 (free on Tue). 🖳

An elegant piazza with a fountain, Plac Szczepański, contains a number of interesting buildings that are used as arts venues and is well worth exploring.

At No. 1, the **Old Theatre** (Teatr Stary) is the oldest theatrical building in Poland. It opened in 1798 and has since been rebuilt twice – most recently between 1903 and 1905, when it was remodelled by Franciszek Mączyński and Tadeusz Stryjeński in the Art Nouveau style. The frieze on the façade is by Józef Gardecki.

Exhibitions are regularly held at the **Fine Arts Society Building** (Pałac Sztuki) at No. 4. Built by Franciszek Mączyński in 1901, this too is in the Art Nouveau style. Interesting exhibitions of contemporary art are also on display for viewing at **The Bunker of Arts** (Bunkier Sztuki), a Brutalist building erected in the 1960s, located at No. 3a.

Mieczysława Gajewicza, a portrait by Stanisław Ignacy Witkiewicz

⑬ Szołaysky House

pl. Szczepański 9. **Tel** 12 433 54 50. 🚋 2, 4, 14, 18, 24. **Open** 10am–6pm Tue–Sat, 10am–4pm Sun. 🏛 (free on Sun). 🎫 ♿ 🖥 🅦 mnk.pl

This 15th-century mansion on the corner of plac Szczepański is now one of Krakow's most important venues for visiting international art exhibitions or themed exhibitions celebrating prominent cultural figures from Poland. There's a beautiful garden courtyard at the back of the building.

⑭ Church of St Anne

ul. św. Anny 11. **Tel** 12 422 53 18. 🚌 124, 152, 504. 🚋 2, 8, 13, 18, 20. **Open** 1:30–7pm Tue–Thu, 9am–7pm Sat, 2–7pm Sun.

In the narrow Ulica św. Anny, it is impossible to miss the imposing Baroque façade of the twin-towered Church of St Anne (Kościół św. Anny). The architect was Tylman van Gameren. In designing the façade, he took into account the fact that any view of it would be acutely foreshortened by virtue of the narrowness of the street.

The church building was erected between 1689 and 1703, although work on the decoration was not completed until much later.

The interior has murals by Karol and Innocenti Monti and a fine high altar by Baldassare Fontana. The painting of St Anne that adorns it is by Jerzy Eleuter Siemigonowski. Also notable are the Baroque choir stalls, decorated by Szymon Czechowicz, and the pulpit, which was carved by Antoni Frączkiewicz.

In the south transept is the shrine and reliquary of St John of Cantinus, a 15th-century theologian and the patron of St Anne's. The church was built after the saint's beatification.

Baroque shrine of St John of Cantinus in the Church of St Anne

⑮ Collegium Maius

ul. Jagiellońska 15. **Tel** 633 15 21. 🚌 124, 152, 504. 🚋 2, 8, 13, 18, 20. **Open** Apr–Oct: 10am–5:20pm Mon–Fri (to 1:30pm Sat); Nov–Mar: 10am–2:20pm Mon–Fri (to1:30pm Sat). 🏛 🎫 compulsory. ♿ 🖥 🅦 maius. uj.edu.pl

The Collegium Maius is the oldest surviving college of the Jagiellonian University, which grew from the Krakow Academy established by Kazimierz the Great in 1364.

Auditorium of the Collegium Maius, with Renaissance coffered ceiling

Queen Jadwiga, wife of Władysław Jagiełło, bequeathed her personal fortune to the Academy in 1399. In the second half of the 15th century the Collegium Maius acquired new premises, which incorporated the walls of several older buildings. Its present appearance is largely due to a 19th-century restoration in a Romantic style, although the building's Gothic structure survives. Copernicus *(see p279)* undoubtedly walked in the cloistered courtyard when he was a student here. In the **Jagiellonian University Museum** are numerous exhibits documenting the rich history of the university.

⑯ Józef Mehoffer House Museum

ul. Krupnicza 26. **Tel** 12 433 58 80. 🚋 4, 8, 13, 14, 24. **Open** 10am–4pm Wed–Sun. 🏛 (free on Sun). 🎫 🖥

This small museum is located in the house where Józef Mehoffer (1854–1946), the leading Art Nouveau stained-glass artist, lived from 1932 until his death. It contains furnishings made by Mehoffer, as well as examples of his artistic output, including the captivating *Portrait of the Artist's Wife*. The house was the birthplace of the well-known artist and writer Stanisław Wyspiański (1869–1907).

⑰ National Museum in Krakow

al. 3 Maja 1. **Tel** 12 433 55 00. 🚌 124, 144, 152, 173, 179, 194, 502. 🚊 20. **Open** 10am–6pm Tue–Sat, 10am–4pm Sun. 🎟 (free on Sun). ⬛ ♿ ⬛ 🎬 **w** muzeum.krakow.pl

The enormous edifice that dominates this part of the city is the main building of Krakow's National Museum. Building began in the 1930s but was not finished until 1989.

The exhibits are divided into three main sections. The first is devoted to the applied arts. The second comprises an interesting collection of militaria and objects of historical interest, such as the military jacket of Józef Piłsudski *(see p57)*. The third has an important collection of 20th-century painting and sculpture. The work of the artists of the Young Poland movement is particularly well represented. The display also features pieces by artists active in the interwar years, and some fine examples of the art of the postwar period.

⑱ Ulica Retoryka

🚌 124, 144, 152, 164, 173, 179, 194. 🚊 1, 2, 6, 20.

Take a walk down Ulica Retoryka and it is impossible to miss the remarkable houses that were designed and built here by Teodor Talowski (1857–1910) in the late 19th century. The architect had an exuberant imagination and a lively sense of humour; the houses that he designed are in an unusual mixture of the Neo-Gothic and Neo-Mannerist styles. They have startling ornamentation, sometimes artificially damaged so as to bestow a patina of age.

At No. 1, for example, is the house **"At the Sign of the Singing Frog"**. Close by is the house **"At the Sign of the Donkey"**, with a motto in Latin that translates as "Every man is master of his own fate". The architect gave to his own house the motto "Festina lente", or "Make haste slowly".

Stained-glass window in the Franciscan church

⑲ Franciscan Church

pl. Wszystkich Świętych 5. **Tel** 12 422 53 76. 🚌 124, 152, 304, 502. 🚊 1, 6, 8, 10, 13, 18, 20. **Open** 6am–7:45pm daily. **Closed** during services. **w** franciszkanska.pl

The origins of the Gothic Franciscan church go back to the 13th and 15th centuries, although rebuilding in the 17th and 19th centuries has considerably altered its appearance. The church, however, is renowned more for its interior decoration than for its architecture and attracts many visitors from all over the world.

A number of interesting features from different ages have been preserved, although the most notable are the Art Nouveau murals and stained-glass windows by Stanisław Wyspiański, dating from around 1900. The chancel and transept are decorated with a vertiginous scheme featuring entwined flowers, heraldic motifs and religious scenes. The stained-glass windows are monumental compositions of great expressive power and represent one of the highest achievements of the Art Nouveau stained-glass movement. Particularly noteworthy is *Let there be Light (see p55)*, which shows the figure of God the Father creating the world. The cloisters are lined with murals that include the Gallery of Krakovian Bishops, in which the finest portrait is that of Bishop Piotr Tomicki, painted by Stanisław Samostrzelnik some time before 1535.

"At the Sign of the Singing Frog"

⑳ Ulica Grodzka

🚊 1, 6, 8, 10, 13, 18, 20.

Many interesting buildings give this picturesque, winding street leading from the Main Market Square to the Wawel a historical atmosphere. At No. 53 is the cloistered courtyard of the **Collegium Iuridicum**, a law college founded in the 15th century and rebuilt in 1718. A little further along rises the façade of the Church of Saints Peter and Paul, with the white stone tower of the 13th-century Romanesque **Church of St Andrew** (Kościół św. Andrzeja) gleaming behind it. The walls of the latter conceal an earlier, late 11th-century building. The interior was radically altered around 1702 by Baldassare Fontana. The adjacent Baroque building is the former Catholic **Church of St Martin** (Kościół św. Marcina). Built between 1637 and 1640 for the Discalced Carmelites, it is now in the hands of the Evangelical Church of the Augsburg Confession.

The Church of St Andrew in Ulica Grodzka

㉑ Church of Saints Peter and Paul

ul. Grodzka 54. **Tel** 12 422 65 73. 🚊 6, 8, 10, 13, 18. **Open** 9am–7pm Mon–Fri, 9am–5:30pm Sat, 1:30–5:30pm Sun; also during services. 🎟

The Church of Saints Peter and Paul (Kościół sw. Piotra i Pawła) is one of the most beautiful

Baroque façade of the Jesuit Church of Saints Peter and Paul

early Baroque churches in Poland. It was built for the Jesuits soon after their arrival in Krakow.

Work began in 1596, but after a structural disaster in 1605, the church was almost completely rebuilt to the design of an architect who remains unknown to this day.

The church is enclosed by railings, topped with the twelve figures of the apostles, dating from 1715–22. The interior of the building contains fine stuccowork by Giovanni Battista Falconi and rich Baroque furnishings. The high altar and the organ screen, designed by Kacper Bażanka, are particularly noteworthy.

Among the many funerary monuments, the most striking is the black-and-white marble tomb of Bishop Andrzej Tomicki, dating from 1695–6.

㉒ Ulica Kanonicza

🚋 1, 6, 8, 10, 13, 18, 20. Archdiocesan Museum: **Tel** 12 421 89 63. **Open** 10am–4pm Tue–Fri, 10am–3pm Sat & Sun. Palace of Bishop Erazm Ciołek: **Tel** 12 433 59 20. **Open** 10am–4pm Tue–Sun. **W** mnk.pl

Ulica Kanonicza is named after the canons of the Krakow Chapterhouse, who once had their houses here. Most of the houses were established in the Middle Ages, but in the course of later rebuilding they were embellished with Renaissance, Baroque and Neo-Classical elements. They constitute one of the most important groups

of historical buildings in Krakow today.

The finest of these houses is considered to be the **Deanery**, at No. 21. Its present form dates from the 1580s – a rebuilding project probably undertaken by the Italian architect Santi Gucci that preserved the arcaded courtyard and the mysterious decoration of the façade.

During the 1960s, Karol Wojtyła – later Pope John Paul II – lived in this house. The adjacent house at No. 19, with a modest Neo-Classical façade, contains the **Archdiocesan Museum**, which has many valuable religious artifacts and a reconstruction of the room at No. 21 where the future pontiff lived.

The house at no. 17 is the former Palace of Bishop Erazm Ciołek (Pałac Biskupa Erazma Ciołka), a prominent churchman and patron of the arts. The distinguished residence now houses the National Museum's collection of Polish art from the medieval era to the 18th century. Highlights include a fabulous collection of

The medieval and romantic Ulica Kanonicza in Krakow

late-Gothic altarpieces commissioned by Krakow's guilds and a rich array of Baroque statuary. There's also a room devoted to the funerary customs of 17th century Poland, with robes adorned with embroidered skulls, and coffins decorated with portraits of the deceased. One wing of the museum contains Orthodox and Uniate icons that once decorated the churches of Poland's Ukrainian community.

Monumental portal of the Deanery in Ulica Kanonicza

The Wawel

On the Wawel, the Vistulanians built a citadel. It was replaced by a series of buildings, including the Renaissance castle and Gothic cathedral that stand there today. Once the site of coronations and royal burials, the Royal Cathedral is regarded by Poles as a spiritual shrine. The Wawel Royal Castle beside it, once the hub of cultural and political life in Poland, is a symbol of national identity.

㉖ ★ Wawel Royal Castle (Zamek Królewski)
The Wawel Royal Castle, once home to the Jagiellonian kings, has survived without major damage. It incorporates the walls of older Gothic buildings.

㉓ Fortifications on the Wawel
The Wawel's systems of fortification have been demolished and renewed several times since the Middle Ages – right up to the 20th century.

㉗ ★ Cathedral
The Gothic cathedral, lined with royal burial chapels from different ages, has some extraordinarily valuable furnishings.

㉔ Cathedral Museum
Important artifacts from the cathedral treasury are on display here, including the magnificent robe of Stanisław August Poniatowski (1764–95).

Key

— Suggested route

Visitor Centre

For hotels and restaurants see pp302–3 and pp312–13

Locator Map

㉕ "Lost Wawel" Exhibition
Various finds from archaeological excavations on the Wawel hill are exhibited here.

| 0 metres | 50 |
| 0 yards | 50 |

㉓ Fortifications on the Wawel

Wawel. 🚊 6, 8, 10, 13, 18.
Sandomierska Tower **Open** May–Sep: daily; Oct: Sat & Sun. 🗓

The Wawel was fortified from early times. Only fragments of the oldest Gothic fortifications remain, but three towers raised in the second half of the 1400s survive; they are known as the Sandomierska Tower, the Senators' Tower and the Thieves' Tower. Of the fortifications dating from the 16th to the 17th centuries the most interesting is the Vasa Gate. Since 1921 it has been crowned with a monument to the 18th-century national hero Tadeusz Kościuszko. The Wawel continued to play a defensive role into the 19th century, and a relatively well-preserved system of fortifications dating from the late 18th to mid-19th centuries can still be seen today.

Sandomierska Tower, one of three towers on the Wawel

㉔ Cathedral Museum

Wawel 3. **Tel** 12 429 33 21. 🚊 6, 8, 10, 13, 18. **Open** 9am–5pm Mon–Sat (Oct–Mar: to 4pm). **Closed** 1 Jan, Easter, Corpus Christi, 15 Aug, Christmas. 🗓

This museum is located in buildings near the cathedral and contains a valuable collection of pieces from the cathedral treasury. Here visitors can admire liturgical vessels and vestments; one of the finest is the chasuble of Bishop Piotr Kmita, which dates from 1504 and is ornamented with quilted

Embroidered hood of Bishop Trzebicki's cope, Cathedral Museum

embroidery depicting scenes from the life of St Stanisław (*see pp44–5*). The museum also contains replicas of funeral regalia, royal swords and trophies from battles won.

㉕ "Lost Wawel" Exhibition

Wawel 5. **Tel** 12 422 51 55. 🚊 6, 8, 10, 13, 18. **Open** Apr–Oct: 9:30am–1pm Mon, 9:30am–5pm Tue–Fri, 10am–5pm Sat & Sun; Nov–Mar: 9:30am–4pm Tue–Sat, 10am–4pm Sun. 🗓 (free on Sun Nov–Mar). 🌐 wawel.krakow.pl

For anyone interested in medieval archaeology, this exhibition is a real delight. The display charts the development of the Wawel over a considerable period of time, and includes a virtual image of the Wawel buildings as they existed in the early Middle Ages, archaeological finds from Wawel hill, and a partially reconstructed pre-Romanesque chapel dedicated to the Blessed Virgin (Saints Felix and Adauctus).

Built at the turn of the 11th century, the chapel was discovered during research work carried out in 1917.

Chapel of the Blessed Virgin, part of the "Lost Wawel" exhibition

㉖ The Wawel Royal Castle

One of the most magnificent Renaissance residences in Central Europe, the Wawel Royal Castle was built for Zygmunt I, the penultimate ruler of the Jagiellonian dynasty. The four-winged palace, built in 1502–36 but incorporating the walls of a 14th-century building that stood on the site, was designed and constructed by the Italian architects Francisco Fiorentino and Bartolomeo Berrecci. After the royal court was transferred from Krakow to Warsaw, the palace fell into neglect, and during the era of the Partitions it served as a barracks. At the beginning of the 20th century the castle was given to the city of Krakow, which started a restoration programme and turned it into a museum.

Senators' Hall

Royal Treasury and Armoury
The Royal Armoury has a rich collection of arms and armour. The Royal Treasury has many precious objects, including this chalice from the abbey at Tyniec.

Senators' Staircase

1st floor

Castle Guide

The area open to visitors consists of part of the ground floor of the Royal Castle, where items from the Royal Treasury and Royal Armoury are displayed, as well as the halls on the first and second floors of the east and north wings. The castle's Oriental collection fills the first floor of the west wing.

The Castle Courtyard
A mix of architectural styles can be found at the castle. One of the highlights is the beautiful Renaissance-style courtyard, which was built in the 16th century.

Key

- ☐ Royal Apartments
- ☐ Royal Treasury
- ☐ Royal Armoury
- ☐ Oriental Collection
- ☐ Non-exhibition space

Entrance to courtyard

Entrance to Royal Treasury and Royal Armoury

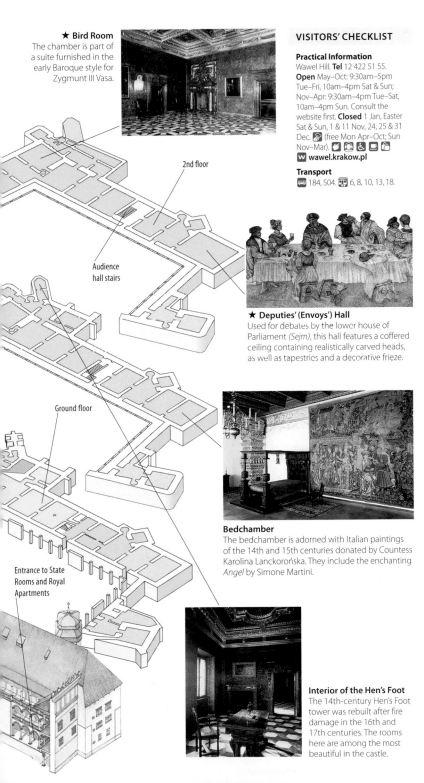

★ Bird Room
The chamber is part of a suite furnished in the early Baroque style for Zygmunt III Vasa.

2nd floor

Audience hall stairs

Ground floor

Entrance to State Rooms and Royal Apartments

★ Deputies' (Envoys') Hall
Used for debates by the lower house of Parliament (Sejm), this hall features a coffered ceiling containing realistically carved heads, as well as tapestries and a decorative frieze.

Bedchamber
The bedchamber is adorned with Italian paintings of the 14th and 15th centuries donated by Countess Karolina Lanckorońska. They include the enchanting *Angel* by Simone Martini.

Interior of the Hen's Foot
The 14th-century Hen's Foot tower was rebuilt after fire damage in the 16th and 17th centuries. The rooms here are among the most beautiful in the castle.

㉗ The Cathedral

The Cathedral of Saints Stanisław and Wacław, which stands on the Wawel in Krakow, is one of the most important churches in Poland. Before the present cathedral was erected (1320–64), two earlier churches stood on the site. The cathedral has many fine features, including a series of chapels founded by rulers and bishops, the most beautiful being the Renaissance Zygmunt Chapel. There are royal tombs in both the cathedral and the Crypt of St Leonard, a remnant of the Romanesque Cathedral of St Wacław begun in 1038.

Zygmunt Bell
This is the largest bell in Poland. It was made in 1520, weighs almost 11 tonnes and has a diameter of over 2 m (6 ft).

Main entrance

★ Tomb of Kazimierz the Jagiellonian
This royal tomb in the Chapel of the Holy Cross, completed in 1492, is one of the last commissions that the German sculptor Veit Stoss fulfilled in Poland.

Shrine of St Stanisław
The silver coffin containing the relics of St Stanisław, the bishop of Krakow to whom the cathedral is dedicated, was made in 1669–71 by Pieter van der Rennen, a goldsmith from Gdańsk.

KEY

① **The top** of the clock tower is decorated with statues of saints.

② **High altar**

Stalls

The early Baroque oak stalls in the chancel were made around 1620.

★ Zygmunt Chapel

The chapel containing the tombs of the two last Jagiellonian kings is the jewel of Italian Renaissance art in Poland. The tomb of Zygmunt the Old was made after 1530 by Bartolomeo Berrecci. That of Zygmunt August was made in 1574–5 by Santi Gucci.

Royal tombs

These Baroque sarcophagi were made for members of the royal Vasa dynasty. The cathedral is the final resting place of most of the Polish kings, as well as national heroes and revered poets.

Crypt of the Pauline Church on the Rock, a pantheon to Polish creativity

㉘ Pauline Church on the Rock

ul. Skałeczna 15. **Tel** 619 09 00.
504. 6, 8, 10, 13. **Open** 9am–
5pm Mon–Sat. Crypt of Honour
Open Apr–Oct: 9am–5pm daily;
Nov–Mar: by appt.

The impressive Baroque Pauline Church on the Rock (Kościół Paulinów na Skałce), with its adjoining monastery complex, was built in 1733–42 by Gerhard Müntzer in collaboration with Antoni Solari. The present church was preceded by two earlier buildings. St Stanisław, Bishop of Krakow, was murdered at the foot of the altar of the Romanesque church, the first to be built on the site (see pp44–5).

The interior includes Baroque stuccowork by Jan Lehnert. The crypt was converted by Teofil Żebrawski into a pantheon to Polish writers and artists, including the painters Jacek Malczewski (1854–1929) and Henryk Siemiradzki (1843–1902), the writers and poets Józef Ignacy Kraszewski (1812–77), Adam Asnyk (1839–97) and Wincenty Pol (1807–72), and the artist and writer Stanisław Wyspiański (1869–1907).

Return along Ulica Skałeczna towards Ulica Augustiańska and take a look at the beautiful Gothic Convent and Church of St Catherine (Kościół św. Katarzyny), begun in the mid-14th century. It once belonged to the Augustinian order, but was deconsecrated and used as a warehouse. Of the original features only the high altar remains. The 15th-century Hungarian Chapel (Kaplica Węgierska) next door is connected by a covered bridge over Ulica Skałeczna to the Baroque Augustinian convent.

㉙ Church of Corpus Christi

ul. Bożego Ciała 26. **Tel** 12 430 59 95. 🚃 504. 🚋 6, 8, 10, 13. **Open** 9am–6pm daily.

The mighty Gothic Church of Corpus Christi was built as the parish church of the town of Kazimierz, which was founded to the south of the castle by Kazimierz the Great in the 14th century. Work on the church began around 1340, continuing into the early 15th century. The basilica-like interior contains some fine works of art in the Baroque style, including the magnificent high altar of 1634–7, with its painting of *The Birth of Christ* by Tomasso Dolabella; a fine mid-18th-century pulpit; and stalls dating from 1632, originally built for the monks (although the church has been in the care of canons since the 15th century). The monastery is on the north side of the church.

㉚ Old Synagogue

ul. Szeroka 24. 🚃 184, 504. 🚋 3, 19, 24, 69. Museum of Jewish History: **Tel** 12 431 05 45. **Open** Apr–Oct: 10am–2pm Mon, 9am–5pm Tue–Sun; Nov–Mar: 10am–2pm Mon, 9am–4pm Tue–Thu, Sat & Sun, 10am–5pm Fri. 🚶 (free on Mon). 🌐 mhk.pl

Built by Matteo Gucci in the mid-16th century in the Renaissance style, the Old Synagogue replaced an earlier Gothic

Gothic-Renaissance bema in the Old Synagogue

synagogue that burned down in 1557. In the Hall of Prayer you will find a reconstructed bema (raised orator's platform) and Torah Ark.

The synagogue houses a branch of the Historical Museum. The displays within consist of some artifacts used in Jewish rituals, and documents relating to the history of Krakovian Jews and their extermination during the Nazi occupation in World War II.

Tomb in Remuh Cemetery from the first half of the 17th century

㉛ Remuh Cemetery and Synagogue

ul. Szeroka 40. **Tel** 12 429 57 35. 🚃 184, 504. 🚋 3, 19, 24. **Open** 9am–6pm Sun–Fri (Oct–Apr: to 4pm). 🚷

The humble prayer house known as the Remuh is one of two synagogues in Krakow that are still in use. It was built around 1557 by Izrael ben Józef for his son Mojżesz Isserles, a famous scholar, rabbi and reputed miracle worker, known as Remuh. Inside, the Renaissance Torah Ark and the bema, rebuilt as a replica of the original, have survived.

Behind the synagogue is one of the most important Jewish cemeteries in Europe. Despite the damage that the cemetery suffered during World War II, many of the tombstones have survived. Fragments of shattered tombstones have been built into the cemetery wall abutting Ulica Szeroka.

This part of town was immortalized in Steven Spielberg's film *Schindler's List*. The district now has shops and

kosher restaurants; the family home of Helena Rubinstein, founder of the cosmetics business, is also here.

㉜ Premonstratensian Church

ul. Kościuszki 88. **Tel** 12 427 13 18. 🚃, 100, 109, 209, 229, 239, 249, 259, 269, 504. 🚋 1, 2, 6.

This church (Kościół Norbertanek) and convent on the banks of the Vistula at Zwierzyniec was founded in 1162. The present appearance of the small nave church is due to rebuilding in 1595–1604. The extensive convent also dates from the early 17th century.

The Chapel of St Margaret (Kaplica św. Małgorzaty), an octagonal building in the early Baroque style, is on nearby Ulica św. Bronisława. Behind the chapel is the Church of Our Saviour (Kościół Najświętszego Salwatora). Built in the second half of the 12th century, it was remodelled at the beginning of the 17th, when it was reduced to a small nave church with a tower at the west end.

㉝ Pharmacy under the Eagle

Pl. Bohaterów Getta 18. **Tel** 12 656 56 25. 🚋 3, 19, 24. **Open** 10am–2pm Mon, 9am–5pm Tue–Sun. 🚶 (free on Mon). 📷 🌐 mhk.pl

Located on the southern side of the Vistula river, the suburb of Podgórze was chosen to be a ghetto by the Nazis in 1941, and the city's Jewish population was relocated here as a result.

Declining to be moved from the area, Dr Tadeusz Pankiewicz, a Gentile, continued to run his pharmacy as the only one left operating in the ghetto. As well as providing medication, often for free, The Pharmacy under the Eagle (Apteka pod Orłem) became a communication hub for the Jewish population.

Now a museum, Pharmacy under the Eagle contains recreations of the interior at the time, and poignant mementos of the ghetto's inhabitants.

❸❹ Camaldolite Monastery in Bielany

ul. Konarowa 1–16. **Tel** 12 429 76 10. 🚌 109, 209, 229, 239, 269. **Open** to men: during services; to women: 2 and 7 Feb, 25 Mar, Easter, Whitsun, 19 Jun, the first Sun after 15 Aug, 8 Sep, 25 Dec.

Seen from afar, this monolithic Mannerist-Baroque monastery set on Srebrna Góra (Silver Mountain) appears to be a tempting tourist attraction. However, the monks, who are the monastery's sole inhabitants, are committed to absolute silence and no contact with the outside world. Visits are therefore severely restricted, especially for women.

The monastery was founded in the early 17th century by Valentin von Säbisch and completed by Andrea Spezza. It is richly adorned with Baroque features, and from the windows of the chapel it is possible to glimpse the monks' dwellings, to which visitors are not admitted.

❸❺ Benedictine Abbey in Tyniec

ul. Benedyktyńska 37. **Tel** 12 688 54 50. 🚌 112. **Open** 10am–6pm daily (Nov–Apr: to 4pm). 🌐 **tyniec. benedyktyni.pl**

This impressive abbey is set on a high chalky outcrop overlooking the River Vistula. The history of the abbey goes back to the mid-11th century. Originally, a Romanesque basilica stood on the site. It was replaced in the 15th century by a Gothic church. The present Baroque abbey was built in 1618–22.

Although in the course of its stormy history the church has lost many fine and valuable features, it still retains its monumental Baroque altars. Some elements of the original Romanesque building have survived in the underground parts of the abbey adjacent to the church.

Benedictine abbey in Tyniec, on a chalky outcrop above the Vistula

❸❻ Schindler's Factory and MOCAK

ul. Lipowa 4. 🚋 3, 19, 24. **Tel** 12 257 00 95. **Open** Apr–Oct: 10am–8pm daily (to 4pm Mon, to 2pm first Mon of month); Nov–Mar: 10am– 6pm daily (to 2pm Mon). 🌐 (free Mon). 💻 🎫 MOCAK: **Open** 11am–7pm Tue–Sun. 🌐 (free Tue). 💻 📷 🌐 **mocak.pl** Schindler's Factory: 🌐 **mhk.pl**

Located in the former industrial district of Zabłocie, next to Podgorze, Schindler's Factory is a symbol of humanitarian courage. In 1943, the factory's German owner, Oskar Schindler, saved over 1000 Jews from deportation to the death camps by employing them in his factory and claiming that they were essential to the running of his business. The story was immortalized in Thomas Keneally's novel *Schindler's Ark*, filmed by Steven Spielberg as *Schindler's List* in 1993.

The factory, now part of the Historical Museum of Krakow *(see p137)*, features an interactive exhibition on the occupation of 1939–45. As well as telling the harrowing story of the city's Jews, it deals with the sufferings of Krakow's Gentile population, many of whom were subjected to forced labour, torture and

Interiors of the popular Schindler's Factory, now a museum

murder. Poignant exhibits include Oskar Schindler's desk, a montage of the metal pots the factory produced, and a wall of photographs of those he saved.

A section of the building now houses MOCAK (Museum of Contemporary Art in Krakow), which displays works by major international artists, as well as hosting temporary exhibitions.

❸❼ Cistercian Abbey in Mogiła

ul. Klasztorna 11. **Tel** 12 644 23 31. 🚋 123, 153, 163. 🚌 15. **Open** 6am–7pm.

Behind the fine Baroque façade of the church, designed and erected by Franciszek Moser in 1779–80, lies a much older interior. Founded by Bishop Iwo Odrowąż, the Cistercian abbey was built in the 13th century; the church was consecrated in 1266. The interior of the early Gothic basilica, which contains a number of Renaissance paintings by Stanisław Samostrzelnik, has survived alongside later, mainly Baroque, features.

Other interesting parts of the abbey are the Gothic cloisters and the chapterhouse, which has paintings by the 19th-century artist Michał Stachowicz. These depict the legend of Wanda, whose patriotism led her to throw herself into the Vistula. Her tomb, situated under a tumulus, is located nearby.

❸❽ Polish Aviation Museum

al. Jana Pawła II 39. 🚋 4, 5, 9, 10, 52. **Tel** 12 640 99 60. **Open** 9am–5pm Tue–Sun. 🌐 (free Tue). 🎫 🌐 **muzeumlotnictwa.pl**

Located on the Rakowice-Czyżyny airfield, one of Europe's oldest military airfields (est. 1912), this museum has more than 200 aircraft, including pre-war Polish fighter planes, Spitfires, German Albatrosses and Soviet Kakaruzniks. There are also 22 aeroplanes that were once part of Hermann Göring's personal collection.

MAŁOPOLSKA (LESSER POLAND)

Małopolska is the country's most picturesque and varied region. Attractions such as the ski resort of Zakopane, hiking trails in the Tatra Mountains, the miraculous Black Madonna of Częstochowa and a lively folk tradition make it Poland's most popular tourist destination. Krakow, not only the region's principal city but the spiritual and historic capital of the Kingdom of Poland, is one of the friendliest cities in the world.

In the 9th century, the Vistulanian tribe established a state in Małopolska. Their capital was Krakow, or Wiślica. In 990, Małopolska became part of the Polanian duchy of Mieszko I, and in 1039, Prince Kazimierz the Restorer made Krakow the centre of his realm of power. For centuries, Małopolska was the heart of Poland. However, its importance began to wane at the end of the 16th century, when the capital of the Republic was moved to Warsaw.

After the Partitions of Poland, Małopolska went into a gradual decline. While Galicia, its southern part, came under Austrian rule, its northern part was incorporated into the Russian Empire. When Galicia gained autonomy within the Austro-Hungarian Empire, Galician towns, and especially Krakow, became important centres of Polish culture, retaining their identity despite a succession of annexations. Not until 1918, when Poland at last regained its independence, did Małopolska again become part of the Polish state.

The Małopolska region is dotted with picturesque towns, ruined castles, palaces, country mansions, great monasteries and pretty wooden churches. The eastern fringes of the region are distinguished by their Uniate Orthodox churches. There are also many monuments to the Jewish population that was present in Małopolska before 1945.

In many parts of the region, folk customs survive and flourish, nowhere more than in the Podhale region. In Zakopane, the regional capital of Podhale, folklore and folk art are a local industry.

Old Gothic Church of St Archangel Michael, a UNESCO World Heritage in Dębno near Brzeska

◄ The verdant landscape around Trzy Korony Peak, in the Pieniny Mountains

Exploring Małopolska

Małopolska, in the south of Poland, is the country's main tourist region. Apart from Krakow, the greatest attractions for visitors are the mountain ski resort of Zakopane, which is the winter sports capital, and the picturesque Tatra Mountains. In summer, many hikers are drawn to the region, and its mountains are traversed by well-marked hiking trails. There are numerous welcoming hostels and excellent mountain lodges for those in need of overnight shelter. Parts of the Beskid Niski Mountains are almost without human habitation, so that it is still possible to walk for several hours without encountering a single living soul. Spiritual relief can be found deep within the forests, where walkers may be surprised to encounter pretty wooden churches.

Interior of a cottage in Zalipie, with traditional decoration

Getting Around

Krakow and Rzeszów can be reached by air. The larger towns all have good rail links with the rest of the country. Some small villages can only be reached by bus or car. The E77 highway goes north and south from Krakow, while the autostrada A4 runs from the German border to the Ukrainian border. This motorway is a part of E40 that goes through Tarnów, Rzeszów and Przemyśl. Parallel to it, but further south, major road 28 connects Nowy Sącz with Biecz, Krosno and Sanok.

Key

════ Motorway

──── Main road

───── Minor road

────── Main railway

────── Minor railway

▬▬▬ International border

═══ Regional border

△ Peak

The magnificent and beautiful Łańcut Castle, Podkarpackie

For hotels and restaurants see p303 and pp313–14

Sights at a Glance

1. Oblęgorek
2. Kielce
3. Holy Cross Mountains
4. Wąchock
5. Opatów
6. Ujazd
7. Sandomierz
8. Baranów Sandomierski
9. *Częstochowa pp160–1*
11. Auschwitz-Birkenau Memorial and Museum *pp164–7*
12. Bielsko-Biała
13. Żywiec

14. Wadowice
15. Kalwaria Zebrzydowska
16. Wieliczka
17. Niepołomice
18. Zalipie
19. Tarnów
20. Dębno near Brzeska
21. Nowy Wiśnicz
22. Chochołów
23. Zakopane
24. Dębno Podhalańskie
26. Stary Sącz
27. Krynica
28. Biecz
29. Krosno

31. Krasiczyn Castle
32. Przemyśl
33. Jarosław
34. Leżajsk
35. *Łańcut pp178–9*
36. Rzeszów

Tours

10. Eagles' Nests Trail *pp162–3*
25. Dunajec Raft Ride
30. Bieszczady Mountains Tour

Niedzica Castle overlooking the artificial lake on the Dunajec

For keys to symbols *see back flap*

The Henryk Sienkiewicz Museum in Oblęgorek

❶ Oblęgorek

Road map E5. 950.

The writer Henryk Sienkiewicz (*see p31*) received a small manor house in the village of Oblęgorek as a gift from the nation in 1900. It is an eclectic building with a tall circular tower. The interior remains as it was when Sienkiewicz lived and worked here. Today it houses the **Henryk Sienkiewicz Museum**.

Sienkiewicz is the best-known Polish novelist. He received the Nobel Prize for Literature for his historical novel *Quo Vadis?* in 1905.

Henryk Sienkiewicz Museum
Tel 41 303 04 26. **Open** Apr–Oct: 9am–5pm Tue–Sun; Nov–Mar: 8am–4pm Tue–Sun. mnki.pl

❷ Kielce

Road map E5. 197,700.
ul. Sienkiewicza 29. **Tel** 41 348 00 60. um.kielce.pl

In a city whose beauty has been defaced by buildings that went up after World War II, the **Bishops' Palace** stands out like a jewel. It is an exceptionally fine example of a well-preserved aristocratic town house of the first half of the 17th century (*see p51*). The early Baroque façades with four corner towers have been preserved almost intact, as has the decoration of the rooms on the first floor. The marble doorways and beamed ceilings are original.

The palace was built in 1637–41, probably by the royal architect Giovanni Trevano, under the direction of Tomasso Poncino, for the Bishop of Krakow, Jakub Zadzik. During the reign of Zygmunt III, this exceptional clergyman was in charge of the Republic's foreign policy, successfully making peace with Russia and establishing a long-standing ceasefire with Sweden. His role as a bishop, however, was inglorious. He contributed to the shameful decision to condemn the Polish Brethren during the Sejm of 1641. These events are illustrated on the palace ceilings, which were painted in 1641.

The period interiors form part of the **National Museum** in the palace. There is also an excellent gallery of Polish painting here.

Next to the palace is the **cathedral**, built on the site of an earlier church of 1632–5, the time of Bishop Zadzik.

Several dozen wooden village buildings from the area around Kielce are laid out over an area of 4.2 sq km (1.6 sq miles) in the **Kielce Rural Museum**.

Kielce Rural Museum
ul. Jana Pawła II 6. **Tel** 41 344 92 97. **Open** 9am–5pm Tue–Sun. (free on Sat). mwk.com.pl *Skansen*: in Tokarnia: **Tel** 41 315 41 71. **Open** Apr, Sep & Oct: 9am–3pm Mon, 9am–5pm Tue–Fri, 10am–6pm Sat & Sun; May & Jun: 9am–5pm Mon–Fri, 8am–6pm Sat, 10am–6pm Sun; Jul & Aug: 9am–5pm Mon, 10am– 6pm Tue–Sun; Nov–Mar: 9am– 3pm daily.

National Museum
pl. Zamkowy 1. **Tel** 41 344 40 15. **Open** May–Aug: 10am–6pm Tue–Sun; Sep–Apr: 9am–5pm Tue–Sun. (free on Sun). mnki.pl

Environs

The ruins of a 13th-century castle dominate the town of **Chęciny**, 15 km (9 miles) to the west of Kielce. **Paradise Cave** (Jaskinia Raj), to the north of Chęciny, contains spectacular stalactites and stalagmites.

The dining hall in the Bishops' Palace in Kielce

❸ Holy Cross Mountains

Road map E5. 🚉 🚌 ℹ️ 41 367 64 36 or 367 60 11.

In geological terms, the Holy Cross Mountains (Góry Świętokrzyskie) – part of the Małopolska uplands – are among the oldest in Europe. Eroded over many thousands of years, they are neither high nor steep, but they are exceptionally rich in minerals, which have been exploited since ancient times. The remains of prehistoric mines and furnaces have been found here. The Łysogóry range, with Mount Łysica at a mere 612 m (2,000 ft), the highest peak in the mountains, lies within the

Broken rock on the Łysogóry slopes, Świętokrzyski National Park

Świętokrzyski National Park. The primeval forest of fir trees that once covered the range was seriously damaged by acid rain in the 1970s and 1980s, so that only vestiges remain today. In ancient times Łysa Góra, the second-highest peak in the Holy Cross Mountains, was a pagan place of worship. Its slopes are covered with *gołoborza*, heaps of broken rock. Legend tells of the witches' sabbaths that are said to have taken place here.

The **Benedictine abbey in Święty Krzyż** on the summit of Łysa Góra was built in the 12th century and extended during the rule of the Jagiellonian dynasty. The building, which replaces an earlier Romanesque church, was built in 1782–9 and has predominantly Baroque and Neo-Classical features. The interior is decorated with paintings by the 18th-century artist Franciszek Smuglewicz. The cloisters and vestry, with late Baroque frescoes, date from the 15th century. The domed chapel of the Oleśnicki family, dating from the 17th century, is the abbey's most outstanding feature. The relic of the Holy Cross, kept in the chapel since 1723, attracts crowds of pilgrims. In the crypt beneath the chapel

Ruins of the Baroque Bishops' Palace at Bodzentyn

is a glass coffin containing the supposedly mummified body of Prince Jeremi Wiśniowiecki. In his novel *With Fire and Sword* Henryk Sienkiewicz portrayed this magnate as a saviour, and hero of the battles against Ukrainian insurgents in 1648. History judges him less kindly: a seasoned soldier, an unimaginative politician and a brute, who by passing sentences of impalement earned himself the nickname Pałej (The Impaler).

Bodzentyn, north of Łysogóry, is worth a visit for its 18th-century Gothic parish church. The Renaissance altar comes from Wawel Cathedral in Krakow. The stately ruins of the Bishops' Palace can also be seen in the town.

Świętokrzyski National Park

The Łysogóry range constitutes the major part of the park. Natural features of particular interest include *gołoborza*, created by the fragmentation of quartzite sandstone, and vestiges of the primeval fir forest. Native Polish larch can be seen on Chełmowa Góra.

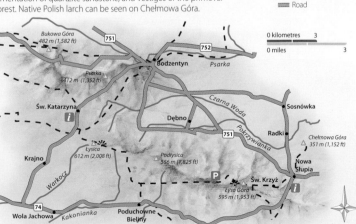

Key

-- Hiking trail

▬ Road

0 kilometres 3

0 miles 3

Bukowa Góra 482 m (1,582 ft)
751
752
Bodzentyn
Psarka
Psarka 412 m (1,352 ft)
Czarna Woda
Św. Katarzyna ℹ️
Sosnówka
Dębno
751
Radki
Pokrzywianka
Chełmowa Góra 351 m (1,152 ft)
Krajno
Łysica 612 m (2,008 ft)
Podłysica 556 m (1,825 ft)
Nowa Słupia
Warkocz
🅿️
Św. Krzyż ℹ️
Łysa Góra 595 m (1,953 ft)
74
Wola Jachowa
Kakonianka
Poduchowne Bieliny

❹ Wąchock

Road map E4. 👤 2,800. 🚃 🚌
Cistercian Abbey: ul. Koscielna 14.
Tel 41 275 02 00. **Open** daily.

Wąchock is a neat town with a well-preserved **Cistercian abbey**. It was founded in 1179 by Gedko z Gryfitów, Bishop of Krakow. The church, built in the early 13th century, has Romanesque and Gothic features. Although the architect is unknown, the inscription "Simon" that can be seen on the façade is thought to be his signature. The interior is decorated with mural paintings. The most important Romanesque interiors of the abbey – those of the chapter house and the rooms off the cloisters – have been preserved almost intact. After the abbey burnt down in a fire, it was fully-restored from 1636 to 1643, only to be damaged again in the Swedish Flood of 1656. It underwent a second restoration in 1659 and has been open ever since.

❺ Opatów

Road map E5. 👤 6,600. 🚌

The collegiate church of St Martin (Kolegiata św. Marcina), built in the first half of the 12th century, is among the best-preserved Romanesque churches in Poland. The façade has two quadrilateral towers and representations of dragons and plants on its borders. The interior contains interesting tombs, the most eminent being the one with the bronze effigy of Krzysztof Szydłowiecki, the royal chancellor who became the owner of Opatów. The tomb

Collegiate Church of St Martin in Opatów

dates from 1533–6 and bears a relief known as the Opatów Lament (see pp48–9). The marble tombstone of Anna Szydłowiecka carved by Bernardino de Gianotis in 1536 is also noteworthy.

The curious holes and ruts in the walls of the church are an unusual mark of the past. Noblemen would use the church walls to sharpen their sabres, which they would often do on horseback. This explains why the holes are so high.

❻ Ujazd

Road map E5. 👤 500. 🚌
Krzyżtopór Castle: **Tel** 15 860
11 33. 🌐 **krzyztopor.org.pl**

The main attraction in Ujazd are the ruins of **Krzyżtopór Castle**, built for the Palatine Krzysztof Ossoliński, probably by Agostino Locci the Elder in 1621–44. It is one of the most eccentric residences of its time in Europe (see pp50–51). Having been attacked during the Swedish Deluge (see p50), the castle fell into neglect. The palace was enormous, and for 300 years its walls provided the surrounding villages with vast amounts of building material. However, the magnificent ruins are still extremely impressive.

Environs
Ossolin, situated 15 km (9 miles) to the east of Ujazd, is the town from which the Ossoliński family came. The historic remains here are much more modest. It survived an explosion in 1816, inflicted by subsequent owners who sought to blow it up in search of the treasure rumoured to be hidden there.

The stately ruins of Krzyżtopór Castle in Ujazd

The Mannerist and Baroque collegiate church in **Klimontów**, 13 km (8 miles) east of Ujazd, and begun in 1643, is something of an architectural curiosity. The elliptical nave with galleries is an unusual combination, and the columns sunk into niches hollowed out in the pillars make a mockery of the principles of tectonics.

❼ Sandomierz

Road map F5. 🚇 24,100. 🚉 🚌
ℹ️ PTTK, Rynek 12 (15 832 26 82). Underground Tourist Route: ul. Oleśnickich 1. **Tel** 15 832 30 88. **Open** 10am–5pm Mon–Fri, 10am–7pm Sat & Sun (Oct–Apr: to 5pm). ⓦ sandomierz.pl

The best view of this small, ancient town is from the River Vistula. In 1138, Sandomierz became the capital of an independent duchy, and from the 14th century until the Partitions of Poland it was a regional capital. The **Underground Tourist Route**, a network of underground passages that runs beneath the town, dates from the 15th to 17th centuries.

The main entrance to the old town is the gothic **Opatów Gate**. The charming, slightly sloping **Market Square** is surrounded by elegant houses. In the centre stands the 14th-century town hall, with its splendid Renaissance parapet. It houses the **Regional Museum**. The most important building in the town is the **cathedral**, built around 1360 on the site of an earlier Romanesque cathedral and later altered. The 15th-century Ruthenian-Byzantine frescoes in the chancel depict scenes from the lives of Christ and the Virgin, and there are also some beautiful carvings.

The **Church of St James** (Kościół św. Jakuba), built in brick, is an exceptionally fine late Romanesque aisled basilica that was begun in 1226. Its ceramic decoration and beautiful portal are evidence that it was built by master craftsmen from Lombardy. The remains of 49 Dominican friars murdered by Tatars in 1260 lie in the Martyrs' Chapel.

Gothic Opatów Gate, defending the old town of Sandomierz

🏛 Diocesan Museum

ul. Długosza 9. **Tel** 15 833 26 70. **Open** May–Sep: 9am–4:30pm Tue–Sat, 1:30–4:30pm Sun; Oct–Apr: 9am–3:30pm Tue–Sat, 1.30–3:30pm Sun. 🅿

The museum is in the Gothic house of Jan Długosz (1415–80), the celebrated chronicler of Poland. It features religious paintings and sculptures from the Middle Ages to the 19th century, including *Madonna with the Christ Child* and *St Catherine* by Lucas Cranach the Elder.

🏛 Regional Museum

Castle: **Tel** 15 644 57 57/58. **Open** 1–3pm Mon, 9am–4pm Tue–Fri, 10am–4pm Sat & Sun (May–Sep: 10am–5pm Tue–Fri, 10am–6pm Sat & Sun). 🅲 (free Mon). ⓦ zamek-sandomierz.pl

The Regional Museum comprises an underground tourist tour and the refurbished Gothic and Renaissance castle. The museum

contains archaeological, ethnographic and historical displays.

❽ Baranów Sandomierski

Road map E5. 🚇 1,500. 🚉 3 km (2 miles) from the centre. 🚌
ⓦ baranow.com.pl

Leszczyński Castle, built in Baranów Sandomierski for the Leszczyński family in 1591–1606, is one of the finest examples of Mannerist architecture in Poland. The castle consists of four wings arranged around a rectangular arcaded courtyard. The grand exterior staircase and the façades, with their elaborate attics giving the impression of a massive (but in fact delicate) curtained wall, are striking. The square tower in the central façade serves a purely decorative purpose. On account of its architectural ornamentation, featuring spheres, rosettes and strange creatures, the castle is thought to have been designed by Santi Gucci. The **Sulphur Basin Museum** on the ground floor contains furniture, suits of armour and other objects from the castle's heyday, as well as exhibits relating to the history of sulphur exploitation in the huge quarries nearby.

🏛 Sulphur Basin Museum

ul. Zamkowa 20. **Tel** 15 811 80 39. **Open** Apr–Sep: 9am–6pm daily; Oct: 9am–5pm daily; Nov–Mar: 9am–4pm Tue–Sun. 🅿 🅲 (compulsory, every hour). 🅿 📷 🖥

Staircase in the courtyard of Leszczyński Castle in Baranów Sandomierski

❾ Częstochowa

The monastery of Jasna Góra in Częstochowa is the most famous shrine of the Virgin in Poland and the country's greatest place of pilgrimage – for many, its spiritual capital. The image of the Black Madonna of Częstochowa, to which miraculous powers are attributed, is Jasna Góra's most precious treasure. Founded in 1382 by Pauline monks who came from Hungary at the invitation of Władysław, Duke of Opole (who probably brought the image of the Black Madonna to Częstochowa), the monastery withstood several sieges, including the legendary 40-day siege by the Swedes in 1655 *(see p50)*.

Knights' Hall
The hall contains a series of late 17th-century paintings depicting major events in the monastery's history.

Refectory
The ceiling is decorated with rich frescoes by the 17th-century painter Karl Dankwart. In 1670, a wedding reception was held here for the Polish king Michał Korybut Wiśniowiecki and his bride, Eleanor.

Stations of the Cross
The 14 Stations of the Cross standing on artificial rocks in the moat were created by the architect Stefan Szyller and the sculptor Pius Weloński in 1900–13. Every day, groups of pilgrims attend a religious service here.

KEY

① **Arsenal**

② **The 600th Anniversary Museum** has an impressive display of artifacts made by concentration camp inmates.

③ **Bastion of St Roch (belonging to Morsztynowie)**

④ **The outdoor altar** is where services are held for the pilgrims.

⑤ **Confessional**

★ Black Madonna

The most important icon of the Catholic faith in Poland, depicting the Virgin with the Christ Child, was probably painted in 1434 on top of an older Byzantine icon – the original Black Madonna, which was damaged by robbers in 1430.

VISITORS' CHECKLIST

Practical Information
Road map D5. 231,000. **i** al. Najświętszej Marii Panny 65 (34 368 22 50); Jasna Góra, Pauline Monastery: ul. Kordeckiego 2 (34 377 77 77). Jasna Góra: **Open** 5am–9:30pm. Black Madonna of Częstochowa: (unveiling times) 6am–noon daily (to 1pm Sat & Sun), 3–9:30pm (May–Sep: from 2pm). Times may vary. Treasury, Arsenal, 600th Anniversary Museum: **Open** 9am–4pm daily (May–Oct: to 5pm). "Gaude Mater" International Festival of Religious Music (early May).
w czestochowa.pl
w jasnagora.pl

Transport

Treasury

Gold and silver vessels, church vestments, tapestries and votive offerings are among the items on display.

Chapel of the Last Supper

This chapel was designed by Adolf Szyszko-Bohusz in the 20th century.

★ Basilica of the Holy Cross and the Nativity of the Virgin Mary

The present basilica dates from 1692–1728. The Baroque decoration of the high altar and of the ceiling, the latter by Karl Dankwart, is rich in detail.

Monastery Gates

The Lubomirski Gate, the Stanisław August Gate, the Gate of the Sorrowful Virgin Mary and the Bank (or Jagiellonian) Gate all lead to the monastery hill.

⑩ Eagles' Nests Trail

The Krakow-Częstochowa upland is a limestone mountain range formed in the Jurassic period. Perched on rocky outcrops, some of the castles, most of which were built in the Middle Ages and ruined during the Swedish Deluge of the 1650s *(see p50)*, resemble eagles' nests. Ojców National Park, with Pieskowa Skała Castle, encompasses some of the most beautiful upland areas. This castle was once the stronghold of kings, but at the end of the Middle Ages it passed into the hands of bandits – Piotr Szafraniec and his son Krzysztof – who lured rich merchants to their deaths. Today, all is peaceful and the area offers tourist trails, rock climbing and beautiful scenery.

① Olsztyn
Every autumn, thousands of spectators gather to watch as a magnificent firework display and laser show illuminate the stately ruins of the castle.

② Mirów
This 14th century gothic castle once belonged to the Myszkowski family. It is perched on a rocky ridge, turning the natural lie of the land to defensive advantage.

0 kilometres   5

0 miles   5

Tips for Drivers

Length of trail: 190 km (118 miles).
Stopping-off points: Many bars and restaurants are to be found along the trail. There is a café and restaurant in Pieskowa Skała Castle.

③ Bobolice
Today, jousting tournaments and outdoor games take place in the surroundings of the splendid ruins of the castle built by Kazimierz the Great in the 14th century.

Map labels: Częstochowa, Janów, Potok Złoty, Czestochowa, 46, 793, 78, Warta, Czarna Przemsza, Dąbrowa Górnicza, Błedows Desert, ①, ②

④ Ogrodzieniec
In the 16th century, the castle belonged to the Boner family of Krakow. With its gate, towers and galleries, it is one of the most picturesque castles on the trail.

⑤ Błędowski Desert
This miniature desert is 320 sq km (123 sq miles) of drifting sand and dunes. Unique in Central Europe, it is slowly becoming choked with vegetation.

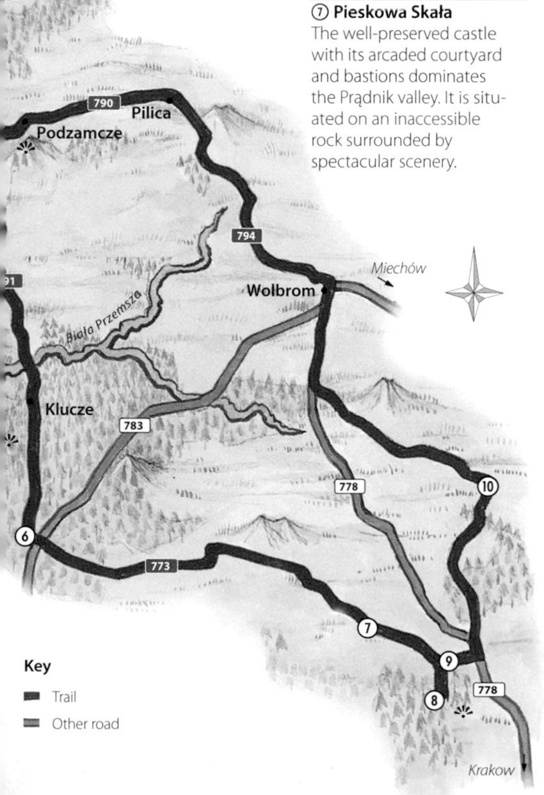

⑥ Olkusz
The town is well endowed with historic buildings. It owes its prosperity to silver and lead mining.

⑦ Pieskowa Skała
The well-preserved castle with its arcaded courtyard and bastions dominates the Prądnik valley. It is situated on an inaccessible rock surrounded by spectacular scenery.

⑧ Ojców National Park
The Prądnik valley has a karst landscape; there are outcrops of limestone, a multitude of gorges and caves with bats. The most famous rock is the pillar known as Hercules' Club.

⑨ Grodzisko
The obelisk with a stone elephant is an unusual monument. It was made in 1686 and stands next to the Church of the Assumption.

⑩ Imbramowice
This small village has a late Baroque Premonstratensian convent that was built in the 18th century.

Map labels: Pilica, Podzamcze, Wolbrom, Miechów, Klucze, Krakow

Key

▬ Trail
▬ Other road

⑪ Auschwitz-Birkenau Memorial and Museum

Over 1.1 million people died here between 1940 and 1945, 90 percent of whom were Jews. Auschwitz began as a camp for Polish political prisoners, and subsequently it became a camp for Soviet prisoners of war, many of whom died of malnourishment, overwork or torture. From 1942 onwards, Auschwitz-Birkenau camp was built to deal with the vast numbers of Jews brought to be murdered as part of the Nazi's Final Solution. Auschwitz is now a UNESCO World Heritage site.

Exhibitions
The daily horrors of life in the camp are today displayed in some of the barracks.

The Camp

Auschwitz I opened in 1940 on the site of former Polish army barracks. Originally built to incarcerate Polish political prisoners, further buildings were added in the spring of 1941 as the number of prisoners dramatically increased. Camp administration was also based at Auschwitz I.

| 0 metres | 100 |
| 0 yards | 100 |

Gas Chambers and Crematoria
The entire Auschwitz complex had seven gas chambers and five crematoria. Six of the gas chambers were in Birkenau but the first was at Auschwitz, operating from 1941.

The Two Camps

Though part of the same camp complex, Auschwitz and Birkenau are in fact 3 km (2 miles) apart, on the western

suburbs of the bustling town of Oświęcim (Auschwitz in German). Birkenau was opened in March 1942 in the village of Brzezinka, where the residents were evicted to make way for the camp. There were an additional 47 sub-camps in the surrounding area.

Aerial view of the complex taken by the Allies in 1944. The yellow dotted line marks Birkenau; the blue shows Auschwitz I.

KEY

① **SS Guard house and office of the camp supervisor**

② **"Arbeit Macht Frei" entrance**: the words above the infamous entrance to Auschwitz translate as "Work makes you free". This was certainly not the case for the prisoners transported here, who were often worked to death.

③ **Block 11** was the central jail that housed prisoners from all over the camp complex.

④ **Store containing the poison, Zyklon B**, first used at Auschwitz to kill prisoners.

⑤ **Camp kitchen**

⑥ **Present-day Information Centre for visitors**

The "Wall of Death"

This is a reconstruction of the wall near Block 11 used for the summary executions by shooting. Usually covered in flowers, it now serves as a place of remembrance.

VISITORS' CHECKLIST

Practical Information
Oświęcim. **Road map** D5. **Tel** 33 844 81 00. **Open** Feb: 7:30am–4pm; Mar & Oct: 7:30am–5pm; Apr, May & Sep: 7:30am–6pm; Jun, Jul & Aug: 7:30am–7pm; Nov & Jan: 7:30am–3pm; Dec: 7:30am–2pm. **Closed** 1 Jan, Easter Day, 25 Dec. ◪ Call to arrange, or check website for details.
W **auschwitz.org**

Transport
🚌 Bus to Auschwitz from Krakow Bus Station; bus to Birkenau from Information Centre.

Maksymilian Kolbe
The camp jail, in Block 11, was used for those who broke camp rules. Few emerged alive. Father Kolbe died here after sacrificing his life for another inmate's.

Roll Call Square
Roll call took place up to three times a day and could last for hours. Eventually, due to the increasing numbers of prisoners, roll call was taken in front of individual barracks.

1939	1940	1941	1942	1943	1944	1945
1939 1 Sep, Hitler invades Poland	**1940** First deportation of German Jews into Nazi-occupied Poland	**1941** First gas chamber goes into operation	**1942** The implementation of the Final Solution is agreed at the Wannsee Conference and mass deportation to Auschwitz begins		**1944** As the Soviet Army closes in, the SS begin destroying all evidence of the camp	**1945** 27 Jan, Soviet soldiers liberate the few remaining prisoners at Auschwitz
	1940 Oświęcim chosen as the site of the Nazis' new concentration camp	**1941** Himmler makes first visit to Auschwitz and orders its expansion	**1942** First section of Birkenau camp completed	**1943** Four gas chambers built for mass murder	**1945** 18 Jan, 56,000 prisoners evacuated on "Death March"	**1945** 7 May, Germany surrenders to the Allies

Auschwitz II–Birkenau

Birkenau was primarily a place of execution. Most of Auschwitz's machinery of murder was housed here. In the six gas chambers in use at different stages of the camp's construction, over one million people were killed, 98% of whom were Jewish. Victims included people from over 20 nations. Birkenau was also an enormous concentration camp, housing 90,000 slave labourers by mid-1944 and providing labour for many of the factories and farms of southwestern, Nazi-occupied Poland. The gas chambers were quickly destroyed by the Nazis shortly before the Soviet Army arrived in January 1945.

Hell's Gate
In 1944 the numbers arriving began to increase dramatically. A rail line was extended into the camp. The entrance gate through which the trains passed was known as "Hell's Gate".

Visiting Birkenau
There is little left of the camp's buildings today; its main purpose is for remembrance. Most visitors come to pay their respects at the Monument to the Victims of the Camp, near the site of the gas chambers.

The Unloading Ramp
Arriving at the ramp was a terrifying experience It was here that SS officers separated the men from the women and children, and the SS doctors declared who was fit for work. Those declared unfit (as many as 70 or 80 per cent) were taken immediately to their death.

The Camp

Birkenau was the largest camp in Nazi-occupied Europe. In 1944 it held more than 90,000 prisoners, the majority of whom were murdered or taken on forced marches to other camps. From the unloading ramp to the gas chambers, the crematoria to the ash dumping grounds, the whole process of murder was carried out systematically and on an enormous scale. This reconstruction shows the camp at its peak in 1944, when as many as 5,000 people could be killed every day.

The Liberation of the Camps

With the war all but lost, in mid-January 1945 the Nazi authorities gave the order for all the camps to be destroyed. Such was the speed of the collapse of the German army, however, that only part of Birkenau was destroyed. Between 17–21 January more than 56,000 inmates were evacuated by the Nazis and forced to march west; many died en route. When the Soviet army entered the camps on 27 January 1945, they found just 7,000 survivors.

Survivors of Auschwitz II-Birkenau, filmed by Soviet troops

For hotels and restaurants see p303 and pp313–14

Kanada

"Kanada" was the nickname of the barracks where property stolen from prisoners was stored. It was the preferred place to work at Auschwitz II-Birkenau as it offered opportunities for inmates to pilfer items to barter for food or medicine later.

0 metres 200
0 yards 200

The Sauna

New arrivals selected for work were deloused and disinfected in this building, which became known as the "sauna". Periodic disinfections of existing prisoners were also carried out here.

The Ash Pond

Tons of ash – the remains of hundreds of thousands of Auschwitz victims – were dumped in ponds and troughs dug around the outskirts of the camp.

KEY

① **Towers and barbed wire** isolated the camps from the outside world.

② **Large gas chambers and crematoria** (from 1943)

③ **Area of expansion**, nicknamed "Mexico", never completed.

④ **Wooden barracks**, with 500–600 people living in each.

⑤ **Hell's Gate**

Barracks

The conditions of the living quarters at the camps were terrible. With little or no sanitation, poor nutrition and no medical care, diseases such as typhus spread rapidly. This image shows a typical wooden barracks at Birkenau shortly after liberation.

⑫ Bielsko-Biała

Road map D6. 172,400.
ℹ Plac Ratuszowy 4 (33 819 00 50).
🌐 bielsko.biala.pl

The city was created by joining the Silesian town of Bielsko and the Galician town of Biała. It was once an important centre for the production of textiles and wool.

The **Castle of the Sułkowski princes**, built in the Middle Ages and altered in the 19th century, is also of interest. The unusual hilltop Church of St Nicholas (Kościół św. Mikołaja) began as a modest 15th-century Gothic church and was extensively remodelled in 1907–10.

Bielsko-Biała is a good starting point for excursions into the Beskid Śląski Mountains. The chair lift from the suburbs takes visitors to the Szyndzielnia peak, 1,026 m (3,365 ft) above.

⑬ Żywiec

Road map D6. 31,700.
ℹ ul. Zamkowa 2 (33 861 43 10).
🌐 zywiec.pl

The town of Żywiec is associated with one of the best locally brewed Polish brands of beer. It is a good starting point for excursions into the Beskid Żywiecki Mountains. Lake Żywiecki, with its water-sports facilities, is another tourist attraction. This is also a town of thriving folk traditions; a particular high point is Corpus Christi, when women dressed in traditional costumes take part in a festive procession. Local monuments include the **Market Square**,

Arcaded courtyard of the Renaissance castle in Żywiec

the 19th-century **town hall**, and the **Church of the Nativity of the Virgin Mary** (Kościół Narodzenia Najświętszej Marii Panny), built in 1582–3. Not far from the Market Square is the **Gothic Church of the Holy Cross** (Kościół św. Krzyża).

The most important buildings are the Renaissance **castle** and the 19th-century **palace**. In the mid-17th century, Jan Kazimierz, King of Poland, was the owner of Żywiec.

The town became the property of the Habsburgs in the 19th century, who built a palace next to the castle.

🏛 Town Museum

ul. Zamkowa 2. **Tel** 33 861 21 24.
Open 9am–4pm Mon–Fri, 10am–4pm Sat & Sun. 🌐 muzeum-zywiec.pl

⑭ Wadowice

Road map D6. 18,500.
ℹ ul. Koscielna 4 (33 873 23 65).
🌐 it.wadowice.pl

Karol Wojtyła, who became Pope John Paul II in 1978, was born in Wadowice in 1920. His childhood home is now the **Museum of the Holy Father John Paul II**, with objects relating to his early life. He was christened in the late Baroque **Church of the Presentation of the Virgin Mary** (Kościół Ofiarowania NMP), near the Market Square. The church, built in 1791–8, replaces an early Gothic church, of which only the chancel remains. The tower, with Baroque cupola, was built by Tomasz Pryliński in the late 19th century.

🏛 Museum of the Holy Father John Paul II

ul. Kościelna 7. **Tel** 33 823 26 62.
Open Apr & Oct: 9am–6pm (May–Sep: to 7pm; Nov–Mar: to 4pm). 🌐 domjp2.pl

⑮ Kalwaria Zebrzydowska

Road map D6. 4,600.
ℹ ul. Bernardyńska 46 (33 876 63 04).
🌐 kalwaria.eu

Kalwaria Zebrzydowska is the oldest and most unusual **calvary**

Bernardine church in Kalwaria Zebrzydowska

in Poland. It was commissioned in 1600 by Mikołaj Zebrzydowski, the ruler of Krakow.

The calvary (built 1605–32) consists of 40 chapels, set on the surrounding hills. The most distinctive are the work of the Flemish architect and goldsmith Paul Baudarth. Some have unusual shapes: the House of the Virgin Mary takes the form of the Mystic Rose, and the House of Caiaphas that of an ellipsis. The large Baroque monastery church dates from 1702; the monastic buildings were constructed by Baudarth and Giovanni Maria Bernadoni in 1603–67.

Passion plays are performed here during Holy Week, and the Feast of Assumption is celebrated in August.

⑯ Wieliczka

Road map D5. 20,000.
ℹ ul. Dembowskiego 2a (12 288 00 52). 🌐 wieliczka.eu

Wieliczka is famous for its ancient **salt mine**, which was opened 700 years ago and is still being exploited. Unique in the world, it has been listed by UNESCO as a World Heritage Site.

The 2-km- (1½-miles-) long route is an ideal opportunity to see the network of underground galleries and chambers. They reach a depth of 135 m (442 ft) and have a stable temperature of 13–14° C (55–57° F). The highlights include the Chapel of St Kinga, with altarpieces, chandeliers and sculptures made of salt.

The Staszic Chamber has the highest ceiling, at 36 m (115 ft). There is also an underground sanatorium where respiratory diseases are treated.

The Salt Mine Castle at Ulica Zamkowa 8 is worth a visit, too. From the 13th century right up until 1945 it was a base for the management of the salt mine. Today it houses a museum with – among other things – a collection of antique salt mills.

Salt Mine
ul. Daniłowicza 10. **Tel** 12 278 73 02. **Open** Apr–Oct: 7:30am–7:30pm; Nov–Mar: 8am–5pm. **Closed** 1 Jan, Easter, 1 Nov, 24–26 Dec. 🚫 🎥 (compulsory, book ahead) 🏛 📷 📶 **w** wieliczka-saltmine.com

⑰ Niepołomice

Road map E5. 🗺 11,700. 🚉 🚌 **w** niepolomice.eu

In the 14th century, the **royal castle** at Niepołomice was the hunting base of Kazimierz the Great. Between 1550 and 1571 it was converted into a Renaissance palace by Zygmunt August. The entrance gate, dating from 1552, was once decorated with a Jagiellonian eagle; the plaque, with the Latin inscription "May the King Win and Live", hints at its former splendour. The monarchs loved hunting in the **game park** nearby.

Today, the forest is much smaller than it was in the time of the Jagiellonians. It is still, however, a sizeable nature reserve with plenty of secluded areas, and bison are raised there.

⑱ Zalipie

Road map E5. 🗺 739. 🚌 🚉 6 km (4 miles) from the village. **w** dommalarek.pl

Zalipie has a unique folk art tradition: cottages, barns, wells and fences are painted with colourful floral, animal, geometric and other motifs. The painters are predominantly the women of the village. Every year in June, a competition called the Painted Cottage is organized and exhibitions of paintings are held.

The Gothic-Renaissance town hall in Tarnów

⑲ Tarnów

Road map E5. 🗺 110,000. 🚌 🚉 ℹ Rynek 7 (14 688 90 90). **w** it.tarnow.pl

Tarnów received its municipal charter in 1330; the medieval layout of the old town is perfectly preserved. Those around the arcaded **Market Square** are among the finest. The **town hall**, in the centre, dates from the 15th century and was remodelled in the second half of the 16th century.

The late Gothic **Cathedral of the Nativity of the Virgin Mary** (Katedra Narodzenia NMP), the grandest building in Tarnów was built in 1400. Its **Diocesan Museum** is worth a visit. The monuments, epitaphs and tombstones within are mostly those of the Tarnowski family, who at one time owned the town.

🏛 Diocesan Museum
pl. Katedralny 6. **Tel** 14 621 99 93. **Open** 10am–3pm Tue–Sat, 9am–2pm Sun. **w** muzeum.diecezja.tarnow.pl

⑳ Dębno near Brzeska

Road map E6. 🗺 1,600. 🚌

This well-proportioned castle surrounded by a moat was built in 1470–80 for the castellan and royal chancellor Jakub Dębiński. It survives in an excellent state of preservation.

The **Museum of Period Interiors** installed in the castle re-creates the atmosphere of noble houses of the 15th to 18th centuries. Not only the living quarters but also the castle's kitchen, pantry and wine cellar are included in the exhibition.

🏛 Museum of Period Interiors
Tel 14 665 80 35. **Open** Mar–Dec: 9am–4pm Tue–Fri, 11am–3pm Sat & Sun. **Closed** Jan, Feb. 🚫 🎥 **w** muzeum.tarnow.pl

㉑ Nowy Wiśnicz

Road map E6. 🗺 2,700. 🚌

The enormous **Nowy Wiśnicz Castle** and the **Monastery of the Discalced Carmelites** overlook this town from the hills above. The **parish church** stands in the Market Square below. Each of these early Baroque buildings was raised by Stanisław Lubomirski, Palatine of Krakow, in the 17th century. This wise magnate earned renown in the Battles of Chocim against the Turks. Twice the emperor bestowed a dukedom on him. The castle, which previously belonged to the Kmita family, was extended by Lubomirski after 1615. It has four corner towers, an arcaded courtyard and an entrance gate, framed by enormous volutes. Now a prison, the monastery is not open to visitors. The façade of the parish church is one of the most unusual pieces of architecture in Poland, combining Baroque elements in a Mannerist style.

Nowy Wiśnicz Castle, towering above the town

Old cottages along the main street of Chochołów

㉒ Chochołów

Road map D6. 🗺 1,100. 🚌

Along the main street of the 16th-century village stand traditional wooden cottages, the best examples of highland architecture in the whole Podhale region. One of the cottages, at No. 75, is open to the public. It dates from 1889 and has "white" and "black" rooms, a vestibule and a cellar. It also houses the **Museum of the Chochołów Insurrection**, which took place in 1846 against Austrian rule.

Chochołów has a curious local custom that involves cleaning the walls of the building once a year until they are white.

🏛 **Museum of the Chochołów Insurrection**
Chochołów 75. **Open** 10am–2pm Wed–Sun. 📷 🌐 **muzeumtatrzanskie.pl**

㉓ Zakopane

Road map D6. 🗺 27,000. 🚏 🚌
ℹ ul. Kościuszki 17 (18 201 22 11).
🎿 Autumn in the Tatras; International Festival of Mountain Folklore (end Aug). 🌐 **zakopane.pl**

For over 100 years, the Polish people have regarded Zakopane as their country's winter capital, on a par with alpine resorts as an upmarket winter sports and leisure centre.

Many tourists also appreciate Zakopane in the summer. While some go hiking in the mountains, most are content to admire the scenery from the windows of their cable cars gliding to the summit of Mt Kasprowy Wierch or from the funicular railway ascending Mt Gubałówka. Later

Entrance to the Villa Koliba Museum

Cable-car line from Kuźnice to Kasprowy Wierch, Zakopane

in the day, many tourists gather in Krupówki, the town's central pedestrianized area, which is lined with cafés, restaurants, exclusive souvenir shops and art galleries.

Walking down Krupówki it is impossible to resist the market near the funicular railway station. Here you can buy leather *kierpce* (traditional moccasins), woollen pullovers, wooden *ciupagi* (sticks with decorative axe-like handles), and *bryndza* and *oscypek* (regional cheeses made from sheep's milk).

Villa Atma, the wooden house where the composer Karol Szymanowski *(see p32)* lived from 1930 to 1936, is now a museum dedicated to this eulogist of the Tatra Mountains. It is worth a visit since it is in typical Zakopane style.

In 1992, the Polish and Slovakian national parks in the Tatra Mountains were jointly designated a biosphere reserve by UNESCO. The Tatra National Park can be accessed from Zakopane. The largest lake in the Tatra Mountains, Morskie Oko (Sea Eye), is one of

Panorama from Mount Gubałówka

The finest panorama of the Tatra Mountains from the northern, Polish side of the range is from Mt Gubałówka or Głodówka pod Bukowiną. The Tatras, the highest mountains in Central Europe, with alpine landscapes, lie within Polish and Slovak national parks. The main attractions for tourists include the excursion to the Lake Morskie Oko (Eye of the Sea) and the ascent by cable car to the summit of Mount Kasprowy Wierch. In summer, hikers can follow the many designated trails. In winter, the mountains offer favourable conditions for skiing.

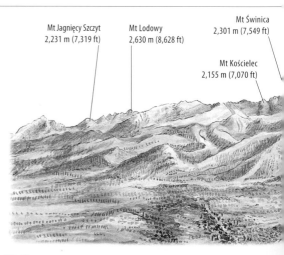

Mt Jagnięcy Szczyt
2,231 m (7,319 ft)

Mt Lodowy
2,630 m (8,628 ft)

Mt Świnica
2,301 m (7,549 ft)

Mt Kościelec
2,155 m (7,070 ft)

For hotels and restaurants see p303 and pp313–14

the most popular attractions. Visitors can take the carriage from road or hike to the lake.

🚌 **Villa Atma**
ul. Kasprusie 19. **Tel** 18 202 00 40.
Open 10am–5pm Tue–Sun (summer 2–6pm Fri). 🎫 (free Sun).

㉔ Dębno Podhalańskie

Road map E6. 🚗 790. 🚌

The picturesque larch timber **Parish Church of St Michael the Archangel** (Kościół parafialny św. Michała Archanioła), dating to the middle of the 15th century, is one of the most highly regarded examples of wooden Gothic architecture in Europe. The ceiling, walls and furnishings are covered with colourful geometric, figural and floral motifs painted at the end of the 1500s. A magnificent domed tower rises over the church. The church is still used for religious services.

The Convent of the Order of St Clare in Stary Sącz

㉕ Dunajec Raft Ride

See pp172–3.

㉖ Stary Sącz

Road map E6. 🚗 9,000. 🚉 🚌
ℹ️ ul. Rynek 5 (18 446 18 58).
🎵 Early Music Festival (Jun–Jul).
🌐 wstarymsaczu.pl

This charming Galician town has a cobbled Market Square surrounded by small houses that in summer are bedecked with flowers. Were it not for the presence of cars, tourists and modern shops, one might imagine that time had stood still here. The town's finest buildings include the **Convent**

Wooden Gothic church in Dębno Podhalańskie

of the Order of St Clare (Klasztor Sióstr Klarysek), founded in 1208 by the Blessed Kinga. The Gothic church was consecrated in 1280 and the vaulting dates from the 16th century. Its altars, with stuccowork ornamentation made by Baldassare Fontana in 1696–9, and a pulpit from 1671 showing a depiction of the Tree of Jesse, complement the modern decoration of the church.

Environs
Nowy Sącz is situated 8 km (5 miles) northeast of Stary Sącz. In the large **Market Square** stands the Neo-Baroque **town hall** of 1895–7. The town's major buildings are the old collegiate church, now the parish Church of St Marguerite (Kościół parafialny św. Małgorzaty), founded by Zbigniew Oleśnicki in 1466, and a fine synagogue.

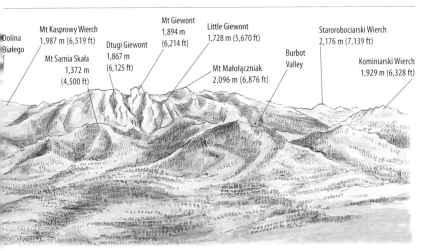

🟪 Dunajec Raft Ride

The Pieniny Mountains form a small range famous for its spectacular landscapes cut through by the Dunajec valley. The raft ride on the river that flows through the limestone mountain gorges is one of the best-known tourist attractions in Poland. At first the rafts move with deceptive calm, but as they approach the gorge behind the cloister ruins the water becomes rougher as the river twists and winds. This lasts for about 8 km (5 miles), after which the water once again flows more slowly. The exhilarating ride ends in Szczawnica, a well-known health resort.

① Czorsztyn Castle
The castle was built in 1330 for the Hungarian Berzevicy family. It now houses the Museum of the Spisz Region.

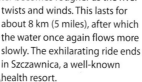

Lake Czorsztyńskie

Czorsztyn

Łapsze

Lake Sromowskie

Sromowc Wyżne

② Niedzica Castle
The castle once guarded the Polish border with Hungary. Its ruins perch on a precipitous outcrop of rock.

0 km   1
0 miles   1

Key

– – Raft ride route

▬ Tour route

▬ Other road

③ Dunajec Dam
Despite protests, the building of this dam went ahead. On the day of its opening in 1997, it saved the Dunajec valley from a disastrous flood.

🟪 Krynica

Road map E6. 🗺 11,000. 🚍 🚌
ℹ️ ul. Zdrojowa 4/2 (18 472 55 77).
🎵 concerts by spa orchestras (all year round). 🌐 krynica.pl

Well-equipped with sanatoria and pump rooms, Krynica is one of the largest, as well as the most modern health and ski resorts in Poland. Fashionable and luxurious pre-war boarding houses stand next to old wooden villas. The best known is "Patria", built by Bohdan

One of Nikifor's paintings on view at the Nikifor Museum

Pniewski in the Art Nouveau style, and owned by singer Jan Kiepura (1902–66). The **New Sanatorium** near the pedestrian promenade (Deptak) is also worth a visit. Completed in 1939, it retains its original furnishings and decor. The Great Pump Room nearby is always very popular with visitors.

The town is surrounded by tree-covered mountains. Mt Jaworzyna, at 1,114 m (3,654 ft) the highest peak in the area, can be reached by cable car, departing from Czarny Potok. In winter, the mountain turns into a skier's paradise. Remote areas of the mountains are inhabited by lynxes, wolves and bears, so caution should be exercised away from the established trails.

The work of amateur painter Nikifor (d. 1968) is displayed in the "Romanówka" villa, now the **Nikifor Museum**.

🏛 Nikifor Museum
Bulwary Dietla 19. **Tel** 18 471 53 03.
Open 10am–1pm & 2–5pm Tue–Sat, 10am–3pm Sun. **Closed** pub hols. ♿

🟪 Biecz

Road map E6. 🗺 4,500.
🚍 🚌 City bus from Gorlice.
🎵 Pogórze Folklore Days.

In the 16th century this small town was one of the most important centres of cloth manufacture in Poland. It is dominated by the **town hall tower**, built in 1569–81, and the **Parish Church of Corpus Christi** (Kościół farny Bożego Ciała). The church, one of the most magnificent late Gothic churches in all of Małopolska, was built at the turn of the 15th century in a style that seeks to reconcile the Gothic tradition with the new canons of the Renaissance. The first pharmacy in the Carpathian foothills was located in the **Renaissance house** at Ulica Węgierska 2, dating from 1523; it now houses a division of the **Regional Museum**.

🏛 Regional Museum
ul. Kromera 3. **Tel** 13 447 10 93.
Open May, Jun & Sep: 8am–5pm Tue–Fri, 9am–5pm Sat & Sun; Jul & Aug: 8am–7pm Tue–Fri, 10am–7pm Sat & Sun; Oct–Apr: 8am–4pm Tue–Sun.
🌐 muzeum.biecz.pl

⑧ **Szczawnica**

Neighbouring Slovakia, this well-known health resort is mainly a centre for the treatment of respiratory diseases. It is also the disembarkation point for the Dunajec river raft ride.

⑦ **Ostra Skała**

After Ostra Skała (Sharp Rock) the River Dunajec turns sharply as it flows through the narrowest part of the gorge.

Tips for Drivers

Raft ride: 2.25–2.75 hours.
Length: 18 km (11 miles) to Szczawnica; 23 km (14 miles) to Krościenko. **Tel** 18 262 97 21 or 262 97 93. **Starting point:** Sromowce Wyżne–Kąty. Apr–Nov: daily. 🚗 🅦 flisacy.com.pl

Stary Sącz

969

Krościenko • on the Dunajec

⑧

Three Crowns

⑥

⑦

Dunajec

Sromowce Średnie · Niżne

⑤

④ **Kąty**
Departure point for the raft ride.

⑥ **Trzy Korony**

Trzy Korony (Three Crowns) is the most beautiful massif in the Pieniny range. In 1287, the Blessed Kinga took refuge from the Tatars in the Castle of the order of St Clare, whose ruins stand on one peak.

⑤ **Cerveny Kláštor**
The ruins of the Red Monastery can be seen on the Slovak side of the Dunajec.

The Parish Church of Corpus Christi in Biecz

Environs

In the village of **Harklowa** there is a late Gothic wooden church dating from the turn of the 15th century.

㉙ Krosno

Road map F6. 🗻 47,000. 🚌 🚗 ℹ️
ul. Rynek 5 (13 432 77 07). 🎪 Krosno Fair (Jun); Krosno Music Autumn (Oct).

Krosno was once the centre of the Polish oil industry, but there is more to the town than its industrial past. The finest historical monument is the

Oświęcim Chapel in the Gothic Franciscan church. Completed in 1647, the chapel is decorated with exquisite stuccowork by Giovanni Battista Falconi. It contains the tombs of the half-siblings Anna and Stanisław, whose love ended in tragedy. The Market Square is surrounded by old arcaded houses, the most interesting of which is No. 7, with its Renaissance doorway.

Environs

In **Odrzykoń**, 10 km (6 miles) north of Krosno, stand the ruins of Kamieniec Castle. Kamieniec

was the setting for *Revenge* (1834), the most popular comedy by the 19th-century writer Count Aleksander Fredro (*see p31*), the plot of which involves a dispute over the hole in the wall dividing the courtyard of the castle.

In the **geological park** not far from the castle stands a group of sandstone and shale structures known as Prządki (The Spinners), which have unusual, sometimes quite startling shapes.

Iwonicz Zdrój and **Rymanów**, 15 km (9 miles) east of Krosno, are very popular health resorts. At **Dukla**, there is the Baroque Mniszcha Palace, which today houses a historical museum, and an 18th-century Bernardine church, which features the charming Rococo tomb of Maria Amalia Brühla Mniszkowa, with its peaceful effigy.

In **Bóbrka**, 12 km (7 miles) south of Krosno, an industrial *skansen* has been created in what is certainly one of the oldest oil wells in the world, established in 1854.

For keys to symbols *see back flap*

㉚ Bieszczady Mountains Tour

The Bieszczady Mountains, together with the neighbouring Beskid Niski, are the wildest in Poland. Tourists return with blood-curdling tales of encounters with bears and wolves, or the discovery of a skeleton in the forest undergrowth. Needless to say, these stories are often exaggerated. Before World War II, the region was densely populated by Ukrainians and ethnic groups known as the Boyks and the Lemks. After the war, because of fighting and resettlements, it became deserted, and farming had largely disappeared from the region by the 1970s. Pastures and burned-out villages became overgrown as the forest encroached and wild animals returned to the mountains.

⑦ Komańcza
Cardinal Stefan Wyszyński, Primate of Poland, was sent into exile to this village, deserted after World War II. He was interned by the Communist authorities in 1955–6.

⑥ Połonina Wetlińska
Known as "połoniny", these elongated ranges with their picturesque alpine meadows above forest level are a characteristic feature of the Bieszczady Mountains. The most interesting, 1,250 m (4,100 ft) up, are Caryńska and Wetlińska.

⑤ Bieszczady National Park
With an area of 300 sq km (116 sq miles), this area is part of the "East Carpathian" International Biosphere Reserve, the first UNESCO reserve to be located in three countries (Poland, Slovakia and Ukraine). In summer, many tourists walk the hiking trails. The main tourist base is in the small village of Ustrzyki Górne.

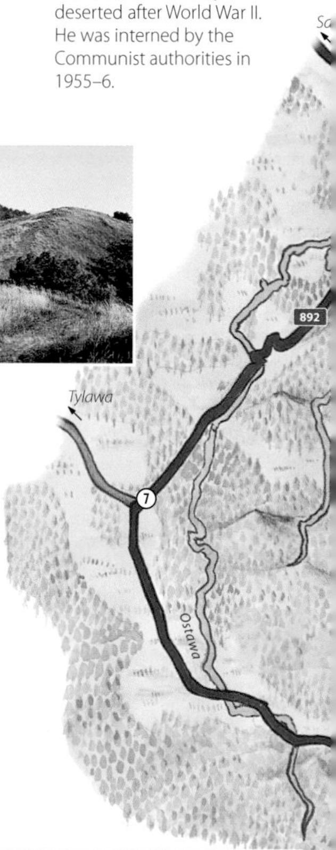

Bieszczady Mountain Animals

The lynx, the emblem of Bieszczady National Park, is not the only feline to make its home in these mountains. Wildcats also live here. They are rarely seen because they are very shy, concealing themselves in the forest undergrowth. Carpathian deer, with a population of 5,000, are more often encountered. Roe deer are also abundant and relatively tame. Wolves, a protected species numbering about 100 here, are more cautious. Bison, kings of the Polish forest, number up to 120, and brown bear may also be seen. The Bieszczady Mountains are also popular with ornithologists for the many species of birds of prey: eagles, including the golden eagle, falcon and hawk.

A wild mountain wolf

④ Równia
The most beautiful Orthodox churches in the Bieszczady Mountains are vestiges of the numerous villages of the Boyks and the Lemks.

① Zagórz
Zagórz, dominated by the ruins of the 18th-century Baroque fortified Church of Discalced Carmelites, is the starting point of hiking trails into the Bieszczady Mountains.

Tips for Drivers
Tour length: 106 km (66 miles)
Stopping-off points:
Restaurants, boarding houses and inns can be found in Polańczyk, Lesko, Wetlin, Ustrzyki Dolne and Ustrzyki Górne. In the summer season, bars also open.

② Lesko
This charming town has many fine buildings, including a castle and a 16th-century parish church. The Baroque synagogue houses a museum, and the Jewish cemetery is also of interest.

③ Solina
The highest dam in Poland – 82 m (269 ft) high and 664 m (2,178 ft) long – was built at Solina. The reservoir that was created is ideal for sailing. The dam is surrounded by magnificent forests with nature reserves.

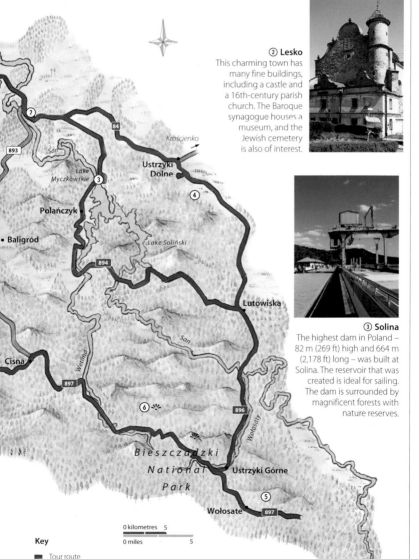

Krościenko

Ustrzyki Dolne

San

Lake Myczkowskie

Polańczyk

● Baligród

Lake Soliński

Lutowiska

San

Cisna

Wetlina

Bieszczadzki National Park

Ustrzyki Górne

Wołosate

Wołosaty

Key
■ Tour route
■ Other road

0 kilometres 5
0 miles 5

The Divine Tower, one of four towers in Krasiczyn Castle

❸ Krasiczyn Castle

Road map F6. 440. Castle: **Tel** 16 671 83 12. **Open** mid-Apr–mid-Oct: 9am–4pm; mid-Oct–Mar: by appt only. compulsory. krasiczyn.com.pl

Krasiczyn Castle is one of the most magnificent late Renaissance castles in the old Ruthenian territories of the Polish crown. Building began in 1592 on the site of an earlier castle by Stanisław Krasicki, castellan of Przewór. It was continued by his son Marcin and completed in 1608. The architect was Galeazzo Appiani.

The castle takes the form of an arcaded courtyard, with a tall clock tower over the gate and four stout cylindrical towers at the corners. The Divine Tower contains a chapel. The Papal Tower is crowned by a dome and decorated with a parapet symbolizing the papal tiara. The Royal Tower has a crown-shaped dome, and the Tower of the Gentry is topped with sword pommels.

The Baroque sgraffito on the walls is striking. Mythological scenes are depicted on the upper tier; the central tier is filled with portraits of the kings of Poland from the 14th-century Jagiellonian monarchs to Jan III Sobieski, King of Poland at the time, as well as portraits of nobles. In the lowest tier are medallions with the busts of Roman patricians. Little of the original decoration of the interior

survives, as it was destroyed by fire in 1852, on the eve of the marriage of a later owner, Duke Leon Sapieha. The castle is ideal for visitors who are looking for some peace and quiet.

Environs
In Krzywcza, 10 km (6 miles) west of **Krasiczyn**, stand the ruins of the castle of the Kącki family. About 12 km (7 miles) south of Krasiczyn, in **Posada Rybotycka**, is the only stone fortified Uniate church in Poland. In **Kalwaria Pacławicka**, the 18th-century Franciscan monastery has about a dozen chapels marking the Stations of the Cross. Passion plays are performed here on Good Friday and many processions and plays are organized during the year for different church festivities.

The funeral of the Virgin enacted in a passion play in Kalwaria Pacławicka

❸ Przemyśl

Road map F6. 62,400. ul. Grodzka 1 (16 675 21 63). Canoe rally (Apr, May); Gitariada International Festival (Jul). przemysl.pl

The history of Przemyśl, picturesquely laid out on a hill and the

banks of the River San, goes back to prehistoric times. In the Middle Ages it was a regional capital and lay on a busy trade route. The object of dispute between Poland and Ruthenia, it became part of Poland in 1340, later passing into Austrian control.

During World War I, the strongly fortified city successfully held out against the besieging Russian army. The **fortifications** from that time survive. From 1939 to 1941 the River San, which flows through the city, constituted a border between territory held by the Soviet Union and Germany.

The city's Catholic and Orthodox churches, together with its synagogues, are evidence of its multicultural history. Today, a Ukrainian minority lives alongside the city's Polish population.

The **cathedral**, remodelled in 1718–24, is predominantly in the Baroque style; of its earlier Gothic form only the chancel remains. Notable features of the interior include the Renaissance tomb of Bishop Jan Dziaduski, by Giovanni Maria Padovano, and the late Gothic alabaster figure of the Virgin from Jacków. Near the cathedral are the Baroque Church of the Discalced Carmelites and the former Jesuit church, now Uniate, dating from 1627–48. The castle, founded by Kazimierz the Great in the 1340s, stands on a hill above the city. The top of its tower offers a panorama of the city and the San valley.

Przemyśl, on the banks of the River San

Orsetti House, a palace in the Renaissance style, in Jarosław

㉝ Jarosław

Road map F5. 🔼 38,200. 🚉 🚌
Jarosław Museum in the Orsetti House
Rynek 5: **Tel** 16 621 54 37. **Open** May–
Sep: 9am–5pm Tue–Sat, 10am–5pm
Sun; Oct–Apr: 9am–3pm Tue–Sun.
🐾 (free on Sun). **W** muzeum-
jaroslaw.pl 🎵 Early Music Festival
(Aug). **W** jaroslaw.pl

The city of Jarosław owes its
wealth to its location on the
River San and the trade route
linking the east with western
Europe. In the 16th and 17th
centuries, the largest fairs in
Poland were held here. When
Władysław IV attended a fair in
Jarosław, he mingled with an
international crowd and con-
versed with merchants from as
far away as Italy and Persia. The
Orsetti House, built in the style
of an Italian Renaissance palazzo,
testifies to the wealth of the city's
merchants. Built in the 16th
century and extended in 1646,
it is crowned with a Mannerist
parapet. The **town hall**, with
coats of arms on the corner
towers, stands in the centre
of the broad **Market Square**.

㉞ Leżajsk

Road map F5. 🔼 14,000. 🚉 🚌
ℹ ul. Rynek 1a (17 787 70 67).
🎵 Organ recitals in the basilica
(Jun–Aug: 7pm; booking required).

The major attractions of Leżajsk
are its Bernardine basilica and
monastery, built by the architect
Antonio Pellacini, and the organ
recitals that take place in the

basilica, which was built in
1618–28. Its interior decoration
and the furnishings, such as
the oak stalls, pulpit and high
altar, are mostly the work of the
monks themselves. The basilica
was established by Łukasz
Opaliński, who earned renown
through his defeat of the
lawless magnate Stanisław
Stadnicki in mortal combat.

The west end of the nave is
filled with the complex organ,
completed in 1693 and said
to be the finest in Poland. The
central theme of the elaborate
Baroque casing is Hercules' fight
with the Hydra, the nine-headed
monster of Greek mythology.
Not only is this a symbol of
the age-old struggle of virtue
against vice but also of Polish
victory over the Turks, who were
threatening Europe at the time.

The Jewish cemetery in Leżajsk
is a place of pilgrimage for Jews
from all over the world, who
come to visit the tomb of
Elimelech, the great 18th-
century Orthodox rabbi.

㉟ Łańcut

See pp178–9.

㊱ Rzeszów

Road map F5. 🔼 188,000. 🚉 🚌
❌ ℹ ul. Rynek 26 (17 875 47 74).
W rzeszow.pl

The dominant building in this
town is the Gothic **Church of
Saints Stanisław and Adalberg**
(Kościół św. Stanisława i
Wojciecha), dating from the
15th century and with a later
Baroque interior. The former
Piarist **Church of the Holy
Cross** (Kościół św. Krzyża),
extended in 1702–07 by
Tylman van Gameren, and
the Baroque monastery and
Bernardine church of 1624–9
are also worth a visit. The
latter contains the unfinished
mausoleum of the Ligęz family,
where there are eight alabaster
statues carved by Sebastian
Sala around 1630.

The remains of the old
castle of the Ligęz family can
still be seen. It later passed
into the ownership of the
Lubomirskis, who surrounded
it with bastions in the 17th
century. The Market Square,
with an eclectic town hall
remodelled in 1895–8, is
another interesting feature.

Highlights of the **Muzeum
Miasta Rzeszowa** include
the gallery of 18th- to 20th-
century Polish painting and
the collection of glass, china
and faïence.

🏛 **Muzeum Miasta Rzeszowa**
ul. 3 Maja 19. **Tel** 17 853 52 78.
Open 9am–3:30pm Tue–Thu, Sun;
10am–5:30pm Fri. 🐾 (free Sun). 🛍

Fair in Leżajsk, a centre of folk pottery

㉟ Łańcut

The town of Łańcut was purchased by Stanisław Lubomirski in 1629. Securing the services of the architect Maciej Trapola and the stuccoist Giovanni Battista Falconi, this powerful magnate went about building a fortified residence in the town. It was completed in 1641. After 1775 the palace, by then owned by Izabella Lubomirska, was extended and the interiors remodelled. The Neo-Classical Ballroom and the Great Dining Room were created during this period, and the magnificent gardens with their many pavilions laid out. In the 19th century, ownership of the palace passed to the Potocki family. From 1889 to 1914, the penultimate owners, Roman and Elżbieta Potocki, modernized the residence. The palace, now a museum, attracts numerous visitors.

★ Column Room
The statue in this room is that of the young Henryk Lubomirski, carved by Antonio Canova in around 1787.

Mirror Room
The walls are lined with Rococo panelling brought back to Łańcut by Izabella Lubomirska – probably from one of her visits to France.

Carriage
The largest collection of carriages in Poland is displayed in the coach house. It comprises 120 different types of coaches, carriages and other horse-drawn vehicles.

KEY

① Library

② **Corner tower known as the Hen's Foot**

For hotels and restaurants see p303 and pp313–14

★ **Theatre**
The small court theatre was built around 1800. Its present appearance is the result of remodelling carried out by the eminent Viennese workshop of Fellner & Helmer.

Sculpture Gallery
Many pieces, mostly 19th-century, make up the collection on display; among them is this statue of Psyche carried by Zephyrs, a copy of a piece by John Gibson.

The main entrance

★ **Ballroom**
The Neo-Classical ballroom was designed by Christian Piotr Aigner in 1800. The stuccowork is by Fryderyk Baumann.

Neo-Rococo Clock
This typically French Neo-Rococo gilt clock is mounted in the mirror that hangs over the fireplace in the Billiard Room.

Façade
The palace façades are fundamentally Baroque. The rustication of the lower storey, however, is typical of French Renaissance style – part of the remodelling that the palace underwent at the end of the 19th century.

SILESIA

Silesia's great wealth of architectural monuments, its eventful history and its beautiful and varied landscape distinguish it from other regions of Poland. The region's well-preserved historic towns and the many hiking trails in the picturesque Sudeten Mountains make it an area that invites long exploration.

The stormy history of Silesia (Śląsk) and the great variety of cultural influences that have flourished here have given this region a rich heritage. It belonged initially to the Bohemian crown and passed into Polish control around 990. When Poland split into principalities, Silesia began to gain independence. Divided into smaller independent duchies, it returned to Bohemian rule in the 14th century. After 1526, together with other Bohemian territories, it became part of the Habsburg Empire. During the Reformation, many of its inhabitants were converted to Lutheranism. The Thirty Years' War (1618–48) inflicted devastation on Silesia, bringing in its wake the repression of Protestantism. While Jesuits and Cistercians erected magnificent Baroque monasteries at that time, under the terms of the Peace of Westphalia of 1648, Protestants were limited to building the three "peace churches". The Habsburgs lost Silesia to Prussia in 1742. Although the main language was German, many areas, especially the Opole region and Upper Silesia, were inhabited by an influential Polish minority. After World War I, as a result of the Silesian Uprisings of 1919–21, the eastern part of Upper Silesia, together with Katowice, was included within Polish borders. After 1945, nearly all of historical Silesia joined Poland, and its German population was deported. Poles who had been resettled from Poland's eastern provinces (which had been annexed by the Soviet Union) took their place.

Silesia is an enchanting region, not only for the breathtaking beauty of its mountain landscapes but also for its outstanding architecture. The medieval castles built to defend ancient borderlands, the grand Renaissance manor houses and impressive Baroque residences, the great Gothic churches and stately monasteries all provide ample attractions and a historic atmosphere.

The snow capped Karkonosze Mountains on a sunny day

◀ The Kamienczyk waterfall, in the Karkonosze National Park

Exploring Silesia

The most attractive part of the region is Lower Silesia. A good starting point for exploration is Wrocław, the provincial capital and a city full of historic buildings as well as interesting 20th-century architecture. From here, the area of Kotlina Kłodzka, with the fantastically shaped Table Mountains, is within easy reach. Not far away lies Jelenia Góra, a good base for hiking in the Karkonosze Mountains in summer or for skiing on the nearby slopes in winter. The visitor to Silesia will also find beautiful palaces and churches in almost every village. Many fine residences, however, are gradually falling into ruin.

Sheep in the alpine pastures of the Beskid Śląski Mountains

Key

=== Motorway

— Main road

— Minor road

⋯ Main railway

— Minor railway

■■ International border

== Regional border

Sights at a Glance

Getting Around

There are rail links between all the major Silesian cities, so that it is possible to travel by train from Wrocław to Jelenia Góra, Legnica, Głogów, Świdnica, Wałbrzych and Kłodzko. There are also good connections between Katowice, Opole and Wrocław, and trains also stop in Brzeg. Although smaller towns are accessible by bus, the service can be very infrequent, so that outside the major cities the best way to travel is by car. The A4 motorway links several major cities, while smaller roads provide more scenic routes.

The Baroque plague column in the Market Square in Świdnica

Poznań

Góra
Rawicz
36
Milicz
Żmigród
5
va
Wołów
BIĄŻ   TRZEBNICA 21
3
20 WOJNOWICE   22 OLEŚNICA
Syców
Środa   94
Śląska   23 WROCŁAW
A8   Jelcz-Laskowice   Namysłów   Byczyna   Praszka
orzyna 35   Kluczbork   11
OLNOŚLĄSKIE   Odra (Odra)
19 MT ŚLĘŻA   45   Olesno   Częstochowa
8   Wiazów   24 BRZEG   46
WIDNICA
Strzelin   OPOLSKIE   Dobrodzień
AGÓRZE   Niemcza   Grodków   Lubliniec
LĄSKIE   31 OPOLE   46   11
25 HENRYKÓW   A4   94   Strzelce   ŚLĄSKIE
KAMIENIEC   45   Opolskie   Tarnowskie
ABKOWICKI 26   414   Krapkowice   Góry
dzko   PACZKÓW 28 29   30 NYSA   32 GÓRA ŚWIĘTEJ   Bytom
27 OTMUCHÓW   Głogówek   ANNY A4   Zabrze   Chorzów
trzyca   Lądek   Głuchołazy   Prudnik   Kędzierzyn-   UPPER 35 Katowice
odzka   Zdrój   Koźle   SILESIAN   S1   A4
33   Głubczyce   INDUSTRIAL
REGION
Racibórz   Rybnik   78
A1   Żory   1
Ostrava   PSZCZYNA 34
S1   Bielsko-
33 CIESZYN   Biała
Wisła

0 kilometres   25
0 miles   25

The house of Gerhard Hauptmann in Jagniątków

The Baroque-Neo-Classical palace of the Talleyrand family in Żagań

❶ Żagań

Road map B4. ⛫ 26,200. 🚌 🚋
ℹ️ ul. Szprotawska 4 (68 477 10 01).
🌐 **um.zagan.pl**

The origins of Żagań go back as far as the 13th century. A particularly happy episode in the history of this pretty town on the River Bóbr was the period from 1845 to 1862, thanks to the beautiful Dorothea Talleyrand-Périgord, the youngest daughter of Peter Biron, Duke of Kurland.

Dorothea was something of a social magnet. She was a friend of Maurice Charles de Talleyrand, one of Louis Napoleon's ministers, and his nephew's wife. Her circle attracted the most eminent composers and writers of the day, among them Franz Liszt and Giuseppe Verdi. Her residence was the **palace** built for Albrecht von Wallenstein, a commander in the Thirty Years' War (1618–48). Dorothea had alterations made, and the palace's present Neo-Classical appearance and the layout of the rooms were commissioned by her in the mid-19th century. It now houses the **Cultural Institute**.

Other prominent buildings in the town are the Franciscan **Church of Saints Peter and Paul** (Kościół św. Piotra i Pawła), built in the Gothic style and dating from the 14th century. The enormous **Church of the Assumption** (Kościół Wniebowzięcia NMP), which once belonged to the Augustinians, also merits attention. It was built in stages from the late 13th to the early 16th century, although the finely furnished interior dates

from the 1830s. The library of the monastery next to the church contains works by the 18th-century painter George Wilhelm Neunhertz and items connected to the German astronomer Johannes Kepler, who worked in Żagań between 1628 and 1630.

🏛️ **Church of the Assumption**
pl. Klasztorny 2. **Tel** 68 444 31 14.

🏛️ **Church of Saints Peter and Paul**
ul. Łużycka.

🏛️ **Cultural Institute**
ul. Szprotawska 4. **Tel** 68 477 64 75.
Open 7:30am–3:30pm Mon–Fri. 🅿️

❷ Głogów

Road map B4. ⛫ 66,400. 🚌 🚋 ℹ️
ul. Koszarowa 1 (76 726 54 51). 🎷 Jazz in Głogów (Oct, Nov). 🌐 **glogow.pl**

This town on the Odra River was established about 1,000 years ago but fell into ruin during World War II. Two Gothic churches, the collegiate Church

Old and new architecture on a street in the old town in Głogów

of the Assumption, set on an island in the Odra, and the Church of St Nicholas in the old town, have not been rebuilt. However, the beautiful Jesuit Baroque **Church of Corpus Christi** (Kościół Bożego Ciała), built in 1694–1724 to a design by Giulio Simonetti, has been reconstructed. Its original twin-tower façade was added in 1711 by Johann Blasius Peintner. The picturesque town hall with its slender tower owes its present form to remodelling carried out by Augustus Soller in 1831–4. It too has been reconstructed. On the bank of the Odra stands the castle of the dukes of Głogów, with its original 14th-century medieval tower and Gothic cellars, and later Baroque walls. It houses the **Archaeological and Historical Museum**. Among the exhibits are a collection of instruments of torture.

🏛️ **Archaeological and Historical Museum**
ul. Brama Brzostowska 1. **Tel** 76 834 10 81. **Open** 10am–5pm Wed–Sun. 🅿️ (free Sat).

🏛️ **Church of Corpus Christi**
ul. Powstańców. **Tel** 76 833 36 01.

❸ Lubiąż

Road map B4. ⛫ 2,300. 🚌 Malczyce. 🚋 Abbey. Lubiąż Foundation: **Tel** 71 322 21 29. **Open** Apr–Sep: 9am–6pm daily; Oct–Mar: 10am–3pm daily. 🅿️

The gigantic Cistercian monastic complex situated on the high bank of the River Odra comes into view from a great distance. Cistercian monks first settled in Lubiąż in 1175. They built a Romanesque church followed by a Gothic basilica, of which the twin-tower façade and ducal chapel remain. The present abbey dates from 1681–1715. After World War II, it was used as a warehouse for unsold books, mostly works by Lenin. Its restoration began in the mid-1990s. An exhibition of Silesian sculpture as well as certain rooms of the monastery, including the refectory and the Ducal Hall, are now open to the public.

Refectory of the Cistercian Abbey in Lubiąż

The ceiling of the refectory is decorated with paintings by Michael Willmann, whose work is also to be seen on the altars of the parish church in Lubiąż. The great Ducal Hall is a magnificent example of the late Baroque style, its purpose being to glorify the faith and the feats of the Habsburg dynasty.

❹ Legnica

Road map B4. 🅜 100,700. 🚂 𝒊
Brama Głogowska (76 854 20 36).
🅦 portal.legnica.eu

Legnica, after Wrocław and Opole Silesia's third-largest city, became the capital of the independent duchy of Legnica in the 13th century. Today it is a large administrative centre and copper-mining town, as evidenced by the displays in the **Copper Museum**.

The **Parish Church of John the Baptist** (Fara św. Jana Chrzciciela) is one of the most beautiful Baroque shrines in Silesia, built for the Jesuits in 1714–27. The presbytery of the original church was converted into a chapel, the Mausoleum of the Silesian Piasts (1677–8).

In the northern part of the old town stands the **Dukes' Castle**. It has medieval origins and was remodelled many times. The fine Renaissance gate was added by George von Amberg in 1532–3. From here, Ulica Mariacka leads to the Gothic **Church of the Virgin Mary** (Kościół NMP), which dates from the 14th century; it was remodelled in the first half of the 15th century.

In the Market Square stand the Baroque town hall, from 1737–46, which houses a theatre, and the Gothic **Cathedral of Saints Peter and Paul** (Katedra św. Piotra i Pawła), built in the 14th century and preserving a 13th- century baptismal font. In the centre of the Market Square are eight narrow arcaded houses known as he **Herring Stalls** and, at No. 40, a 16th-century house known as **Under the Quail's Nest House**, with sgraffito decoration.

🔼 **Cathedral of Saints Peter and Paul**
ul. św. Piotra 2a. **Tel** 76 724 42 81.

🔼 **Church of the Virgin Mary**
pl. Mariacki 1. **Tel** 76 855 34 40.
Closed to the public.

🏛 **Copper Museum**
ul. Partyzantów 3. **Tel** 76 862 49 49.
Open 9am–4pm Tue & Wed,
11am–6pm Thu, 11am–5pm
Fri & Sat. 🎫 (free on Sat and
first Wed of the month).
🅦 muzeum-miedzi.art.pl

🔼 **Parish Church of John the Baptist**
ul. Zbigniewa i Michała 1. **Tel** 76 724 41 88.

❺ Legnickie Pole

Road map B4. 🅜 1,300. 🚌

It was at Legnickie Pole that a great battle between the Poles, led by Henry II, the Pious, and the Tatars took place on 9 April 1241. Despite the Turks' defeat of the Poles and the death of their commander, Poland prevented westward Tatar expansion. The **Museum of the Battle of Legnica** details this event.

The Benedictine abbey, dating from 1727–31 and built by Kilian Ignaz Dientzenhofer in the Baroque style, is the greatest attraction of this small village. The abbey church, dedicated to St Jadwiga, has an elliptical nave and undulating vaulting covered with trompe l'oeil paintings by Cosmas Damian Asam. Its furnishings are equally fine.

🏛 **Museum of the Battle of Legnica**
pl. Henryka Pobożnego 3. **Tel** 76 858 23 98. **Open** 11am–5pm Wed–Sun. 🎫 (free on Wed).

The Baroque façade of the Benedictine abbey church in Legnickie Pole

Tower of the Baroque Church of Peace in Jawor

Church of St Martin (Kościół św. Marcina), and the late 15th-century Church of St Mary (Kościół Mariacki). The best place to finish a walk around the town is the Market Square, which is surrounded by arcaded Baroque houses.

Ⅲ Gallery of Silesian Ecclesiastical Art

ul. Klasztorna 6. **Tel** 76 870 30 86 or 870 23 21. **Open** Apr–Oct: 10am–5pm Wed–Sun; Nov–Mar: 10am–4pm Wed–Sun. 🎟 (free Wed).

❻ Jawor

Road map B4. 🏛 23,500. 🚍 🚌
ℹ️ Rynek 3 (76 870 33 71).

The capital of an independent duchy in the Middle Ages, Jawor is dominated by a castle that is a vestige of those times. Reconstruction has robbed the castle of much of its original splendour, but other buildings, which were painstakingly restored after World War II, enhance the town's historic atmosphere.

The most picturesque building is the large **Church of Peace** (Kościół Pokoju). It was one of three Protestant "peace churches" erected in Silesia after the Peace of Westphalia that marked the end of the Thirty Years' War (1618–48). It was built by Andreas Kempner, to a design by Albrecht von Säbisch, in 1654–6. With the church in Świdnica *(see p191)*, it is among the world's largest timber-framed structures. Other notable buildings in Jawor are the 14th-century

❼ Złotoryja

Road map B4. 🏛 15,700.
🚍 🚌 ℹ️ Basztowa 15 (76 878 18 73). 🎿 World Gold-Panning Championships (May).

Derived from the Polish word *złoto*, meaning gold, the town's name reflects the fact that the gold-rich sands of the River Kaczawa, which flows through Złotoryja, have been exploited since the early Middle Ages. Even today gold-seekers flock to contests organized by the local gold-panning association.

Features of interest in Złotoryja include the Gothic **Church of St Mary** (Kościół NMP), which has a 13th-century presbytery, and the remains of the town walls.

Environs

The volcanic **Wilcza Góra Geological Park**, also known as Wilkołak, lies 2 km (1¼ miles) south of Złotoryja. Unusual basalt formations known as "basalt roses" can be seen in the western part of the park.

Gothic doorway of the 15th-century Grodziec Castle

❽ Grodziec

Road map B4. 🏛 500. 🚍 Złotoryja. 🚌 Castle: **Open** Feb & Mar: 10am–5pm daily; Apr–Oct: 10am–6pm daily; Nov–Jan: 10am–4pm daily.
🌐 grodziec.com

An imposing fortification crowning a basalt hill, Grodziec Castle was built in the 15th century in the Gothic style as the seat of the dukes of Legnica. It was extended in 1522–4 and over the next four centuries it was destroyed several times, once during the Thirty Years' War (1618–48). It was rebuilt in the Romantic style in 1906–8.

The walls, which follow the contours of the hill, are irregular. The castle's tower and living quarters survive.

At the bottom of the hill is the magnificent, although neglected, palace built for the Frankenberg family by Johann Blasius Peintner in 1718–27. Its overgrown surroundings were once attractive gardens.

❾ Lwówek Śląski

Road map B4. 🏛 9,000. 🚍 🚌
ℹ️ pl. Wolności 1 (76 647 79 12).
🌐 lwowekslaski.pl

Lwówek Śląski is a small town set on a precipice overlooking the River Bóbr, in the foothills of the Izerski Mountains. Remnants of the stone walls that once surrounded the settlement can be seen all around.

The centrepiece of the town is its Gothic-Renaissance **town hall**. Built in the 15th century, it was

Gold-panning competition in Złotoryja

Gothic-Renaissance town hall in Lwówek Śląski

extended in 1522–5 and restored in 1902–5, when the delightful arcades around the building were added. Several town houses of historical interest stand in the Market Square.

The twin-towered **Church of the Assumption** (Kościół Wniebowzięcia) has an imposing Romanesque façade which dates from the 13th century. The tympanum over the portal depicts the Coronation of the Virgin. The main body of the church was not added until the turn of the 16th century. The Gothic chapel on the south side, which dates from 1496, has vaulting with beautiful 16th-century frescoes.

The ruins of another Gothic church also survive in Lwówek Śląski. The church was built by Franciscan monks but fell into disuse in 1810.

Environs
The castle at **Płakowice**, 2 km (1¼ miles) south of Lwówek Śląski, is one of the finest Renaissance castles in Silesia. It was built in 1550–63 for the von Talkenberg family.

❿ Czoch Castle

Road map B4. 🚌 Sucha. **Tel** 75 721 15 53. **Open** Apr–Oct: 10am–6pm daily; Nov–Mar: 10am–5pm daily. 🖉
W zamekczocha.com

Czoch Castle (Zamek Czocha) is one of Silesia's major tourist attractions. Standing in a picturesque location on the banks of Lake Leśniańskie, it can be seen for miles around.

The castle dates from the 14th century, and because it was destroyed and rebuilt several times over many centuries, it incorporates a range of architectural styles. It was most recently renovated in the early part of the 20th century, when the Gütschoff family of Dresden had their dilapidated family seat rebuilt by Bodo Ebhardt in 1904–14. Ebhardt's Romantic vision restored Zamek Czocha to its former glory and the castle has since been used as the setting for several films. It is now an atmospheric hotel.

⓫ Lubomierz

Road map B4. 🚶 1,900. 🚉 🚌
ℹ ul. Wacława Kowalskiego 1 (75 783 35 73). 🎬 Review of Polish Comedy Films (Aug).

A sleepy little town in the foothills of the Izerskie Mountains, Lubomierz boasts a picturesque **market square** lined with large arcaded houses. The Baroque Benedictine church built by Johann Jakob Scheerhof in 1727–30 dominates the town.

Many Polish films have been shot in Lubomierz. The popular comedy film *Sami swoi* ("Just Our Own") brought it the greatest renown. The film follows the fortunes of displaced persons from Poland's eastern territories – which were lost to the Soviet Union after World War II – as they settle in the town, itself a former German territory ceded to Poland.

🏛 The Kargul and Pawlak Museum
ul. Wacława Kowalskiego 1. **Tel** 75 783 35 73. **Open** 10am–4pm Mon–Fri, 9am–5pm Sat & Sun. 🅿 **W sami-swoi.com.pl**

This museum is housed in Płóciennik House, built in the 16th century and reconstructed around 1700. Its collection includes items used during the making of Sylwester Chęciński's film *Sami swoi*.

The imposing outline of Czoch Castle in Sucha

⑫ The Foothills of the Karkonosze Mountains

The Karkonosze Mountains, the highest in the Sudeten (Sudety) chain, draw holiday-makers all year round. There are many footpaths and good facilities for hikers throughout the summer, while in winter skiers come to enjoy the exhilarating pistes. The upper parts of the Karkonosze Mountains are a national park, recognized by UNESCO as a World Biosphere Reserve.

In the lower parts of the mountains are several attractive small towns, such as Karpacz and Szklarska Poręba, as well as Cieplice and Sobieszów in Jelenia Góra district *(see p190)*.

① Cieplice
This popular spa town has a number of fine Baroque buildings, including Schaffgotsch Palace and its Cistercian and Protestant churches. There is also a natural history museum.

② Szklarka Waterfall
A forest of fir trees provides a scenic setting for the 15-m (45-ft) waterfall.

Jakuszyce ← E 65 ③ ②

Piechowice

Szklarka

③ Szklarska Poręba
This health resort is a good starting point for excursions into the Karkonosze Mountains. It is also famous for its glassworks – handmade crystal artifacts are available in local kiosks.

④ Jagniątków
A picturesque villa was built here by the Nobel Prize-winning author Gerhart Hauptmann for his second wife in 1900–02. It now houses a gallery of paintings illustrating scenes from Hauptmann's works.

⑥ Miłków
A Baroque palace and church surrounded by stone walls covered in penitentiary crosses are the main attractions of this village.

⑤ Sobieszów: Chojnik Castle
Situated on a high escarpment, this 14th-century castle was built for Duke Bolko II. In the 15th and 16th centuries it was renovated by the Schaffgotsch family, but in 1675 was gutted by a fire after being struck by lightning.

⑧ Mysłakowice

The village is noted for its Neo-Gothic palace, which once belonged to Kaiser Friedrich Wilhelm IV, for a church designed by Karl Friedrich Schinkel, and for Tyrolean-style houses built by religious refugees fleeing persecution in the Tyrol.

Tips for Drivers

Tour length: About 70 km (46 miles).

Stopping-off points: Bars and restaurants can be found in Szklarska Poręba, Cieplice and Karpacz. The Spiż restaurant in Miłków is recommended.

Other attractions: Karpacz also has a chair lift to Kopa, which is one hour's walk from Mt Śnieżka. Another chair lift from Szklarska Poręba goes to Szrenica.

Key

■ Scenic route
■ Other road

| 0 Kilometres | 5 |
| 0 miles | 5 |

⑦ Karpacz

The buildings of this popular health resort are concentrated along a single street 7 km (4.5 miles) long. The wooden Romanesque church here was brought from Vang, in Norway, in 1842–4.

Interior of the Cistercian Church of St Mary in Krzeszów

⑬ Krzeszów

Road map B5. ▲ 1,300. 🚐 Kamienna Góra. 🚍 Church of St Mary, Church of St Joseph: and Mausoleum of the Silesian Piasts: **Tel** 75 742 32 /9. **Open** May–Oct: 8am–6pm daily; Nov–Apr: 8am 1pm daily). 🚫 📷

This tiny village in the Góry Kamienne Mountains has one of the most picturesque groups of historic buildings in Poland. Benedictine monks settled here in 1242, followed by Cistercian monks in 1292. They were responsible for building the Church of St Joseph (Kościół św. Józefa), which has frescoes by Michael Willmann, in 1690–96. They also built the abbey **Church of St Mary** (Kościół NMP Łaskawej) in 1727–35. The interior is decorated with vertiginous trompe l'oeil paintings by Georg Wilhelm Neunhertz; sculptures by Anton Dorazil and Ferdinand Maximilian Brokoff make the pilasters, cornices and vaulting appear to float in mid-air. The figures of saints on the stalls in the chancel are of particular interest.

Behind the presbytery is the **Mausoleum of the Silesian Piasts** (Mauzoleum Piastów Śląskich), with the Gothic tombs of Bolko I (d. 1301) and Bolko II (d. 1368), dukes of Świdnica-Jawor. Figures of their wives, Agnieszka and Beatrycze, stand opposite the tombs. On the wall is an epitaph by the son of Bolko II, the last member of the Piast dynasty.

For keys to symbols see back flap

Arcaded houses around the Market Square in Jelenia Góra

⓮ Jelenia Góra

Road map B4. 🏔 80,800. 🚍 🚌
ℹ️ pl. Ratuszowy 6/7 (519 509 343).
Open Jun–Sep: 8am–8pm daily; Oct–May: 9am–7pm daily. 🎭 Cieplice Spring (May); International Street Theatre Festival (Jul); Jelenia Góra (Aug). 🖥 jeleniagora.pl

Situated at the foot of the Karkonosze Mountains, Jelenia Góra is a favourite tourist destination and a major starting point for mountain hikers. The town was granted city status at the end of the 13th century. It was once renowned for its textiles – delicate batiste and voile that were exported as far as Africa and America. It was also one of the main centres of engraved glassware, examples of which can be seen in the **Regional Museum**.

Silesian glassware

The town's historic centre is the Market Square, with a Baroque town hall surrounded by arcaded town houses. In Ulica Maria Konopnicka, east of the Market Square, is the **Church of Saints Erasmus and Pancras** (Kościół św. Erazma i Pankracego), a Gothic basilica of the late 14th to early 15th centuries. The line of the old defensive walls here is marked by a chapel that was once a keep.

In Ulica 1 Maja, on the same axis, is the Church of Our Lady, with two penitentiary crosses set into the outer walls. The street then leads to the Baroque former Protestant **Church of the Holy Cross** (Kościół św. Krzyża),

known also as the Church of Peace.

The town boundaries of Jelenia Góra were expanded in 1976 and now include the spa of Cieplice, with its **Natural History Museum**, and the town of Sobieszów (*see p188*), which includes the **Karkonosze National Park Ecological Education Centre**.

🏛 Church of Saints Erasmus and Pancras

pl. Kościelny 1–2.
Tel 75 752 21 60.
This Gothic basilica of the first half of the 14th century features late Gothic vaulting dating from about 1550 and a Baroque altar depicting the Transfiguration.

🏛 Church of the Holy Cross

ul. 1 Maja 45. **Tel** 75 642 32 82.
This church (Kościół św. Krzyża), built by Martin Franze in 1709–18, is modelled on St Catherine's in Stockholm. A triple tier of galleries lines the interior and frescoes by Felix Anton Scheffler and Jozef Franz Hoffman cover the ceilings. The altar, which is structurally integrated with the organ loft, is particularly striking.

🏛 Regional Museum

ul. Matejki 28. **Tel** 75 752 34 65.
Open 9am–5pm Tue–Sun (Nov–Mar: to 4pm). 🏛 (free on Wed).
🖥 muzeumkarkonoskie.pl
Jelenia Góra's Regional Museum contains the largest collection of decorative glassware in the whole of Poland. A traditional Karkonosze hut nearby houses an ethnographical exhibition.

🏛 Karkanosze National Park Ecological Education Centre

Szklarska Poręba ul. Okrzei 28. **Tel** 75 717 21 24. **Open** Jan–Jun, Sep & Oct: 9am–4pm daily; Jul & Aug: 9am–5pm daily; Dec: 9am–3pm daily.

🏛 Natural History Museum

Jelenia Góra – Cieplice, ul. Cieplicka 11a. **Tel** 75 755 15 06. **Open** May–Sep: 9am–6pm Tue–Fri, 9am–5pm Sat, Sun; Oct–Apr: 9am–4pm Tue–Sun.
🏛 🖥 muzeum-cieplice.pl

⓯ Bolków

Road map B4. 🏔 5,100. 🚍 🚌

The great towering **Castle of the Dukes of Świdnica-Jawor** is the main feature of this small town. It was built in stages from the mid-13th to the mid-14th century. Sacked and destroyed several times, in the 16th century it was rebuilt in the Renaissance style by Jakob Paar. Today the castle is a local history **museum**. The Gothic Church of St Jadwiga (Kościół św. Jadwigi) is also worth a visit. In the old town, several fine houses survive.

🏛 Castle Museum

ul. Zamkowa 1. **Tel** 75 741 32 97.
Open May–Oct: 9am–4:30pm Tue–Fri, 9am–5:30pm Sat & Sun; Nov–Apr: closes 1 hr earlier. **Closed** public hols
🏛 (free on Mon).

Environs

In **Świny**, 2 km (1.25 miles) north of Bolków, are the haunting ruins of a castle. The upper part was built in the 14th century. The lower wing is a 17th-century late Baroque palace.

The crenellated tower of Bolków Castle

⑯ Książ

Road map B5. Castle Wałbrzych, ul. Piastów Śl. **Tel** 74 664 38 34.
Open Apr–Sep: 10am–5pm daily (to 6pm Sat & Sun); Oct–Mar: 10am–3pm Tue–Fri, 10am–4pm Sat & Sun. 🏛 Palm House Wałbrzych-Lubiechowo, ul. Wrocławska 158.
Open Apr: 10am– 5pm Tue–Sun; May–Sep: 10am–5pm daily; Oct: 10am–4pm Tue–Sun; Nov–Mar: 10am–3pm Tue–Fri, 10am–4pm Sat & Sun. 🏞 🅲 🆆 ksiaz.walbrzych.pl

Książ Castle, on the outskirts of Wałbrzych, is the largest residential building in Silesia. This huge edifice was built on a rocky hilltop overlooking the surrounding wooded countryside. The late 13th-century Gothic **castle** of Prince Bolko I was rebuilt in the mid-16th century for the Hochberg family of Meissen, who remained its owners until World War II. One of the most powerful Silesian families, they extended the building several times, particularly in 1670–1724 and 1909–23. The Hochbergs' reputation was coloured by several scandals. The penultimate owner of the castle was Hans Henry XV von Pless. After divorcing his wife, he married a much younger Spanish woman. She gave birth to a daughter, but then left the elderly prince for his son Bolko.

During World War II attempts were made to convert the castle into headquarters for Adolf Hitler by drilling tunnels into the rocky hill. Today part of the castle houses a museum, a hotel and a restaurant. The grounds are now the **Książ Nature Park**. The stables and palm house, still in use, are open to visitors.

High altar in the Cathedral of Saints Stanisław and Wenceslas

⑰ Świdnica

Road map B4. 🚐 58,000. 🚉 🚌 🆆 swidnica.pl

For almost 100 years from 1292, Świdnica was the capital of the independent duchy of Świdnica-Jawor. It minted its own coins and was renowned for its beer, which was exported to many cities in Central Europe. The town's mercantile traditions are well illustrated in the **Museum of Silesian Trade** that is housed in the town hall.

From the pretty market square, with its fine Baroque plague column *(see p183)*, Ulica Długa, the main street, leads to the 14th-century **Cathedral of Saints Stanisław and Wenceslas** (Katedra św. Stanisława i Wacława), a Gothic building with the highest tower in Silesia. The interior is richly furnished and decorated in styles ranging from Gothic to Baroque. The altar canopy was made by Johann Riedl in 1694. The town's most impressive

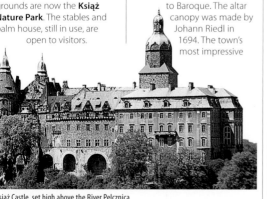

Książ Castle, set high above the River Pełcznica

building, however, is the **Church of Peace** (Kościół Pokoju). With that in Jawor *(see p186)*, it is one of two surviving Protestant "peace churches" built after the Peace of Westphalia that ended the Thirty Years' War (1618–48). The timber-framed church, designed by Albrecht von Säbisch, was built in 1656–7. Its undistinguished exterior conceals an unusual interior, with a two-tiered gallery, fine paintings and furnishings.

🔼 **Cathedral of Saints Stanisław and Wenceslas**
pl. Jana Pawła II. **Tel** 530 853 425.
Open 10am–5:45pm daily. 🅲

🔼 **Church of Peace**
pl. Pokoju 6. **Tel** 74 852 28 14. **Open** Apr–Oct: 9am–1pm and 3–6pm daily (Sun: pm only); Nov–Mar: call first.

🏛 **Museum of Silesian Trade**
Rynek 37. **Tel** 74 852 12 91. **Open** May–Sep: 10am–5pm Tue–Fri, 11am–5pm Sat & Sun; Oct–Apr: 10am–4pm Tue–Fri, 11am–5pm Sat & Sun. 🏞

Environs
Jaworzyna, 10 km (6 miles) northwest of Świdnica, has Poland's largest museum of steam locomotives.

Penitentiary cross in Łaziska, Upper Silesia

Penitentiary Crosses

As a form of punishment, criminals in the Middle Ages sometimes had to make a stone cross and place it at the scene of their crime or near a church. Depictions of the implement used to carry out the deed (such as a crossbow) or a part of the victim's body (such as the feet) were engraved on the cross.

Renaissance gate of Grodno Castle in Zagórze Śląskie

⑱ Zagórze Śląskie

Road map B5. 🚗 430. 🚌 🚆

The main attraction in this small village is **Grodno Castle**. Built by Bolko I at the end of the 13th century, it was altered by later owners and then fell into ruin, but was saved by major restoration work in 1907–29.

Today the castle houses a museum, whose more curious exhibits include the skeleton of a young woman. For the murder of her husband, she was condemned to death by starvation by her own father.

🏰 Grodno Castle

Tel 74 845 33 60. **Open** May–Sep: 9am–6pm daily (to 7pm Sat & Sun); Oct–Apr: 9am–5pm daily (to 6pm Sat & Sun). **Closed** Easter, 1 Nov, 24 & 25 Dec.

Environs

A few kilometres south of Zagórze Śląskie are underground **tunnels** dug secretly in the final year of World War II by prisoners of the Gross-Rosen (Rogoźnica) concentration camp.

🚇 Osowiec Tunnels (Sztolnie w Osówce)

Tel 74 845 62 20. **Open** 10am–6pm daily (Nov–Mar: to 4pm). **Closed** 1 Nov, 24, 25, 31 Dec. 🈂 🅿 **W** osowka.pl

🚇 Walim Tunnels (Sztolnie w Walimiu)

Tel 74 845 73 00. **Open** May–Sep: 9am–5pm Mon–Fri, 9am–6pm Sat, Sun; Oct–Apr: 9am–4pm Mon–Fri, 9am–5pm Sat, Sun. **W** sztolnie.pl

⑲ Mt Ślęża

Road map B4.

Mt Ślęża is a conical peak visible from great distances all around. Used as a location for religious rituals during the Bronze Age (3500–1500 BC), it is crowned with a stone circle, and mysterious statues of unknown origin stand beside the road leading to the summit. The best view of the surrounding countryside is from the terrace of the Neo-Romanesque **church** built on Mt Ślęża in 1851–2. The hill of neighbouring **Wieżyca** has at its summit a tower erected in honour of the German statesman Otto von Bismarck in 1906–7, and is also a good vantage point from which to view the entire area.

In Sobótka, at the foot of Mt Ślęża, a former hospital built by Augustinian monks houses the **Ślęża Museum**. The best place to stay, or stop for lunch, is the hotel Zamek Górka, located in a Gothic-Renaissance Augustinian presbytery that later became the palace of the von Kulmiz family.

🏛 Ślęża Museum

Sobótka, ul. św. Jakuba 18. **Tel** 71 316 26 22. **Open** 9am–4pm Wed–Sun and last Tue in the month.

⑳ Wojnowice

Road map B4. 🚗 400. 🚌 🚆
Mrozów. **Tel** 71 317 07 26. **Open** call in advance. **W** zamekwojnowice.pl

Wojnowice presents a rare opportunity to see a genuine and well-preserved Silesian Renaissance **manor house**. It was built in the early 16th century for Nikolaus von Scheibitz and soon after was acquired by the Boner family, who converted it into a Renaissance castle with a small arcaded courtyard. Compact and moated, it is now a hotel, with an excellent restaurant. It is a superb place for a short break.

Moated Renaissance manor house in Wojnowice

㉑ Trzebnica

Road map C4. 🚗 13,161. 🚆
Oborniki Śląskie. 🚌 **W** trzebnica.pl

In 1203 Jadwiga, wife of Henry I, brought an order of Cistercian monks from Bamberg, in southern Germany, to Trzebnica. Jadwiga was buried here and, after her canonization in 1267, the monastery became an important place of pilgrimage. The entire complex underwent major rebuilding in the second half of the 1600s, obliterating its Romanesque architecture, although the tympanum of the main portal retains a fine relief of around 1230 representing the

Country track in Ślęża

Old Testament figures David and Bathsheba. The Gothic chapel of St Jadwiga contains her Baroque-style tomb, dating from 1677–8. The figure of the saint was carved by Franz Josef Mangoldt in 1750.

Coronation of the Virgin in the portal of the Chapel of St Jadwiga, Trzebnica

㉒ Oleśnica

Road map C4. ㊐ 37,400. ☒ ☒
ⓦ olesnica.pl

The most impressive building in the town is the **Castle of the Dukes of Oleśnica**. While the Gothic interior is original, the exterior, with its circular corner tower, is the result of successive stages of rebuilding from 1542 to 1610 by the Italian architects Francesco Parr and Bernardo Niuron. The castle retains ornamental gables in the attic rooms in the wings and the unusual galleries supported on brackets overlooking the courtyard. Attached to the castle is the **palace** of Jan Podiebrad, built in 1559–63.

A pleasant way of rounding off a visit to Oleśnica is to walk through the old quarter to the Gothic **Church of St John the Evangelist** (Kościół św. Jana Ewangelisty). Beside the presbytery is a chapel built in memory of the dukes of Wurtemberg, and containing the tombs of Jan and Jerzy Podiebrad. Other elements include the Mannerist pulpit and the Gothic stalls from the late 15th and early 16th centuries. Remnants of castle walls, with the tower of the Wrocławski Gate, and the Neo-Classical town hall, rebuilt after World War II, are other features of interest.

🏰 **Castle of the Dukes of Oleśnica**
Tel 605 356 193. **Open** daily.

㉓ Wrocław

See pp194–203.

㉔ Brzeg

Road map C5. ㊐ 36,800. ☒ ☒
ⓦ brzeg.pl

The attractive town of Brzeg, on the River Odra, has an illustrious history. It received its charter in 1245, and from 1311 to 1675 was the capital of the duchy of Legnica-Brzeg. The town's most impressive building is without doubt

Renaissance sculpture on the gate tower of Brzeg Castle

the **Castle of the Dukes of Legnica-Brzeg**. It was built originally in the Gothic style and a 14th century Gothic chapel survives, in whose presbytery a mausoleum to the Silesian Piasts was built in 1567. The castle was transformed into a Renaissance palace in the second half of the 16th century. The three-winged complex features a circular courtyard and a tower over the entrance gate dating from 1554. The walls are decorated with busts of all the ancestors of Duke Jerzy II and his wife Barbara von Brandenburg. Today the castle houses the **Museum of the Silesian Piasts**.

Other buildings of interest are the **town hall**, erected in 1570–7, the 14th-century **Church of St Nicholas** (Kościół św. Mikołaja) and the late Baroque Jesuit church, which was built in 1734–9.

🏛 **Museum of the Silesian Piasts**
pl. Zamkowy 1. **Tel** 77 416 32 57.
Open 10am–5pm Tue–Sun (last adm 4pm). ♿ 📷

Environs

A few kilometres from Brzeg is the small village of Małujowice, or Mollwitz, where on 10 April 1741 a major battle was fought in the Austro-Prussian war. The Gothic church there contains unusual 14th-century frescoes and Renaissance ceilings.

Courtyard of the Castle of the Dukes of Oleśnica

㉓ Wrocław

The city of Wrocław bears the stamp of several cultures. It was founded by a Czech duke in the 10th century and a Polish bishopric was established here in 1000. Later it became the capital of the duchy of Silesian Piasts, and then came under Czech rule in 1335. In 1526, with the whole Czech state, it was incorporated into the Habsburg Empire, and in 1741 was transferred to Prussian rule. The fierce defence that German forces put up here in the last months of World War II left almost three-quarters of the city in ruins. However, reconstruction has largely healed the ravages of the past.

Baroque pietą in the Church of the Holy Name of Jesus

🏛 Wrocław University

pl. Uniwersytecki 1. Aula Leopoldina:
Tel 71 375 26 18. **Open** 10am–4pm Mon, Tue & Thu, 10am–5pm Fri–Sun.
📷 W uni.wroc.pl

Wrocław University was established as an academy by Emperor Leopold I in 1702 and in 1811 became a university. Many of its alumni have gained renown. They include nine Nobel laureates, among them the nuclear physicist Max Born (1882–1970). Since 1945 it has been a Polish centre of learning and university.

Designed by Tausch, an Italian architect, painter and philosopher, the centrepiece of this imposing Baroque building is the assembly hall, the Aula Leopoldina, of 1728–32. It is adorned with frescoes by Christopha Handk, figural sculptures by Franz Joseph Mangoldt and Italian master Ignazio Provisore's stucco and marble sculptures.

The richly ornamented interior of the university assembly hall

For hotels and restaurants see pp303–4 and pp314–15

Central Wrocław

① Wrocław University
② Church of the Holy Name of Jesus
③ Plac Biskupa Nankera
④ National Museum
⑤ Panorama of Racławice
⑥ Bernadine Church and Monastery
⑦ Cathedral of St Mary Magdalene
⑧ Kameleon Store
⑨ Market Square
⑩ Town Hall
⑪ Church of St Elizabeth
⑫ Royal Palace
⑬ Church of Saints Wenceslas, Stanisław and Dorothy

🔒 Church of the Holy Name of Jesus

pl. Uniwersytecki 1. **Tel** 71 344 94 23.
Open Mar–Jun, Sep & Oct: 11am–
3:30pm; Jul & Aug: 10:30am–5:30pm.
Closed during services.

This church (Kościół Najświętszego Imienia Jezus), erected for the Jesuits in 1689–98, is an example of Silesian Baroque church architecture. The fine interior was built in 1722–34 by Tausch and vaulting was decorated by Viennese artist Rottmayer in 1704–6.

The Baroque Hochberg Chapel beside the Church of St Vincent

17th-century paintings, including works by the Silesian artist Michael Willmann (1630–1706) and wooden sculptures by Thomas Weissfeldt (1630–1712). The second floor is devoted to works by contemporary Polish artists.

Façade of the National Museum

📍 Plac Biskupa Nankera

The buildings in this square date from various periods. The Gothic **Church of St Vincent** (Kościół św. Wincentego), at No. 5, was erected in the 13th to the 15th centuries. The late 17th-century Baroque monastery is now part of the University of Wrocław.

The group of Baroque monastic buildings at No. 16 encloses the small 13th-century **Church of St Clare** (Kościół św. Klary). The church was used by

the Piasts as a mausoleum, and it still contains Gothic ducal tombs. Next door, at No. 17, is the Gothic **Church of St Maciej** (Kościół św. Macieja), which dates from the 14th and early 15th centuries and was once owned by the Knights Hospitallers of the Red Star. The pavilion of the gallery at No. 8, on the opposite side of the street, contains 13th-century walls of the **House of the Nuns of Trebnica**, the oldest surviving secular building in the city.

🏛️ National Museum

pl. Powstańców Warszawy 5. **Tel** 71 372 51 50. **Open** Apr–Sep: 10am–5pm Tue–Fri, 10am–6pm Sat & Sun; Oct–Mar: 10am–4pm Tue–Fri, 10am–5pm Sat & Sun. 🎫 🅰️ (free on Sat, limited availability). 🌐 mnwr.art.pl

The ground floor contains examples of Silesian and Gothic art, including the tombstone of Henry IV, the Good, dating from 1300. The first floor has a collection of 16th- and

🖼️ Panorama of Racławice

ul. Purkyniego 11. **Tel** 71 344 16 61.
Open 9am–4pm Tue–Sun (summer: to 5pm daily). **Closed** see the website for details. 🎫 (buy tickets online).
🅰️ 🌐 panoramaraclawicka.pl

This painting depicts the Battle of Racławice of 4 April 1794, when the Poles defeated the Russians. It is 114 m (374 ft) long and 15 m (46 ft) high and took the artists Jan Styka and Wojciech Kossak nine months to paint. Unveiled in 1894 in Lviv, in Ukraine, it was brought to Poland in 1946 and put on display in Wrocław in 1985.

Rotunda containing the Panorama of Racławice

Wrocław Old Town

For those who enjoy exploring on foot, the old town of Wrocław is a delightful place. The restored buildings located around the large Market Square have been given over to an assortment of bars, restaurants and cafés with al fresco seating, while the churches nearby contain a wealth of religious art and ecclesiastical furnishings. The impressive Gothic town hall has a finely decorated interior.

On summer evenings, the Market Square in the old town comes alive as local people and tourists alike gather there, some to gossip and exchange news, others to attend the concerts and many cultural events that are held there.

Detail of the ornamental façade of the House of the Seven Electors

Late Gothic portal of the Bernadine church

🏛 Bernadine Church and Monastery

ul. Bernardyńska 5. Museum of Architecture: **Tel** 71 344 82 79. **Open** 11am–5pm Tue–Sun (noon–7pm Thu). 🎟 (half-price Mon, free on Wed). 🌐 ma.wroc.pl

This impressive group of monastic buildings (Kościół i Klasztor pobernardyński) was constructed by Bernadine monks in 1463–1502. Having been rebuilt from their wartime ruins, they now house Poland's only Museum of Architecture. The monastery is of interest for its late Gothic cloisters and the Church of St Bernard of Siena, a towering Gothic basilica with a typically Baroque gable.

🏛 Cathedral of St Mary Magdalene

ul. Oławska 19. **Tel** 71 344 19 04. **Open** 9am–noon, 4–6pm daily.

The great Gothic Cathedral of St Mary Magdalene (Katedra św Marii Magdaleny) was erected between about 1330

and the mid-15th century, incorporating the walls of a 13th-century church that had previously stood on the site. Inside the basilica is a Renaissance pulpit of 1579–81 by Friedrich Gross, a Gothic stone tabernacle and tombstones of various periods. The portal on the north side is a fine example of late 12th-century Romanesque sculpture. It was taken from a demolished Benedictine monastery in Olbina and added in 1546 *(see p26)*. The tympanum, depicting the Dormition of the Virgin, is now on display in the National Museum.

Detail of the Cathedral of St Mary Magdalene

🏢 Kameleon Store

ul. Szewska 6.

The Kameleon store (Dom Handlowy Kameleon) is an unusual building on the corner of Ulica Szewska and Ulica Oławska. Its semicircular bay, formed by rows of windows, juts out dramatically. It was built by the German architect Erich Mendelsohn as a retail store for Rudolf Petersdorf in 1927–8. Nearby, at the intersection of Ulica Łaciarskiej and Ofiar Oświęcimskich, is another interesting example of Modernist architecture, an

office building of 1912–13 by an equally renowned architect, Hans Poelzig.

🏢 Market Square

Rynek.

Wrocław's Market Square is the second-largest in Poland, after that in Krakow. In the centre stand the town hall and a group of buildings separated by alleys. The houses around the square date from the Renaissance to the 20th century. Some still have their original 14th- and 15th-century Gothic vaults. The most attractive side of the square is the west, which features the late Baroque **House of the Golden Sun**, at No. 6, built in 1727 by Johann Lucas von Hildebrandt, as well as the **House of the Seven Electors**, its paintwork dating from 1672. Also to the south is the Griffin House, at No. 2, built in 1587–9. It has a galleried interior courtyard. On the east side, at Nos. 31 and 32, is the Art Nouveau **Phoenix store** of 1904 and, at No. 41, the **Golden Hound**, a rebuilt town house of 1713. The north side was rebuilt after World War II. Just off the corner of the market square, fronting the Church of St Elizabeth (Kościół św. Elżbiety), are two small acolytes' houses, the Renaissance Jaś, of around 1564, and the 18th-century Baroque Małgosia.

🏛 Town Hall

ul. Sukiennice 14/15.
Historical Museum: ul. Kazimierza
Wielkiego 35. **Tel** 71 391 69 40.
Open 10am–5pm Tue–Fri, 10am–
6pm Sat & Sun.
Rynek Stary Ratusz Museum of
Bourgeois Art: **Tel** 71 347 16 91.
Open 11am–5pm Wed–Sat,
10am–6pm Sun. **W** mmw.pl

The town hall in Wrocław is one
of the most important examples
of Gothic architecture in Central
and Eastern Europe. Its present
appearance is the result of an
extensive period of rebuilding
that took place between 1470
and 1510.

The town hall's southern
façade was embellished with
Neo-Gothic stone carvings
in around 1871. Inside are
impressive vaulted halls, the
largest being the triple-aisled
Grand Hall on the ground
floor, and several late Gothic
and Renaissance doorways.

Outside the entrance to
the town hall is a plaque
commemorating the prom-
inent poet and comedy writer
Aleksander Fredro (1793–
1876), who acquired fame
with his comedies about
the Polish upper classes. The
plaque was made in 1879
by Leonard Marconi and
transferred to Wrocław from
Lviv in 1956 (see p31).

Gothic gables of the east façade of the
town hall

🏛 Church of St Elizabeth

ul. św. Elżbiety. **Tel** 71 343 16 38.
The large tower dominating
the market square is that of the
Church of St Elizabeth (Kościół
św. Elżbiety), one of the largest

churches in Wrocław. The Gothic
basilica was built in the 14th
century on the site of an earlier
church, although the tower
was not completed until 1482.
It became a Protestant church
in 1525. Since 1946 it has been
a garrison church.

The church has suffered
damage from a succession of
wars, fires and accidents. A fire
in 1976 destroyed the roof
and the splendid Baroque
organ. Fortunately, more
than 350 epitaphs and tombstones have survived, forming
a remarkable exhibition of
Silesian stone-carving from
Gothic to Neo-Classical times.

Church of St Elizabeth with Jaś and
Małgosia, acolytes' houses

🏛 Royal Palace

ul. Kazimierza Wielkiego 34/35.
Ethnographical Museum:
ul. Traugutta 111/113. **Tel** 71 344
33 13. **Open** 10am–4pm Tue–Sun.
(free on Sat). **W** muzeum
etnograficzne.pl Archaeological
Museum: ul. Cieszyńskiego 9.
Tel 71 347 16 96. **Open** 10am–5pm
Wed–Sat, 10am–6pm Sun.

The Baroque palace, enclosed
by a court of annexes,
was built in 1719. After
1750, when Wrocław came
under Prussian rule, it was
a residence for the Prussian
kings. On the side facing
Plac Wolności, only a side
gallery remains of the Neo-
Renaissance palace built in
1843–6.

The Royal Palace contains
two interesting collections:
the Archaeological Museum
and the Ethnographical
Museum, the latter illustrating
Silesian folk history and art.

The Church of Saints Wenceslas, Stanisław
and Dorothy

🏛 Church of Saints Wenceslas, Stanisław and Dorothy

Plac Wolności 3. **Tel** 71 343 27 21.
Dedicated to three saints, the
Czech St Wenceslas, the Polish
St Stanisław and the German
St Dorothy, this church (Kościół
św. Wacława, Stanisława i
Doroty) was built in 1351 to
cement relations between the
three nationalities in Wrocław.
The church's unusually narrow
interior is Baroque. The Rococo
tombstone of Gottfried von
Spaetgen stands in the nave.

Ossolineum

The National Ossoliński
Institute was founded by
Count Józef Maksymilian
Ossoliński in Vienna in 1817.
In 1827 it moved to Lwów
(later Lviv), where it
assembled collections of
manuscripts, prints, etchings
and drawings, promoted
scientific research and
engaged in publishing.
After World War II most
of the collections were
transferred to the National
Museum in Wrocław, while
the manuscripts were
housed in the Baroque
monastery of the Knights
Hospitallers of the Red Star.

The Baroque monastery that houses
the Ossolineum

Ostrów Tumski and Piasek Island

Ostrów Tumski was once an island in the River Odra, and it is here that the history of Wrocław began. According to legend, the city was founded by Duke Vratislav of Bohemia. In the year 1000 a bishopric was established and the island grew into a centre of ducal power. After the city moved to the left bank of the Odra in 1292, the island remained the base of ecclesiastical authority. In the 19th century the northern arm of the Odra was filled in and Tumski ceased to be an island. Tumski Bridge connects it to Piasek Island, a small sandbank that since the first half of the 12th century has been the location of a monastery for canons regular.

Church of the Holy Cross (Kościół św. Krzyża)
This Gothic church is set on two levels. The upper church is reached via a portal enclosed by a double arch.

Church of St Martin

Tumski Bridge
The present bridge was built in 1888–92. The figures of St Jadwiga and St John the Baptist guarding it are by Gustav Grunenberg.

MOST MŁYŃSKI

ŚW. MARCINA

ŚW. JADWIGI

★ **Church of St Mary on Piasek (Kościół NMP na Piasku)**
The interior of the church was restored after World War II.

Key
— Suggested route

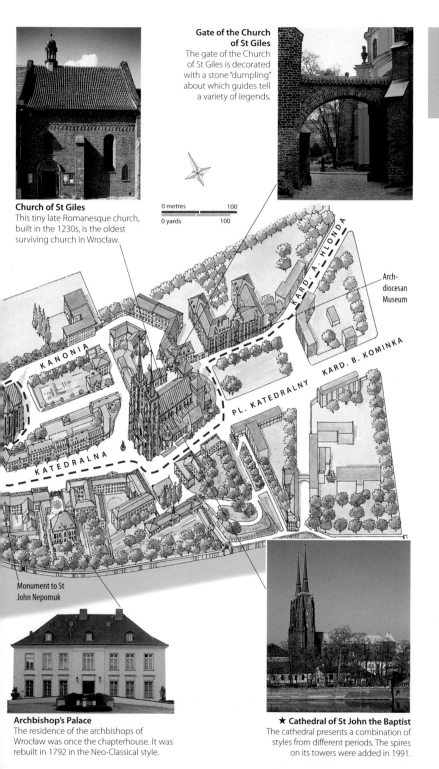

Gate of the Church of St Giles
The gate of the Church of St Giles is decorated with a stone "dumpling" about which guides tell a variety of legends.

Church of St Giles
This tiny late Romanesque church, built in the 1230s, is the oldest surviving church in Wrocław.

0 metres 100
0 yards 100

KANONIA

KATEDRALNA

KARD. A. HLONDA

Arch-
diocesan
Museum

KARD. B. KOMINKA

PL. KATEDRALNY

Monument to St
John Nepomuk

Archbishop's Palace
The residence of the archbishops of Wrocław was once the chapterhouse. It was rebuilt in 1792 in the Neo-Classical style.

★ **Cathedral of St John the Baptist**
The cathedral presents a combination of styles from different periods. The spires on its towers were added in 1991.

Exploring Ostrów Tumski and Piasek Island

Wrocław's islands, bathed by the River Odra, are peaceful places for a stroll away from the bustle of the city. The cathedral, the islands' principal landmark, preserves its valuable interior despite having suffered the ravages of World War II. The Archdiocesan Museum is a rich repository of Gothic art. A walk through the islands' many narrow streets and alleys can be followed by a visit to the Botanical Gardens.

The Gothic Church of the Holy Cross, built on two levels

Gothic portal of the Church of St Mary on Piasek

⛪ Church of St Mary on Piasek
ul. Najświętszej Marii Panny 1.

The rather forbidding bulk of the Church of St Mary on Piasek (Kościół NMP na Piasku) dominates Piasek Island. The church was constructed for canons regular in the second half of the 14th century on the site of a 12th-century Romanesque building whose tympanum is built into the wall over the sacristy in the south aisle.

The Church of St Mary suffered extensive damage in World War II, but some impressive features survive. The asymmetrical tripartite rib vaulting over the aisles is unusual. The church also houses a fine collection of Gothic altars brought here from other churches in Silesia.

⛪ Church of St Martin
ul. św. Marcina 7.

The first ecclesiastical building raised on the site now occupied by the Church of St Martin (Kościół św. Marcina) was a stronghold chapel erected at

the turn of the 11th century. The present church dates from the late 13th century but was rebuilt after World War II because it had suffered major damage. The present building consists of an octagonal nave and an unfinished presbytery.

⛪ Church of the Holy Cross
pl. Kościelny. **Tel** 71 322 25 74.

The two-tiered Church of the Holy Cross (Kościół św. Krzyża) was established in 1288 by Henry IV, the Pious. Building continued in the 14th century, and the south tower was not completed until 1484. The lower church has been used by Uniates since 1956. The upper church, a narrow nave with a transept, was badly damaged during World War II, when most of its interior fittings were lost. The tombstone dedicated to the church's founder has been moved to the National Museum, but the original tympanum, depicting the ducal couple admiring the heavenly Throne of Grace, can be seen in the north aisle. The 15th-century triptych over the high altar comes from a church in Świny.

⛪ Archbishop's Palace
ul. Katedralna 11. **Closed** to visitors.

The present archbishop's residence, once the home of the canons of the cathedral, is a relatively plain building that was reconstructed from a more splendid Baroque edifice in 1792. The old bishop's palace, which stands at Ulica Katedralna 15 nearby, is a fine Neo-Classical building dating from the second half of the 18th century, although three 13th-century wings from the earlier palace remain.

⛪ Cathedral of St John the Baptist
pl. Katedralny. **Tel** 71 322 25 74.
Open daily. Tower: **Open** Jan–Apr: noon–4pm Tue–Sat; Jun–Sep: 10am–5:30pm Mon–Sat, 2–5:30pm Sun; Oct–Dec: noon–4:30pm Mon, 10am–4:30pm Tue–Sat, 2–4pm Sun. **Closed** during services.

The Cathedral of St John the Baptist (Archikatedra św. Jana Chrzciciela) presents a combination of styles from

Ulica Katedralna, with the Cathedral of St John the Baptist

Portal of the Cathedral of St John the Baptist on Ostrów Tumski

The Bridges of Wrocław

Situated on the River Odra, the city of Wrocław boasts more than 100 bridges crossing numerous streams, canals and inlets. The oldest is the Piasek Island bridge, dating from 1845. The best known is Grunwaldzki Suspension Bridge, dating from 1908–10, which under German rule was named the Kaiserbrücke.

Grunwaldzki Suspension Bridge

different periods. The presbytery was built some time between 1244 and 1272; the basilica was built in the first half of the 14th century and the west tower was completed even later. Three-quarters of the cathedral were destroyed in World War II, and most of the present building is the result of post-war reconstruction. The east end, with its interesting chapels accessible from the presbytery, survives in its original form. The Chapel of St Elizabeth in the south aisle was built in the Roman Baroque style by Giacomo Scianzi in 1680. The interior of the chapel is also the work of Italian artists: the tomb of Cardinal Frederyk, a Hessian landowner whose burial chapel this became, is by Domenico Guidi. The altar is by Ercole Ferrata.

The presbytery contains a late Gothic polyptych of 1522, which was brought from Lubin, and Baroque choir stalls from a church of the Premonstratensian order.

🏛 Archdiocesan Museum

ul. Kanonia 12. **Tel** 71 322 17 55. **Open** 9am–3pm Tue–Sat.

The Archdiocesan Museum (Muzeum Archidiecezjalne) stands among a group of buildings dating from three historical periods. The earliest is the Gothic-Renaissance chapterhouse built in 1519–27, which has fine portals and arcades. The later Baroque chapterhouse was completed in 1756. The purpose-built Neo-Gothic museum, libraries and archives of the archdiocese were built in 1896. The museum contains an important and growing collection of Silesian religious art going back to the Gothic period. In addition to altars and sculptures, it has on display one of the earliest cabinets in the world, dating from 1455.

Archdiocesan Museum on Ostrów Tumski

🌿 Botanical Gardens

ul. H. Sienkiewicza 23. **Tel** 71 322 59 57. **Open** Apr–Nov: 8am–6pm daily (May–Aug: to 8pm). 🅿 🅦 ogrod botaniczny.wroclaw.pl

Wrocław boasts the most attractive botanical gardens in Poland. They were established in 1811 by two professors from the University of Silesia in Katowice, and after being totally destroyed in World War II were reverently re-created. The gardens' central area contains picturesque ponds fashioned from what was an arm of the River Odra when Ostrów Tumski was still an island. There are also palms, an alpine garden, cactuses, fountains, bridges and a 19th-century model of the geology of the Silesian town of Wałbrzych. The gardens have 7,000 plant species and a bust of the Swedish botanist Carolus Linnaeus (1708–78), dating from 1871, stands among the greenery. A branch of the gardens, which has an extensive arboretum, has been established in Wojsławice, near Niemcza.

The beautiful Botanical Gardens

Around Central Wrocław

Many places of interest lie within walking distance of central Wrocław. A relaxing day can be spent at the zoo, the museums of natural history, geology and mineralogy and in Szczytnicki Park. The Jewish cemetery gives a fascinating insight into Poland's past. There are also several notable 20th-century buildings, such as the People's Hall and the 1920s Mieszkanie i Miejsce Pracy housing estate.

Some of the exhibits in the Mineralogy Museum

🏛 Geology and Mineralogy Museums

ul. Cybulskiego 30. Geology Museum: **Tel** 71 375 93 27. **Open** 9am–3pm Mon, Wed & Fri; 9am–5pm Tue & Thu; 10am–3pm Sat. Mineralogy Museum: **Tel** 71 375 92 06. **Open** 10am–3:30pm Mon–Fri; Jul & Aug: by appt (71 375 26 68). 🖼

A vast building in a style typical of the German Third Reich houses two interesting museums run by the University of Wrocław. The Geology Museum contains a wealth of rocks and fossils from different geological eras, while the Mineralogy Museum delights visitors with colourful displays of minerals collected from all over the world.

🏛 Natural History Museum

ul. Sienkiewicza 21. **Tel** 71 375 41 45. **Open** 9am–3pm Tue–Fri, 10am–4pm Sat & Sun. 🖳 **muzeum-przyrodnicze.uni.wroc.pl**

This museum, which is very popular with children, has a substantial collection of animals and plants from all continents. The collections of tropical butterflies, shells and mammal skeletons are the largest in Poland. Some date back to the 18th century, and formed the beginnings of the University's Zoological Museum, which was set up in 1820. Since 1904 the exhibits have been displayed in a purpose-built wing of this Art Nouveau building.

🏛 Hydropolis – Waterworks Museum

ul. Na Grobli 19-21, 50-001. **Tel** 71 340 95 15. **Open** 9am–6pm Mon–Fri, 10am–8pm Sat & Sun (last adm: 5pm Mon–Fri; 7pm Sat & Sun). 🖼🖳 🖳 **hydropolis.pl**

Located halfway between the Old Town and the Centennial Hall, this neo-Gothic water tank dating from 1893 has been turned into an ultra-modern museum dedicated to water. The museum has 64 interactive installations that take visitors on a journey from the Big Bang to nucleosynthesis, as well as the formation of planets to the origin of Earth's aqua. It is a child-friendly attraction that allows visitors to see the creatures found in a drop of water, or unwind in the relaxation space, which is accompanied by sea sounds and bioluminescent jellyfish. This is the only such facility in Poland, and one of the few in the world.

🏛 People's Hall

ul. Wystawowa 1. **Tel** 71 347 51 00. **Open** 9am–4pm, except during trade fairs and sports events. 🖼

The People's Hall (Hala Ludowa), originally known as the Century Hall, was intended to be the centrepiece of an exhibition commemorating the centenary of the coalition's victory over Napoleon at Lipsk. It was designed by Max Berg and built in 1911–13. At the time of its construction, it was regarded as one of the finest modern buildings in Europe. The centre of the hall is covered by a reinforced concrete dome with a diameter of 65 m (200 ft). It is lit by a sophisticated method – the openwork design inside the stepped tambour consists of rows of windows that can be shaded or uncovered as required. The auditorium can accommodate up to 5,000 people. The hall has functioned as a concert hall and theatre, and today is used for sports events and trade fairs. Around the hall are some of the pavilions of the Historical Exhibition. It is also worth walking through the old exhibition

A fascinating water presentation at the Hydropolis - Warerworks Museum

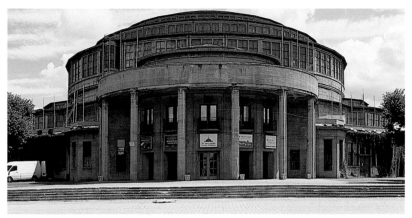

The People's Hall, designed by Max Berg

grounds and seeing the oval pond, which is surrounded by shady pergolas. A steel needle, which is 96 m (316 ft) in height and was made by Stanisław Hempel, stands outside the main entrance. It was erected here in 1948. The hall is a UNESCO World Heritage Site.

🔵 Szczytnicki Park

North of the exhibition area is an extensive park, which back to the 18th century. It was once the site of the residence of Duke Friedrich Ludwig von Hohenlohe-Ingelfingen, but that building was destroyed during the Napoleonic Wars (1799–1815), after which the area was made into a landscaped park.

One of Szczytnicki Park's distinctive features is its delightful Japanese garden, which has been painstakingly restored with the help of Japanese gardening experts.

The footbridges and pathways that run among the pavilions and plants make a charming setting for a leisurely walk. Look out for the rose garden and a small 12th-century wooden church that was brought over from Stare Koźle and reconstructed.

House designed by Hans Scharoun on the Mieszkanie i Miejsce Pracy housing estate

🏠 Mieszkanie i Miejsce Pracy Housing Estate

The Mieszkanie i Miejsce Pracy housing estate is a unique landmark in the development of residential architecture in the 1920s. The houses were examples of different residential buildings designed for the Exhibition of Living and Working Space organized by the Deutscher Werkbund movement in 1929. Many prominent German architects took part in the project. The most impressive building is an apartment block (at Ulica Kopernika 9) designed by Hans Scharoun, architect of several buildings in Berlin, including the National Library and the Berlin Philharmonic Orchestra's Concert Hall. Modern architecture enthusiasts should also visit Sępolno, which was built in 1924–8 and is a fine example of a garden city.

🔵 Jewish Cemetery

ul. Ślężna 37/39. Tel 71 791 59 03. Open 10am–dusk daily (to 6pm summer). 🔲 until noon. Closed Jewish holidays.

This is one of the very few Jewish cemeteries in Poland that escaped destruction at the hands of the Nazis during World War II. Originally opened in 1856, it was the burial place of many celebrated citizens of Wrocław, including the socialist politician Ferdinand Lassalle, the painter Clara Sachs and the parents of Sister Theresa Benedicta of the Cross, who was born in Wrocław as Edith Stein.

Japanese garden in Szczytnicki Park

Façade of the Cistercian church in Henryków

⑳ Henryków

Road map C5. 🚠 1,400. 🚌 🚍
Cistercian Church: pl. Cystersów 1.
Tel 74 810 51 35. **Open** Jul & Aug:
daily; May, Jun, Sep: Sat & Sun. 🎟

The small town of Henryków is known for its **Cistercian church**, founded in 1227 by Henryk the Bearded. A series of allotments surrounding the abbey separate the church and monastery from the street, so that access to the church is by way of a series of gates. The church, originally in the Gothic style, was rebuilt in the early 14th century and remodelled in the Baroque style by Matthias Kirchberger

in 1687–1702. Prominent features of the Baroque interior are the high altar, with *The Birth of Christ in the Vision of St Bernard of Clairvaux* by Michael Willmann, and the large, highly ornamented choir stalls. A plague column outside the church depicts the four archangels.

Other points of interest are the extensive monastery and the scenic park laid out at the rear of the monastery in the early 18th century. A summer-house stands in the park.

㉖ Kamieniec Ząbkowicki

Road map B5. 🚠 4,700. 🚌 🚍

The small town of Kamieniec Ząbkowicki is dominated by the 14th-century Gothic church and Baroque monastery of its Cistercian abbey, which was founded in 1272.

There is also a Neo-Gothic **castle**, perched on a hill but well worth the effort of a climb to visit. It was commissioned by Marianna Orańska in the 1870s, and after her death was completed for her son, Duke Albrecht of Prussia. The architect was Karl Friedrich Schinkel. A massive residence with large circular external towers and two internal piazzas, the castle has an ideal symmetry. Its magnificent ballroom has palm vaulting supported on a single central basalt column.

Unfortunately, the palace's once superb art collection and library were destroyed just after World War II. Today the castle, despite not being yet wholly reconstructed, operates as a hotel. It stands in an attractive overgrown park.

㉗ Kłodzko Valley

See pp206–7.

Gothic town walls and tower in Paczków

㉘ Paczków

Road map C5. 🚠 7,500. 🚌 🚍
ℹ Wojska Polskiego 23 (77 541 86 61). 🌐 **paczkow.pl**

Completely surrounded by a medieval wall set with towers and gates, Paczków has been dubbed the "Carcassone of

Neo-Gothic castle in Kamieniec Ząbkowicki

Silesia" after the medieval walled city in southwest France. Paczków was founded in 1254, and the old town retains its original street layout. It contains many distinctive town houses, a Neo-Classical town hall and the Church of St John (Kościół św. Jana), an originally Gothic church that was rebuilt in the Renaissance style in 1529–36 and fortified for defensive purposes.

㉙ Otmuchów

Road map C5. 🚇 5,000. 🚌 🚍

Otmuchów has a picturesque setting between two lakes, Lake Głębinowskie and Lake Otmuchówskie. In spring and summer the town is filled with flowers, partly as the result of the spring flower festival that is held here.

From the 14th century until 1810, Otmuchów belonged to the bishops of Wrocław. Its historic buildings are all in close proximity around the sloping Market Square. On the lower side is the Renaissance town hall, built in 1538, with a later tower. On the upper side is the Baroque parish church of 1690–6, and the Palace of the Bishops of Wrocław. The adjacent palace, known as the Lower Castle, was the bishops' secondary residence.

The Beautiful Well in Nysa, with Baroque wrought ironwork

㉚ Nysa

Road map: C5. 🚇 45,300. 🚌 🚍
ℹ️ ul. Piastowska 19 (77 433 49 71).
🌐 nysa.eu

Nysa, founded in 1223, was once the capital of the dukes of Wrocław and the see of the duchy of Nysa (Niesse). In the 16th and 17th centuries it became the residence of the Catholic bishops of Wrocław, who were driven there from Ostrów Tumski during the Reformation. After 1742 the Prussians enclosed the town with ramparts. Despite suffering massive destruction during World War II, Nysa retains a number of interesting buildings. The town centre is dominated by the Gothic **Basilica of Saints James and Agnieszka** (Basilica św Jakuba i Agnieszki), with a separate belfry dating from the early 16th century. The well beside it, covered with unusual wrought ironwork, is known as the Beautiful Well and dates from 1686. Of Nysa's many churches, the finest are the

Church of Saints Peter and Paul (Św. Piotra i Pawła) and the Jesuit **Church of the Assumption** (Wniebowzięcia NMP). Also of interest are the bishop's palace and manor, which stand beside a group of Jesuit buildings. The palace houses the **Town Museum**.

🔼 Basilica of Saints James and Agnieszka
pl. Katedralny 7. **Tel** 77 433 25 05.
A number of side chapels containing the tombs of bishops flank the lofty nave of this 14th to 15th-century church (Kościół św. Jakuba i św. Agnieszki). The high altar only survived World War II because it was removed and hidden in the mountains.

🔼 Church of Saints Peter and Paul
ul. św. Piotra. **Tel** 77 448 46 70.
This late Baroque church (Kościół św. Piotra i Pawła) was built by Michael Klein and Felix Anton Hammerschmidt in 1719–27 for the Canons Regular of the Holy Sepulchre. Its original furnishings are intact. Entry is via the office of the seminary situated in the monastery.

🔼 Church of the Assumption
pl. Solny. **Open** daily.
Jesuits were brought to Nysa by Bishop Karol Habsburg. This Baroque Jesuit church (Kościół Wniebowzięcia NMP), built in 1688–92, has a magnificent twin-towered façade. The interior features paintings by Karl Dankwart. It is one of a group of buildings known collectively as the Carolinum College.

🏛 Town Museum
pl. Bpa Jarosława 11. **Tel** 77 433 20 83. **Open** 9am–3pm Tue–Fri, 10am–3pm Sat & Sun. 📷 (free Wed). 🌐 muzeum.nysa.pl
The Town Museum is located in the former bishop's palace, which dates from 1660–80. It contains a fine collection of European painting, including pictures from the studios of Lucas Cranach the Elder (1472–1553) and Hugo van der Goes (c.1440–82).

Renaissance town hall in Otmuchów

㉗ Kłodzko Valley

Located only 100 km (62 miles) from Wroclaw, Kłodzko Valley is renowned for its architecture and spas as well as for its breathtaking views. Sharing its border with Czech Republic, the valley is dotted with castles. Many dignitaries, attracted by its favourable climate and its mineral springs, built splendid residences here. The area has several well-equipped hiking trails, particularly on Góry Stołowe (Table Mountains), and a number of ski resorts.

② Góry Stołowe
The Table Mountains are an unusual geological phenomenon – the strange shapes of the sandstone and marl hills were created by erosion. At Szczeliniec Wielki and Błędne Skały, fissures form natural mazes.

① Wambierzyce
The village is an ancient town of pilgrimage. The Pilgrimage Church dates from 1695–1710, although its oval nave was built in 1715–20. In the village and nearby hills are more than 130 Stations of the Cross.

③ Kudowa Zdrój
Built in 1776, the Chapel of Skulls (Kaplica czaszek) near Kudowa Zdrój contains 3,000 skulls and other bones of victims of the Thirty Years' War (1618–48) and ensuing plagues.

④ Duszniki Zdrój
Features of interest in this health spa are the Baroque pulpit in the Church of Saints Peter and Paul (Kościół św. Piotra i Pawła), by Michael Kössler, and a historical paper mill.

Map labels: 387 · Kudowa · Nachod · Lewin Kłodzki · Szczytna · E67 · E67 · Stara Łomnica

Tips for Drivers

Length of trail: 216 km (135 miles).
Stopping-off points: Restaurants are easy to find in towns such as Kudowa Zdrój, Lądek Zdrój, Kłodzko or Bystrzyca Kłodzka.
Other attractions: Bear's Cave at Jaskinia Niedźwiedzia, near Kletno; pre-booking **Tel** 74 814 12 50. Underground walk in Kłodzko **Open** Apr–Oct: 9am–6pm daily; Nov–Mar: 9am–3pm daily.
Closed Mon.

⑤ Polanica Zdrój
Founded in the early 19th century, this world-renowned spa is considered to be the most attractive in the whole Kłodzko Valley.

⑩ Kłodzko
The large 18th-century Kłodzko Fortress commands a panoramic view over the town. There is also a Gothic bridge with Baroque carving and an underground passage.

⑧ Kletno
Formed 50 million years ago, Bear's Cave, the largest in the Sudeten range, has 3 km (2 miles) of subterranean passages on four different levels with stalactites and stalagmites in a variety of shapes.

⑨ Lądek Zdrój
This picturesque resort has luxurious mineral baths and a historic market square. For the energetic, the ruins of Karpień Castle are within walking distance.

⑦ Międzygórze
This town, which seems Austrian, is located at the foot of the Śnieżnik massif in the Wilczka River Valley is an ideal starting point for mountain hiking.

⑥ Bystrzyca Kłodzka
The town's Museum of Fire-Making, the only one of its kind in Europe, is devoted to the manufacture of matches and cigarette lighters. The Gothic church that towers over the old town has an unusual double-nave interior.

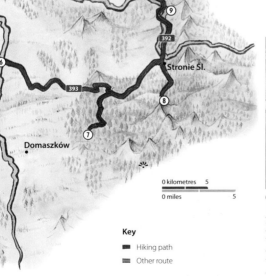

Wrocław

Biała Lądecka

Nysa Kłodzka

Stronie Śl.

Domaszków

0 kilometres 5
0 miles 5

Key

■ Hiking path
▬ Other route

⑪ The Gold Mine
Enticing over 250,000 tourists every year, this mine is one of the biggest attractions of the region. Designed for children, it offers an underground waterfall, an "Titanic" boat tour, as well as panning for gold and the casting of gold bars.

❸❶ Opole

Road map C5. 🏔 118,900. 🚉 🚌
ℹ️ 77 451 19 87, Rynek 23. 🎭
Festival of Polish Song (Jun).
🅦 opole.pl

The origins of Opole, on the River Odra, go back to the 8th century. Once the seat of the Piast duchy, from 1327 it was ruled by Bohemia, from 1526 by Austria, and from 1742 by Prussia. Although it has been part of Poland only since 1945, it has always had a sizeable Polish population. The town hall was built in 1936 in imitation of the Palazzo Vecchio in Florence. Other notable buildings include the **Cathedral of the Holy Cross**, a Gothic church with a Baroque interior, and the late Gothic Franciscan church, containing the tombs of the dukes of Opole. On Pasieka Island, near the park's amphitheatre, stands the Piast Tower, all that remains of the Gothic ducal castle.

🏛 **Regional Museum**
ul. św Wojciecha 13. **Tel** 77 453 66 77.
Open 9am–4pm Tue–Fri, 11am–5pm Sat & Sun (Jul–Sep: to 6pm Fri). 🎨 (free Sat). ♿

Opole sitting on the bank of the River Odra

◀ The interior of the Cathedral of St John the Baptist in Wrocław

❸❷ Góra Świętej Anny

Road map C5. 🚉 Leśnica.
🅦 swanna.pl

Góra Świętej Anny is a place of pilgrimage for Catholics and a centre of commemoration of the Silesian uprisings of 1919–21. The great Pilgrimage Church of St Anne was built here by the Gaschin-Gaszyński family in the second half of the 1600s. The Stations of the Cross that make up the 18th-century Calvary are placed around the church and monastery. The Calvary draws large numbers of pilgrims.

During the Third Silesian Uprising in May and June 1921, two major battles were fought in the mountains near Góra Świętej Anny. They are commemorated by a commanding monument carved by Xawery Dunikowski in 1955 on the mountainside above a gigantic amphitheatre built in 1930–34. A **museum** contains records relating to the uprising.

🏛 **Museum of the Uprising**
Góra Świętej Anny, ul. Leśnicka 28.
Tel 77 461 54 66. ⭕ 9am–3pm Tue–Fri, 10am–4pm Sat & Sun. 🎨 (free Sat).

Romanesque Rotunda of St Nicholas in Cieszyn

❸❸ Cieszyn

Road map D6. 🏔 35,100. 🚉
🚌 ℹ️ 33 479 42 49. 🎭 Bez Granic Theatre Festival (Jun); Viva il Canto Festival of Vocal Music (Oct); Cieszyńska Jazz Autumn Festival (Nov). 🅦 cieszyn.pl

This delightful town on the Czech–Polish border was founded in the 9th century. From the 13th to 17th centuries it was the capital of a Silesian duchy and in 1653 fell under Habsburg rule. On a hill where a castle once stood is the 11th-century Romanesque **Rotunda of St Nicholas** (Rotunda św. Mikołaja), the Piast Tower, in the Gothic style, and a hunting palace built by Karol Habsburg in 1838.

The Market Square has some fine town houses and a Neo-Classical town hall. Cieszyn also has several churches, most importantly the Protestant **Church of Grace** (Kościół Łaski), of 1709.

The town is well kept, with a number of pedestrianized streets. Czech as well as Polish is heard in its homely pubs, bars and restaurants.

❸❹ Pszczyna

Road map D5. 🏔 24,850. 🚉 🚌
ℹ️ Brama Wybrańców (32 212 99 99).
🅦 pszczyna.info.pl

Pszczyna, on the edge of the ancient Pszczyna Forest, is named after a residence that was built within the walls of a Gothic castle in the area. The building, situated next to the forest and its wildlife, was used as a hunting lodge for many centuries. From

1846 Pszczyna was ruled by the Hochbergs of Książ *(see p191)*. The palace was rebuilt for them in 1870–76 in the French Neo-Renaissance style.

Today the palace houses a **museum** with an interesting and well-stocked armoury, a collection of hunting trophies and a fine array of period furniture. The centrepiece of the palace is the extraordinary Hall of Mirrors, which contains two vast mirrors, each with a surface area of some 14 sq m (150 sq ft).

The striking exterior of the Museum of Silesia

🏛 Palace Museum

ul. Brama Wybrańców 1. **Tel** 32 210 30 37. **Open** Jan–Mar & Nov–mid-Dec: Tue–Sun; Apr–Oct: daily. For opening hours, please consult the website. **Closed** 1 and 3 May, Easter, Corpus Christi, 1 and 11 Nov, 15–31 Dec. 🖼 (free on Mon Apr–Oct; Tue Nov–Mar). **W** zamek-pszczyna.pl

Portrait of Princess Daisy in the Palace Museum in Pszczyna

㉟ Upper Silesian Industrial Region

Road map D5. 🚉 🚌 ✈ Katowice.

The vast conurbation of 14 towns that make up the Upper Silesian Industrial Region (Górnośląski Okręg Przemysłowy) was created by the coal-mining industry, which has been active in the area since the 18th century. The area's hardworking inhabitants have their own unique dialect, which is spoken especially by the older generation. After World War I and following the three Silesian uprisings of 1919–21, almost the entire region was incorporated into Poland. Although the towns, with their mines, steelworks and power stations, seem unappealing, the region is of interest to tourists. Katowice, the capital, has particularly interesting buildings dating from the interwar years. In Kościusz Park there is a wooden church from 1510 that was moved here from Syryna, a Silesian village, as well as the **Archdiocesan Museum** and **Museum of Silesia**. The museum in Bytom has some interesting works of art. In Chorzów the main attraction is a park with a funfair. The **Coal Museum** demonstrates the importance of mining in Upper Silesia.

🏛 Archdiocesan Museum

Katowice, ul. Jordana 39. **Tel** 519 546 023. **Open** 2–6pm Tue & Thu; 11am–3pm Sat.

The museum has a collection of ecclesiastical art, the most outstanding piece being *Head of a Monk* by José de Ribera (1591–1652).

🏛 Museum of Silesia

Katowice, ul. Korfantego 3. **Tel** 32 779 93 00. **Open** 10am–8pm Tue–Sun. **W** muzeum slaskie.pl

Among the displays at the Silesian Museum is a varied collection of 19th and 20th-century Polish painting.

🏛 Coal Museum

Będzin, ul. Świerczewskiego 15. **Tel** 32 267 47 31. Castle and Palace **Open** 8am–4pm Tue, Thu & Fri; 9am–5pm Wed, Sat & Sun (Jul & Aug: 10am–6pm Tue–Sun). **W** muzeum. bedzin.pl

Będzin Castle was founded by Kazimierz the Great. Constructed from roughly hewn boulders, it was erected in stages between 1250 and 1350. In 1834 it was restored in the romantic Neo-Gothic tradition by Franciszek Maria Lanci. The castle now houses the fascinating Coal Museum. Another branch of the museum is to be found in the Mieroszewski Palace.

Będzin Castle, now the home of the Coal Museum

WIELKOPOLSKA (GREATER POLAND)

Wielkopolska (Greater Poland) is the cradle of Polish statehood. It was here in the mid-10th century that the Polonians, the strongest of the Polish tribes, set up an enduring state structure. It was also in this region that the Piast dynasty, the first Polish dynasty, emerged to rule the country in the 10th century. The first two capitals of Poland, Gniezno and Poznań, lie in Wielkopolska.

During the Thirty Years' War of 1618–48, the region of Wielkopolska was settled by large numbers of dissenting Germans, particularly from neighbouring Silesia. The Protestant faith of the incomers set them apart from the existing inhabitants, who were Catholics.

During the Partitions of Poland, Wielkopolska was divided. Under the terms of the Congress of Vienna of 1815, the larger western part fell under Prussian rule, and the smaller eastern part came under Russian control. In the second half of the 19th century the Prussian part of Wielkopolska was subjected to repeated, but unsuccessful, campaigns of Germanization. Polish activists fought back in the courts and laid the economic foundations for the Polish section of the population. At the end of 1918, an insurrection broke out in the western part of Wielkopolska and almost the entire region as it had been before the Partitions was reincorporated into the Polish state.

The inhabitants of Wielkopolska have a long-standing reputation for thrift and orderliness. The years of Soviet domination that followed World War II strained these qualities to the limit, although the local state-owned farms worked more efficiently than those in other parts of the country and many palaces and country mansions have survived in better condition than was the case elsewhere.

Poznań, the capital of Wielkopolska, is not only an ebullient commercial and cultural centre, but also abounds in historic buildings. Almost every town, however small, contains something of interest. Wielkopolska maintains its identity: to this day the customs preserved in many of the region's towns and villages are distinct from those in other parts of Poland.

Old windmills in a typical Wielkopolska scene

◀ The colourful façades of the 16th-century merchants' houses lining Poznań's Old Market Square

Exploring Wielkopolska

Wielkopolska's extensive territory is mainly low-lying, but the landscape is far from monotonous. The vast forests and lakes of northern Wielkopolska are ideal for a walking or cycling holiday. Besides Poznań, the regional capital, other towns of interest include Gniezno, seat of an archbishopric and the first capital of Poland. In the area around Gniezno traces of the rise of Polish statehood can be seen on Ostrów Lednicki, in Strzelno, and in Kruszwica on Lake Gopło. Located outside the heartland of Wielkopolska, the former textile city of Łódź is a showcase of post-industrial regeneration.

Getting Around

Wielkopolska is situated on main transport routes between eastern and western Europe. The efficient express train service from Berlin to Poznań takes just under 3 hours, and the journey from Warsaw by express train takes just over 2 hours. All the larger towns of the region have rail connections, while smaller ones can be reached by bus. Roads are generally good, although Poznań suffers from almost permanent traffic jams. Poznań can also be reached by air, although the number of international connections is limited.

Skansen on Lake Lednicki

For hotels and restaurants see p304 and pp315–16

Sights at a Glance

1. Łagów
2. Leszno
3. Rydzyna
4. *Raczyński Palace, Rogalin pp218–19*
5. *Poznań pp220–25*
6. Kórnik
7. Koszuty
8. Gułtowy
9. Czerniejewo
10. Ostrów Lednicki
11. *Gniezno pp228–9*
12. Biskupin
13. Lubostroń
14. Ląd
15. Śmiełów
16. Gołuchów
17. Kalisz
18. Antonin
19. Piotrków Trybunalski
20. Sulejów
21. *Łódź pp234–5*
22. Łęczyca

Tours

14. Romanesque Architecture Tour *pp230–31*

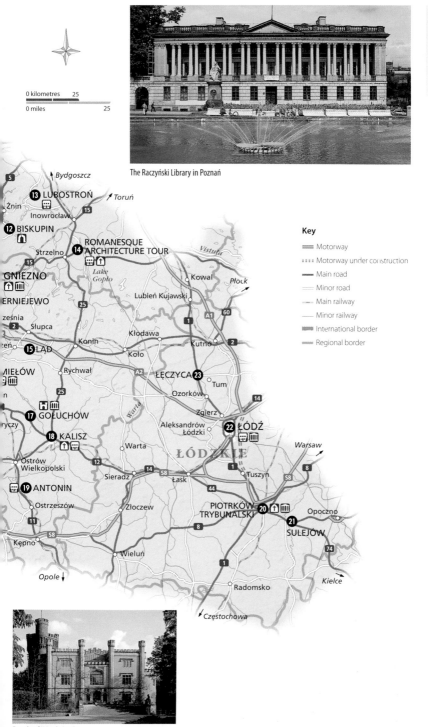

The Raczyński Library in Poznań

Key

━━ Motorway

┅┅┅ Motorway under construction

━━ Main road

━━ Minor road

┅┅ Main railway

━━ Minor railway

▬▬ International border

━━ Regional border

Façade of Kórnik Castle

❶ Łagów

Road map B3. 🗺 1,600. 🚌 🚆 ℹ️ 68 341 20 62 (Jun–Sep). 🎬 Lubuskie Film Festival (Jun). 🌐 **lagow.pl**

Łagów, situated in woodland between lakes Łagów and Ciecz, is known for its film festival.

The tower of the 14th-century **castle** built by the Knights Hospitallers affords a magnificent view of the surrounding countryside, as does the 19th-century tower of the Neo-Classical Church of St John the Baptist (Kościoł św. Jan Chrzciciela), dating from 1726. Around the town are also remains of the 15th-century town walls, with their gate towers, the Polish Gate and Marchian Gate.

Environs
Łagów Nature Park, near the town, contains protected areas of woodland and wild flowers.

About 16 km (10 miles) east of the town are the remains of a system of **fortifications** erected by the Germans just before World War II. Its surviving corridors and bunkers are now inhabited by thousands of bats.

❷ Leszno

Road map B4. 🗺 64,500. 🚌 🚆 ℹ️ ul. Słowiańska 24 (65 529 18 91). 🎭 Days of Leszno (May); Summer of Folklore (Aug). 🌐 **leszno.pl**

In the 17th century Leszno gave asylum to religious dissidents fleeing the ravages of the Thirty Years'War (1618–48) in Silesia. Apart from Lutheran Protestants, they included a group known as the Bohemian Brethren, who founded the Arian Academy that gained renown across Europe. One of its members was Jan Amos Komeński (Commenius), a prominent philosopher of the Reformation.

The town was destroyed by fire in 1707, so that none

Palace in Rydzyna, former seat of the Sułkowski family

of its monumental buildings dates from earlier than the 18th century. The Baroque **town hall** was built just after the fire to a design by Pompeo Ferrari. Beside the market square is the distinctive Baroque **parish church**, built by Jan Catenaci at the turn of the 18th century. It has a delightful façade and interior with Baroque altars and tombs. Ferrari also designed the former Lutheran **Church of the Holy Cross** (Kościoł luterański św. Krzyża), which was built after 1707.

The **Regional Museum's** finest collection is in the Polish Portrait Gallery, and features 18th-century coffin portraits of the Bohemian Brethren.

🏛 **Regional Museum**
pl. Metziga 17. **Tel** 65 529 61 40. **Open** 9am–4:30pm Tue, 9am–2:30pm Wed–Fri, 10am–2pm Sat, 2–6pm Sun. 🔲 (free on Tue). Judaic section: ul. Narutowicza 31. **Tel** 65 529 61 43. **Open** 10am–3pm Tue & Thu, 9am–2pm Wed & Fri, 10am–2pm first Sun of the month. **Closed** Day after public holiday. 🔲 (free 1st Sun each month). 🌐 **muzeum. leszno.pl**

Leszno's Baroque town hall

❸ Rydzyna

Road map B4. 🗺 2,500. 🚆 🚌 🌐 **rydzyna.pl**

This small town is dominated by the **palace**, built in the 15th century. Its present late Baroque appearance dates from after 1737; further building work was carried out by Karl Martin Frantz in 1742, when paintings by Wilhelm Neunhertz were added to the ballroom ceiling. The ballroom was destroyed by fire in 1945.

The ceiling was painted in honour of the palace's owner, Prince Józef A. Sułkowski. A member of a noble family of relatively low rank, he was catapulted to success at the court of August III, but fell from the king's favour in 1738 and was replaced by Henryk Brühl. The palace remained in the possession of the Sułkowskis into the early 20th century, when it was sold to the Prussian rulers. It is now a hotel.

The Market Square is lined with Baroque houses, the **town hall** and two Baroque churches: the **Parish Church of St Stanisław** (Kościoł św. Stanisława) designed by Karl Martin Frantz and Ignacy Graff in 1746–51, and the **Protestant church**, dating from 1779–83, also by Graff.

❹ Raczyński Palace, Rogalin

See pp218–19.

❺ Poznań

See pp220–25.

A room with coffered ceiling and ornate floor in Kórnik Castle

⑥ Kórnik

Road map C3. 🚂 6,900. 🚌 🚍
W kornik.pl

Set on an island and surrounded by a landscaped park, Kórnik Castle is one of the most picturesque castles in Poland. Its present appearance dates from the 19th century, when it was rebuilt in the English Neo-Gothic style by Karl Friedrich Schinkel. There have also been some subsequent alterations.

The castle's original interior survives: the Moorish Hall is decorated in the style of the Alhambra Palace in southern Spain and in the dining room the ceiling is covered with the coats of arms of all the Polish knights who fought at the Battle of Grunwald (1410). An inscription in Turkish on the ceiling of one hall is an expression of thanks to Turkey, which refused to recognize the Partitions of Poland. The castle also contains a collection of 18th- and 19th-century porcelain and other pieces.

The castle became the repository of the art treasures that were once kept at

Czartoryski Palace in Puławy (see p125). In order to acquire the library at Puławy, Tytus Działyński persuaded his son Jan to marry Izabella, heiress to the Czartoryski fortune.

The castle has an extensive library and a museum. The museum's collections include a display of 16th to 19th century Polish and foreign paintings, as well as sculpture, drawings and an intriguing array of militaria, including a complete suit of armour. The **Kórnik Library** contains manuscripts of Polish poets' works and a substantial collection of prints and maps. There is also a park that contains

Suit of armour, Kórnik Castle Museum

an arboretum with many rare species of trees, and a walk here is a relaxing way to round off a visit.

🏛 Kórnik Library
ul. Zamkowa 5. **Tel** 61 817 00 81 or 817 19 30. **Open** 10am–4pm Tue–Sun. **Closed** public hols, Easter, 1 Sep, Dec–Feb.
W bkpan.poznan.pl

Environs
There are several holiday villages scattered along the shores of lakes Kórnik and Bniń, to the south of Kórnik. The best known of them is **Zaniemyśl**, which boasts both a bathing beach and a holiday camp among its attractions. On Edward Island there is a 19th-century wooden pavilion built in the style of a Swiss chalet.

⑦ Koszuty

Road map C3. 🚂 400. 🚌 🚍

In an enchanting 18th-century country house, set in a landscaped garden, the interior of a Wielkopolska land-owner's mansion has been reconstructed and is now the **Środa Land Museum**.

🏛 Środa Land Museum
Tel 61 285 10 23. **Open** 9am–3pm Tue–Fri, 11am–3pm Sat & Sun.

Environs
The town of **Środa Wielkopolska**, which is situated just 6 km (4 miles) east of Koszuty, has an interesting Gothic collegiate church dating from the 15th to 16th centuries.

Country house in Koszuty, dating from the 18th century

❹ Raczyński Palace, Rogalin

Raczyński Palace, in the village of Rogalin, is one of the most magnificent buildings in Wielkopolska. It was begun in around 1770 for Kazimierz Raczyński, Palatine of Wielkopolska and Grand Marshal of the Crown. It was designed in the Baroque style, but during construction the architectural ornamentation was abandoned. The imposing main building, however, retains its late Baroque solidity. In 1782–3 curving colonnades were added and complemented by annexes in the classic Palladian style. A drawing room and grand staircase designed by Jan Chrystian Kamsetzer were added in 1788–9.

French Garden
The French garden at the palace's rear is elevated at one end to provide a view of the grounds.

★ Art Gallery
A pavilion built in 1909–12 contains a collection of European and Polish paintings dating from about 1850 to the early 20th century, including works by Jacek Malczewski and Jan Matejko.

0 metres 100
0 yards 100

★ Palace
The main building of the late Baroque palace was given a more fashionable Neo-Classical character by the addition of curving colonnades.

KEY

① **The entrance courtyard** is approached by a tree-lined drive and flanked by coach houses and stables. It also has riding stables on the northeast side.

② **Riding school**

③ **Stable**

④ **Staff cottages**

VISITORS' CHECKLIST

Practical Information
Świątniki nad Wartą, ul.
Arciszewskiego 2. **Road map** C3.
Palace Museum: **Tel** 61 813 88 00.
Open May & Jun: 9:30am–4pm
Tue–Fri, 10am–5pm Sat & Sun;
Jul & Aug: 10am–5pm Tue–Sun;
Sep–Apr: 9:30am–4pm Tue–Sun.
🅿 🚌 **W** rogalin.mnp.art.pl

The Oaks of Rogalin
Rogalin park has one of the largest
protected oak woodlands in Europe.
The three largest trees stand in the
meadow off the park's main avenue.

Bridge and Gateway
A three-arched bridge and a wrought-iron
gateway open onto the entrance courtyard.

Mausoleum Chapel
Designed in the style of a classical
temple and built in 1817–20, the
mausoleum chapel contains
the tombs of prominent members of the Raczyński family.

The Coach House
Built with the stables in around 1801,
the coach house was commissioned
by Filip Raczyński.

❺ Poznań

Poznań is the capital of Wielkopolska and its largest city. A stronghold by the name of Polan stood here in the 8th century, and in the 10th century it was the capital of the emerging Polish state. In 968 it became the seat of the first bishopric in Poland. Poznań has many historic buildings, the finest of which are the cathedral and those in the old town. A visit to the late 19th-century quarter is also rewarding. Today Poznań is Poland's second financial centre after Warsaw and a major centre of commerce. Annual trade fairs attended by producers and traders from all over the world have been held here since 1921.

Some of the houses in the Old Market Square were destroyed during the battles for Poznań in 1945, and were rebuilt after World War II, but others escaped serious damage. They include Mielżyński Palace, which dates from 1796–8, and **Działyński Palace**, both in the Neo-Classical style.

Interior of the former Dominican Church of the Heart of Jesus

🏛 Church of the Heart of Jesus

ul. Szewska 18. **Tel** 61 852 50 76.

The Church of the Heart of Jesus (Kościół Serca Jezusowego) was built in the 13th century. As a result, it is the oldest church in the old town. At first, it was a Dominican church until 1920, when it passed to the Jesuits. During the German occupation in World War II, a repository was set up here for Polish books removed from the libraries of Poznań.

🏛 Old Market Square

The **Old Market Square** (Stary Rynek) is the heart of the old town. It is surrounded by town houses with colourful façades, among which stands the Renaissance town hall. The ground floors of the buildings around the square are filled mainly by banks, cafés and restaurants, and the streets leading off the square contain elegant shops. From spring to autumn the square bustles with life, and the outdoor cafés with their tables and colourful sunshades are permanently busy. Local artists display their paintings, while children play on the steps of the town hall. The square is also a venue for cultural events.

🏛 Działyński Palace

Stary Rynek 78. **Tel** 61 852 48 44.
🌐 **bkpan.poznan.pl**

The palace was built in the late 18th century for Władysław Gurowski, Grand Marshal of Lithuania. The elegant Neo-Classical façade is crowned with a large eagle and set with figures of Roman soldiers made by Anton Höhne in 1785–7. It is worth going inside to see the columned Red Room upstairs. The building is now used as a library, theatre, exhibition and concert hall.

The Old Market Square in Poznań

For hotels and restaurants see p304 and pp315–16

The façade of Działyński Palace

🏛 Town Hall

Stary Rynek 1. Museum of the History of Poznań. **Tel** 61 856 81 93. **Open** 9am–3pm Tue–Thu (Jun–Sep: 11am–5pm), noon–9pm Fri, 11am–6pm Sat & Sun. 🎟 (free on Sat). 🌐 **mnp.art.pl**

Poznań's town hall is one of the finest municipal buildings in Europe. It was built in 1550–60 by the Italian architect Giovanni Battista di Quadro. The façade has three tiers of arcades, topped by a grand attic and a large tower and decorated with portraits of the kings of Poland.

The greatest tourist attraction is the clock tower, where at noon each day two clockwork goats emerge from doors 12 times to butt heads. The Great Hall, or Renaissance Hall, on the first floor was lavishly decorated to reflect the affluence of the city's municipal leaders. The coffered ceiling is covered with an intricate series of paintings. Other important collections can be seen in the Royal Hall and the Courtroom. The centrepiece of the Old Market Square is the Baroque **Proserpine Fountain** of 1766, depicting the abduction of the ancient Roman fertility goddess Proserpine by Pluto, ruler of the underworld. Nearby stands a copy of a stone **pillory** of 1535 and a 20th-century fountain with the figure of a Bamberka, a peasant woman from the Poznań area. It commemorates the Catholic settlers who were sent to Poznań at the beginning of the 18th century from Bamberg, in southern Germany. Soon they became Polonized, although many of the city's inhabitants still claim to be descendants of the Bamberg settlers.

🏛 Church of Saints Mary Magdalene and Stanisław

ul. Gołębia 1. **Tel** 61 852 69 50.
Construction work on this Baroque church, which was originally built for use as a Jesuit chapel, began in 1651 and continued for more than 50 years. Several architects, craftsmen and artists had a role in this extended project, among them Tomasso Poncino, Bartołomiej Wąsowski and Jan Catenaci.

The most impressive aspect of the church is probably its monolithic interior. Gigantic columns along the walls lead the eye towards the illuminated high altar, which was designed and constructed in 1727 by Pompeo Ferrari.

The Baroque buildings of a former Jesuit monastery and college stand close to the church. They were built for the brotherhood in 1701–33. Today, however, they are used for secular business by the members of Poznań's town council.

The Renaissance town hall, with its three tiers of loggias

Central Poznań

For keys to symbols see back flap

Exploring Poznań

Poznań holds much of interest beyond the old town. The Bernadine church in Plac Bernardyński has a remarkably narrow twin-towered façade built in the 18th century by Jan Steyner. It is matched by the former Lutheran Church of the Holy Cross (Kościół św. Krzyża), dating from 1777–83. Walking towards the main railway station, you go through the town centre and across Plac Wolności, a square lined with shops and banks, then following Ulica św. Marcina, where the old Kaiser's palace is located. The trade fair area can be seen on the other side of the railway.

🏠 Przemysław Castle
Góra Przemysła 1. Museum of Applied Art: **Tel** 61 856 81 83. **Open** 9am–3pm Tue–Thu, noon–9pm Fri, 11am–6pm Sat & Sun. 🎟 (free on Sat). **W** mnp.art.pl

Little remains of the original castle built by Przemysław II in the 1200s. The reconstructed castle that now stands on the site houses the Museum of Applied Art, which holds a collection of everyday objects, decorative artifacts and religious items dating from the Middle Ages to the present. The Baroque **Franciscan church** on Ulica Góra Przemysła dates from the early 18th century. Frescoes by the Franciscan painter Adam Swach decorate the nave.

▥ National Museum
al. Marcinkowskiego 9. **Tel** 61 856 80 00. **Open** 9am–3pm Tue–Thu, noon–9pm Fri, 11am–6pm Sat & Sun. 🎟 (free on Sat). **W** mnp.art.pl

The National Museum is housed in what was originally

Statue of Hygeia, Greek goddess of health, outside the Raczyński Library

the Prussian Friedrich Museum, a Neo-Renaissance building of 1900–1903. Its collections of Polish painting are among the best in Poland.

The Gallery of Polish Art includes medieval art of the 12th to 16th centuries and 17th- to 18th-century coffin portraits *(see p35)*. The best examples of painting of the Young Poland movement are the canvases of Jacek Malczewski (1854–1929).

The Gallery of European Art, which is housed in its own wing of the museum, contains works from various collections, including that of Atanazy Raczyński, brother of the philanthropist Count Edward Raczyński *(see p218)*. The most outstanding are by Dutch and Flemish painters including Joos van Cleve and Quentin Massys. Italian, French and Spanish painters are also represented.

▦ Raczyński Library
pl. Wolności 19. **Tel** 61 852 98 68. **Open** 9am–8pm Mon–Sat. **W** bracz.edu.pl

With its façade of columns, the Raczyński Library combines grandeur with elegance, and cannot be compared with any other building in Poznań. The idea for a library was initiated by Count Edward Raczyński in 1829. The aim of this visionary aristocrat was to turn Poznań into a "New Athens"; the library was to be a centre of culture and "a shrine of knowledge". Although the library's architect is unknown, it is thought to have been built by the French architects and designers Charles Percier and Pierre Fontaine. A seated **figure of Hygeia**, the ancient Greek goddess of health, with the features of Konstancja z Potockich, wife of Edward Raczyński, was installed in front of the library in 1906.

Another element of the "New Athens" of Poznań was to be a gallery (now non-existent) for the outstanding art collection owned by Edward Raczyński's brother, Atanazy.

▦ Former Kaiser District
After the Second Partition of Poland in 1793, Poznań came under Prussian rule. In the second half of the 19th century, Prussia heightened its policy of Germanization in Wielkopolska. One of its instruments was the Deutscher Ostmarkenverein ("German Union of the Eastern Marches"), which the Poles called the "Hakata" colonization commission, from the acronym

The elegant entrance of Raczyński Library with its façade of columns

 uf the initials of its founders. When the city's ring of 19th-century fortifications was demolished, a decision was made to use the space for government buildings. Designed by the German town planner Josef Stübben, they were built in 1903–14 and today stand amid gardens, squares and avenues, with a theatre, the colonization commission, a post office and the royal academy (now the university). Dominating the scene is the Kaiserhaus, designed by Franz Schwechten. The castle was rebuilt by the Germans, but little survives of its original splendour apart from a marble imperial throne and the decor of some of the rooms. The chairs from the Great Hall are now in the Sejm (parliament) in Warsaw. Today, the Kaiserhaus houses the Kaiserhaus Cultural Centre.

Beside it, in Plac Mickiewicza, stands the evocative Monument to the Victims of June 1956, which takes the form of two large crosses. The monument was unveiled in 1981 to commemorate the violent suppression of the workers' uprising in Poznań in 1956 *(see p58)*.

The Opera, built in 1910, is flanked by statues of lions

Monument to the Victims of June 1956

Hill of St Adalbert

The hill is said to be the spot where, 1,000 years ago, St Adalbert gave a sermon before setting off on his campaign to evangelize the Prussians. On the summit two churches face each other across a small square. One is the Discalced Carmelites' Church of St Joseph, built by Cristoforo Bonadura the Elder and Jan Catenaci in 1658–67. It contains the tomb of Mikołaj Jan Skrzetuski, who died in 1668 and on whom Henryk Sienkiewicz *(see p31)* based the hero of his historical saga *With Fire and Sword*.

The other is the small Gothic Church of St Adalbert, forming a pantheon with practically the same function as the Pauline Church on the Rock in Krakow *(see p149)*. In the crypt are the remains of great figures in the history of Wielkopolska. They include Józef Wybicki (1747–1822), who wrote the Polish national anthem, and the traveller and scientist Paweł Edmund Strzelecki (1797–1873). A striking contrast to the rest of the building is the ultramodern glass, concrete and stainless steel entrance to the crypt, which was designed by Jerzy Gurawski in 1997.

The 16th century wooden belfry of the Church of St Adalbert

The Poznań Trade Fair

The trade fair area is in the city centre, the main entrance lying opposite Dworcowy Bridge. The Poznań International Trade Fair has been held here every year since 1921. It takes place in June, and for its duration the surrounding area is filled with an international throng of businessmen. If you visit at this time you will find that the local cafés and restaurants are often full and hotel accommodation can be extremely hard to come by.

The symbol of the Trade Fair is a steel needle erected over the lower part of the Upper Silesian Tower in 1955, the main part having been destroyed during World War II. When the tower was built in 1911, to a design by Hans Poelzig, it was considered by admiring critics to be a masterpiece of modern architecture in reinforced concrete.

The needle rising over the Poznań International Trade Fair

Poznań Cathedral

The first church on this site, a pre-Romanesque basilica, was built in Poznań in 966, shortly after Poland adopted Christianity, and the first rulers of Poland were buried there. In 1034–8 the basilica was destroyed during pagan uprisings and the campaign of the Czech prince Brzetysław. It was then completely rebuilt in the Romanesque style. It was remodelled in the Gothic and Baroque periods, and after suffering war damage was restored to its earlier Gothic form. Vestiges of the pre-Romanesque and Romanesque churches can be seen in the crypt.

Coffin Portrait
The cathedral has a display of these portraits, which were used during funeral ceremonies in the 17th and 18th centuries.

Tomb of the Górka Family
The tomb of the Górkas, a prominent Wielkopolska family, was made in the Chapel of the Holy Cross by Girolamo Canavesi in 1574.

Main entrance

High Altar
The late Gothic polyptych on the high altar was probably carved in the workshop of Jacob Beinhart in Wrocław and painted in the Pasje studio of Upper Silesia. It was brought to the cathedral in 1952.

VISITORS' CHECKLIST

Practical Information
Ostrów Tumski. **Tel** 61 852 96 42.
Open Mar–Oct: 9am–6pm
Mon–Sat, 2–6pm Sun; Nov–Feb:
9am–4pm Mon–Sat, 2–6pm Sun.
W katedra.archpoznan.pl

★ **Tomb of Bishop Benedykt Izdbieński**
The tomb was made by Jan Michałowicz of Urzędów, the most celebrated sculptor of the Polish Renaissance, in 1557–62.

★ **Golden Chapel**
The chapel, built in 1834–41, contains the tombs of two of Poland's first rulers, Mieszko I and Bolesław the Brave. Their statues were carved by Chrystian Rauch.

Gothic Church of St Mary, with the cathedral in the background

Ostrów Tumski Island
Ostrów Tumski Island is the oldest part of Poznań. In the 10th century it was the site of one of the first capital cities of the Polish state.

Today the island is dominated by the Gothic towers of the cathedral, which contains many fine works of art. Near the cathedral stands the small Gothic **Church of St Mary** (Kościół halowy NMP), which was built in the years 1431–48 for Bishop Andrzej Bniński by Hanusz Prusz, a pupil of the notable late medieval architect Heinrich Brunsberg.

In the gardens on the other side of Ulica ks. I. Posadzego stand a number of canons' and vicars' houses which are charming in appearance – if a little neglected. One of them contains the collections of the **Archdiocesan Museum**.

The late Gothic **Psalter**, which was built in around 1520 by Bishop Jan Lubrański, is another of Ostrów Tumski Island's notable buildings. Its fine stepped and recessed gables are enclosed by ogee arches.

🏛 Archdiocesan Museum
ul. Lubrańskiego 1. **Tel** 61 852 61 95.
Open 10am–5pm Tue–Fri, 9am–3pm Sat. **Closed** public hols. 🗺
🗂 **W** muzeum.poznan.pl

The superb collection of religious art on display in the Archdiocesan Museum includes examples of medieval painting and sculpture, pieces of Gothic embroidery and some fine *kontusz* sashes

(see pp34–5). The most important pieces in the museum are probably the *Madonna of Ołobok*, a Romanesque-Gothic statue dating from about 1310–29, and a fascinating group of coffin portraits *(see p35)*.

The modern interior of Brama Poznania museum

🏛 Brama Poznania
ul. Gdanska 2. **Tel** 61 647 76 34.
Open 9am–6pm Tue–Fri, 10am–7pm Sat & Sun. **Closed** Mon. 🗺 ♿ 🎧
W bramapoznania.pl

Housed in a cube-like concrete building, just across the water from Ostrów Tumski, this stunning contemporary museum opened in 2013. The museum narrates the history of Ostrów Tumski through a series of themed multimedia displays that are more like art installations than traditional exhibits.

Façade of the Baroque and Neo-Classical palace in Gułtowy

❽ Gułtowy

Road map C3. ⚠ 1,490. 🚌
🚉 **Tel** 61 818 01 80. **Open** by
appointment only.

The pretty Baroque and
Neo-Classical palace at
Gułtowy was built in
1779–83 for Ignacy Bniński
to a design by an unknown
architect and subsequently
altered by Ignacy Graff. The
most striking feature of its
interior is the two-tiered
ballroom decorated with
delicate trompe l'oeil paintings
dating from about 1800.

❾ Czerniejewo

Road map C3. ⚠ 2,600. 🚉 4.5 km
(3 miles). 🚌 Palace Hotel: **Tel** 61 876
84 05. 🌐 czerniejewo.pl

Czerniejewo has one of the
finest Neo-Classical palaces
in Wielkopolska. It was built
for General Jan Lipski in
1771–80, and the monumental
four-columned portico was
added in 1789–91. Situated
in a large park and connected
to the town by a wide scenic
avenue, it makes a grand
impression. Within, the unusual
circular ballroom is probably
its finest feature. Today the
palace is a hotel, a restaurant
and a conference venue.

❿ Ostrów Lednicki

Road map C3. 🚌 🚉 🚉
Closed 1 Nov–14 Apr.

The small island in Lake Lednickie
has special significance as
the place where Poland is
believed to have adopted
Christianity. In the 10th century
a fortified town stood on
the island, surrounded by
earth ramparts enclosing
the earliest known Christian
buildings in Poland. Archaeologists have uncovered the
foundations of a rotunda
and a rectangular hall identified
as a baptistery and palace.
The remains of a church were
also found.

The town is assumed to
have been the seat of the Piasts
(see pp44–5). The baptism of
Poland, by which the country
adopted Christianity, is believed
to have taken place in this
baptistery in 966. The island, as
a result, has now become the
Museum of the First Piasts.

🏛 **Museum of the First Piasts**
Lednogóra. **Tel** 61 427 50 10.
Open Apr & Sep: 10am–5pm Tue–
Sun; May–Aug: 10am–6pm daily.
Closed Oct–mid-Apr. 🌐
🌐 lednicamuzeum.pl

⓫ Gniezno

See pp228–9.

⓬ Biskupin

Road map C3. ⚠ 320. 🚌 🅵 052
302 50 55. **Open** summer: 9am–6pm
daily; winter: 8am–dusk daily. 🌐
🎟 Archaeology Gala (Sep).
🌐 biskupin.pl

The remains of a 2,500-year-old
Iron Age fortified settlement
can be seen on an island in Lake
Biskupinskie. The settlement was
built entirely of wood and was
inhabited for about 150 years by
people of the Lusatian culture.
It was surrounded by a stockade
and a wall of earth and wood
6 m (18 ft) high. Access was
over a bridge and through a
gateway. The wall enclosed
more than 100 houses built
in 13 terraces, and the streets
were paved with wood. The
population was about 1,000.

When the water level rose,
the lake flooded the houses
and covered the settlement
with a layer of silt, so that the
site was abandoned. It was
rediscovered in 1934 by a local
teacher, Walenty Szwajcer. It is
the earliest known settlement
in Poland and one of the most
interesting prehistoric sites in
the whole of Europe.

Some of the buildings have
been reconstructed and there
are pens with small ponies,
goats and sheep similar to those
that the inhabitants would have
raised. The annual Archaeology
Gala features exhibitions – of
Iron Age hairstyles and archery,
for example – and workshops
where artifacts are made by
prehistoric methods.

Reconstructed fortifications of the Iron Age lake settlement in Biskupin

Lubostroń Palace viewed from the courtyard

⓭ Lubostroń

Road map C2. 790. **Tel** 52 384 46 23. **palac-lubostron.pl**

In 1795–1800 Fryderyk Józef Skórzewski, a landowner, commissioned Stanisław Zawadzki to build a palace here in the Neo-Classical style. It has a square floor plan with a central rotunda and columned porticos on all four sides, and is an outstanding imitation of the Villa Rotonda built in Vicenza, Italy, by the Italian Renaissance architect Andrea Palladio.

Lubostroń Palace has a rather severe and monumental appearance, but its interior is one of the finest surviving examples of Polish Neo-Classical architecture. It is decorated with a bas-relief depicting the history of the Wielkopolska region.

The palace is set in land-scaped grounds which date from about 1800. Today it is used for conferences and also has guest rooms for hire.

⓮ Romanesque Architecture Tour

See pp230–31.

⓯ Ląd

Road map C3. 530.

Ląd was settled by Cistercian monks after 1193. The monastery retains a number of Romanesque and Gothic buildings, one of which contains a Gothic fresco of about 1372 commemorating the benefactors of the church. The Baroque church is considerably later. The twin-towered façade by Giuseppe Simone Belloti does not do justice to the ornately decorated nave, which was built in 1730–33. Commissioned by the abbot Mikołaj A. Łukomski, Pompeo Ferrari designed a single interior space covered by a large dome rising to a height of 36 m (119 ft); the paintings by Georg Wilhelm Neunhertz depict the Church Fathers during the land seizures and give visual expression to the methods by which the Counter-Reformation would triumph in Poland: by teaching and persuasion rather than by militancy.

Environs

In Ciążeń, 5 km (3 miles) west of Poznań, there is a late Baroque bishop's palace, now owned by Poznań University Library. **Nadwarciański Nature Reserve** nearby is one of the world's most scenic refuges for wading and aquatic birds.

Ornately decorated interior of the Baroque church in Ląd

⓰ Śmiełów

Road map C3.

The Neo-Classical palace in Śmiełów, built by Stanisław Zawadzki for Andrzej Ostroróg Gorzeński in 1797, is associated with the Romantic poet Adam Mickiewicz, who stayed here in 1831, hoping to cross into the annexed part of the country where the November Insurrection against Russian rule was taking place.

His plan failed, but the palace at Śmiełów, with its landscaped grounds, became the back-drop to Mickiewicz's love for Konstanta Łubieńska. Today, fittingly, the palace houses the **Adam Mickiewicz Museum**, dedicated to the poet's life and works and containing exhibits from the age of Romanticism.

🏛 **Adam Mickiewicz Museum**
Żerków. **Tel** 62 740 31 64. **Open** 10am–4pm Tue–Sun (May–Sep: to 8pm Sun). (free Wed). **mnp.art.pl**

Neo-Classical palace in Śmiełów, today the Adam Mickiewicz Museum

⓫ Gniezno

The 14th-century Gothic Cathedral of the Assumption (Archikatedra Wniebowzięcia NMP) stands on the site of two earlier churches. The first was a pre-Romanesque church built some time after 970, and the second a Romanesque church dating from the mid–11th century. When Princess Dąbrówka, wife of Mieszko I, was buried here in 977, Gniezno was the first capital of the Polonians. Its importance increased further when in 997 the relics of St Adalbert were laid in the church. From 1025 to the 14th century Poland's royal rulers were crowned in the cathedral.

Potocki Chapel
The chapel of Archbishop Teodor Potocki was built by Pompeo Ferrari in 1727–30. It is decorated with Baroque paintings by Mathias Johannes Mayer.

★ Bronze Doors
The bronze doors of the cathedral, made in the late 12th century and depicting scenes from the life and martyrdom of St Adalbert, are among the finest examples of Romanesque art in Europe.

★ Tomb of Archbishop Zbigniew Oleśnicki
This tomb was carved in red marble by the late Gothic sculptor Veit Stoss in 1495.

KEY

① **Baroque towers** were reconstructed after the originals of 1779.

② **Original Gothic arches** have been preserved in the aisles and the ambulatory.

St Adalbert

St Adalbert (St Wojciech in Polish) was a bishop from Prague. In 977, at the suggestion of Bolesław the Brave, he left Poland for the heathen lands of Prussia, where he converted the inhabitants to Christianity but was martyred. Bolesław bought the saint's body from the Prussians, giving them in return its weight in gold, and laid the remains in Gniezno. Pope Sylvester II acknowledged the bishop's martyrdom and canonized him.

In 1038, when the Czech prince Brzetysław invaded the city, the cathedral was sacked and the saint's relics taken to Prague.

Baptism of the Prussians, a scene from the cathedral doors

Nave
The arcades separating the nave from the aisles have rich sculptural decoration made from artificial stone and dating from the second half of the 14th century.

Visitors' entrance

Shrine of St Adalbert
The silver casket, made in 1662 by Peter van der Rennen, contains a box with the relics of St Adalbert.

Exploring Gniezno

Besides its magnificent cathedral, Gniezno has many historic buildings and fine museums, making for a pleasant walk around the city. **Gniezno Archdiocesan Museum**, next to the cathedral, has religious artifacts, including paintings, sculpture, textiles and coffin portraits (see p35). A smart street leads off the Market Square to the Gothic **Church of St John** (Kościół św. Jana), which has 14th-century murals. It is hard to imagine that this small town was once the capital of the Polish nation. The **Museum of the Origins of the Polish State** in Piast Park tells the history of the city. In the park are the remains of a late medieval fortified town.

Gniezno Archdiocesan Museum

ul. Kolegiaty 2. **Tel** 61 426 37 78. **Open** May–Oct: 9am–5pm daily (to 4pm Sun); Nov–Apr: 9am–4pm Tue–Sat. (free for clergy).
muzeumag.com

An impressive collection of religious art, including artifacts from the cathedral treasury, is displayed in this museum.

Monument to Bolesław the Brave

Museum of the Origins of the Polish State

ul. Kostrzewskiego 1. **Tel** 61 426 46 41. **Open** 9am–5pm Tue–Sun (Apr–Sep: to 6pm). (free on Sun).
muzeumgniezno.pl

This archaeological museum documents the early history of the town of Gniezno, as well as the period when it was the capital of Poland.

⑭ Romanesque Architecture Tour

Sadly, few buildings survive in Wielkopolska from the earliest days of the Polish nation in the 10th century. For hundreds of years most building in Poland was in wood, and more durable brick or stone architecture was rare. A tour of pre-Romanesque and Romanesque buildings in Wielkopolska might start at Gniezno, then take in Trzemeszno and Mogilno. The finest Romanesque architecture in Poland is to be found in Strzelno – examples are the Rotunda of St Procopius and the Church of the Holy Trinity, with its remarkable Romanesque pillars. Another town of interest is Kruszwica, setting for the legend of King Popiel and home to the "Mouse Tower" of that tale.

① Gniezno
By the 14th century, Gniezno's Romanesque church had been replaced by a Gothic cathedral, but the bronze doors of the earlier building survive (see pp228–9).

② Trzemeszno
In the 12th century an order of Augustinian canons regular settled here on the site of a pre-Romanesque basilica and Benedictine monastery that had been demolished in 1038. In 1782–91 the church was rebuilt in the Baroque style.

③ Mogilno
The Benedictine church probably dates from the 11th century. After many phases of rebuilding it finally acquired a Baroque façade, although many Romanesque elements remain, in particular the crypt.

④ Strzelno
The Rotunda of St Procopius in Strzelno dates from the turn of the 13th century. In the Church of the Holy Trinity 12th-century carvings, discovered in 1946, depict personifications of the virtues and vices of Christian tradition.

Poznań

⑦ Lake Gopło
This narrow lake is surrounded mostly by marshy meadows. It is home to many birds, including bitterns, marsh harriers, lapwings and wild geese.

⑥ Kruszwica
Kruszwica was briefly the seat of a bishopric and the mid-12th-century Church of St Peter may well have been its cathedral. The shell and the interior of the church are built of granite ashlars, which survive, remarkably, almost in their original state.

Key

 Tour route
 Other road

Toruń
Bydgoszcz
Barcin
Kanał Notecki
Lake Pakoskie
Lake Gopło
Radziejów
Konin

0 kilometres 5
0 miles 5

The Legend of King Popiel

The legend of King Popiel was recorded in the early 12th century by Gall Anonim, the first Polish chronicler. According to the legend, Siemowit Piast, founder of the Piast dynasty, was a peasant from Kruszwica. The Polonians, terrified by the atrocities committed by their king, Popiel, decided to depose him and chose Siemowit Piast as his successor. Popiel fled to his tower but the rebels turned into mice and devoured him. The Gothic tower overlooking Lake Gopło in Kruszwica is called the "Mouse Tower" but was in fact built in the 14th century, a few hundred years after these events were said to have taken place.

The Mouse Tower

⑤ Inowrocław
The most historic building in this health resort is the Church of Our Lady, dating from the turn of the 13th century, built in the time of the dukes of Inowrocław.

Castle in Gołuchów, home of the Działyński family

⑰ Gołuchów

Road map C4. 🚩 1,500.
🚌 **W** goluchow.pl

The castle at Gołuchów looks as if it belongs in the Loire Valley, in France, alongside the other Renaissance châteaux for which that region is celebrated. Although the castle at Gołuchów was built in the mid-16th to 17th centuries, its present exterior dates only from 1872–85, commissioned by the owners, Izabella Czartoryska and her husband, Jan Działyński. Izabella was the daughter of Adam Czartoryski, a Polish émigré leader in Paris, and was educated in France; her wish was to turn the residence into a "paradise on earth" according to her own tastes. She also built a museum that was open to the public. Initial plans for the renovation of the castle were made in around 1871 by the French architect Eugène Viollet-le-Duc. The rest of the castle was designed by his son-in-law, Maurice August Ouradou, after plans by Polish architects. Today the **castle museum** contains European and Oriental works of art from the collection of the Działyński family.

🏛 **Castle Museum**
ul. Działyńskich 2. **Tel** 62 761 50 94.
Open 10am–4pm Tue–Sun (May–Sep: to 6pm Sun). 🎫 (free on Tue).
🅿 **W** mnp.art.pl

Environs
In **Dobryczy**, 23 km (14 miles) to the west of Gołuchów, is the Neo-Classical residence of Augustyn Gorzeński, a freemason, built in 1798–9.

⑱ Kalisz

Road map C4. 🚩 103,000. 🚌
🅿 **ℹ** ul. Zamkowa (62 598 27 31). 🎭 Theatre Festival (May); International Jazz Festival (Nov–Dec). **W** cit.kalisz.pl

Kalisz, a settlement on the amber route between the Baltic Sea and Rome, has ancient origins. It is mentioned as Calisia by Ptolemy in his *Geography* of AD 142–7. However, a town did not grow up here until the 13th century, and it did not really develop until the 15th century, when Kalisz became a provincial capital. During the Partitions of Poland, Kalisz was the furthest outpost of the Russian empire. In 1914, just after the start of World War I, it was severely bombarded by Prussian artillery. Its rebuilding began in 1917, and the present city centre, with town houses surrounding the **Market Square**, the **town hall** and the Bogusławski Theatre, dates from that time. A substantial number of earlier buildings survive. These include the Gothic **Cathedral of St Nicholas** (Katedra św. Mikołaja), the late Baroque collegiate **Church of the Assumption** (Kościół Wniebowzięcia NMP), and the neighbouring Mannerist **church**, formerly a **Jesuit college**. The group of Bernadine monasteries and

Bernadine church in Kalisz

the late Renaissance **Church of the Annunciation** (Kościół Nawiedzenia NMP) are also worth a visit.

🏛 **Cathedral of St Nicholas**
ul. Kanonicka 5. **Tel** 62 757 59 74.

Antoni Radziwiłł's hunting lodge in Antonin

⓲ Antonin

Road map C4. 🏔 320. 🚆 🚌
🎵 Chopin Festival (Sep).

When Duke Antoni Radziwiłł asked Karl Friedrich Schinkel to build him a hunting lodge, it was an unusual commission for the architect. The small larchwood building, dating from 1822–4, has a cruciform plan and an octagonal centre. The octagonal hall is surrounded by galleries supported by a large central pillar. It was here that, in 1827, Fryderyk Chopin taught Wanda, Duke Radziwiłł's daughter, with whom he fell in love. The piano on which the great composer played was chopped up for firewood by soldiers of the Red Army who were billeted in the lodge. The building now houses a hotel and is the venue for concerts and festivals in honour of Chopin, as well as hunting balls.

Environs
In the village of Bralin, 36 km (22 miles) north of Antonin, there is a delightful wooden church called Na Pólku, dating from 1711.

⓴ Piotrków Trybunalski

Road map D4. 🏔 77,000. 🚆 🚌
ℹ Zamurowa 11 (44 732 60 50).
🌐 cit.piotrkow.pl

Before the Partitions of Poland, this was the town where sessions of the royal court and parliament were held, and after 1578 it was the seat of the Crown Tribunal. The town flourished and many magnificent churches bear witness to those times. Above **Tribunal Square** (Rynek Trybunalski) rises the brick tower and Baroque roof of the Gothic **Parish Church of St James**. Synods and official ceremonies were conducted here. The large **Jesuit church**, dating from 1695–1727, contains remarkable *trompe l'oeil* paintings by Andrzej Ahorn, himself a Jesuit and a self-taught painter. The scheme includes a painting of a monk looking into the church through a painted grille. Other interesting churches include the **Piarist church and monastery**, now a Protestant church, a 17th-century **Dominican monastery complex** and the former **Dominican Church of Saints Jacek and Dorothy** (Kościół św. Jacka i Doroty), with Rococo interior. There is also a **Regional Museum** located in a Gothic-Renaissance castle that is essentially a large brick tower designed as

Detail from the castle in Piotrków Trybunalski

a residence. The most interesting part of the museum is the exhibition of grand interiors of the 16th to 20th centuries.

🏛 **Church of St James**
ul. Krakowskie Przedmieście 2. **Tel** 44 646 51 40.

🏛 **Jesuit church**
ul. Pijarska 4. **Tel** 44 647 01 51.

🏛 **Regional Museum**
pl. Zamkowy 4. **Tel** 44 646 52 72. **Open** 10am–3pm Tue–Sun (to 4pm Tue & Sat). **Closed** pub hols & day after pub hols. 🅿 🅲

㉑ Sulejów

Road map D4. 🏔 6,400. 🚌
🌐 sulejow.pl

In 1177 a Cistercian abbey was founded here by Kazimierz the Just and the church was consecrated in 1232. It is in the Romanesque-Gothic style and has remained almost unaltered across the centuries, although the interior does contain Baroque altars and paintings in the same style.

The Romanesque portal in the west front bears what are said to be sword marks made by knights who in 1410 went to war with the Teutonic Knights. The monastery fell into ruin, although the remaining parts of it have been renovated and are now a hotel and **museum**. Near the abbey is a large artificial lake made in the 1970s on the River Pilica. It is a popular holiday spot.

🏛 **Abbey Museum**
Tel 44 616 25 84. **Open** 9am–6pm Mon–Sat & 1–6pm Sun (call first). 🅿

Cistercian abbey in Sulejów

⑳ Łódź

The centre of the Polish textile industry, Łódź developed at an astonishing rate as the industry thrived. Its population grew from just 15,000 in 1850 to more than half a million in 1914. It was a place of great contrasts, which were vividly documented in the novel *The Promised Land* (1899) by the Nobel Prize-winning author Władysław Reymont. The contrasts can still be seen in the architecture of the city, where vast fortunes and abject poverty existed side by side. Factories and opulent mansions sprang up in their hundreds, contrasting with the ramshackle homes of the factory workers.

VISITORS' CHECKLIST

Practical Information
Road map D4. 🚆 700,000.
ℹ️ ul. Piotrkowska 87 (42 638
59 55). 🎭 International Ballet
Festival (May).

Transport
🚉 Railway information: **Tel** 42
205 55 15 (local trains) or 19 575
(Intercity trains). 🚌 Coach
information: PKS **Tel** 42 631 97 06.
W cit.lodz.pl

Exploring Łódź

The city's main thoroughfare is Ulica Piotrkowska, which is several kilometres long. Its most important section stretches from **Plac Wolności** to Aleje Piłudskiego. It is Poland's longest pedestrianized street and is lined with shops, cafés, restaurants and banks.

Behind the town houses, the brick factory buildings still stand, many of them now converted into stores. A noteworthy example is the one at **Piotrkowska 137/139**, built in 1907 for the cotton manufacturer Juliusz Kindermann by the architect Gustav Landau-Gutenteger, and featuring a gold mosaic frieze depicting an allegory of trade. In Plac Wolności there is a **Monument to Tadeusz**

Colourful Art Nouveau stained-glass window in Poznański Palace

Kościuszko from 1930, rebuilt after its destruction in 1939 and a favourite meeting place for the city's youth. Beside it stands the modest Neo-Classical **town hall**, which dates from 1827,

when the foundations of industry were being laid in Łódź.

The city's **cemeteries** – the Catholic and Protestant cemeteries in Ulica Srebrzyńska and the Jewish cemetery in Ulica Bracka – contain some exceptionally interesting monuments that bear witness to the variety of cultures and nationalities that existed in Łódź before 1939, when it was a city with one of the largest Jewish populations in Europe. The grand mausoleums were built for local industrialists, who before 1914 were the wealthiest people in the Russian empire.

The **Leopold Kindermann Villa** at Ulica Wólczańska 31/33 is an Art Nouveau building designed by Gustav Landau-Gutenteger. It was built in 1902 and features fine stained-glass windows. Today it houses an art gallery.

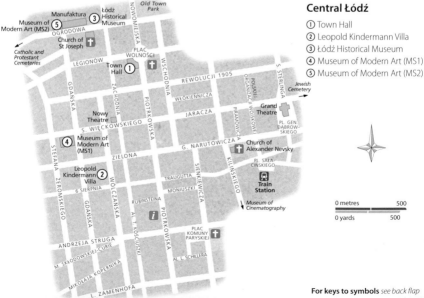

Central Łódź

① Town Hall
② Leopold Kindermann Villa
③ Łódź Historical Museum
④ Museum of Modern Art (MS1)
⑤ Museum of Modern Art (MS2)

0 metres   500
0 yards   500

At the turn of the 20th century the townscape of Łódź was dominated by the industrialists' palaces. The finest surviving examples are the residences of the textile-factory-owner Izrael Kalmanowicz Poznański, at Ogrodowa 15 and Gdańska 36, and a remarkable palace at Plac Zwycięstwa 1 that rivals the one built by Karol Scheibler, the merchant celebrated as the "cotton king" of Poznań.

🏛 Łódź Historical Museum

ul. Ogrodowa 15. **Tel** 42 254 90 00. **Open** 10am–2pm Mon, 10am–4pm Tue & Thu, 2–6pm Wed, 11am–6pm Sat & Sun. 🚲 🏛 🌐 **muzeum-lodz.pl**

The museum is located in Poznański Palace, beside a group of brick factory buildings. Alongside the palace stands a former spinning mill, a vast Neo-Renaissance edifice designed by Hilary Majewski in 1876. The eclectic palace, with twin cupolas, was built in stages from 1888 onwards. Notable features of the interior are the grand staircase, the series of private apartments, the beautifully restored reception rooms, and the *belle époque* furniture.

The museum contains exhibits associated with the pianists Władysław Kędra and Artur Rubinstein, who was born in Łódź.

Elaborate Moorish stove in the Scheibler Palace, Łódź

Romanesque basilica at Tum, near Łęczyca

🏛 Museum of Modern Art

MS1: ul. Więckowskiego 36. **Tel** 42 633 97 90. MS2: ul. Ogrodowa 19 **Tel** 42 634 39 48. **Open** 10am–6pm Tue, 11am–7pm Wed–Sun. 🚲 (free Thu). 🏛 🌐 **msl.org.pl**

The Museum of Modern Art has two branches, MS1 and MS2. The first is housed in another of Izrael Poznański's palaces, this one built in imitation of a Florentine Renaissance palazzo. This is usually used for high-profile temporary exhibitions.

MS2 is in part of the restored factory complex, now known as Manufaktura, and contains one of Poland's best collection of modern art, featuring the likes of Hans Arp, Piet Mondrian, Max Ernst and Joseph Beuys.

🏛 Museum of Cinematography

pl. Zwycięstwa 1. **Tel** 42 203 24 50. **Open** 10am–5pm Tue, 9am–4pm Wed & Fri, 11am–6pm Thu, Sat & Sun. 🚲 (free on Tue). 🌐 **kinomuzeum.pl**

Situated in the eclectic palace of Karol Scheibler, the museum contains a rich collection of films and film posters from the earliest days of cinematography to modern times. It also documents the works of Łódź's renowned film school, whose graduates include the directors Andrzej Wajda, Roman Polański, Krzysztof Kieślowski and Jerzy Skolimowski, and the much-praised cameraman Witold Sobociński.

㉓ Łęczyca

Road map D3. 🚏 16,500. 🚉 🚌

The royal castle at Łęczyca, built in 1357 by Kazimierz the Great, was the third fortified building to be raised in the town. Little is known about the first. The second was the seat of the rulers of another duchy. The castle, with its brick tower, served as a jail for imprisoned aristocrats. The **Regional Museum** within it contains artifacts from prehistoric times to the present. The main attraction is the unusual exhibition dedicated to the devil Boruta, legendary guardian of the treasure hidden in the castle's cellar.

The devil Boruta at Łęczyca royal castle

🏛 Regional Museum

ul. Zamkowa 1. **Tel** 24 721 24 49. **Open** May–Sep: 10am–5pm Tue–Sun (from 11am Sat & Sun); Oct–Apr: 10am–4pm Tue–Sun (to 5pm Fri, to 3pm Sat & Sun). **Closed** public hols. 🚲 🏛 🏛 🌐 **zamek.leczyca.pl**

Environs

In **Tum**, 3 km (2 miles) from Łęczyca, there is a splendidly preserved Romanesque church. This granite building, consecrated in 1161, was remodelled several times, but its current form is close to the original. It consists of a triple-nave basilica with two circular and two square towers and an apse at the west and east ends. The west apse has a remarkable Romanesque fresco of *Christ in Glory*, painted in 1161.

For hotels and restaurants see p304 and pp315–16

GDAŃSK

Gdańsk is among the finest cities of northern Europe, distinguished by beautiful buildings and a history that stretches back more than 1,000 years. For many centuries the wealthiest city in Poland. In 1939, this prosperity was abruptly bought to a close as the first shots of World War II were fired in the city. The end of the conflict brought destruction, but Gdańsk recovered as settlers moved in from other parts of Poland.

The earliest mention of Gdańsk occurs in 997. For more than 300 years it was the capital of a Slav duchy in Pomerania, and in 1308 it was taken over by the Teutonic Knights. Under their rule, the city grew.

In 1361 Gdańsk became a member of the Hanseatic League (a trade association of Baltic towns), further bolstering its economic development. From 1466 until the Second Partition in 1793, the city belonged to Poland; it was the country's largest Baltic port and an important centre of the grain and timber trade between Poland and the rest of Europe.

A wealthy city, Gdańsk played a pivotal role in the Republic of Two Nations (see p48). It also became a major centre of the arts – goldsmiths fashioned fine jewellery for the royal courts of Europe, and the city's gemstone and amber workshops won great renown. From 1793 it was incorporated into Prussia, only becoming a free city under the Treaty of Versailles after World War I. It was almost totally destroyed during World War II, but a post-war rebuilding programme has restored many of the city's finest buildings and much of its historic atmosphere.

Today Gdańsk, attractively set between the coast and wooded hills, is renowned for its mercantile traditions and its openness to the world. Together with the coastal resort of Sopot and the port of Gdynia (see p269), it forms the conurbation known as Trójmiasto ("the Tri-City").

The beautiful main town of Gdańsk

◄ The majestic medieval port crane over Motlawa River

Exploring Gdańsk

The most important buildings in terms of the history of Gdańsk are to be found in the city centre, which can be reached by taking a bus or tram to the Main Station (Dworzec Główny), the Highland Gate (Brama Wyżynna) or the Podwale Przedmiejskie, and continuing on foot from there. The bus, tram or urban railway (SKM) are all useful for travelling to outlying parts of the city. You can also take the SKM to reach Oliwa in the northwest, which has a fine group of cathedral buildings, one of which contains a famous organ, and a good park for walking.

Ulica Długie Pobrzeże on the River Motława

Getting There

Gdańsk has good transport links. There are rail services to and from all the major cities in Poland – the express train from Warsaw takes less than 3 hours. There is an international airport at Rębiechowo, near Gdańsk. It is also easy to reach Gdańsk by car, whether from Warsaw (route E77), central Poland (route E75), Szczecin (route E28) or Berlin (route 22).

Key

- ■ Major sight
- ▫ Other sight
- ═ Railway line
- ─ Pedestrian street

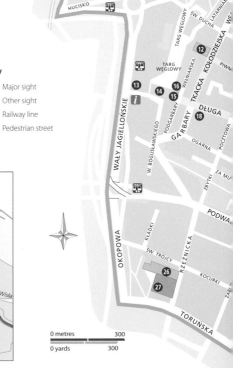

Panoramic shot of Gdansk City Centre

Sights at a Glance

Museums and Galleries

❷ European Solidarity Center
❷④ *National Maritime Museum p251*
❷⑦ *National Museum p253*

Churches

❺ Church of St Catherine
❻ Church of St Bridget
❿ *Church of St Mary pp244–5*
❷⑥ Church of the Holy Trinity
❷⑧ *Oliwa Cathedral pp254–5*

Historic Buildings

❶ Monument to the
   Shipyard Workers
❸ Old Town Hall
❹ Great Mill
❼ Polish Post Office
❽ Gdańsk Crane
⑪ Royal Chapel
⑫ Arsenal
⑬ Highland Gate
⑭ Prison Tower
⑮ Golden Gate
⑯ St George's Court
⑱ Uphagen House
⑲ Main Town Hall
㉑ Artus Court
㉒ Golden House
㉓ Green Gate

Major Streets and Districts

❾ Ulica Mariacka
⑰ Ulica Długa
⑳ Długi Targ
㉕ Spichlerze Island
㉙ Westerplatte
㉚ Wisłoujście Fortress

For keys to symbols *see back flap*

Street-by-Street: Along Raduna Canal

Despite wartime destruction, some fine buildings have survived on either side of the Raduna Canal. It was dug in about 1338, one of the greatest projects undertaken by the Teutonic Knights in Gdańsk *(see p27)*, and for many centuries it was of great importance to the city's economy. The current in the canal was used to supply power for local mills, grindstones and a sawmill. Among the buildings look out for the Mannerist-style House of the Abbots of Pelplin, the Great Mill, which dates from the rule of the Teutonic Knights, and the enormous churches of St Catherine and St Bridget.

The Church of St Joseph is a former Carmelite church, built in 1482. It was burned down by Red Army Soldiers in 1945 and then rebuilt by the Church Fathers.

❸ ★ Old Town Hall
The Lord's Blessing in one of the rooms is from the ceiling of the house at Ulica Długa 39. It is ascribed to the workshop of 17th-century Pomeranian artist Hermann Hahn.

The Church of St Elizabeth was built in 1417 beside a *leprosorium*, or lepers' sanctuary.

Small Mill

ELZBIETANSKA

KORZENNA

RAJSKA

NA PIASKACH

WIELKIE

GARNCARSKA

KOWALSKA

House of the Abbots of Pelplin

0 metres 50
0 yards 50

❹ ★ Great Mill
Today this medieval brick mill houses a modern shopping centre.

Locator Map
See pp238–9

❻ Church of St Bridget
This church was used as a place of worship by Solidarity members.

❺ ★ St Catherine's Church
The memorial to astronomer Johannes Hevelius (1611–87) was installed in 1780 by Daniel G. Davisson, his great-grandson.

Key

— Suggested route

❶ Monument to the Shipyard Workers

Plac Solidarności Robotniczej. 🚌 🚋 to Dworzec PKP.

The monument was built a few months after the famous Gdańsk Shipyard workers' strike of 1980 and the creation of the independent Solidarity trade union *(see p59)*. It was erected in honour of the shipyard workers who were killed during the strike and demonstrations of December 1970; it stands 30 m (100 ft) from the spot where the first three victims fell. Its three stainless steel crosses, 42 m (130 ft) high, were both a warning that such a tragedy might happen again and a symbol of remembrance and hope.

The monument was designed by the shipyard workers and a group of artists including Bogdan Pietruszka, Wiesław Szyślak, Robert Pepliński and Elżbieta Szczodrowska. It was built by a team of workers from the shipyard. In the 1980s, the cross was the rallying point for Solidarity demonstrations, which were suppressed by the police.

❷ European Solidarity Centre

Pl. Solidarności 1, 80-863. **Tel** 58 772 41 12. **Open** May–Sep: 10am–7pm daily; Oct–Apr: 10am–5pm daily. 🚻 🖥 ⧉ 🇼 ecs.gda.pl

Dedicated to the history of Solidarity, the Polish Trade Union and Civil Resistance Movement, the European Solidarity Centre is located next to Gdańsk shipyards. The museum is not only devoted to Solidarity, but also takes visitors on a historical journey of other opposition movements, which led to the democratic transformation of many countries in Central and Eastern Europe. It was constructed with the ambition of becoming a world centre for the ideas of freedom, democracy and solidarity.

Visitors can enjoy the views of the remains of the shipyards from its viewing terrace or the rooftop bar.

❸ Old Town Hall

Nadbałtyckie Centrum Kultury, ul. Korzenna 33/35. **Tel** 58 301 10 51. 🚻 🖥 ⧉ 🇼 nck.org.pl

Built by Antonis van Opbergen in 1587–95, the Old Town Hall in Gdańsk is an outstanding example of Dutch Mannerist architecture. It is a compact, plain building with no distinctive ornamentation, and is equipped with a defence tower. The stone doorway was probably made by Willem van der Meer. Beneath each bracket are two distorted masks personifying vice, and two smiling, chubby masks, personifying virtue. Within the town hall, the painting, sculpture and furniture are very interesting, although little is left of the original decorative scheme of 1595. Of particular interest is the painted ceiling in one of the rooms which is by Hermann Hahn, a 17th-century Pomeranian artist. It was removed from a house at Ulica Długa 39 and transferred to the Old Town Hall some time after 1900. The theme of the ceiling paintings is allegorical: the central one depicts *The Lord's Blessing* and a figure of Zygmunt III Vasa also appears.

The magnificent European Solidarity Centre

The Great Mill from the Raduna Canal

❹ Great Mill

ul. Wielkie Młyny 16. **Tel** 58 305 24 05.
Open 10am–7pm Mon–Fri,
10am–4pm Sat. 🚻 📷 🏛 🔁 🚹

The Great Mill (Wielki Młyn)
was one of the largest industrial
buildings in medieval Europe. It
was constructed during the rule
of the Teutonic Knights, being
completed in around 1350. It is
built in brick and is crowned by
a tall, steeply pitched roof.

At the front of the building
stood a two-storey bakery with
a chimney set against the gable
of the mill which reached the
height of its roof. Beside
the mill stood 12, later 18,
large poles to which millstones
were attached for grinding
various types of grain. The mill
was destroyed by fire in 1945,
but was restored after World
War II. This remarkable old
building now contains a
modern shopping centre.

❺ Church of St Catherine

ul. Profesorka 3. **Tel** 58 301 15 95.

The Church of St Catherine
(Kościół św. Katarzyny) is the
oldest and also the most
important parish church in
the old town. It was built
in 1227–39 by the dukes
of Gdańsk-Pomerania and
underwent major rebuilding
in the 14th century.

Most of the Gothic, Mannerist
and Baroque furnishings that
the church once contained
were pillaged or destroyed
in 1945. The most notable
surviving pieces are the

paintings by Anton
Möller and Izaak
van den Blocke, the
Baroque memorials to
various townspeople,
and the tombstone
of the astronomer
Johannes Hevelius,
dating from 1659.

The tower, 76 m (250 ft)
high, was first built in
1486. Demolished
in 1944 and later
rebuilt, it is once again
a major landmark. It
is well worth climbing
to the top of the tower;
the effort is rewarded
by wonderful views
of the city. The
presbytery on
the east side
of the church
has a fine late
Gothic gable.

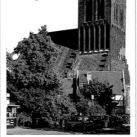

Gothic tower of the Church of
St Catherine

❻ Church of St Bridget

ul. Profesorska 17. **Tel** 58 301 31 52.

The Church of St Bridget
(Kościół św. Brygidy) was well
known in Poland in the 1980s
as a place of worship and
sanctuary for members of
Solidarity. It was built on
the site of a 14th-century
chapel dedicated to St Mary
Magdalene, where in
1374 the remains
of the visionary
St Bridget
were

displayed as they were being
taken from Rome to Vadstena
in Sweden. Soon afterwards a
monastery for the Sisters of
St Bridget was founded here.
The church built beside it was
completed in around 1514.

The brick shell of the Gothic
church contrasts with the more
recent belfry, built in 1653 by
Peter Willer. The church's stark
interior is an effective foil for the
modern altars, tombstones and
sculptures that it now contains.
The most impressive of these
are the high altar and the
monument to Father Jerzy
Popiełuszko, who was murdered
in 1984 by Polish security
service officials.

❼ Polish Post Office

pl. Obrońców Poczty Polskiej 1/2.
Post Office Museum: **Tel** 51 241 87 57.
Open 10am–1pm Tue, 10am–4pm
Wed & Fri–Sun, 10am–6pm Thu.
📷 (free on Tue). **W** mhmg.pl

The Polish Post Office was
the scene of some of the
most dramatic events of
the first days of World War II.
At daybreak on 1 September
1939, German troops attacked
the Polish Postal Administration
that had its base here, in what
was then the free city of Gdańsk.
For 15 hours the postal workers
resisted the onslaught, but
they were finally overwhelmed.
On 5 October more than
30 of them were executed
by Nazi soldiers at the Zaspa
Cemetery. Their heroism
is commemorated in the
Post Office Museum and
by a monument depicting
an injured postal worker
atop scattered mail, handing
over his rifle to Nike, Greek
goddess of victory. It was
designed by Wincenty Kućma
in 1979 and bears an epitaph
written by Maria
and Zygfryd
Korpalski
in 1979.

Monument to Father Jerzy Popiełuszko in the Church of St Bridget

Ulica Mariacka, once the haunt of writers and artists

❽ Gdańsk Crane

ul. Szeroka 67/68. Maritime Museum: **Tel** 58 301 69 38. **Open** May, Jun & Sep–Nov: 10am–4pm Tue–Sun; Jul & Aug: 10am–6pm daily; Dec–Apr: 10am–3pm Tue–Sun. **Closed** public hols. 🅿 🍴 W nmm.pl

The Gdańsk crane (Żuraw), icon of the city, is one of its finest buildings and a medieval structure almost unique in Europe. Built in the 14th century and renovated in 1442–4, when it acquired its present appearance, it combined the functions of a city gate and a port crane.

The crane, an entirely wooden structure, is set between two circular brick towers. It was operated by men working the huge treadmills within, and was capable of lifting weights of up to 2 tonnes to a height of 27 m (90 ft). The crane was used not only to load and unload goods but also in fitting masts to ships.

The crane was destroyed by fire in 1945. As part of the rebuilding programme after World War II it was repaired and reconstructed, together with its internal mechanism. It is now part of the collection of the National Maritime Museum (see p251). The Crane Tower looks out over Ulica Długie Pobrzeże, which runs alongside the River Motława. Once known as the Long Bridge, it was originally a wooden footbridge that functioned as a quay where ships from all over the world tied up. Today a fleet of yachts and small pleasure boats offering trips around the harbour in the Port of Gdańsk is moored here.

❾ Ulica Mariacka

Ulica Mariacka, regarded as Gdańsk's finest street, runs eastwards from the Church of St Mary to Długie Pobrzeże, terminating at the Mariacka Gate on the riverfront. Rebuilt from the ruins that resulted from World War II, the street contains outstanding examples of traditional Gdańsk architecture. Here, town houses that were once owned by wealthy merchants and goldsmiths have tall, richly ornamented façades; others are fronted by external raised terraces with ornamented parapets. It is small wonder that this picturesque street has for centuries inspired writers and artists.

The neighbourly porch gossip that once upon a time filled the evening air is, sadly, no more. Today, however, the street is a favourite haunt of lovers as well as tourists, most of whom are looking for picturesque subjects to photograph or browsing through the amber jewellery for which Ulica Mariacka is now celebrated. During the long summer evenings, a number of musicians provide free open-air concerts, and the welcoming street cafés stay open until late at night.

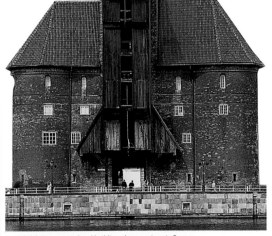

The Gdańsk Crane, a medieval building almost unique in Europe

⑩ Church of St Mary

The Church of St Mary (Kościół Mariacki) is the largest medieval brick-built church in Europe. Building work began in 1343 and took 150 years to complete. The final stage of construction, involving the 100-m (325-ft) long nave, was carried out by Henryk Hetzel. From 1529 to 1945, when it was destroyed, St Mary's was a Protestant church. Like so many other parts of Gdańsk, it was rebuilt after World War II. The interior contains furnishings in the Gothic, Mannerist and Baroque styles. Look out for the memorial tablets to prominent local families.

★ **Astronomical Clock**
The clock, made by Hans Dürunger in 1464–70, shows the hour and also the days, dates of moveable feasts and phases of the moon. At noon a procession of figures representing Adam and Eve, the Apostles, the Three Kings and Death appears.

★ **Tablet of Charity**
This ornate panel, made by Anton Möller in 1607, once hung over the church collection box. Its purpose was to encourage churchgoers to be generous.

★ **Tablet of the Ten Commandments**
This panel of around 1480–90 depicts each of the Ten Commandments in two scenes, illustrating obedience to, and disregard of, the laws.

The Beautiful Madonna of Gdańsk
The Chapel of St Anne contains this 15th-century figure of the Virgin and Child by an unknown artist.

Gothic Sacrarium
The sacrarium, in the shape of an open-work tower decorated with pinnacles, is over 8 m (26 ft) high.

Epitaph to Valentin von Karnitz
The memorial tablet to Valentyn von Karnitz, of around 1590, has many Dutch Mannerist features. The centre painting depicts the biblical tale of the Lamentation of Abel.

⑪ Royal Chapel

ul. św. Ducha 58. **Tel** 58 301 67 55.

The Royal Chapel (Kaplica Królewska) was built by Jan III Sobieski as a place of worship for Catholics of the parish of St Mary's, which had become a Protestant church in 1529. The Baroque chapel was built in 1678–81 to designs by the great royal architect Tylman van Gameren.

The carving in the Kaplica Królewska is by Andreas Schlüter the Younger. The chapel itself is enclosed within a chamber and is situated on a raised floor. The interior is less ostentatious than the façade.

The façade of the Dutch Mannerist Arsenal seen from Targ Węglowy

⑫ Arsenal

ul. Targ Węglowy 6. Academy of Fine Arts: **Tel** 58 301 28 01.
w asp.gda.pl

The Arsenal is the finest example of the Dutch Mannerist style in Gdańsk. It was built, probably to plans by Antonis van Opbergen in collaboration with Jan Strakowski, in 1600–9.

Today the ground floor of the former weapons and ammunition store is filled with shops, while the Academy of Fine Arts occupies the upper storeys. The building has a finely decorated façade, with fascinatingly original carvings by Wilhelm Barth.

Street-by-Street: Długi Targ and Ulica Długa

Długi Targ and Ulica Długa, its continuation, are the most attractive streets in Gdańsk. Długi Targ leads westwards from the Green Gate on the River Motława to join Ulica Długa, which runs as far as the Golden Gate. These two pedestrianized streets are lined with old town houses that were once the residences of the city's wealthiest citizens. Most of the Main City's principal buildings, including the town hall and Artus Court, are on Długi Targ. Together the streets formed an avenue that was used for parades, ceremonies and sometimes public executions and, from 1457, for the processions that accompanied royal visits – which is why the two streets were known as the Royal Way.

⑯ St George's Court
Built for the patricians of Gdańsk in 1487–98, the name derives from the exclusive Fraternity of St George, whose seat it was.

⑬ Highland Gate
The gate, built in 1574–5, has relief decoration with inscriptions and sculptures in the Italian Renaissance and northern Mannerist style.

⑮ Golden Gate
This ceremonial gateway to the city, made in 1612–14 and surmounted by allegorical sculptures, embodies the spirit of Gdańsk's golden age.

⑭ Prison Tower
This was once used to hold prisoners sentenced to death. The tower currently houses the Amber Museum.

Key

— Suggested route

⑱ ★ Uphagen House
The interior of this restored town house features 18th-century Rococo panelling, which survived wartime destruction.

⑲ ★ Main Town Hall
The Allegory of Justice by Hans Vredeman de Vries decorates the main council chamber, also known as the Red Room.

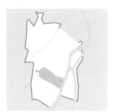

Locator Map
See pp238–9

㉑ ★ Artus Court
The bench of the Brotherhood of St Christopher, in this meeting house for dignitaries, is adorned with the story of Lot and his daughter by Laurentius Lauenstein.

⑰ Ulica Długa
Rebuilt after wartime destruction, this is the main street of old Gdańsk.

㉒ Golden House
The unusual façade of the house was once completely covered in gilt stone carvings.

㉓ Green Gate
This building in the Mannerist style was the official residence of the Polish kings when they came to Gdańsk on state visits.

KUŚNIERSKA

DŁUGI TARG

NICZA

MIESZCZAŃSKA

Fountain of Neptune

0 metres 100
0 yards 100

⑳ Długi Targ
When the street was rebuilt after World War II, the houses and their stepped terraces were reconstructed.

The Highland Gate, part of the new fortifications of 1571–6

⑬ Highland Gate

ul. Wały Jagiellońskie.

The Highland Gate marks the beginning of the Royal Way that, following Ulica Długa and Długi Targ, descends eastwards to the Green Gate *(see p250)*. It was built by Hans Kramer of Saxony as part of the fortifications that were erected along the western limits of the city in 1571–6. Originally built in brick, the gate acquired its present appearance in 1588, when the Flemish architect Willem van den Blocke faced it with stone on its western side, making it look as if it were made of masonry blocks.

The upper level is decorated with cartouches containing coats of arms: that of Poland, held by two angels (on the breast of the eagle the coat of arms of Stanisław August, a bull calf, is visible) are flanked by the Prussian coat of arms, borne by unicorns, and those of Gdańsk, borne by lions.

⑭ Prison Tower

ul. Długa–Przedbramie. **Tel** 58 301 47 33. Amber Museum: **Open** 10am–3pm Tue, 10am–6pm Wed–Sat, 11am–6pm Sun. ⚡ (free on Tue).

The mix of architectural styles in the Prison Tower is the result of several rebuildings. The tower was originally built as part of the now-destroyed Ulica Długa Gate that was erected in the second half of the 14th century as part of the medieval fortifications of the Main Town.

In the 15th and 16th centuries, the tower was heightened several times and the surrounding buildings altered accordingly. When the new fortifications were built in 1571–6 the entire complex lost its purpose. It began to be used as a prison, court and torture chamber.

It was remodelled for its new purpose in 1604 by Antonis van Opbergen, who gave it a northern Mannerist form, and by Willem van der Meer, who added decorative detail. The tower was the scene of many blood-curdling interrogations. There is a whipping post on the western wall, which was also the site of many executions. At the turn of the 20th century, in accordance with the new functions of the buildings, a stonecutter's workshop was installed in the courtyard.

The Prison Tower now houses the Amber Museum.

⑮ Golden Gate

ul. Długa.

The Golden Gate was built in 1612–14 on the site of the medieval Ulica Długa Gate. The architect, Abraham van den Blocke, devised the new construction in the style of a classical Roman triumphal arch through which the Royal Way would enter the city of Gdańsk.

The arches of the gate are framed by Ionic columns in the lower tier surmounted by composite columns in the upper tier. The gate is crowned

with statues carved by Piotr Ringering in 1648 and reconstructed after the originals were damaged in World War II. The statues on the outer side of the gate, facing away from the city, depict peace, freedom, prosperity and glory, while those on the inner side, facing the city, represent prudence, piety, justice and harmony. The carved decoration is complemented by inscriptions in both Latin and German on the theme of civic virtue. The whole gate was designed and constructed in the Neo-Classical style but with Mannerist elements.

The Golden Gate, so called because of the gilding on its façade

⑯ St George's Court

ul. Targ Węglowy 27. **Closed** to visitors.

The fraternity of St George, an association of archers and the oldest of its kind in medieval Gdańsk, originally met in Artus Court. However, in 1487 the fraternity acquired its own premises, St George's Court, which was built under the direction of Hans Glothau in the Flemish style. It was completed in 1494.

The first floor contained an archery range and storerooms for archery equipment. Members of the fraternity met in the Great Hall on the first floor. The hall was also used for ceremonies, meetings and banquets and for the performance of plays.

In 1566 it was crowned by a figure of St George and the Dragon, which was removed and is now on display in the National Museum (the figure on the small tower is a copy). In the 19th century the building housed the School of Fine Art. Today, Artus Court is the premises of the Gdańsk branch of the Association of Polish Architects.

Looking down Ulica Długa from the Golden Gate to Długi Targ

⑰ Ulica Długa

Today, as in the past, Ulica Długa ("Long Street") is the Main Town's principal thoroughfare. The houses that line the street were once inhabited by the foremost burghers of Gdańsk, and virtually every one has its own colourful history. Although the oldest surviving houses on the street date from the Middle Ages, most were built during the heyday of the Hanseatic League.

With their narrow façades crowned by a variety of elements – from coats of arms and symbols to animals, allegorical figures and the heroes of classical mythology – the houses on Ulica Długa are typical of the architecture of Gdańsk. Unfortunately, when they were modernized in the mid-19th century, all the stepped terraces that originally fronted the entrances to the houses were removed.

After the carnage of World War II, almost every building on Ulica Długa was left in ruins. Many of the houses were later reconstructed, but only the finest buildings were rebuilt in architectural detail.

The Red Room in the Main Town Hall

⑱ Uphagen House

ul. Długa 12. **Tel** 78 944 96 65. Part of the Museum of the History of Gdańsk: **Open** 10am–1pm Tue, 10am–4pm Wed, Fri & Sat, 10am–6pm Thu, 11am–4pm Sun. 🖼 (free Tue). 🅦 mhmg.pl

The house that originally stood at Ulica Długa 12 was acquired by Johann Uphagen, a town councillor, in 1775. He had it demolished, and a new residence was built in its place. The architect, Johann Benjamin Dreyer, completed the project in 1787. The result was an attractive building combining Baroque, Rococo and early Neo-Classical features.

The sole ornamentation of the restrained façade is the Rococo decoration to the door, which is inscribed with the initial A, for Abigail, the owner's wife. The interiors, featuring Rococo and Neo-Classical elements, are splendid.

The Rococo doorway of Uphagen House

⑲ Main Town Hall

ul. Długa 47. Museum of the History of Gdańsk: **Tel** 58 573 31 28. **Open** 10am–1pm Tue, 10am–4pm Wed, Fri & Sat, 10am–6pm Thu, 11am–4pm Sun. 🖼 (free Tue). 🅰 🅼 🅦 mhmg.pl

The city's first town hall was built after 1298 on the orders of Świętopełk II, Duke of Gdańsk-Pomerania. It functioned as an office of the Hanseatic League.

Work on the current building was begun in 1327. An elegant tower was added in 1486–8, during one of several phases of rebuilding. After a fire in 1556, this Gothic town hall was remodelled in the Mannerist style. The interior was lavishly decorated in 1593–1608 by the most prominent painters and craftsmen of the day, including Hans Vredeman de Vries, Izaak van den Blocke and Simon Herle. Their combined genius produced one of the finest town halls in all of northern Europe, proof of the city's wealth and power. It also served as a royal residence.

The highlight of the town hall is without doubt the Red Room, which was once the Great Council Chamber. The Renaissance fireplace is by Willem van der Meer and the centrepiece of the ceiling paintings is the *Apotheosis of Gdańsk* by Izaak van den Blocke. After being destroyed in 1945, the town hall was rebuilt and many of its furnishings reconstructed. It now houses the Museum of the History of Gdańsk. Today, the Town Hall functions as the headquarter of Historical Museum of Gdansk.

⑳ Długi Targ

Długi Targ, a broad short street that runs on from Ulica Długa and terminates at the Green Gate on the River Motława, is the final part of the Royal Way leading from the Golden Gate through to the city centre. It also functioned as a marketplace as well as a site for the public execution of aristocratic prisoners. The town houses on Długi Targ, like those elsewhere in the old town, were destroyed in 1945 but have been restored. Today the square is filled with souvenir shops. Its focal point is the Fountain of Neptune, which was installed outside Artus Court in 1633. According to legend, Neptune hit the water with his trident and shattered the gold of the coins into fine flakes to create the famous Gdańsk Goldwasser liquor. The shine of these flakes has since decorated the wonderful herbal liquor.

㉑ Artus Court

ul. Długi Targ 44. Museum: **Tel** 78 944 96 54 . **Open** 10am–1pm Tue, 10am–4pm Wed, Fri & Sat, 10am–6pm Thu, 11am–4pm Sun. 🖼 (free on Tue). 🖾 🏕 🏠 🏛

Artus Court was a meeting place for the wealthy burghers of Gdańsk, who were inspired by the chivalrous traditions of King Arthur and the Knights of the Round Table. Similar fraternities were set up throughout Europe, and they were particularly fashionable in the cities of the Hanseatic League. Visitors to the court came to discuss the issues of the day and to enjoy the fine beer that was served there in unlimited quantities. The first Artus Court in Gdańsk was established in the 14th century, but the original building was destroyed by fire in 1477. The present building opened in 1481. Its rear elevation preserves the building's original Gothic style, but the façade was twice rebuilt, first in 1552 and again in 1616–17 by Abraham van den Blocke. The interior furnishings were renewed several times, funded mainly by individual

St George killing the Dragon, a carving of 1485 in Artus Court

fraternities, who would gather for meetings seated on benches along the walls of the court. Despite wartime destruction, reconstruction has succeeded in re-creating something of the court's historic atmosphere. A highlight of the interior is the intricately decorated 16th-century Renaissance tiled stove, 12 m (40 ft) high.

㉒ Golden House

ul. Długi Targ 41. **Closed** to the public.

The Golden House, also known as Speimann House or Steffens House after its owners, was built in 1609–18 for Jan Speimann, mayor of Gdańsk and a wealthy merchant and patron of the arts, and his wife Maria Judyta. The architect was Abraham van den Blocke, who also executed some of the stone carving. The most impressive feature

of the house is its façade, which is covered in intricate gilt carvings, and which fortunately escaped the fires that ravaged the building in 1945.

Today the building houses the Maritime Institute. Local people claim that it is haunted; in one of the corridors the shining figure of the former lady of the house, Maria Judyta Speimann, is said to appear and can be heard whispering the words "A just deed fears no man".

㉓ Green Gate

ul. Długi Targ 24. **Tel** 58 307 59 12. **Open** 9am–5pm Tue–Sun. 🖼 Ⓦ mhmg.pl

With its pinnacled roof and elaborate decorative stonework, the Green Gate hardly resembles the usual city gate – it is more like a mansion. There is good reason for this, because the gate was intended to serve as a residence for visiting royalty. In the event it was used in this way only once – when Maria Louisa Gonzaga arrived in Gdańsk from France in order to marry Władysław IV in 1646.

The gate was designed in the Mannerist style by the architect Johann Kramer from Dresden, and built in 1564–8 by Regnier from Amsterdam. Its windows provide a magnificent view of Ulica Długi Targ and the town hall in one direction, and the River Motława and Spichlerze Island in the other.

The Green Gate now houses a branch of the National Museum (see p253).

The Green Gate, not only a city gate but also a royal residence

㉔ National Maritime Museum

In the 17th century Poland strove to be "master of the Baltic Sea" and her seafarers were dedicated to maintaining Poland's maritime presence. The themes of the displays in the Maritime Museum are Gdańsk's seafaring traditions and navigation on the Vistula. Exhibits include a reconstruction of scenes from a sailor's life aboard the Swedish ship *Solen*, sunk at the Battle of Oliwa in 1627 and raised from the seabed in the Gulf of Gdańsk in 1970.

VISITORS' CHECKLIST

Practical Information
ul. Ołowianka 9–13. **Tel** 58 301 86 11. **Open** 10am–6pm daily (winter: 10am–4pm Tue–Sun). **Closed** pub hols. 🅿 ♿ W nmm.pl

Transport
🚌 106, 111, 138

Period Gdańsk
This reconstruction of a merchant's office is in the Harbour Town Life exhibition. It is part of the display in the Gdańsk Crane.

Poles on the World's Seas
The Granaries contain wax-work exhibitions depicting the lives of Poles at sea

Sołdek
The Sołdek, the first Polish ocean-going ship to be built after World War II, was built in the Gdańsk Shipyard in 1948. Its holds are now used for exhibitions.

Maritime Culture Centre

Museum Guide

The museum consists of several buildings either side of the River Motława, with the head office on Ołowianka Island. There is a Polish naval exhibition in the Gdańsk Crane. Skład Kolonialny hosts a collection of boats from distant parts of the world. The exhibition in the granaries is dedicated to Poland and Gdańsk at sea from the Middle Ages to the present.

Ferry
An easy way from one building to another is by ferry.

★ **The Grain Warehouse**
The naval weapons displayed here include 17th-century Polish and Ruthenic cannons, as well as cannons from the Swedish warship *Solen*.

Key
— Suggested route

ⓩ Spichlerze Island

🚌 106, 111, 112, 138, 166, 178, 186.
🚋 8, 9.

Once joined to the mainland, Spichlerze Island was created when the New Motława Canal was dug in 1576. A centre of trade developed here at the end of the 13th century. What was then a relatively small number of granaries had grown to more than 300 by the 16th century. Each granary had a name and each façade was decorated with an individual emblem. The purpose of digging the canal, and thus of surrounding the district with water, was not only to protect the granaries against fire but also to safeguard their contents against thieves.

Everything was destroyed in 1945. Today a main road bisects the island, and the charred stumps that can still be seen in many places are all that remain of the granaries. The name signs on some ruins – such as Arche Noah ("Noah's Ark") on Ulica Żytnia ("Wheat Street") – remain legible. Reconstruction began several years ago. The first granaries to be rebuilt were those between the Motława and Ulica Chmielna ("Hop Street"). One of them is now the headquarters of ZUS, the Polish social security organization. Restoration of a group of buildings on Ulica Stągiewna was completed in 1999. Two 16th-century Gothic castle keeps, survivors of World War II, are in this street. They are known as the Stągwie Mleczne ("Milk Churns").

Chapel of St Anne, near the Church of the Holy Trinity

㉖ Church of the Holy Trinity

ul. św. Trójcy 4. **Tel** 58 320 79 80.
🚌 106, 111, 112, 138, 166, 178, 186.
🚋 8, 9.

The imposing Church of the Holy Trinity (Kościół św Trójcy) was built by Franciscan monks in 1420–1514. In 1480, the Chapel of St Anne was constructed alongside the church. Protestantism quickly spread to Gdańsk, and one of its most ardent proponents in the region was the Franciscan friar Alexander Svenichen. When congregations declined because of Svenichen's activities, the Franciscans decided in 1556 to hand the monastery over to the city as a theological college. The head of the Franciscan order did not agree with the Gdańsk friars' decision to cede the monastery but the order's petitions to the Polish kings to have the property returned bore no result. As a result, the church was transferred to the Protestants. The grammar school that was established here later became the widely celebrated Academic Grammar School. It also came to house the first library in Gdańsk. However, centuries later in 1945 it was returned to the Catholics, after the violence of World War II had reduced it to a ruin.

Monkey from the stalls of the Church of the Holy Trinity

The aisled church has a distinctive exterior with ornamental Gothic spires. They crown the elongated presbytery, the façade and the walls of the adjacent Chapel of St Anne. The presbytery, which was occupied by the friars, was separated from the aisles by a wall. Interesting features of the interior are the many tombstones that are set into the floor and the numerous works by Gdańsk artists. The very fine Gothic stalls were made by local craftsmen in 1510–11. Their carved decorations depict a wide variety of subjects, among them animals including a monkey, a lion fighting a dragon and several birds.

The church contains the oldest surviving pulpit in Gdańsk – it dates from 1541 and is another remarkable example of local woodcarving. In the north aisle is the marble tomb made by Abraham van den Blocke in 1597 for Giovanni Bernardo Bonifacio, Marquis d'Orii, a restless spirit and champion of the Reformation who founded the Gdańsk library. "Bones long since thrown ashore here finally rest from their earthly wanderings" reads the poetic Latin inscription.

Beside the church is a half-timbered galleried house dating from the 17th century.

The Milk Churns, two medieval keeps on Spichlerze Island

🅐 National Museum

The National Museum is laid out mainly in a former Gothic Franciscan monastery of 1422–1522. It contains a wealth of artifacts, from wrought-iron grilles to sculpture and painting. The museum's most prized piece is *The Last Judgement* by the Flemish painter Hans Memling (c.1430–94). In 1473, it was plundered by privateers from Gdańsk from a ship bound for Italy.

VISITORS' CHECKLIST

Practical Information
ul. Toruńska 1. **Tel** 58 301 70 61.
Open May & Sep: 10am–5pm
Tue–Sun; Jun–Aug: noon–7pm
Thu; Oct–Apr: 9am–4pm Tue–Fri,
10am–5pm Sat, Sun. 🖾 (free Fri).
🔇 🖋 🖥 🅦 mhmg.pl

Transport
🚌 106, 111, 112, 121, 138, 166,
178, 186 🚊 8, 9.

★ **The Last Judgement**
Hans Memling painted this monumental triptych in 1467–71. The left-hand side panel represents the Gates of Heaven, while the right-hand one shows the torments of Hell.

Museum Guide

The exhibits on the ground floor include Gothic art and gold jewellery. The first floor has more recent paintings. The upper floor displays temporary exhibitions.

"The Griffin's Talons"
This bison-horn cup was made in the 15th century and belonged to a sailing fraternity.

Longcase Clock
A Rococo clock made c.1750 is decorated with scenes from the biblical story of Tobias and the Raising of the Copper Snake.

Key

- ☐ Pomeranian medieval art
- ☐ Goldsmithery
- ☐ Metalwork
- ☐ Gdańsk and northern European furniture, 15th–18th centuries
- ☐ Ceramics
- ☐ Dutch and Flemish painting
- ☐ Gdańsk painting, 16th–18th centuries
- ☐ Polish painting, 19th and 20th centuries
- ☐ 19th-century Gdańsk artists (temporary exhibitions)
- ☐ Furniture-making in Gdańsk and eastern Pomerania in the 18th century
- ☐ The Last Judgement

㉘ Oliwa Cathedral

Oliwa, a district to the northwest of Gdańsk, was once the base of wealthy Cistercians, who built a cathedral and monastery here. The present cathedral, built in the 14th century in the Gothic style, replaced the original 13th-century Romanesque church that was destroyed by fire in 1350. While the exterior has survived without major alteration, the interior has been redecorated in the Baroque style. Its famous organ can be heard in recitals. The monastery buildings are now occupied by branches of the Diocesan, Ethnographical and Contemporary Art museums. Oliwa Park, with lakes and wooded hills, is a pleasant place for a walk.

Mannerist Stalls
The stalls in the chancel, decorated with bas-reliefs of the Apostles, were made in 1604.

Tomb of the Kos Family
The tomb was carved in around 1599, probably by the prominent Gdańsk sculptor Willem van den Blocke.

Main entrance

KEY

① **The former high altar**, built in 1604–6, has a depiction of the Holy Trinity.

★ **Organ Loft**
The organ loft was made by local Cistercian monks in 1763–88. The organ, made by Jan Wulff and Fryderyk Rudolf Dalitz and completed in 1793, was the largest in Europe at the time.

VISITORS' CHECKLIST

Practical Information
ul. Biskupa Edmunda Nowockiego
5. **Tel** 58 552 47 65. **Open** daily.
Organ recitals: noon Mon–Sat, 3pm
Sun (Jun–Aug: 11am, noon, 1pm,
3pm, 4pm Mon–Sat, 3pm, 4pm,
5pm Sun), except on public hols.

Transport
🚋 🚋 2, 6, 11, 12. 🚌 117, 122,
169, 171, 179, 622.

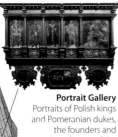

Portrait Gallery
Portraits of Polish kings
and Pomeranian dukes,
the founders and
benefactors of the
cathedral, hang in the
presbytery.
They were
painted by
Hermann
Hahn in 1613.

★ High Altar
The altar itself is thought to be by
Andreas Schlüter. It was decorated
by Andreas Stech with images of
the Virgin and St Bernard, patrons
of the monastery at Oliwa.

The Monument to the Defenders
of Westerplatte

㉙ Westerplatte

🚌 106, 138, 606. Ferries in summer
season at Green Gate. Guardhouse
No. 1 Museum: ul. Mjr. H. Sucharskiego.
Tel 58 767 91 64. **Open** Apr–Oct:
9am–4pm daily (Jun–Sep: to 7pm).
W mhmg.pl

It was at Westerplatte that the
first shots of World War II were
fired, on 1 September 1939. The
German battleship *Schleswig
Holstein* opened fire on Polish
ammunition dumps in the Free
City of Gdańsk. The Germans
expected the capture of the
Westerplatte to take a matter of
hours, but the 182-man garrison
under Major Henryk Sucharski
resisted for seven days, their
heroism becoming a symbol of
Polish resistance in the struggle
against the Nazi invasion.

Today, ruined barracks and
concrete bunkers, together
with a huge Monument to
the Defenders of Westerplatte
unveiled in 1966, bear witness
to that struggle.

㉚ Wisłoujście Fortress

ul. Stara Twierdza 1. **Tel** 53 107 76 92.
🚌 106, 606. **Open** Oct–Apr:
9am–4pm daily. W mhmg.pl

Fortifications were first built on
this strategic point at the mouth
of the River Vistula in the time of
the Teutonic Knights. Work on the
construction of a brick tower
began in 1482. From here, a
duty was levied on passing
ships using a simple enforcement method that was
impossible to avoid – a chain
was stretched across the river,
preventing the ship's passage,
and released only when the
captain had made the required
payment. Equipped with a
brazier in which a fire was lit,
the tower was also used as
a lighthouse.

In 1562–3 the tower was
surrounded by a system of
defences, and afterwards
was repeatedly fortified and
refortified as military technology
advanced. In 1586–7 the entire
complex was reinforced by
four bastions, designed
by Antonis van Opbergen
and Jan Strakowski, and an
outer moat was added. This
was followed by the addition
of a ditch in 1624–6. Also in
the 17th century, 15 tall barrack
buildings were added around
the now-ageing tower.

Over the following years,
constant building, often by
prominent fortification engineers
of the time, steadily enlarged
the fortress. It withstood several
sieges and was often used to
accommodate visiting royalty.

Wisłoujście Fortress, which once defended the mouth of the River Vistula

POMERANIA

Beautiful beaches and the resorts of the Baltic are Pomerania's main attractions, which every summer draw large numbers of holiday-makers in search of sand and sun. A less crowded but equally attractive aspect of the region are the Drawsko Lakes and the alpine scenery of Szwajcaria Kaszubska, west of Gdańsk.

Polish Pomerania is divided into the two regions of Western and Eastern Pomerania, each with an ethnically diverse population. The border between the two regions is in the districts of Bytów and Lębork.

Christianity was introduced to Western Pomerania by Bishop Otto of Bamberg, who founded a bishopric in Wolin in 1140. The Duchy of Pomerania, established in the 12th century, maintained its independence for several centuries and secured its economic development through the strength of its port cities, which were part of the Hanseatic League. The Thirty Years' War (1618–48) and the death of the last duke of the Gryfici dynasty brought this independence to an end. Most of Western Pomerania came under the rule of Brandenburg, while Szczecin and the surrounding area was engulfed by Sweden until 1713. In the 18th and 19th centuries, Western Pomerania became first Prussian, then German, territory. It was returned to Poland in 1945.

Eastern Pomerania was Christianized in the 10th century. Although it originally belonged to Poland, it became an independent duchy from the 12th century. Overrun by the Teutonic Knights in 1306, it then enjoyed strong economic development. In 1466, after the Second Peace of Toruń, areas of Eastern Pomerania, including Royal Prussia, were ceded to Poland. However, during the Partitions of Poland *(see p52)*, Eastern Pomerania became part of Prussia. It was finally returned to Poland in 1919. Gdańsk was given the status of a free city and only became part of Poland in 1945.

Pomerania's landscape was formed by the movement of glaciers. Its hilly countryside with small, clear lakes and its varied Baltic coastline make the region outstandingly beautiful.

Malbork Castle, the great fortress of the Teutonic Knights, on the River Nogat

◄ A sandy beach fringed by pine trees along the Baltic Sea

Exploring Pomerania

Pomerania is one of Poland's most attractive regions, and in summer resorts such as Międzyzdroje, Kołobrzeg, Ustka, Łeba and Sopot teem with sunbathers and watersports enthusiasts. The most popular holiday spots are on the Hel Peninsula, where swimmers can choose between the open waters of the Baltic Sea or the calm of the Gulf of Gdańsk. For sightseeing at a slower pace there are the villages of Kashubia. The shady, tree-lined lanes in the region of Słupsk and Koszalin make for enjoyable cycle tours, while the clean rivers are attractive for canoeing. Those with an interest in history will not be disappointed with the great variety of historic buildings, from castles and cathedrals to small village churches and the stately houses of old seaside resorts.

A half-timbered house, typical of the Gdańsk region, in Różyny

Getting Around

Szczecin and Gdańsk can be reached by air (see pp344–5). The best way to tour Pomerania is by car. The E28 connects Gdańsk with Słupsk, Koszalin and Szczecin. Parallel to it but further to the south is route 22, which is part of the old German A1 from Berlin to Kaliningrad (Królewiec). The E75 goes south from Gdańsk to Gniew. All larger towns and cities have rail links. In the Gulf of Gdańsk there are also ferries to Sopot and Hel.

Key

- ▬ Motorway
- ▬ Main road
- ═ Minor road
- ── Main railway
- ── Minor railway
- ▬ International border
- ▬ Regional border

Fishermen's buoys on a Baltic beach

For hotels and restaurants see p305 and pp317–19

The lakes of Szwajcaria Kaszubska, in Kashubia, in autumn

Sights at a Glance

- **1** *Szczecin pp260–61*
- **3** Stargard Szczeciński
- **4** Drawsko Lakes
- **5** Kołobrzeg
- **6** Darłowo
- **7** Słupsk
- **8** Słowiński National Park
- **9** Bytów
- **11** Hel Peninsula

- **12** Gdynia
- **13** Sopot
- **14** *Malbork pp270–71*
- **15** Pelplin
- **16** Gniew
- **17** Kwidzyn
- **18** Grudziądz
- **19** *Chełmno pp274–5*
- **20** Bydgoszcz

- **21** *Toruń pp276–9*
- **22** Golub-Dobrzyń
- **23** Ciechocinek

Tours
- **2** Around Wolin
- **10** Kashubia

For keys to symbols *see back flap*

❶ Szczecin

Szczecin, on the river Odra, is a major port even though it is more than 65 km (40 miles) from the sea. It serves both ocean-going vessels and river traffic, and is linked with Berlin by the Odra and by canals. A castle and a fishing village existed here in the 9th century. Szczecin was granted a municipal charter in 1243 and soon after it joined the Hanseatic League. It became the capital of a Pomeranian duchy and in 1673–1713 was overrun by the Swedes. Under Prussian rule it became a major port. The city suffered severely during World War II; post-war restoration has been confined to its more important buildings.

The Gate of Prussian Homage, once known as the Royal Gate

The Castle of the Dukes of Pomerania, rebuilt in the Renaissance style

Exploring Szczecin

The old town of Szczecin is picturesquely laid out on a steep escarpment. The large **Castle of the Dukes of Pomerania** was founded in the mid-13th century and was rebuilt in the Renaissance style by Guglielmo di Zaccharia in 1575–7. It consists of five wings, with two interior courtyards and two towers. The east wing dates from the 17th century. After damage suffered during World War II, the castle was almost completely rebuilt and its once-magnificent interior re-created. The basement of the east wing houses the Castle Museum. In a Baroque building near the castle is the main section of the **National Museum**. The castle balcony overlooks the Odra and

offers a view of the **Tower of the Seven Cloaks**, the only remaining part of the city's medieval fortifications. Across the road is the **Gate of Prussian Homage**, formerly the Royal Gate, one of a pair that was built under Swedish rule in 1726–8. The architect was Gerhard Cornelius de Wallrawe, and the sculptor Berhold Damart. North of the castle is the red-brick late Gothic **Church of Saints Peter and Paul** (Kościół św. Piotra i Pawła), while further along the banks of the Odra is **Ulica Wały Chrobrego**. This boulevard, an impressive municipal project of 1902–13, was known in German times as the Hakenterrasse ("Haken's

Terrace") in honour of the mayor who initiated it. One of the buildings on the boulevard houses the **Maritime Museum**. From the terraces, with their decorative pavilions and a statue of *Hercules Fighting the Centaur* by Ludwig Manzel, there is a fine view of the harbour below.

North of the castle stands **Loitz House**, a sumptuous late Gothic town house built for the Loitz banking family in 1547. Further down, among the newly built town houses in the old style, is the mainly 15th-century Baroque **Town Hall**. It houses the **Szczecin History Museum**. The **Cathedral of St James** (Katedra św. Jakuba) was also rebuilt after almost complete wartime destruction; only the presbytery and west tower survived the bombing. It was originally erected in stages from the late 13th to the 15th centuries, with the involvement of the architect Heinrich Brunsberg. The cathedral has several Gothic altars originating from other churches in Pomerania. From the

Ulica Wały Chrobrego, with the Maritime Museum and local government offices in the distance

cathedral it is possible to walk southwards towards the Gothic Church of St John (Kościoł św. Jana), founded by the Franciscans, or to wander through the part of the city stretching out to the west that was built in the late 19th century. Many town houses and villas in a variety of styles have been preserved here, and the area has numerous bars and restaurants.

National Museum

ul. Staromłyńska 27. **Tel** 91 431 52 00.
Open 10am–6pm Tue–Thu & Sat; 10am–4pm Fri & Sun. (free Sat). **muzeum.szczecin.pl**

The museum's extensive collections comprise arti-facts mainly from Western

Loitz House, once the home of a family of bankers

Pomerania. Among the many interesting exhibits are the displays of Gothic ecclesiastical art and jewellery and the ornate costumes of Pomeranian princes.

Maritime Museum

ul. Wały Chrobrego 3. **Tel** 91 431 52 67.
Open 10am–6pm Tue–Thu & Sat; 10am–4pm Fri & Sun.
(free on Sat). **muzeum.szczecin.pl**

The museum's principal theme is the history of seafaring in the Baltic sea. The archaeological displays include amber and silver jewellery and a medieval boat. There are also models of ships, nautical instruments and an ethnographical section. Boats and fishing vessels are displayed in a *skansen* behind the museum.

Castle Museum

ul. Korsarzy 34. **Tel** 91 489 16 30.
Open 11am–6pm Tue–Sun. **zamek.szczecin.pl**

This museum is housed in the former crypt of the dukes of Pomerania. Among the exhibits are the tin coffins of the last of the Gryfici dynasty, and a special exhibition on the history and the restoration of the castle.

VISITORS' CHECKLIST

Practical Information
Road map A2. 407,000.
Castle: ul. Korsarzy 34.
Tel 91 489 16 30.
Harbour boat trips: ul. Jana z Kolna 7. **Tel** 91 434 55 61.
International Passion Music Festival (Mar); Days of the Sea (late Jun). **szczecin.pl**

Transport
33 km north in Goleniów.
ul. Kolumba. **Tel** 91 946 00 11. pl. Grodnicki.
Tel 91 434 66 25.

Portal of the Cathedral of St James

Szczecin History Museum
ul. Mściwoja 8. **Tel** 91 431 52 55.
Open 10am–6pm Tue–Thu & Sat; 10am–4pm Fri & Sun. (free Sat).

Szczecin City Centre

① National Museum
② Gate of Prussian Homage
③ Church of Saints Peter and Paul
④ Maritime Museum
⑤ Tower of the Seven Cloaks
⑥ Castle of the Dukes of Pomerania
⑦ Loitz House
⑧ Town Hall (Szczecin History Museum)
⑨ Cathedral of St James

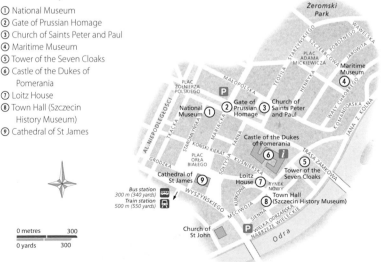

0 metres 300
0 yards 300

For keys to symbols *see back flap*

❷ Around Wolin

Wolin's forests, deserted sandy beaches and picturesque, sometimes dramatic, coastal cliffs delight walkers and inspire photographers. Wolin also has plenty to offer those with an interest in historic buildings – the cathedral in Kamień Pomorski is one of the finest in Poland.

④ **Wolin National Park**
Apart from its beaches and lakes, the park is known for its bison, which can be seen in a special reserve. The bird life includes the rare sea eagle.

③ **Międzyzdroje**
This renowned health resort was created in 1830. It has a seafront promenade and a pier from which the cliffs can be admired. It is also a good base for hiking in Wolin National Park.

Lake Wicko Wielkie

② **Świnoujście**
The town straddles Poland's two islands – Wolin and Uznam. The only way of moving between the two parts of the town is by ferry. It has a large port, wide beaches and the elegant buildings of a coastal resort.

① **Wolin**
In the early Middle Ages this small town was a major Baltic port. Today it is the venue for the Viking Festival that takes place every July as a reminder of the settlement's historic importance *(see p39)*.

---

❸ Stargard Szczeciński

Road map B2. 🗺 68,500. 🚗 🚌
ℹ Rynek Staromiejski 4 (91 578 54 66). 🌐 **stargard.pl**

With its own port in the Szczecin Lagoon at the mouth of the River Ina, Stargard Szczeciński once rivalled Szczecin as a merchant town of the Hanseatic League.

Almost three-quarters of the old town was destroyed during World War II, although the Gothic defensive walls with their towers and gates survived. The town's finest building is the Gothic **Church of St Mary** (Kościół Mariacki), which was founded in the late 13th century but only given its present appearance by Heinrich Brunsberg in the mid-15th century. The rich decoration of glazed and

moulded brick is quite striking. The magnificent town hall, built in the 16th century and then remodelled in 1638, has a gable with intricate tracery. A particularly pleasant way to round off a trip to Stargard Szczeciński is to visit the café in the former salt

Interior of the Gothic Church of St Mary in Stargard Szczeciński

granary, a Gothic building overlooking a spur of the Ina.

The **Regional Museum** has some militaria and an archaeological and ethnographical display.

🏛 **Regional Museum**
Rynek Staromiejski 3. **Tel** 91 578 38 35. **Open** 10am–5pm Tue–Fri & Sun (Oct–Apr: to 4pm), 10am–2pm Sat. 🎟 (free on Thu). 🌐 **muzeum-stargard.pl**

❹ Drawsko Lakes

Road map B2.

The Drawsko Lakes are an oasis of quiet, unspoiled scenery. Their crystal-clear waters teem with fish and, in season, the forests are carpeted with mushrooms. The area is ideal for a canoeing or rowing holiday.

Key

- Tour route
- Other road

Trzebiatów

Gryfice

0 km 5

0 miles 5

⑥ Kamień Pomorski
The town was the seat of a bishopric from 1176. Its widely admired cathedral contains a well-preserved collection of fine late Gothic murals as well as famous organs.

⑤ Dziwnów
A swing bridge across the River Dziwna links Wolin Island with the mainland.

Tips for Drivers

Tour length: 103 km (65 miles).
Stopping-off points: Plenty of good cafés and restaurants are to be found in Kamień Pomorski and Międzyzdroje.
Additional features:
Golf course at Kołczewie.
Bison reserve: **Open** May–Sep: 10am–6pm Tue–Sun; Oct–Apr: 8am–4pm Tue–Sat.

⑦ Świerzno
The modest timber-frame palace here was built for the Fleming family in 1718–30. In the 17th century the family also founded the timber-framed church that stands nearby.

Lake Drawsko, the second-deepest lake in Poland

The largest of the lakes is Drawsko, on whose shores stands Stare Drawsko, with ruins of a once-impressive 14th-century Teutonic Knights' castle. In the delightful spa town of **Polczyn Zdrój** the mineral springs are surrounded by a park and there are some elegant early 20th-century sanatoria. **Złocieniec** has an outstanding example of Baroque architecture in the form of a palace that was built here in 1704–45.

❺ Kołobrzeg

Road map B1. ⚐ 46,600. 🚆 🚌
ℹ️ ul. Dworcowa 1 (94 35 279 39); ul. Armii Krajowej 12 (94 354 72 20).
🎵 Kołobrzeg Summer Music Festival.
🌐 **kolobrzeg.turystyka.pl**

The fine sandy beaches of Kołobrzeg make it one of the most popular health resorts on the Baltic coast. It has a full complement of hotels, sanatoria, holiday homes and fried-fish stalls, but it is also a working fishing port. In the past it was a fortified coastal town of strategic significance. In summer the long promenade, leading to the **lighthouse**, is crowded with holiday-makers. The brick-built **Cathedral of the Virgin Mary** (Katedra NMP) was begun in 1255 and later altered and extended. Among the remarkable objects it contains is a chandelier made by Johann Apengheter of Lübeck in 1327 depicting the Virgin and St John the Baptist. The Neo-Gothic **town hall** was built by the Berlin architect Karl Friedrich Schinkel in 1829–32. It is surrounded by alleys lined with old houses. The **fortress**, now in ruins, was unsuccessfully besieged by Napoleon's troops in 1807.

The sturdy brick-built lighthouse in Kołobrzeg harbour

❻ Darłowo

Road map B1. 🏔 13,900. 🚌 🚃
ℹ️ ul. Zamkowa 4 (94 314 35 72).
🌐 darlowo.pl

Darłowo, set 2.5 km (1.5 miles) inland on the banks of the River Wieprza, is one of the most attractive towns of coastal Pomerania. In summer the waterfront district swarms with tourists and the fish stalls do a brisk trade, but the town's real charm lies in its old riverside district, where there are many historic buildings. The most prominent of these is the Gothic **Castle of the Dukes of Pomerania**. Founded in the 14th century, it was rebuilt several times and partially demolished in the 19th century; its surviving parts now house a museum.

The castle is associated with Erik of Pomerania, the warlike Duke of Słupsk, whose royal blood enabled him, in 1397, to hold the thrones of Denmark, Sweden and Norway. His turbulent rule was marked by constant warfare. He was finally deposed and returned to Darłowo, where he established the Duchy of Słupsk, crowning himself Erik I, and retaining his rule over Gotland. He was buried in the Church of St Mary (Kościół Mariacki), and his sarcophagus, made in 1888, can be seen here in the sepulchral chapel. Erik may also have been the founder of the late Gothic **Chapel of St Gertrude** (Kaplica św. Gertrudy) on Ulica Tynickiego, an unusual 12-sided building.

Shifting dunes in Słowiński National Park

❼ Słupsk

Road map C1. 🏔 92,100. 🚌 🚃
ℹ️ ul. Starzyńskiego 8 (59 728 50 41).
🎵 International Festival of Organ Music (Jun–Aug). 🌐 slupsk.pl

From 1368 to 1648, this town on the River Słupia was the capital of the Duchy of Western Pomerania. The Renaissance ducal castle was built by Antonio Guglielmo di Zaccharia in 1580–87. Today it is the **Museum of Central Pomerania**, which, besides items of local interest, has the country's largest collection of portraits by the painter and writer Stanisław Ignacy Witkiewicz (1885–1939), better known as Witkacy.

The watermill opposite the castle, dating from about 1310, is one of the oldest in Poland. Now a branch of the museum, it houses an ethnographical collection. In the Dominican Church of St Hyacinthus (Kościół św. Jacka) nearby are the black marble and alabaster tombs of Bogusław de Croy, the last of the dukes of Pomerania, and his mother, the Duchess Anna de Croy. They were carved by Kasper Gockhaller of Gdańsk in 1682. The 14th-century Church of St Mary (Kościół Mariacki) is also of interest.

🏛 **Museum of Central Pomerania**
ul. Dominikańska 5/9. **Tel** 59 842 40 81. **Open** Jul & Aug: 11am–3pm Mon, 10am–6pm Tue–Sun; Sep–Jun: 10am–4pm Wed–Sun.
📷 (free Sat). 🎫 🌐 muzeum.slupsk.pl

Effigy of Anna de Croy in the Church of St Hyacinthus

❽ Słowiński National Park

Road map C1. 🚌 **Tel** 59 811 72 04.
🌐 slowinskipn.pl

Słowiński National Park is renowned for its large, shifting sand dunes, which move at a rate of about 9 m (30 ft) a year, leaving the stumps of dead trees behind them. The area was once a gulf, of which the glacial lakes Łebsko and Gardno are vestiges. The park, a World Biosphere Reserve, is a haven for wild birds; more than 250 species, including the rare sea eagle, are found here.

The park's highest point, Rowokół, offers a fine view of the village of Smołdzino, which has a small Baroque church founded by Duchess Anna de Croy in the 17th century.

In the hamlet of Kluki, on Lake Łebsko, is a *skansen* dedicated to the ancient local Slovincian culture. Fishing equipment and agricultural implements are exhibited in the farmsteads. An electric train runs to the park from Rąbka,

The castle of the Dukes of Pomerania, Duke of Słupsk, in Darłowo

near the resort of Łeba. The town of Nowęcin, also near Łeba, has a Neo-Gothic palace built for the Wejher family in 1909. It now houses a hotel and restaurant.

Corner tower of the Gothic castle of the Teutonic Knights in Bytów

❾ Bytów

Road map: C1.  17,000.
i ul. Zamkowa 2 (59 822 68 39).
w bytow.pl

Bytów, with nearby Lębork, was the westernmost outpost of the territory held by the Teutonic Knights. The town, which after its conquest in 1466 was established as a Polish fiefdom, was ruled by the dukes of Pomerania, and later by Brandenburg and Prussia. It has been part of Poland since 1945.

Few of Bytów's historic buildings survive. The most interesting is the **castle** of the Teutonic Knights, which was built in 1390–1405 and was one of the first castles in Europe to be adapted for the use of firearms. It has four circular corner towers and a residential

Timber-framed fishermen's cottages in Jastarnia, on the Hel Peninsula

wing was added in about 1570. It houses the **Museum of Western Kashubia**, which contains a collection of artifacts relating to the ancient Kashubian culture.

Museum of Western Kashubia
ul. Zamkowa 2. **Tel** 59 822 26 23.
Open Oct–Apr: 10am–4pm daily;
May–Sep: 10am–6pm daily (to 4pm Mon). (free on Mon).
w muzeumbytow.pl

❿ Kashubia

See p268.

⓫ Hel Peninsula

Road map D1. Hel, ul. Wiejska 78 (58 675 10 10); Jastarnia, ul. ks. Pawła Stefańskiego 5 (58 675 23 40); ul. Kuracyjna 26 (666 871 622).
w jastarnia.pl

The Hel Peninsula is about 34 km (22 miles) long and in width ranges from just 200 m (650 ft) to 3 km (2 miles). It is made up of sandbanks formed by sea currents; in the 1700s it was no more than a chain of islets. The peninsula is now the Nadmorski Park Krajobrazowy, an area of outstanding natural beauty.

When the railway line to Hel was completed in 1922, resorts began to appear on the peninsula. Their main attraction was the double beach – one part facing the sea, the other the Gulf of Gdańsk. At the base of the peninsula is the town of Władysławowo, named after Władysław IV, who founded a now-vanished fortress here. Today the town's boundaries embrace many resorts, such as Jastrzębia Góra, Cetniewo and Chałupy. Jastarnia is the most popular resort, as it still retains many of its original fishermen's cottages. The elegant resort of Jurata was established in 1928; Modernist hotels dating from the 1930s can be seen here. At the very end of the peninsula is the fishing port and tourist resort of Hel, with its towering lighthouse and timber-framed fishermen's cottages. The former Protestant church, built in the 1400s, is now the **Fisheries Museum**. From Hel, passenger and tourist boats cross to Gdynia and Gdańsk.

Fisheries Museum
Hel, ul. Bulwar Nadmorski 2.
Tel 58 675 05 52. **Open** Feb–Jun & Sep–Nov: 10am–4pm Tue–Sun; Jul & Aug: 10am–6pm Tue–Sun; Dec: 10am–3pm Tue–Sun. **w** nmm.pl

The narrow Hel Peninsula, separating Puck Bay from the Baltic Sea

⑩ Kashubia

A trip to the part of Kashubia known as Szwajcaria Kaszubska ("Kashubian Switzerland") is a chance to experience the culture of a people who have inhabited this area for centuries. The Kashubian Museum in Kartuzy has a collection of original embroidery, toys and snuffboxes carved from horn, there are working potteries in Chmielno and in Wdzydze Kiszewskie there is a *skansen* with traditional Kashubian cottages.

① Kartuzy
The town takes its name from the Carthusians, who founded a monastery here in the 1380s. The collegiate church still stands. The Kashubian Museum re-creates the daily life of the region.

② Chmielno
This village has several workshops producing traditional Kashubian pottery. Potters can be seen at work, and their products are for sale.

③ Kashubian Park Krajobrazowy
The national park in Szwajcaria Kaszubska offers some breath-taking views from the summit of its moraine hills.

④ Wdzydze Kiszewskie
As well as traditional peasant farmsteads, this *skansen* has a windmill, an inn, a school and a small church.

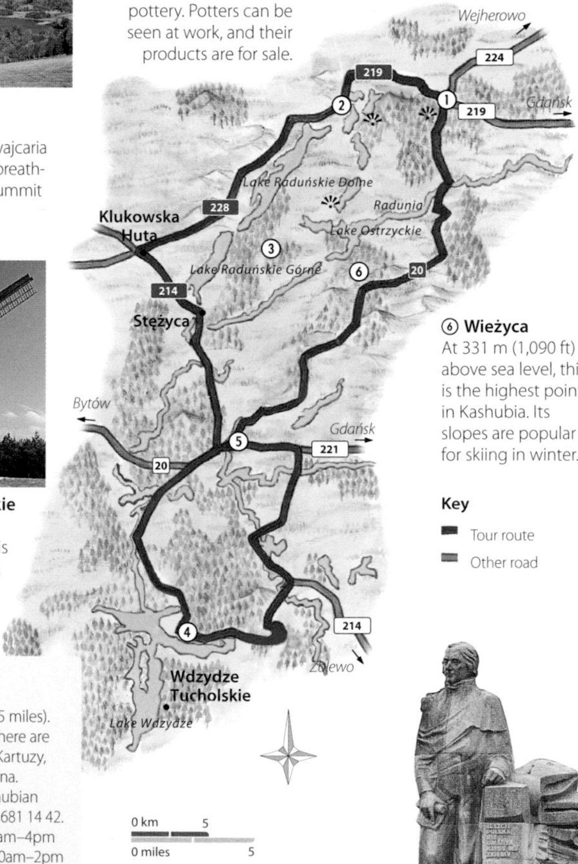

⑥ Wieżyca
At 331 m (1,090 ft) above sea level, this is the highest point in Kashubia. Its slopes are popular for skiing in winter.

Key

■ Tour route

▢ Other road

Map labels: Wejherowo · 224 · Gdańsk · 219 · 219 · Lake Raduńskie Dolne · Radunia · Lake Ostrzyckie · 20 · Klukowska Huta · 228 · Lake Raduńskie Górne · 214 · Stężyca · Bytów · Gdańsk · 221 · 20 · 214 · Żełewo · Wdzydze Tucholskie · Lake Wdzydze

Tips for Drivers

Tour length: 120 km (75 miles).
Stopping-off points: There are bars and restaurants in Kartuzy, Chmielno and Kościerzyna.
Places of interest: Kashubian Museum, Kartuzy. **Tel** 58 681 14 42. **Open** May, Jun & Sep: 8am–4pm Tue–Fri, 8am–3pm Sat, 10am–2pm Sun; Jul & Aug: 8am–6pm Tue–Fri, 9am–5pm Sat & Sun; Oct–Apr: 8am–4pm Tue–Fri, 8am–3pm Sat.
🅿 🅶 🛈 Ⓦ **muzeum-kaszubskie.gda.pl** Kashubian Pottery Museum, Chmielno. **Tel** 58 684 22 89. **Open** 9am–6pm Mon–Sat.

0 km   5
0 miles   5

⑤ Kościerzyna
Although not in itself a scenic town, Kościerzyna is a good stopping place on a tour of Kashubia. A monument to Józef Wybicki, author of the Polish national anthem, stands in the town.

The three-masted training ship *Dar Młodzieży* moored in Gdynia

⑫ Gdynia

Road map D1. 🚉 247,000. 🚌 💬
ℹ️ ul. 10 Lutego 24 (58 622 37 66). 🎬
Days of the Sea (Jun); Festival of Polish
Feature Films (Oct). 🆆 **gdynia.pl**

Gdynia, until 1918 a small
fishing village, is one of the
most recently developed towns
in Poland. When, after World
War I, Poland regained independence but did not control
the port of Gdańsk, the authorities decided to build a major
port at Gdynia. During World
War II Gdynia and its shipyard
were used by the German
Kriegsmarine, and the town
was renamed Gotenhafen by
the Germans. A landmark in
Gdynia's post-war history came
in December 1970, when striking
workers were fired on by the
militia. In 1980 a monument
in their honour was erected.

A walk along the Northern
Pier offers an overview of the
port at work and a sight of
the town's most important

landmarks. There are two
floating museums by the quay,
the ships **ORP Błyskawica** and
Dar Pomorza. The *Błyskawica* is
a destroyer that saw action in
World War II alongside Allied
forces in Narvik, Dunkirk and
during the Normandy landings.
Dar Pomorza is a three-masted
training vessel, built in 1909
and decommissioned in 1981.
It was replaced by the *Dar
Młodzieży*, which can sometimes
also be seen moored in the
port. At the end of the pier is
a statue of the writer Joseph
Conrad (1857–1924), who was
born in Poland as Teodor
Josef Konrad Korzeniowski.
Beyond the pier stands the
Aquarium Gdyńskie.

You can walk along
Gdynia's seafront
promenade all the
way to the islet of
Kępa Redłowska. A
wander around the
city's shopping
area, with its
boutiques and
bars, is equally
enjoyable.

🏛️ **Aquarium Gdyńskie**
al. Jana Pawła II 1. **Tel** 58
732 66 01. **Open** Apr, May
& Sep: 9am–7pm daily; Jul
& Aug: 9am–9pm daily; Oct–Mar:
10am–5pm daily. 🆆 **akwarium.
gdynia.pl**

💬 **Dar Pomorza**
al. Jana Pawła II. **Tel** 58 620 23 71.
Open Feb–Apr, Sep & Oct: 10am–
4pm Tue–Sun; May & Jun: 10am–6pm
Tue–Sun; Jul & Aug: 10am–6pm daily.
Closed Nov–Jan. 🆆 **nmm.pl**

💬 **ORP Błyskawica**
al. Jana Pawła II. **Tel** 58 620 13 81.
Open May–Oct: 10am–1pm, 2–5pm
Tue–Sun. 🆆 **muzeummw.pl**

A street ornament
in Gdynia

⑬ Sopot

Road map D1. 🚉 37,000. 🚌
💬 ℹ️ Plac Zdrojowy 2 (79 028
08 84). **Open** 10am–6pm daily.
🎼 International Festival of Song
(Aug). 🆆 **sopot.pl**

Sopot is the most popular
resort on the Baltic coast. It was
established as a sea-bathing
centre in 1824 by Jean Georges
Haffner, a physician in the
Napoleonic army who chose a
spot on the coast that since the
17th century had been favoured
by the wealthy burghers of
Gdańsk for their mansions. Its
heyday came in the interwar
years, when it attracted some
of the richest people in
Europe. The pier is a
continuation of the
main street, Ulica
Bohaterów Monte
Cassino, colloquially
known as Monciak. The
pier is 512 m (1,680 ft long)
and the bench running
all the way around it is
the longest in Europe.
The pier is filled with
bars, restaurants and
cake shops as well as
antique shops and
boutiques selling amber.
It is a pleasant place
to enjoy a beer and the sea air.
An alternative is coffee at the
Grand Hotel, built in 1924–7,
which overlooks the beach.
This splendid Neo-Baroque
building once housed a casino.

The town's narrow streets
hide many delightful guesthouses. In the wooded hills
behind the town is the Opera
Leśna ("Opera in the Woods"),
built in 1909 and the venue
of the International Song
Festival (see p39).

The Grand Hotel in Sopot, overlooking the beach and the Gulf of Gdańsk

For hotels and restaurants see p305 and pp317–19

⓮ Malbork

Malbork, the castle of the Teutonic Knights, was begun in the 13th century. In 1309 it was made capital of an independent state established by the order. The first major phase of building was the Assembly Castle, a fortified monastery later known as the Upper Castle. The Middle Castle was built some time after 1310, and the Palace of the Grand Master was begun in 1382–99 by Konrad Zöllner von Rotenstein. In 1457 the castle was taken by Poland and used as a fortress. It was restored in the 19th century, and again after World War II. In December 1997, UNESCO declared the castle a World Heritage Site.

Summer Refectory
It has double rows of windows and late Gothic palm vaulting supported on a granite central column. The Winter Refectory adjoins it on its eastern side.

★ **Palace of the Grand Master**
The grandeur of the four-storey palace was almost without equal in medieval Europe.

★ **Golden Gate**
Built in the late 13th century, this gate is enclosed by a porch. The keystone in the vaulting is carved with the figure of Christ.

Cloistered Courtyard
The inner courtyard of the Upper Castle is surrounded by slender Gothic arches with triangular vaulting.

KEY

① Upper Castle
② Church of St Mary

Lower Castle

These partly reconstructed farm buildings, abutting the former Chapel of St Lawrence, have been converted into a hotel.

Battlements

A good view of the towers and walls surrounding the castle can be had from the east side.

VISITORS' CHECKLIST

Practical Information
Road map D1. 38,900.
ul. Kościuszki 54 (55 647 47 47; 8am–4pm Mon–Fri). Castle Museum: ul. Starościńska 1. **Tel** 55 647 09 78. **Open** 9am– 7pm daily (Oct–Apr: 10am–3pm). **Closed** 1 Jan, 8 Apr, 1 Nov, 25 Dec. Courtyard: **Open** 1 hr longer. 🅿️ 📷 🍴 Son et Lumière show: 1 May–15 Sep.
Ⓦ **zamek.malbork.pl**

Transport
🚌 🚉

Teutonic Knight

The Teutonic Knights, or the Knights of the Teutonic Order of the Hospital of St Mary in Jerusalem, had a strict monastic code. In battle they were distinguished by the black crosses on their white cloaks.

Chapel of St Anne

Built in 1331–44 beneath the choir of the Church of St Mary, this chapel contains the tombs of eleven Grand Masters.

The Altar of St Mary in the south aisle in Pelplin cathedral

⑮ Pelplin

Road map: D2. 🏛 8,000.
🚉 🚌 ⓦ pelplin.pl

The beautiful Cistercian abbey at Pelplin is one of the finest examples of Gothic architecture in Poland. Work on the monastery began in 1276, when the Cistercians came to Pelplin.

The brick-built church, now a **cathedral**, dates largely from the 14th century, although its late Gothic vaulting was not completed until the late 15th and early 16th centuries. The imposing triple-naved basilica has no tower, and the west and east fronts are almost identical. The interior contains an outstanding collection of finely crafted furnishings, including Gothic stalls with a rare carving of the Holy Trinity in which the Holy Ghost is depicted not as the customary dove but as a man. Other fine pieces include the 17th-century Mannerist and Baroque altar and a pulpit supported on a figure of Samson in combat with a lion. There are several paintings by Hermann Hahn, including a large *Coronation of the Virgin* on the high altar. The monastery was dissolved in 1823, and in 1824 the church became the **Cathedral of the Virgin Mary** (Katedra NMP). The monastery buildings now accommodate the **Diocesan Museum,** whose carved gallery contains a handsome collection of ecclesiastical art as well as illuminated manuscripts. The most highly prized exhibits are a Madonna cabinet from Kolonówka, a rare original Gutenberg Bible of 1435–55 and a 17th-century musical manuscript, the *Pelplin Tabulature for Organ*. A range of goldwork and liturgical objects are also displayed in the cathedral treasury.

🏛 Cathedral of the Virgin Mary
pl. Mariacki. **Tel** 58 536 15 64. **Open** 9am–5:30pm Mon–Sat, 9am–6pm Sun. 📷 🚫 (except on Sun).

🏛 Diocesan Museum
ul. ks. Biskupa Dominika 11. **Tel** 58 536 19 49. **Open** 9:30am–4:30pm Tue–Sat, 11:30am–4:30pm Sun. **Closed** Mon & religious feast days. 📷 🚫 ⓦ muzeum. diecezja.org

⑯ Gniew

Road map: D2. 🏛 6,870. 🚉 🚌
🗓 International Tournament for the Sword of Sobieski (May/Jun).
ⓦ gniew.pl

This pretty little town on the River Vistula retains a medieval atmosphere. Founded by the Teutonic Knights in 1276, it was later the seat of a commander of the order and in 1466 became part of Poland. The town's narrow alleys lead into the **Market Square**, which is lined with arcaded buildings. While most date from the 18th century, some, like the town hall, have Gothic elements. Traces of the 14th- to 15th-century fortifications that once protected Gniew from invaders still remain. The Gothic **Church of St Nicholas** (Kościół św. Mikołaja) towers over the town. Probably built in the first half of the 14th century, it retains its magnificent interior, which includes Gothic vaulting and Mannerist, Baroque and Neo-Gothic altars. The town's most distinctive feature is the **castle** of the Teutonic Knights. This imposing fortress was begun in 1283 and completed in the mid-14th century. The castle has a regular plan, with four corner turrets and the remains of a mighty keep in the northeastern corner.

Samson fighting a lion, Pelplin Cathedral

Gniew seen from the River Vistula, framed by the Church of St Nicholas and the castle of the Teutonic Knights

Kwidzyn Cathedral, seat of the bishops of Pomerania in the 13th century

In summer the castle hosts festivals, jousting tournaments and reconstructions of medieval banquets.

🏛 Castle Museum
ul. Zamkowa 3. **Tel** 58 535 25 37.
Open Apr–Nov: 9:30am–4:30pm
Tue–Sun. 📷 compulsory. 🖊
W zamek-gniew.pl

🏠 Church of St Nicholas
ul. Ks. Benona Kursikowskiego 8.
Tel 58 535 22 16 or 609 566 333.

🔟 Kwidzyn

Road map: D2. 🏔 38,600.
🚆 🚌 **W** kwidzyn.pl

From 1243 until 1525, the small town of Kwidzyn was the capital of the Pomezania bishopric, one of four to be established in the territory ruled by the Teutonic Knights. After the order was dissolved, the town passed in turn to Prussia, Germany and Poland.

The **cathedral** standing on a high escarpment and the **castle** attached to it are fine examples of Gothic architecture. The cathedral was built in the 14th century on the site of an earlier church, of which only the narthex (a portico or porch separated from the nave by a screen) remains. The porch dates from 1264–84.

In 1862–4 the cathedral was remodelled in the Neo-Gothic style by Friedrich August Stüler. The interior of this vast pseudo-basilica has Gothic murals, which unfortunately were excessively repainted in the 19th century. Many of the earlier furnishings are still in place, including a late Gothic bishop's

throne of about 1510 and Baroque altars and tombs. The presbytery gives access to the tiny cell of the Blessed Dorothy of Mątowy, who ordered that she be immured there in 1393. By the north nave is the Baroque chapel of Otto Frederick von Groeben, which contains a tomb depicting the deceased accompanied in death by his three wives.

The castle resembles a knights' fortress, although it was in fact the seat of a chapter. It was built in 1322–47 and partially demolished in the 18th century. Among the interesting features of the castle are the well tower and the exceptionally tall latrine tower, which is connected to the castle by a gallery supported on large arches.

🏛 Castle Museum
ul. Katedralna 1. **Tel** 55 646 37 80
or 646 37 97. **Open** May–Sep:
9am–4:30pm; Oct–Apr: 9am–2:30pm
Tue–Sun. 🖊

🔞 Grudziądz

Road map: D2. 🏔 96,000. 🚆 🚌
🛈 56 461 23 18. **W** grudziadz.pl

Grudziądz, situated on an escarpment overlooking the River Vistula, was once a major port. It was founded by the Teutonic Knights and became part of Poland in 1466. As a result of the Partitions of Poland (see p52), it became part of Prussia from 1772 and in 1918 was returned to Poland. Despite the damage it suffered during World War II, the town has some fine buildings. The Gothic **Church of St Nicholas** (Kościoł św. Mikołaja) was begun in the late 13th century and completed in the second half of the 15th. It contains a late Romanesque font from the 14th century. The former Benedictine abbey, including the Palace of the Abbesses of 1749–51, is also of interest. Part of the abbey now houses a museum and art gallery.

The huge complex of **harbour granaries**, 26 brick buildings built side by side along the waterfront, fulfilled a defensive function as well as being used for storage – seen from the river, the granaries appear to surround the entire hillside. They were built mostly in the 17th and 18th centuries, but some are significantly older.

🏛 Grudziądz Museum
ul. Wodna 3/5. **Tel** 56 465 90 63.
Open from 10am Tue–Sun; closing times vary (see website). 🖊 (free on Tue). **W** muzeum.grudziadz.pl

The granaries in Grudziądz

⑲ Chełmno

The lands of Chełmno that Konrad, Duke of Mazovia, presented to the Teutonic Knights in 1226 were the beginning of the vast state established by the order. The knights' first city, Chełmno, was founded in 1233 and was initially intended to be the capital of their state but this honour went to Malbork (see p270). The civic laws of Chełmno became a model for other cities.

Exploring Chełmno

Chełmno's medieval street plan and 13th- to 15th-century fortifications survive virtually intact. The town walls are set with 23 towers and a fortified gate, the **Grudziądz Gate**, which was converted into a Mannerist chapel in 1620. The town's finest building is the **Town Hall**, a late Renaissance building of 1567–72 with traces of earlier Gothic elements. It houses the **Chełmno Museum**. At the rear of the town hall is an iron measuring stick equalling 4.35 m (just over 14 ft) and known as the Chełmno Measure, or pręt. The Baroque building on Ulica Franciszkańska,

The late Renaissance town hall in the Market Square

dating from the turn of the 18th century, once housed the **Chełmno Academy**, which was founded in 1692.

Six Gothic churches have been preserved in Chełmno. The largest is the **Church of the Assumption** (Kościół Wniebowzięcia NMP) of 1280–1320, a fine aisled building containing early Gothic frescoes and stone carvings. Two monastery churches, the **Church of St James** (Kościół św. Jakuba) and the **Church of Saints Peter and Paul** (Kościół św. Piotra i Pawła), date from the same period. The Abbey of the Cistercian Nuns, established in the late 13th century, is an exceptional group of buildings. It was later transferred to Benedictine

Baroque high altar in the Church of the Assumption, Chełmno

monks and then passed to the Catholic sisters who run a hospital here today. The entrance on Ulica Dominikańska leads to an internal courtyard, which in turn gives access to the **Church of St John the Baptist** (Kościół św. Jana Chrzciciela), built in 1290–1340. It has two storeys, the

Chełmno Town Centre

① Grudziądz Gate
② Church of Saints Peter and Paul
③ Town Hall (Chełmno Museum)
④ Church of the Assumption
⑤ Chełmno Academy
⑥ Church of St James
⑦ Church of St John the Baptist

0 metres 300
0 yards 300

lower one having two naves, and the upper a single nave that was reserved for the choir of the Order of Teutonic Knights.

🏛 Chełmno Museum
Rynek 28. **Tel** 56 686 16 41. **Open** 10am–4pm Tue–Fri, 10am–4pm Sat, 11am–3pm Sun (Apr–Sep). 🅿

Environs
In Chełmża, 23 km (14 miles) north of Chełmno, stands the Gothic Cathedral of the Holy Trinity, built in 1251–1359 and rebuilt after 1422.

⓴ Bydgoszcz
Road map C2. 🅰 354,900. 🚉 🚌 ℹ ul. Stefana Batorego 2 (52 340 45 50). 🎭 Bydgoszcz Music Festival (Sep); Musica Antiqua Europae Orientalis (every 3 years, Sep). 🆆 **bydgoszcz.pl**

Bydgoszcz lies at the confluence of the River Brda and the Bydgoszcz Canal, which then flow into the Vistula. The city was only briefly part of the state of the Teutonic Knights, after which its fate was linked with that of the rest of Poland. It was the scene of dramatic events on 3 September 1939, when the town's German minority attempted to stage a coup. The Nazis entered the town and massacred thousands of the Polish population.

The **old town** of Bydgoszcz is set on a bend of the Brda. It has several monumental town houses, the late Gothic church of Saints Nicholas and Martin (Kościół św. Mikołaja i Marcina) and two monasteries: a Bernadine monastery with a church of 1545–52, and the Church and

Convent of the Poor Clares (Kościół Klarysek), which today houses a **Regional Museum**. The half-timbered **granaries** on the banks of the Brda, built in the 18th and 19th centuries, were used for the salt and wheat that the town traded and to store the beer for which it was renowned.

🏛 Regional Museum
ul. Gdańska 4. **Tel** 52 585 99 66. **Open** 10am–6pm Tue, Wed, Fri (Nov–Mar: to 4pm); 10am–7pm Thu; 11am–6pm Sat & Sun (Oct–Mar: to 4pm). 🅿 (free on Sat). 🆆 **muzeum.bydgoszcz.pl**

⓴ Toruń
See pp276–9.

⓶ Golub-Dobrzyń
Road map D2. 🅰 12,800. 🚉 🚌 ℹ 56 683 54 10 (May–Sep: 48 603 227 369). 🎭 International Jousting Tournament (Jul). 🆆 **golub-dobrzyn.pl**

This picturesque town was originally two separate settlements, one on either side of the River Drwęca. During the Partitions, Golub was part of Prussia and Dobrzyń part of Russia *(see p52)*. Golub's main feature is the large **castle** built by the Teutonic Knights in 1293– 1310. From 1466 Golub was part of Poland, and in the 17th century the castle became the residence of Queen Anna Vasa of Sweden, sister of Zygmunt III Vasa. The castle was rebuilt for her in 1616–23 in the Renaissance style. Highly educated and with an interest in botany and natural medicine, Anna Vasa was an unusual woman for her time. She remained a

spinster, reputedly because of her ugly appearance. Today the castle hosts such events as jousting tournaments and oratory competitions, as well as New Year's balls, at which revellers say that the ghost of Queen Anna appears. Ironically, the Miss Poland beauty contests are also held here.

🏛 Castle Museum
ul. PTTK 13. **Tel** 56 683 24 55. **Open** May–Sep: 9am–7pm daily; Oct–Apr: 9am–3pm daily. 🅿 📷 (compulsory, every hour).

Graduation tower for the production of salt in Ciechocinek

⓷ Ciechocinek
Road map D3. 🅰 10,600. 🚉 🚌 ℹ ul. Zdrojowa 2 (54 416 01 60). 🎭 Festival of Kujawy and Dobrzyń Folklore (Jul); International Festival of Gypsy Song and Culture (Aug). 🆆 **ciechocinek.pl**

Ciechocinek is one of Poland's best-known spa towns, which grew and prospered thanks to its iodine-rich salt springs. It is not strictly part of Pomerania but of Kujawy, and has always been a Polish town. The town came into being in 1824, when Stanisław Staszic started to build saltworks and the first of three salt graduation towers. The "towers" are huge wooden frames filled with thorny brushwood which, washed with brine, accumulates salt crystals. Each "tower" is more than 1.7 km (1 mile) wide.

Other features of Ciechocinek are the group of baths built in a variety of styles between 1845 and 1913, a fine park with a flower clock, a pump room designed by Edward Cichocki, a bandstand and open-air theatre, and numerous elegant boarding houses, sanatoria and hotels dating from the start of the 20th century.

The castle built by the Teutonic Knights in Golub-Dobrzyń

㉑ Toruń

Toruń's principal claim to fame is as the birthplace of the astronomer Nicolaus Copernicus *(see p279)*, but it is also renowned for its architecture. The city was founded by the Teutonic Knights in 1233 and quickly became a major centre of trade; in 1454, when its citizens rebelled against the knights' rule, it passed to the kings of Poland. The old town of Toruń, picturesquely situated on the banks of the River Vistula, retains its medieval street plan, and has a rare calm, since most of the streets are closed to traffic.

Star House, an early Baroque town house in the Old Market Square

The Wilam Horzyca Theatre

🎭 Wilam Horzyca Theatre
pl. Teatralny 1. **Tel** 56 622 50 21.
The delightful theatre, in the Art Nouveau style with Neo-Baroque elements, was built in 1904 by the Viennese architects Ferdinand Fellner and Hermann Helmer. The Kontakt Theatre Festival is held here each year in early summer, bringing together theatre performers from all over Europe and drawing large and enthusiastic audiences to its performances.

🏛 Church of the Virgin Mary
ul. Marii Panny. **Tel** 56 622 26 03.
The Gothic Church of the Virgin Mary (Kościół NMP) was built for Franciscan monks in 1270–1300. It has an unusually richly ornamented east gable. Late 14th-century wall paintings can be seen in the south aisle, while in the north aisle is a 16th-century Mannerist organ loft, the oldest in Poland. By the presbytery is the mausoleum of Anna Vasa *(see p275)*, sister of Zygmunt III, which was made in 1636. She was of royal blood but could not be buried at Wawel Castle because she was of the Protestant faith.

🏛 Old Market Square
The Old Market Square is the city's finest open space and still the vibrant heart of its historic district. The centrepiece is the town hall, but on all four sides of the square there are fine buildings. On the south side, at No. 7, is the Meissner Palace, built in 1739 for Jakob Meissner, mayor of Toruń, and given a Neo-Classical façade in 1798. Many of the town houses retain their original details,

The elaborate east end of the Church of the Virgin Mary

such as that at No. 17, which has a portal made in 1630. The most attractive house in the square is Star House, at No. 35 on the east side, built in 1697. It has a richly ornamented façade, with stuccowork motifs of fruit and flowers. In the square stands a monument to Nicolaus Copernicus made by Friedrich Tiecek in 1853, and a fountain with the figure of a raftsman who, according to legend, rid the citizens of Toruń of a plague of frogs by playing his fiddle.

The town hall in the Old Market Square

🏛 Town Hall
Rynek Staromiejski 1. Regional Museum: **Tel** 56 660 56 12.
Open 10am–6pm (Oct–Apr: to 4pm) Tue–Sun. **Closed** see website for details. 🎫 (ground floor free on Wed). Tower: **Open** 10am–8pm daily (Nov–Apr: to 4pm). 🎫 🌐 **muzeum. torun.pl**

The town hall, an imposing building with an internal courtyard, was erected in 1391–9 as a two-storey edifice. In 1602–5 the Gdańsk architect Antonis van Opbergen added the third floor and gave the building its current Mannerist appearance. The lower parts of the tower date from the 13th century. Standing 42 m (138 ft) high, it commands a fine view over the city of Toruń.

The town hall now houses a museum featuring Gothic art, 19th-century paintings and local crafts. The building's original interiors are also noteworthy, especially the vaulting of the former bakery and wool stalls on the ground floors of the east and west wings.

The town hall also features a restaurant and a popular pub in the basement.

Toruń City Centre

1. Wilam Horzyca Theatre
2. Church of the Virgin Mary
3. Old Market Square
4. Town Hall
5. Church of the Holy Spirit
6. Copernicus House
7. Gothic Granary
8. Crooked Tower
9. Palace of the Bishops of Kujawy
10. Cathedral of Saints John the Baptist and John the Evangelist
11. Castle of the Teutonic Knights
12. New Market Square
13. Church of St James
14. Ethnographical Museum

For keys to symbols see back flap

0 metres 100
0 yards 100

The Church of the Virgin Mary seen from the top of the town hall tower

Exploring Toruń

Toruń survived World War II relatively unscathed. It has well-preserved city walls and a series of gates that once opened onto the quayside. Granaries dating from the 15th to the 19th centuries still line the streets leading down to the river. The Cathedral of Saints John the Baptist and John Evangelist and the richly ornamented Palace of the Bishops of Kujawy are two of Toruń's finest buildings and the Copernicus Museum stands as a memorial to the city's most famous son.

🏛 Church of the Holy Spirit
ul. Piekary 24. **Tel** 56 655 48 62.
The Baroque Church of the Holy Spirit (Kościoł św. Ducha) in the Old Market Square was built in the mid-18th century for the Protestant community of Toruń. It was begun by Andreas Adam Bähr, and completed by Ephraim Schroeger.

🏛 Copernicus House
ul. Kopernika 15/17. **Tel** 56 660 56 13. **Open** 10am–4pm Tue–Sun (May–Sep: to 6pm). 🎫 (free Wed).
🌐 **muzeum.torun.pl**

These two Gothic town houses from the 15th century are outstanding examples of Hanseatic merchants' houses. The painted façades and fine carving of the arched gables bear witness to the city's former wealth. The house at No. 17 was that of Mikołaj Kopernik, a merchant and the father of the boy who was to become the famous astronomer. The house, although it may not be the one in which the younger Mikołaj was born, is now a museum.

The Crooked Tower, part of the fortifications on the River Vistula

🏛 Gothic Granary
ul. Piekary 4.
The most remarkable of the many Gothic granaries still standing in Toruń is that on the corner of Ulica Piekary and Ulica Rabiańska. Although the granary was rebuilt in the 19th century, it retains its towering ornamental gable with fine pointed arches.

🏛 Crooked Tower
ul. Pod Krzywą Wieżą.
The Crooked Tower is one of Toruń's greatest attractions.

It is part of the town's old fortifications system, and was probably built in the first half of the 14th century. Although it leans significantly from the perpendicular, the floors that were added later are perfectly level – so that beer glasses in the pub that it now houses can be set down on the tables without danger of sliding off.

🏛 Palace of the Bishops of Kujawy
ul. Żeglarska 8.
The palace was built by Bishop Stanisław Dąmbski in 1693. In the 19th century it was converted into a hotel and then into a mess for military officers. Subsequent restoration work undid the damage inflicted by these conversions and returned the building to its former elegance. It is now the Academy of Fine Arts.

Cathedral of Saints John the Baptist and John the Evangelist

🏛 Cathedral of Saints John the Baptist and John the Evangelist
ul. Żeglarska 16. **Tel** 56 657 14 80.
The origins of the Cathedral of Saints John the Baptist and John the Evangelist (Kościoł św. Janów) go back to 1250. The oldest surviving part of the cathedral is the presbytery. The nave, with its numerous side chapels, was completed by Hans Gotland in about 1500, long after the tower had been finished in 1433. The interior is a treasury of art. The presbytery contains some fine 16th-century mural

A room in the Copernicus House

Nicolaus Copernicus

Nicolaus Copernicus (Mikołaj Kopernik; 1473–1543), astronomer, mathematician, economist, doctor and clergyman, was born in Toruń. For most of his life he lived in Warmia. He wrote treatises on economics, but gained the greatest renown for his astronomical observations. His heliocentric theory of the universe, which he expounded in *De Revolutionibus Orbium Celestium* (1543), posited the fact that the planets rotate around the Sun.

Renaissance epitaph to Copernicus in Toruń

paintings. There are also altars, chandeliers, stained-glass windows, sculpture and many paintings. In one of the side chapels in the south aisle is the Gothic font where Nicolaus Copernicus was baptized and a memorial to him from about 1580. He was buried in Frombork Cathedral *(see p284)*.

🏰 Castle of the Teutonic Knights

ul. Przedzamcze. **Tel** 56 621 08 89.

Little more than ruins remain of the castle that the Teutonic Knights built in Toruń. Before the castle at Malbork *(see pp270–71)* was built, Toruń was the knights' capital.

The castle was built in the 13th century and extended in the 14th. However, it was destroyed in 1454 when the people of Toruń rose up in rebellion against the knights. Only the latrine tower – a tower overhanging a stream

that acted as a sewer – were left standing, although part of the cellars and cloisters survive. The late Gothic house that was built on the site in 1489, probably with materials scavenged from the castle, was the meeting place of the Brotherhood of St George.

🏛 New Market Square

The new town emerged as a separate civic entity in 1264. Although it does not have as many historic buildings as the old town, there is a good deal of interest here. In summer the square is filled with fruit and vegetable stalls. In the centre, where the town hall once stood, is a former Protestant church, built in 1824, probably by the German architect Karl Friedrich Schinkel. It has been converted into a gallery of contemporary art. Fine houses, some with ornate façades like that of the Baroque house at No. 17, surround the square.

On the corner of Ulica Królowej Jadwigi and the square is the Golden Lion pharmacy, a brick-built house originating in the 15th century.

🏛 Church of St James

ul. Rynek Nowomiejski 6.
Tel 56 622 29 24.

The Gothic Church of St James (Kościół św. Jakuba) was built in the first half of the 14th century as the new town's parish church. It was first used by Cistercian monks, and then by Benedictines. It contains wall paintings of the second half of the 14th century. In the south aisle is a late 14th-century Gothic crucifix in the form of the Tree of Life, in which the figure of Christ is nailed to the branches of a tree containing the figures of the prophets. Above the rood beam is a rare depiction of the Passion of about 1480–90, consisting of 22 scenes of the Stations of the Cross.

Gothic tower of the Church of St James in the new town

🏛 Ethnographical Museum

ul. Wały gen. Sikorskiego 19. **Tel** 56 622 80 91. **Open** mid-Apr–Jun: 9am–5pm Tue & Thu (to 4pm Wed & Fri), 10am–6pm Sat & Sun; Jul–Sep: 10am–6pm Tue, Thu, Sat & Sun, 9am–4pm Wed & Fri; Oct–mid-Apr: 9am–4pm Tue–Fri, 10am–4pm Sat & Sun. 🎫 (free Wed). 🌐 etnomuzeum.pl

The museum contains fishing tools and folk art. There is also a *skansen*, in which wooden houses from the region of Kujawy, Pomerania and Ziemia Dobrzyńska are displayed.

Latrine tower, the surviving part of the Castle of the Teutonic Knights

WARMIA, MAZURIA AND BIAŁYSTOK REGION

Known as the land of a thousand lakes, northeastern Poland has no major industrial areas and is blessed with vast forests and undulating moraine hills as well as a large number of lakes and rivers. Its three regions, Warmia, Mazuria and Białostocczyzna, are ethnically different and have had divergent histories.

Warmia, the western part of the region, was once inhabited by the early Prussians, and in the 13th century was taken over by the Teutonic Knights, who established a bishopric here. Warmia became part of Poland in 1466, was transferred to Prussia under the Partitions, and was not returned to Poland until 1945. There are many historic churches in the region.

Mazuria and the Iława Lake District at its southern and eastern fringes were also once controlled by the Teutonic Knights. When the order was secularized in 1525, the region became known as ducal Prussia and was ruled by the Hohenzollern family, although until 1657 it was a Polish fiefdom. The area's subsequent history is linked to that of Germany, and it did not become part of Poland again until 1945.

Many castles were built by the Knights and some Prussian mansions can be seen here today.

The Suwałki and Augustów lakelands and Białostocczyzna form the region's eastern part, which once belonged to the grand duchy of Lithuania. The area was covered in primeval forests, and three – the Augustów, Knyszyńska and Białowieża forests – remain today. The Biebrza valley contains Poland's largest stretches of marshland and peat swamps and offers plenty for naturalists. Those interested in religious culture are also well served: the Orthodox church in Grabarka, the old monastery of the Orthodox order of St Basil in Supraśl, the mosque in Kruszyniany and the synagogue in Tykocin represent a panoply of faiths.

View of Frombork Cathedral from the belfry

◀ The Ostróda-Elbląg Canal, which connects a number of lakes in Western Mazuria with the Vistula Bay

Exploring Warmia, Mazuria and Białystok Region

Northeastern Poland is an ideal place for a longer holiday. It is suitable for watersports such as sailing trips on the Mazurian Lakes or canoeing expeditions down the Czarna Hańcza or Krutynia rivers, and there are also plenty of opportunities for cycling tours. For unspoiled primeval scenery, the Białowieża Forest National Park with its bison reserve and the Biebrza marshes, with their population of nesting birds, are almost without equal.

Szczurkowo, a village where storks outnumber people

Sights at a Glance

1. Frombork
2. Braniewo
3. Elbląg
4. Morąg
5. Dobre Miasto
6. Lidzbark Warmiński
7. Olsztyn
8. Grunwald
9. Nidzica
10. Reszel
11. Święta Lipka
12. Kętrzyn
13. The Great Mazurian Lakes pp290–91

15. Biebrza National Park
16. Łomża
17. Tykocin
18. Białystok
19. Kruszyniany
20. Białowieża National Park
21. Grabarka
22. Drohiczyn

Tours

14. Canoeing on the Czarna Hańcza River and Augustów Canal pp292–3

Baroque façade of the Jesuit church in Święta Lipka

Getting Around

The main road is Highway No. 16 from Grudziądz via Olsztyn to Augustów. Highway E77 goes from the south to Elbląg, highway 51 runs from Olsztyn to the border with the Russian Kaliningrad District, while highway 8 links Augustów with Białystok. Charter flights depart from Szymany, the region's only airport, near the town of Szczytno, and there are also connections with some airports in Germany. There are rail links with all major towns, and buses link other towns in the region.

The forests of Suwalszczyzna, carpeted with mushrooms

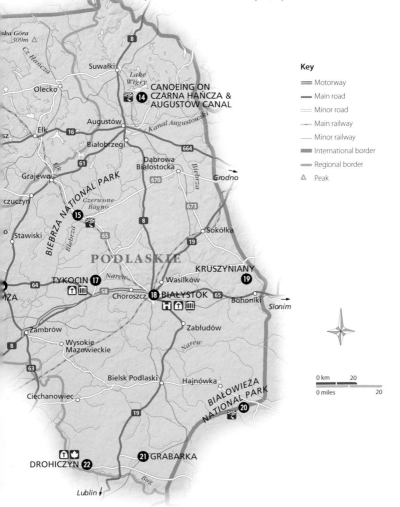

Key

- ▰▰▰ Motorway
- ▬▬ Main road
- ▭▭ Minor road
- ▬▪▬ Main railway
- ▭▭ Minor railway
- ▰▰▰ International border
- ▬▬ Regional border
- △ Peak

❶ Frombork

The history of this fortified town goes back to the second half of the 13th century, when it became a Warmian chapter (diocesan capital). Erected in 1342–88, the Gothic cathedral has an unusual form, with no towers on its west end, giving it the appearance of a Cistercian monastery. Its building houses the Museum of Nicolaus Copernicus and the Copernicus Tower, where he lived and worked from 1510–43. The Museum's collection includes two copies of *De Revolutionibus Orbium Coelestium*, postage stamps pertaining to astronomy and medicine, instruments and replicas of the devices used by the famous scholar.

VISITORS' CHECKLIST

Practical Information
Road map D1. Cathedral:
Open 9am–5pm Mon–Sat (8:30am–3pm winter). Copernicus Tower: **Open** 9:30am–5pm Tue–Sat (summer). Museum: **Tel** 55 244 00 71. **Open** May–Aug: 9am–4:30pm Tue–Sun (Sep–Apr: to 3:30pm). 🏛 (first floor free on Wed). 🅦 frombork.art.pl Planetarium: **Tel** 55 244 00 83. **Open** 9:30am–4pm daily. 🏛 Organ recitals: noon, 3pm (summer). 🎟

Former High Altar
Commissioned by Bishop Łukasz Watzenrode, uncle of Nicolaus Copernicus, the high altar was made in Toruń in 1504. It is in the form of a polyptych and is now in the south aisle. The central panel has a carving of the Virgin, depicted as a Maiden of the Apocalypse.

Altar of St Anne
The Altar of St Anne, in the north aisle, has as its focal point this subtle painting of 1639 by the Gdańsk artist Bartholomäus Strobel.

Bishop's Palace
The palace now houses the Copernicus Museum.

Organ
The instrument was made by Daniel Nitrowski of Gdańsk in 1683–4.

Main gate

Copernicus Tower

The Belfry
Also known as the Copernicus Tower, it houses a planetarium.

High Altar
Designed by Franciszek Placidi in 1742–52, the high altar is almost identical to that in the collegiate church at Dobre Miasto *(see p286)*. The central panel is a painting of the Virgin by Stefan Torelli.

❷ Braniewo

Road map D1. 🗺 17,400.
🚌 🚆 🖥 braniewo.pl

The fortified town of Braniewo was founded by the Teutonic Knights in 1240. It was the seat of the bishops of Warmia and later became the diocesan capital of Warmia. A member of the Hanseatic League, the town was a busy port and grew prosperous through the linen trade. During the Counter-Reformation it played an important role as the first Jesuit centre in Poland: the Hosianum Jesuit College was founded here in 1565, and a papal college set up in 1578.

Church of St Catherine in Braniewo

Just 8 km (5 miles) from the Russian border, Braniewo has become an important transit point for travellers crossing from one country into the other. Although it suffered severe damage during World War II, several fine buildings are still there.

🏛 Church of St Catherine

ul. Katedralna 3. **Tel** 51 253 89 78.
The nave of the Gothic Church of St Catherine (Kościół św. Katarzyny) dates from 1343–81 and the vaulting and tower from the 15th century. War damage reduced the church to little more than ruins, but it has been extensively restored.

🏛 Church of St Anthony

ul. Królewiecka 24.
Tel 55 243 23 61.
The Neo-Classical Church of St Anthony (Kościół św. Antoniego) was built in 1830–38 by the German architect Karl Friedrich Schinkel. Originally Protestant, it is now a Catholic church.

🏛 Tower of the Bishop's Castle

ul. Gdańska. **Closed** to the public.
The tower, built in the 13th century as a town gate, led from the Castle of the Bishops of Warmia to a close linking it to the town walls.

❸ Elbląg

Road map D1. 🗺 122,000. 🚌 🚆
🖥 elblag.pl

Once a large port on a par with Gdańsk, Elbląg is today known for its large ABB engineering plant, its restored old town and for producing the

Postmodern houses in the old town of Elbląg

beer Specjal, which is popular in the Pomerania region. Founded in 1237 by the Teutonic Knights, the town was part of the Polish Republic from 1466 to 1772, when under the Partitions it passed to Prussian rule. After the devastation of World War II, only the most important old buildings of Elbląg were rebuilt. The Brama Targowa tower is all that remains of the former Gothic fortifications that surrounded the town.

In the old town, just a few town houses, on Ulica Wigilijna, survive. Today, a programme of rebuilding is under way; houses in the style of the old Hanseatic merchants' houses, with stairways and their typical gables, are revitalizing the old town. The quarter is well provided with friendly bars and good restaurants.

🏛 Church of the Virgin Mary

ul. Kuśnierska 6. **Tel** 55 625 67 84.
Open 10am–6pm Tue–Sat, 10am–5pm Sun. 🖼 🖥 galeria-el.pl
This Gothic church with a double aisle was built for Dominican monks in the 14th century. After World War II it became the EL art gallery.

🏛 Church of St Nicholas

ul. Mostowa 18. **Tel** 55 232 72 44.
The Church of St Nicholas (Kościół św. Mikołaja) was begun in the 13th century and completed in 1510. The interior includes a font from 1387 by Bernhuser, a *Crucifixion* ascribed to Jan van der Matten and a late Gothic altar with the Adoration of the Magi.

The EL art gallery in the Church of the Virgin Mary

The Elbląg Canal

The Elbląg Canal is one of the most extraordinary feats of hydraulic engineering in Poland. A network of canals and locks connecting a number of lakes, it was built in 1848–72 by the Dutchman Georg Jacob Steenke. Including its branches, its total length is 212 km (133 miles). Ingenious slipways enable barges to be hauled overland from one lake to another where the difference in the water levels is too high for conventional locks to be built: there are five slipways along the 10-km (6-mile) section

between Buczyniec and Całuny, and from the canalside ships can be seen being hauled along them. You can book a boat trip along the canal that will take you through the Vistula valley and Iława Lake District.

❹ Morąg

Road map: E2. 14,500. pl. Jana Pawła II 1 (89 757 38 26). **W** morag.pl

Located in the lakelands of Iławski Morąg, the town of Morąg was founded by the Teutonic Knights – like all other towns in the region. It received its municipal charter in 1327. Despite joining the Prussian Union, Morąg remained part of the state of the Teutonic Knights, and up until 1945 its history was linked to that of ducal Prussia. In the town are the remains of a 14th-century Teutonic castle, a Gothic town hall that was rebuilt after World War II, and the Church of St Joseph (Kościół św. Józefa), built in the 14th century and extended in the late 15th, with Gothic polychromes from that time.

Morąg is the birthplace of the German philosopher Gottfried von Herder. A **museum** dedicated to him is housed in a Baroque palace that once belonged to the Dohn family.

Johann Gottfried von Herder Museum
ul. Dąbrowskiego 54. **Tel** 89 757 28 48. **Open** 9am–5pm Tue–Sun (Oct–May: to 4pm).

❺ Dobre Miasto

Road map: E2. 10,500. **W** dobremiasto.com.pl

Founded in 1326, Dobre Miasto owes its historical importance to the fact that, in 1347, it became the seat of a college of canons of the diocese of Warmia. The vast Gothic collegiate church that they

Interior of the Gothic collegiate church in Dobre Miasto

established was built in the second half of the 1300s.

Its impressive interior includes two Gothic side altars as well as a Baroque high altar almost identical in design to that made by Franciszek Placidi for Frombork Cathedral (see p284). The church also possesses richly decorated Baroque stalls down each side, which have remarkable Gothic steps carved into them in the shape of lions.

❻ Lidzbark Warmiński

Road map: E1. 16,800. **W** lidzbarkwarminski.pl

From 1350 to 1795 Lidzbark was the main residence of the bishops of Warmia, and one of the region's major towns. Picturesquely set on a bend of the River Łyna, the town is dominated by the medieval Bishops' Castle. The massive edifice with corner towers was built in the second half of the

14th century. Of special interest are the Palace of Bishop Grabowski and the Great Refectory in the east wing, the castle's Rococo chapel and armoury in the south wing, the Small Refectory in the west wing and the bishops' private apartments located in the north wing. The cloistered courtyard is decorated with murals. The astronomer Nicolaus Copernicus (see p279) lived here as secretary and physician to his uncle, Bishop Łukasz von Wantzenrode, in 1503–10. The castle now houses the **Warmia Museum** and a bar and art gallery in its cellars.

On the opposite bank of the Łyna, in the historic town centre, stands the fine Gothic **Church of Saints Peter and Paul** (Kościół św. Piotra i Pawła). There are also remnants of the city walls, and the main gate, the Brama Wysoka, still stands. The former Protestant church (now Orthodox) nearby was built in 1821–3 by Karl Friedrich Schinkel.

Church of Saints Peter and Paul
ul. Kościelny 1. **Tel** 89 767 23 15. **Open** 9am–5pm Tue–Sun (Sep–19 May: to 4pm).

Warmia Museum
pl. Zamkowy 1. **Tel** 89 767 21 11. **Open** May–Oct: 9am–5pm Wed–Fri & Sun, 10am–6pm Tue & Sat. (free on Thu). **W** muzeum.olsztyn.pl
On display is a selection of Warmian art and a unique collection of icons from the Convent of the Old Believers' in Wojnowo (see p290).

The Gothic cloisters of the Bishop's Castle in Lidzbark

Johann Gottfried Von Herder (1744–1803)

The German writer and philosopher Johann Gottfried von Herder, who was born in Morąg, was one of the great figures of the Enlightenment. He studied theology in Königsberg (Kaliningrad) before entering the priest-hood. He saw the importance of nations in the making of history and the role of culture and language in preserving national identity. While living in Riga, he recorded Latvian folk songs.

❼ Olsztyn

Road map: E2. 🚗 175,000. 🚌 🚆
ℹ️ ul. Jana Pawła II (89 521 03 98).
Open Jan–May & Oct–Dec:
10am–4pm Mon–Sat; Jun–Sep:
10am–6pm Mon–Fri, 10am–4pm Sat
& Sun. 🎭 Olsztyn Blues Nights; Castle
Poetry Readings (Jul).
W olsztyn.eu

Olsztyn is the largest city in
Warmia and Mazuria and the
main town of the two regions.
It is a centre of both academic
and cultural life as well as a
major city. It is also associated
with several sporting heroes,
particularly in speedway and
aerobatics. It hosts the Olsztyn
Summer Arts festival from mid-
June to mid-September.

The Gothic Castle of the
Warmian Chapter, which
was built in the 14th century,
formed the beginning of the
city. The castle was built on a
hill on the banks of the Łyna.
It was a four-sided fortress of
modest proportions with
residential quarters in the north
wing and a service wing to the
south. The palace in the east
wing was added in 1756–8.
The finest part of the building
is the refectory, which has
intricate crystalline vaulting.
On the wall of the cloister is
a remarkable diagram of an
equinox probably drawn by
Nicolaus Copernicus, who
combined his duties as an
administrator of the chapter in
Olsztyn with his astronomical
observations. The castle now
houses the
Museum of

The High Gate, part of the defences
of Olsztyn old town

Warmia and Mazuria, which
has a special section dedicated
to Nicolaus Copernicus. The first
floor contains an ethnographical
and natural history collection.

The castle's fortifications
were linked to the city walls,
which were built after 1353
on the far side of the moat.
The moat today has an open-
air theatre that is used for
concerts in summer.

In the picturesque old town
of Olsztyn, set on a slope, are
remnants of the walls and the
High Gate. The quaint little Market
Square surrounded by arcaded
houses was built during the post-
war reconstruction of the city,
but the houses retain their
original cellars, which today
are given over to bars, restaurants and cafés. Standing in
the middle of the square is a
Baroque town hall, whose
wings were added in 1927–9.

Another important building
in the Market Square is the
Gothic **Cathedral of St James**
(Katedra św. Jakuba), most
probably built between
1380 and 1445. The very fine
crystalline vaulting was added
in the early 16th century.

🏛️ **Cathedral of St James**
ul. Staszica 125. **Tel** 89 527 32 80.

🏛️ **Museum of Warmia
and Mazuria**
ul. Zamkowa 2. **Tel** 89 527 95 96.
Open May, Jun & Sep: 9am–5pm Tue–
Sat, 10am–6pm Sun; Oct–Apr:
10am–4pm Tue–Sat, 10am–6pm Sun.
📷 W muzeum.olsztyn.pl

Environs
Barczewo, 10 km (6 miles) east
of Olsztyn, is the birthplace of
Feliks Nowowiejski (1877–1946),
composer of the *Rota*, a patriotic
Polish anthem. His family home
contains a small **museum**.

Halfway between Olsztyn and
Nidzica, in the local Ethnography
Park, lies the country's oldest
skansen, **Budownictwa Ludowego
Open Air Museum**, including
traditional wooden windmills,
arts and crafts.

🏛️ **Budownictwa Ludowego
Open Air Museum**
ul. Leśna 23. **Tel** 89 519 21 64. **Open**
mid-end Apr, Sep, Oct: 9am–4pm
Tue–Sun; May & Jun: 9am–5pm daily;
Jul & Aug: 10am–6pm daily. 📷 🚫
W muzeumolsztynek.com.pl

🏛️ **Feliks Nowowiejski Museum**
ul. Mickiewicza 13. **Tel** 89
674 04 79. **Open**
9am–5pm Tue–
Fri, 8am–4pm Sat,
Sun by appt
(89 660 017
208).📷

The Castle of the Warmian Chapter in Olsztyn

The monument to the Battle of Grunwald outside the town

❽ Grunwald

Road map E2. 🏛 420. 🚌
🎏 Battle of Grunwald (15 Jul).

The fields between Grunwald and Stębark (Tannenberg in German) were the scene of one of the major battles of the Middle Ages. On 15 July 1410, the forces of the Teutonic Knights – some 14,000 cavalry plus infantry commanded by Ulrich von Jungingen – faced 24,000 Polish-Lithuanian and Ruthenian cavalry and several thousand infantry led by Władysław II Jagiełło. The knights suffered a resounding defeat, and the Grand Master himself was killed. Historians believe that during World War I, in August 1914, the German Field Marshal Hindenburg deliberately chose this site for his victorious battle against the Russians in order to negate the memory of that

defeat. The monument to the medieval Battle of Grunwald that stands on the site was designed by Jerzy Bandura and Witold Cęckiewicz and unveiled in 1960. Nearby is a small **museum** with a collection of documents about the battle and archaeological finds from the site. For several years the battle's anniversary has been marked by re-enactments of the engagement as it is described in chronicles.

🏛 **Museum of the Battle of Grunwald in Stębark**
Stębark 1. **Tel** 89 647 22 27. **Open** 10 Apr–Sep: 9:30am–6:30pm daily (8:30pm on 15 Jul). 🎟 (free on Wed).
W **muzeumgrunwald.fbrothers.com**

❾ Nidzica

Road map E2. 🏛 14,200. 🚉 🚌
ℹ pl. Wolności 1 (89 625 03 70). 🎏 Nidzica Festival (May). W **nidzica.pl**

The main feature of Nidzica is the Teutonic Castle, which overlooks the town from a hill. It was built in the late 1300s and altered in the 16th century. Reduced to ruins, it was rebuilt in the 1800s and again after World War II. Part of it is now a hotel. Some of the town's medieval fortifications also survive.

Environs
The **Tatars' Stone** lies 2 km (just over 1 mile) south of Nidzica. This large rock, with a circumference of 19 m (63 ft), marks the spot where, according to legend, the leader of the Tatars was killed in 1656, thus sparing Nidzica from invasion in the same year.

Castle for the Bishops of Warmia, built to repulse Lithuanian attacks

❿ Reszel

Road map E1. 🏛 4,800.
🚌 ℹ Rynek 24 (89 755 00 97).
W **reszel.pl** or **ugreszel.pl**

This little town was once a major Warmian city. In 1337, Reszel was granted a municipal charter, and in the second half of the 14th century a Gothic **castle** was built here for the Bishops of Warmia. The castle's tower commands a splendid view over the town. The castle is now a hotel, and it also houses a **gallery** of contemporary art.

There are two churches in the town: the Gothic Church of Saints Peter and Paul, built in the 1300s with the addition of late 15th-century vaulting, and the former Church of St John the Baptist, now an Orthodox church, built in 1799–1800 in the Baroque style.

The Gothic Castle of the Teutonic Knights in Nidzica

Trompe l'oeil paintings in the pilgrimage church in Święta Lipka

🏛 Castle Gallery

ul. Podzamcze 4. **Tel** 89 755 01 09.
Open 9am–6pm Tue–Sun. 📷 🎫 ♿
🌐 **zamek-reszel.com**

⓫ Święta Lipka

Road map E2. 🚶 190. 🚌 🚃 Święta
Lipka Music Evenings (Jun–Aug).
🌐 **swlipka.org.pl**

Święta Lipka has one of the most important shrines of the cult of the Virgin in Poland. The name of the town means "holy lime" (or linden tree), and the legend that grew up concerns a miraculous sculpture of the Virgin that was carved by a prisoner in the 15th century and hung from a roadside lime tree. A chapel containing the statue of the Virgin, destroyed during the Reformation, was built around it. In 1619 a temporary chapel was built here, followed in 1687–93 by a proper **church**, which was cared for by the Jesuits. In 1694–1708 cloisters and outside chapels were added and the façade and belfry were completed in 1729.

During the Counter-Reformation Święta Lipka was a Catholic stronghold within Protestant ducal Prussia. Large donations were made for decorating the church, resulting in one of the finest and most intriguing examples of Baroque art in Poland.

The magnificent interior contains frescoes, including trompe l'oeil paintings in the dome by Mathias Mayer, and the high altar has an image of the Virgin dating from about 1640. The organ, with its moving figurines of angels, built in 1721 by Johann Mosengel of Królewiec (Königsberg), is a great attraction for both tourists and pilgrims. In summer, about eight organ recitals are given every day, and during some of them, the figures in the organ loft are set in motion.

⓬ Kętrzyn

Road map E1. 🚶 28,300. 🚌 🚃
ⓘ pl. Piłsudskiego 10/1 (89 751 47 65). 🌐 **it.ketrzyn.pl**

From the 14th century, Kętrzyn was the seat of the Prosecutor of the Teutonic Knights, who built the castle that can still be seen today. Kętrzyn then passed to Prussia and later Germany, but retained a sizeable Polish population. The original name for the town was Rastembork; in 1946 it was renamed in honour of Polish national activist Wojciech Kętrzyński. The old town was almost entirely flattened during World War II: only the town walls and the Church of St George (Kościół św. Jerzego) survived. Its exterior is modest, but the interior is impressive – its finest decoration is the crystalline vaulting of around 1515.

Environs

Ten km (6 miles) east of Kętrzyn is **Gierłoż**, location of the "Wolf's Lair", Adolf Hitler's headquarters in 1940. It consisted of dozens of reinforced concrete bunkers built in woodland. There was also an airfield, railway lines and a power station. Here, on 20 July 1944, the German officer Claus von Stauffenberg made an unsuccessful attempt on Hitler's life. The lair was never discovered by the Allies, and the bunkers were blown up by the withdrawing Germans in January 1945.

Crystalline vaulti[ng...]
St George in Ke[...]

⓲ The Great Mazurian Lakes

The Great Mazurian Lakes are the largest in Poland and a popular holiday spot in summer. Despite this, the countryside remains largely unspoiled, and many rare plants and birds thrive here. The lakes are interlinked by rivers and canals, and are suitable for yachting or canoeing trips. Another way to see the region is to take a cruise aboard a ship of the Mazurian Shipping Company or to drive along the roads that wind among the lakeside trees.

The district is a paradise for ramblers and for those who delight in discovering secret spots. Its woods conceal overgrown bunkers built by the Germans in World War II.

Ryn

The castle that towers over the town was built by Konrad Wallenrod, Grand Master of the Teutonic Knights, for his brother Frederick in 1394. It was rebuilt in the English Gothic style in 1853.

Mikołajki

The summer capital of the Mazurian Lake District is the location of its main yachting marina. A variety of vessels – from sailing dinghies, yachts and canoes to motorboats – are available for hire.

KEY

① **The Pranie Forester's House Museum** honours the poet Konstanty Ildefons Gałczyński (1905–53), who spent the last days of his life here.

② **Sztynort**, once the residence of ...he Prussian Lehndorff family, stands a large peninsula. Some of the ...rees in the park surrounding ...use are three centuries old.

Śniardwy is not very ...covering an area of ...4 sq miles), it is ...oland.

... **museum** in Pisz ...column with ...n as the

Wojnowo

The church, cemetery and convent at Wojnowo were built by the Old Believers, who fled Russia in the 18th and 19th centuries.

... p305 and p319

Giżycko
In the woods beside the town, on an isthmus between the lakes, is the grim Prussian Boyen Castle, which was built in 1844.

Lake Niegocin
Like most others in the region, the lake is popular with water-sports enthusiasts and swimmers. Holiday resorts and campsites are scattered around the lakes.

Water Lilies
Several varieties of water lily can be seen in the region's lakes.

| 0 kilometres | 10 | |
| 0 miles | | 10 |

Key
■■■ Major road
═══ Minor road

Wild Swans

Lake Łuknajno, which is listed by UNESCO as a World Biosphere Reserve, has become one of Poland's finest nature reserves for wild swans. The fact that the lake is shallow – its average depth does not exceed 1.5 m (4 ft) – makes it easy for the birds to feed on the weed that grows on the lakebed. In 1922, eggs laid by the swans of Lake Łuknajno were used to regenerate Berlin's swan population. Lake Łuknajno attracts wildlife photographers from all over the world, lured by the chance of an unforgettable shot. To safeguard the natural habitat, boats are not allowed on the lake.

A swan on Lake Łuknajno

⑭ Canoeing on the Czarna Hańcza and Augustów Canal

This is one of the most beautiful canoeing routes in Poland. In some places the narrow, winding River Czarna Hańcza is as swift as a mountain stream; in others its course slows as its banks widen. The route downstream passes swamps and lakes and goes through locks on the Augustów Canal that have remained almost unchanged since the time that they were built at the beginning of the 19th century. Canoe trips may be made individually or in organized groups.

① Lake Wigry
Lake Wigry, in Wigry National Park, is the largest lake in the Suwałki region. Part of the "silent zone", it has numerous islands.

② Camaldolite Monastery
This monastery stands on the peninsula in Lake Wigry. The monastery buildings have been converted into a hotel. Beyond, the Czarna Hańcza River flows from the lake.

③ The Czarna Hańcza River
The most beautiful stretch of the Czarna Hańcza, beyond the village of Wysoki Most, takes a meandering route. All around is the Augustów Forest.

④ Rygol
Here the river forks, its right arm joining the Augustów Canal. Canoeists may stray off the route and follow the canal leading to the border with Belarus, but they must turn back at the last lock before the border, which is closed.

⑤ Locks
The Augustów Canal connects the River Niemen with the River Biebrza and, further on, with the Vistula, passing through several locks on the way. Built in 1823–39, the canal was a great engineering achievement.

Map labels: 658, 653, 654, 660, Suwałki, Lake Krzywe, Lake Petry, Stary Folwark, Lake Długie, 660, Sej, Lake Gremzdy, Olecko, Wigry National Park, Lake Wigry, ①, ②, ③, 8, Fracki, Lake Blizno, Lake Busznica, Blizno, Lake Serwy, Lake, Rospuda, 16, Lake Długie, Lake Biała, Augustów Canal, Lake Necko, Lake Studzieniczne, ⑤, ⑥, 61, Lake Sajno, 664, Grodno, Grajewo, ⑦, 8, Białystok

Tips for Walkers

Starting point for canoe trips:
Stary Folwark or Wigry.
Length: About 100 km (62 miles).
Stopping-off places: There are campsites and bivouacs along the route. You may also stay by the locks and PTTK riverside hostels.

Meadows covered by the floodwaters of the River Biebrza

Typical landscape of the Augustów lake district

⑥ Augustów

Augustów is a major tourist town with many hotels, guesthouses and rest centres. There is a large yachting marina on the canal.

⑦ Białobrzegi

Canoeing trips usually end in Augustów, but canoeists may continue along the Augustów Canal through Białobrzegi southwards to the swamps on the River Biebrza.

0 kilometres   5
0 miles   5

Key

■ ■ Canoeing route
■ Main road
▬ Other road

⑮ Biebrza National Park

Road map F2. 🚌 ℹ️ Osowiec National Park Management (85 738 06 20). 🎫 tickets available in the management office, foresters' lodges and gamekeepers' cottages.
🌐 biebrza.org.pl

Biebrza National Park is one of the wildest places in Europe, untouched by human activity. It stretches for 70 km (50 miles) along the banks of the River Biebrza and contains Poland's largest swamps, which are home to a wide variety of wildlife. A close encounter with a moose is a distinct possibility. The greatest attraction of the swamps, however, is their rich bird life; over 260 species live here, and bird-watchers from afar come to the swamps to observe them. The most interesting swamp for bird life is **Red Swamp** (Czerwone Bagno), part of a strictly protected nature reserve accessible only by means of a wooden walkway. Walkways have also been installed in other parts of the park. A walk along the red tourist trail holds a range of attractions – although you may have to wade through mud to reach them. Visitors may hire a guide and tour the swamps in a punt, or descend the River Biebrza in a canoe, for which a ticket and the permission of the park management are required.

In **Osowiec**, in the middle of the swamps, there is a beaver reserve. Nearby stand the partly blown-up walls of a Russian redoubt. Although it was impregnable, the Russians, fearful of the German offensive, abandoned it in 1915.

⑯ Łomża

Road map F2. 🚶 62,000. 🚌 🚏
ℹ️ ul. Krzywe Koło 9 (86 216 70 50).
🌐 lomza.pl

Łomża is a large provincial town with many distinguished buildings. Its Gothic **cathedral**, built in the 16th century by the last dukes of Mazovia, has a number of notable features: in particular, the cellular and star vaulting of its interior, the silver reliefs on the high altar, and the tombs of Andrzej Modliszewski, mayor of Łomża, his wife and their son. The tombs are the work of Santi Gucci. The Capuchin church and regional museum are also of interest.

Environs

In **Nowogród**, on a high bank of the River Narew, 15 km (9 miles) northwest of Łomża, is a *skansen* in which the houses and other buildings of a typical Kurpie village are displayed. Opened in 1927, it is one of Poland's oldest *skansens*.

Star vaulting over the nave of Łomża Cathedral

The synagogue in Tykocin, now a museum

⑰ Tykocin

Road map F2. 🏛 2,000. 🚌
ⓘ ul. Złota 2 (85 718 72 32).

The town of Tykocin was granted a municipal charter in 1425. In 1659 it was given to Stefan Czarnecki, hero of the bitter wars with Sweden, in recognition of his service to the king and to Poland. It later passed to the royal field commander Jan Klemens Branicki. The town owes its present appearance to renovation – financed by Branicki – that was carried out after a fire in 1741.

In the centre of the Market Square there stands a Baroque monument to Stefan Czarnecki that was carved between 1761 and 1763 by the court sculptor Pierre Coudray. The **parish church** on the east side of the square was built a little earlier, in 1750. The Baroque **synagogue**, which dates from 1642, is a relic of the town's former Jewish population. Inside, the walls are inscribed with religious quotations in Hebrew and Aramaic. The synagogue now contains the **Tykocin Museum**.

Ⅲ **Tykocin Museum**
ul. Kozia 2. **Tel** 85 718 16 26.
Open 10am–6pm Tue–Sun (Oct–Apr: to 5pm). 🖾 (free on Sat.) 📷

⑱ Białystok

Road map F2. 🏛 295,000. 🚌 🚆
ⓘ ul. Kilińskiego 1 (85 869 62 58).
🎪 Białystok Days (around 20 Jun).
W **bialystok.pl**

Białystok is the largest town in northeast Poland. Its population is both Polish and Belarussian, something that can easily be read in the cityscape: the domes of the Orthodox church rise up next to the towers of the Catholic church, and there are many Belarussian cultural institutions. Białystok was once owned by the Branicki family; indeed, the layout of the town is dominated by their former residence, **Branicki Palace.**

The Baroque palace was built by Tylman van Gameren in the 17th century and extended by Jan Zygmunt Deybel – who gave it the appearance of a royal mansion – between 1728 and 1758. It was modelled on the Palace of Versailles, and a formal park, with terraces, canals, fountains, summerhouses and numerous sculptures, was laid out around it. Like other members of the high aristocracy, Jan Klemens Branicki, royal field commander and an extremely wealthy man in his own right, maintained his own private army. He was also a connoisseur of art. In political circles, however, he was unpopular, opposing

Statue by JC Redler at Branicki Palace in Białystok

reform and contributing to the ruin of Poland. Parts of the palace now house the town's medical academy.

Another interesting building is the **Church of St Roch** (Kościół św. Rocha), in reinforced concrete, designed by Oskar Sosnkowski, and built between 1927 and 1946. The Baroque town hall in the Market Square houses a **Regional Museum**.

🏰 **Branicki Palace**
ul. Kilińskiego 1. **Tel** 85 748 54 67.
Open 10am–5pm Tue–Fri, 9am–5pm Sat & Sun. 🖾

⛪ **Church of St Roch**
ul. ks. Abramowicza 1. **Tel** 85 652 10 58.

Ⅲ **Regional Museum**
Rynek Kościuszki 10. **Tel** 85 742 14 73.
Open May–Aug: 10am–5pm daily (to 6pm Fri); Sep–Apr: 10am–5pm Tue–Sun. 🖾 (free Sun).

⑲ Kruszyniany

Road map G2. 🏛 110.

Kruszyniany and nearby **Bohoniki** count among their inhabitants the descendants of the Tatars who settled here in the 17th century. Although they became fully integrated into the community a long time ago, their Muslim faith and customs live on. Descendants of the Tatars also live in the Podlasie villages of Nietupy, Łużyny and Drahle. Kruszyniany has a charming wooden **mosque**, originating in the 18th century and rebuilt in 1843. The tombstones in the Muslim graveyard face Mecca.

Wooden mosque in Kruszyniany, built by the descendants of the Tatars

⑳ Białowieża National Park

Road map G3. 🚌 **ℹ️** Park Pałacowy 11 (85 681 29 01). **W** bpn.com.pl

The Białowieża Forest, covering almost 1,500 sq km (580 sq miles), is Europe's largest natural forest. It lies partly in Poland and partly in Belarus. The larger – Belarussian – part is virtually inaccessible to tourists; the Polish part became a national park in 1932. Many parts of the park have preserved their natural character – that of a primeval forest. The areas of greatest interest may be visited only with a guide. Recently, the park's borders have been extended on the Polish side.

The forest has an impressive abundance of flora and fauna. There are several thousand species of plants and 11,000 species of animals, including many very rare birds, such as the capercaillie, black stork and golden eagle. Larger mammals include elk, deer, roe deer, wild boar, wolf, lynx and, most famously, the European bison.

On the road through the forest there is a bison-breeding centre and enclosures of bison, deer, wild boar and Polish ponies. The park also has a **forest museum**, whose exhibits were once housed in a brick hunting lodge used by the tsars. It was torched by German forces in 1944. Only an Orthodox church remains.

Białowieża National Park has been listed by UNESCO as a World Biosphere Reserve.

🏛️ **Białowieża Forest Museum**
Palace Park Botanical Gardens. **Tel** 85 682 97 04. **Open** mid-Apr–mid-Oct: 9am–4:30pm Mon–Fri, 9am–5pm Sat & Sun; mid-Oct–mid-Apr: 9am–4pm Tue–Sun. 🖼️

㉑ Grabarka

Road map F3. 🚠 50. 🚉 Nurzec. 🚌 Orthodox convent: **Tel** 85 655 00 10. **W** grabarka.pl

For Poland's Orthodox Christians, there is no more important place of pilgrimage in the country than the Holy Mountain outside Grabarka. The story goes that in 1770, when the plague was ravaging the town, the inhabitants of Grabarka were directed by a heavenly sign to erect a cross on the hill. The plague

Part of the forest of crosses on the Holy Mountain outside Grabarka

Baroque façade of the Benedictine church in Drohiczyn

passed and the hill became a hallowed site.

To this day its slopes are covered with hundreds of votive crosses. The original wooden church, destroyed by an arsonist in 1990, was replaced by a brick-built church. The Orthodox convent next to it is the only one in Poland.

㉒ Drohiczyn

Road map F3. 🚠 2,055. 🚌 **ℹ️** ul. Kraszewskiego 13 (85 655 70 69). **W** drohiczyn.pl

Drohiczyn, set on a high bank of the Bug River, is today a small, quiet town. As early as the 13th century, however, it was a major centre of trade, and in 1520 it became the provincial capital of Podlasie. In 1795, with the Third Partition of Poland, it was demoted to the status of an ordinary village.

The oldest surviving church in the town is the Baroque **Franciscan church**, dating from 1640–60. The cathedral, originally a Jesuit church, dates from 1696–1709. Nearby stands the former **Jesuit monastery**, later taken over by the Piarists. The striking **Benedictine church**, begun in 1744, has a typically Baroque undulating façade and elliptical interior. The **Orthodox church**, originally Greek Catholic, dates from 1792. To the east of the town, along the winding Bug River, lies a park, the **Podlasie Bug River Gorge**.

European Bison

The European bison *(Bison bonasus)* is the largest mammal native to Europe. The weight of an adult bull may reach 1,000 kg (2,200 lb). The largest population of bison ever recorded – 1,500 animals – was in Białowieża in 1860. Hunting these animals has always been restricted, but by World War I (1914–18) the species faced extinction. In 1929, several bison were brought to Poland from zoos in Sweden and Germany to be bred in their natural habitat. The first were set free in Białowieża National Park in 1952. Today bison can also be seen in the other great forests of Poland, including Borecka, Knyszyńska and Niepołomice *(see p169).*

The European bison

TRAVELLERS' NEEDS

WHERE TO STAY

The accommodation industry in Poland has come a long way since the fall of Communism in 1989. The country is now home to big international chains, such as Radisson Blu and Sheraton, as well as many superbly renovated 19th-century hotels, renowned for their *fin-de-siècle* atmosphere. The best of these have managed to recapture the magnificence that was lost during the period of Communist rule. In addition to these renovated historic hotels, many new hotels have sprung up in cities and resorts throughout the country. The number of backpacker hostels has also mushroomed, ensuring that there is a broad choice of accommodation for all budgets. Visitors can still expect to pay a premium for hotels in the city centre, but the increased competition is helping to keep prices in check. From all the hotels in Poland, this section highlights some of the best; they have been categorized according to location and price on pages 302–5.

The façade of the Hotel Wolne Miasto, in Gdańsk *(see p304)*

Hotels

Poland offers some of the most atmospheric and characterful places to stay in the whole of Central Europe. The country boasts an impressive number of historic, mostly 19th-century hotels, especially grand old places like the Hotel Bristol in Warsaw *(see p302)* and the Pollera hotel in Krakow *(see p303)*, which has preserved the decor and atmosphere of the *belle époque*. There are also a lot of luxury establishments, notably the Hotel Stary in Krakow *(see p303)*, that have made good use of old buildings, adapting medieval and Renaissance town houses to the needs of the modern hospitality industry, while leaving a lot of the original exposed-brick and stone features intact. Many former manor houses in the Polish countryside now serve as luxury hotels and conference centres.

Modern five-star chains such as Radisson Blu and Sheraton are also present in Poland, alongside a lot of the more budget-oriented hotel chains, such as Ibis and Mercure. Lake and mountain resorts have seen an increase in the number of spa hotels offering indoor pools, wellness treatments and saunas in an unspoiled setting.

Finally, a new breed of boutique and design hotels aims to make good use of local artistic traditions; alongside these is a healthy quantity of B&Bs, offering cosy, characterful and informal accommodation in rural areas and mountain resorts.

Making a Reservation

Almost all of Poland's hotels, B&Bs and hostels are featured on international booking sites such as **Booking**, **Airbnb** and **Hostelworld**. Reservations can also be made by contacting the establishment directly by phone or email.

Early booking is advisable with most hotels, especially during high summer, when finding vacancies in some establishments can be quite a challenge. Peak times are July and August, the period around the May Day public holiday and New Year's Eve. Accommodation in mountain resorts tends to be scarce during the Christmas period and the skiing season. In

The warm Art Deco ambience at the Rialto hotel in Warsaw *(see p302)*

◀ A selection of traditional Polish handmade pottery

Prettily decorated room at the Oki Doki hostel, Warsaw *(see p302)*

Warsaw there is a constant flow of international conferences, meetings and festivals, and finding a hotel on arrival may prove difficult at any time, so booking in advance is vital. In Poznań, accommodation is hard to find during the trade fairs that take place here throughout the year.

Facilities

Most of Poland's hotels offer en-suite rooms with satellite or cable television. The provision of Wi-Fi Internet access is also pretty standard throughout the Polish hotel industry. Even in the better hotels, bathrooms may feature a shower rather than a bathtub – if you specifically want a bath-

tub, you should enquire about this when booking. Rooms in the more expensive hotels may have a mini-bar, 24-hour room service and laundry facilities, while some have amenities such as business centres with computers and fax machines. Fitness facilities are increasingly common, and a growing number of hotels in the mid-range and luxury brackets offer spa areas or swimming pools. Tourist information is sometimes available at the reception desk, where it might also be possible to book tickets for various events.

Check-out time is generally noon, but luggage can usually be left with reception if you have an evening flight. Hotel staff frequently speak both English and German.

Discounts

Hotels often advertise rate cuts and budget specials on Internet booking sites. In general, prices tend to fluctuate according to the season, and most hotels in Poland reduce their prices in autumn and winter – except in mountain resorts, where winter is a peak tourist period. Throughout the year, business and con-ference hotels, which are often full on weekdays, tend to reduce their prices at weekends. Note that in Poznań, during the trade fairs,

accommodation prices are usually much higher than at other times. Wherever you are thinking of staying, it is always worth asking for a discount, and you stand a good chance of getting one if you are planning a longer stay.

Hidden Extras

In accordance with Polish law, in every hotel the prices quoted or displayed have to include tax and service. In most establishments, they also include breakfast, but this is not always the case, so it is best to read the details carefully when booking. Telephone calls from hotel rooms are far more expensive than elsewhere and therefore best avoided.

Although free Wi-Fi Internet access is increasingly standard across the Polish hospitality industry, there are still several hotels (mostly in the business category) that charge for this service. Ask before you log on.

On the plus side, however, Polish hospitality almost always extends to providing guests with a free supply of mineral water. Regardless of the standard of the hotel, a fresh bottle of sparkling water is usually left in your room every day. As a rule, if it is not in the mini-bar, it is free.

When it comes to tipping at hotel restaurants, it is cus-tomary to leave 10 per cent. You may, however, choose to give less depending upon the service you have received. It is also worth being aware that saying "thank you" when paying a bill is automatically taken to mean "keep the change". Tips are not offered to hotel staff, except at the most exclusive places.

As a general rule, there is no reduction for single travellers, and the same price will be charged for a double room regardless of whether it is occupied by one or two guests. There are not many single-bed hotel rooms available for solo travellers, although a discount is usually offered when booking a double room for single use.

The Neptun hotel, situated right on the coast in Łeba *(see p305)*

Blow Up Hall 5050, in Poznań's Stary Browar complex *(see p304)*

Mountain Lodges

Hiking along marked mountain trails has long been a popular activity in Poland. The network of mountain lodges is very extensive. It is possible to walk the length and breadth of the Carpathian and Sudeten mountains staying only in mountain hostels.

Standards vary from modest to quite comfortable. It is advisable to book in advance, although after nightfall the staff cannot refuse to let you in, even if all the rooms are occupied. At worst you will end up sleeping on the floor. Mountain lodges usually have bathrooms, as well as buffets serving hot meals. It is also possible to hire equipment.

Disabled Travellers

Newly built and renovated hotels and guesthouses usually have special facilities for disabled travellers, such as wheelchair access and chair lifts. Specially adapted rooms are also increasingly available. However, provision for special needs is by no means universal, so it is advisable to contact the hotel beforehand to check what facilities for disabled people, if any, are provided. The number of rooms equipped for disabled travellers is small even in the best hotels, so reservations should be made as far in advance as possible.

Rooms and Apartments to Let

Many families living on the Baltic coast and around the Mazurian Lakes rent out rooms to tourists during the summer season. Often simply furnished and with a shared bathroom, this accommodation is much cheaper than a hotel room. Look for signs reading *pokoje* ("rooms") or contact the local tourist office.

Numerous apartments in major cities and resorts are made available to tourists for short- or long-term stays. These are often rented out directly by the owner via accommodation websites such as Booking or Airbnb. There are also a number of specialized agents in Krakow, such as **Krakow Apartments**, **Old City Apartments** and **Sodispar**, who rent out holiday apartments in popular central locations. Apartments usually have a fully equipped kitchenette and a TV; many also have Wi-Fi Internet access. Some of the more expensive apartments are serviced, which means that they are cleaned daily or every few days.

Travelling with Children

Children are welcome everywhere in Poland. Most hotels offer additional beds for children, and usually no extra charge is made for this if the child is under the age of seven or eight. However, check that this is the case when making a reservation. Only the very best hotels offer baby-sitting facilities as part of their service.

In hotel restaurants there should be no problem in ordering children's portions, and most places have high chairs.

Hostels

There is an increasing number of backpacker hostels in Poland, especially in major cities, offering cheap, simple dorm accommodation in fun, informal surroundings. A lot of hostels have invested in contemporary design and comforts, and they are similar in style to small boutique hotels. Many hostels offer doubles, triples and quads as well as dorms, and they are increasingly popular with couples and families who enjoy the social aspects of backpacker culture but who want their own room.

Hostels in Poland vary a great deal in terms of character: some have a bar on site and

The communal kitchen area at the Stop Wrocław hostel *(see p304)*

encourage late-night socializing, while others offer a bit more peace and quiet. It will be clear from the description on each hostel's website what kind of atmosphere they favour.

Breakfast is available at some hostels, but not all – this can be checked when making your booking. Beds in hostels can be booked via the hostels' own websites or on specialist sites such as Hostelworld.

Camping

There is a handful of suburban campsites in Warsaw, Krakow and Poznań, and a large number of sites in tourist areas such as the Baltic coast, the Mazurian Lakes and the Tatra Mountains. Most sites are well equipped affairs with good sanitary facilities and electricity for trailers. The larger ones may also offer bungalows, TV lounges, playgrounds and sports pitches. While a few campsites are open all year round, most operate only from early May to the end of September. The **Polish Camping and Caravanning Federation** provides guides and maps detailing all the sites in the country.

Recommended Hotels

The places to stay listed on pages 302–5 are the best from a range of accommodation types, from backpacker hostels

A cosy room at the Kolory B&B in Krakow *(see p302)*

to cosy B&Bs, from boutique hotels to grand historic establishments and the big, luxury business hotels for which Polish cities are increasingly noted. They are listed by price within each area, be that the historic quarters of Gdańsk, Lublin and Krakow, or the blissfully unspoiled lakes and villages of rural Poland.

Throughout the listings certain hotels have been highlighted as DK Choice. These offer a particularly special experience, such as a beautiful location, a historical or characterful setting, outstanding views or a great spa. Whatever the reasons, the DK Choice label is a guarantee of an especially memorable stay.

DIRECTORY

Internet Booking Websites

Airbnb
W www.airbnb.com

Booking
W www.booking.com

Hostelworld
W www.hostelworld.com

Disabled Travellers

Office of the Government Plenipotentiary for the Disabled
Warsaw,
ul. Nowogrodzka 11.
Tel 22 529 06 01.
W niepelnosprawni.gov.pl

Rooms and Apartments to Let

Krakow Apartments
Tel 12 421 48 65.
W krakow-apartments.com

Old City Apartments
Tel 606 941 483.
W oldcityapartments.eu

Sodispar
Tel 600 191 313
W sodispar.pl

Camping

Polish Camping and Caravanning Federation
Warsaw,
ul. Pulawska 102 lok. 2.
Tel 22 810 60 50.
W pfcc.eu

The bright and vibrant interiors of Apple Inn, Warsaw *(see p302)*

Where to Stay

Warsaw

Oki Doki   zł
Hostel   **Map** 1 C5
pl. Dąbrowskiego 3, 00-057
Tel *22 828 01 22*
W okidoki.pl
A budget hostel decorated in
thrift-store style. There's a bar on
site and a fully equipped kitchen.

Apple Inn   zł zł
Historic   **Map** 3 C1
ul. Chmielna 21, lok. 22B
Tel *601 746 006*
W appleinn.pl
Located on one of the most
popular shopping streets, this
hotel offers attic rooms. Breakfast
is served in the café downstairs.

Chopin Boutique   zł zł
B&B   **Map** 4 D2
ul. Smolna 14
Tel *22 829 48 00*
W bbwarsaw.com
Boasting cosy rooms with retro
furniture, this B&B is known for host-
ing piano recitals. Friendly staff.

SleepWell Apartments   zł zł
Boutique   **Map** 4 D1
ul. Nowy Świat 62, 00-357
Tel *600 300 749*
W sleepwell-warsaw.pl
These centrally located studio
apartments have a bold design.

Hilton Warsaw   zł zł zł
Luxury   **Map** 3 A2
ul. Grzybowska 63, 00-844
Tel *22 356 55 55*
W hilton.com
This high-rise hotel with high
standards is situated in the heart
of the new business district.

The elegant Art Deco building housing the
Rialto hotel, Warsaw

Hotel Bristol   zł zł zł
Historic   **Map** 2 D4
Krakowskie Przedmieście 42/44, 00-325
Tel *22 551 10 00*
W hotelbristolwarsaw.pl
This sumptuous *fin-de-siècle*
establishment has welcomed VIPs
such as presidents and rock stars.

Marriott   zł zł zł
Luxury   **Map** 3 A2
al. Jerozolimskie 65/79, 00-697
Tel *22 630 63 06*
W marriott.com
This skyscraper draws celebrity
guests with its superb facilities,
casino and penthouse bar.

Residence St Andrews
Place   zł zł zł
Luxury   **Map** 3 A1
Chmielna 30, 00-020
Tel *22 826 46 40*
W residencestandrews.pl
Enjoy short- or long-term stays in
luxury apartments in a renovated
pre-World War I building.

DK Choice

Rialto   zł zł zł
Boutique   **Map** 3 A3
ul. Wilcza 73, 00 670
Tel *22 584 87 00*
W rialto.pl
An elegant Art Deco vibe runs
through this hotel close to the
central station. Every detail is
a faithful reproduction of
Roaring Twenties style, and
many of the bathrooms have
beautiful tiling. Amenities
include espresso machines
and flat-screen TVs; staff are
helpful and attentive.

Sofitel Victoria   zł zł zł
Luxury   **Map** 1 C5
Królewska 11, 00-065
Tel *22 657 80 11*
W sofitel.com
The well-furnished rooms at this
hotel opposite Warsaw's Saxon
Gardens have all the amenities.

Mazovia and the Lublin Region

KAZIMIERZ DOLNY:
Hotel Villa Bohema   zł zł zł
Boutique   **Map** F4
ul. Małachowskiego 12, 24-120
Tel *81 881 07 56*
W villabohema.pl
A country-house hotel on the
edge of this well-preserved
market town. Good spa facilities.

DK Choice

LUBLIN: Grand Hotel
Lublinianka   zł zł
Historic   **Map** F4
*ul. Krakowskie Przedmieście 56,
20-002*
Tel *81 446 61 00*
W lublinianka.com
This belle epoque building has
been Lublin's finest hotel since
1900. Modern rooms retain the
original marble bathrooms. It is
located on a shopping street.

LUBLIN: Mercure Lublin   zł zł
Chain   **Map** F4
al. Racławickie 12, 20-037
Tel *81 533 20 61*
W mercure.com
Opposite the Saxon Gardens, this
hotel offers contemporary rooms.

ZAMOŚĆ: HOTEL Mercury   zł zł
Chain   **Map** F5
Kołłątaja 2/4/6, 22-400
Tel *84 639 25 16*
W accorhotels.com
Housed in a beautifully renovated
Renaissance building with a glass-
covered atrium in the Old Town.

ZAMOŚĆ: Hotel Senator   zł zł
Historic   **Map** F5
ul. Rynek Solny 4, 22-400
Tel *84 638 76 10*
W senatorhotel.pl
This hotel is a fine example
of a Renaissance design, with
comfortable good-value rooms.

Krakow

Mundo Hostel   zł
Hostel   **Map** D5
ul. Sarego 10, 31-047
Tel *12 422 61 13*
W mundohostel.eu
This boutique hostel offers rooms
decorated with ethnic textiles.

Kolory   zł zł
B&B   **Map** D5
ul. Estery 10, 31-056
Tel *12 421 04 65*
W kolory.com.pl
Located above Les Couleurs café,
this charming B&B has bright en
suites decorated with folk art.

Andel's zł zł zł
Chain **Map** D5
ul. Pawia 3, 31-154
Tel *12 660 01 00*
w viennahouse.com
Jutting out into the plaza in front of the train station like an ocean liner, Andel's has chic rooms in shades of cream and brown.

DK Choice

Hotel Stary zł zł zł
Luxury **Map** D5
ul. Szczepańska 5, 31-011
Tel *12 384 08 08*
w stary.hotel.com.pl
Original features – high ceilings and exposed brick and stone – are mixed with contemporary furniture at this 15th-century merchant's house. Facilities include a subterranean pool, saunas and a spa centre.

Komorowski zł zł zł
Boutique **Map** D5
ul. Długa 7, 31-147
Tel *505 989 371*
w aparthotelkomorowski.com
Rooms at this romantic hotel feature lots of rich colours, plush furnishings and exposed brick.

Pollera zł zł zł
Historic **Map** D5
ul. Szpitalna 30, 31-024
Tel *12 422 10 44*
w pollera.com.pl
An Art Nouveau classic in the Old Quarter, the Pollera was founded in 1834 and has welcomed guests with style ever since.

Małopolska (Lesser Poland)

DK Choice

BIESZCZADY MOUNTAINS, WETLINA: Leśny Dwór zł
B&B **Map** F6
Wetlina 73, 38-608
Tel *13 468 46 54*
w lesnydwor.bieszczady.pl
Well signposted from the western end of the village, this family-run establishment has carefully furnished rooms, a pleasant garden, good home cooking and a small library of local-interest books. The Bieszczady Mountains are a short walk uphill. Half board only.

The warm yet vibrant rooms of Andel's by Vienna House Cracow

CZĘSTOCHOWA: Mercure Centrum zł zł
Chain **Map** D5
ul. Popiełuszki 2, 43-200
Tel *34 360 31 00*
w accorhotels.com
This hotel in a central location has comfy modern rooms and a grand glass-roofed restaurant.

KIELCE: Hotel Dal zł
Business **Map** E5
ul. Piotrkowska 12, 25-510
Tel *41 336 10 00*
w hoteldal.pl
Located near the Market Square, this hotel has excellent transport connections and is housed in a sleek glass-fronted building near the main street.

ŁAŃCUT: Pałacyk zł
Historic/B&B **Map** F5
ul. Paderewskiego 18, 37-100
Tel *17 225 20 43*
w palacyk-lancut.pl
A perfect blend of old noble traditions and modern times, this bijou inn offers a number of timber-beamed attic rooms.

PRZEMYŚL: Europejski zł
Business **Map** F6
ul. Sowińskiego 4, 37-700
Tel *16 675 71 00*
w hotel-europejski.pl
A hotel in a 19th-century building with small but comfortable rooms that are furnished and decorated with warm, pastel colours.

SANDOMIERZ: Pod Ciżemką zł zł
Historic **Map** F5
ul. Rynek 27, 27-600
Tel *15 832 05 50*
w hotelcizemka.pl
Set in a historic building dating back to 1583, this extraordinary hotel offers characterful en-suite rooms.

TARNÓW: Hotel Tarnovia zł zł
Business **Map** E5
ul. Kościuszki 10, 33-100
Tel *14 630 03 50*
w hotel.tarnovia.pl
This hotel near the train and bus stations has simple, comfortable rooms as well as business facilities.

ZAKOPANE: Willa Orla zł
B&B **Map** D6
ul. Kościeliska 50, 34-500
Tel *18 201 26 97*
w orla.com.pl
In a gabled, highland-style property, Willa Orla's breakfast room is full of vintage clocks.

ZAKOPANE: Litwor zł zł zł
Luxury **Map** D6
ul. Krupówki 40, 34-500
Tel *18 202 42 00*
w litwor.pl
Set in a chalet-style building, this hotel offers rooms with mountain views and an indoor pool.

Silesia

JELENIA GÓRA: Hotel Baron zł zł
Historic **Map** B4
ul. Grodzka 4-5, 58-500
Tel *75 752 33 51*
w hotelbaron.pl
The interiors of this hotel in the center of Jelenia Gora combine the roughness of brick walls with wooden furniture, giving Hotel Baron the atmosphere of an old burgher house.

KARPACZ: Hotel Karkonosze zł zł
Resort **Map** B5
ul. Wolna 4, 58-540
Tel *75 761 82 77*
w hotel-karkonosze.com.pl
A charming mountain hotel with a wealth of timber features and comfortable, modern rooms.

For more information on types of hotels *see pages 298–301*

DK Choice

KATOWICE: Monopol　zł zł zł
Historic　Map D5
ul. Dworcowa 5, 40-012
Tel *32 782 82 82*
W monopolkatowice.hotel.com.pl
The Monopol is something of
a treasure, occupying a Neo-
Gothic building with Art Deco
additions. The rooms are classy
and modern; extra luxury is
provided by the underground
pool and the lovely dining
room with exposed brick walls.

LĄDEK ZDRÓJ: Zamek na Skale
Hotel　zł zł
Historic　Map B5
Trzebieszowice 151, 57-540
Tel *74 865 20 00*
W zameknaskale.com.pl
This hotel in the heart of Klodzko
Valley is set in a 16th century
castle. It also has a peaceful park.

OPOLE: Hotel Piast　zł zł
Business　Map C5
ul. Piastowska 1, 45-081
Tel *77 454 97 10*
W hotel-piast.opole.pl
Enjoy the views of Odra and
Młynówka canals from the floral
rooms of this small hotel on
Piaseka Island.

SZCZYRK: Hotel Klimczok　zł zł zł
Resort　Map D6
ul. Poziomkowa 20, 43-370
Tel *33 826 01 00*
W klimczok.pl
A mountain lodge with a cosy
atmosphere and sophisticated art.
It boasts pools, saunas and a spa.

SZKLARSKA PORĘBA:
Hotel Kryształ　zł zł
Resort　Map B4
ul. 1 Maja 19, 58-580
Tel *75 717 49 30*
W hotelkrysztal.pl
An alpine-style hotel near ski lifts,
with bright, air-conditioned rooms,
a sauna and bowling alley.

WROCŁAW: Stop Wrocław　zł
Hostel　Map C4
ul. Sienkiewicza 31, 50-349
Tel *519 115 075*
W stopwroclaw.pl
Set in a 19th-century town house,
Stop Wrocław offers characterful,
individually decorated rooms.

WROCŁAW: Europeum　zł zł
Luxury　Map C4
ul. Kazimierza Wielkiego 27A, 50-077
Tel *71 371 44 00*
W europeum.pl
The stylish rooms here, most
with floor-to-ceiling windows,
are decorated in muted colours.

WROCŁAW: Granary　zł zł zł
Boutique　Map C4
Mennicza 24, 50-057
Tel *71 395 26 00*
W thegranaryhotel.com
This lovingly restored red-brick
granary houses luxurious suites
with kitchenettes.

Wielkopolska

ANTONIN: Pałac
Radziwiłłów　zł zł
Historic　Map C4
ul. Pałacowa 1, 63-421
Tel *62 734 83 00*
W palacantonin.pl
The palace's former hunting
lodge is now a 14-room hotel
with basic comforts, but lots
of atmosphere.

GNIEZNO: Dom Pielgrzyma/
Adalbertus　zł
Historic　Map C3
ul. Tumska 7a, 62-200
Tel *61 426 13 60*
W dompielgrzymagniezno.pl
Housed in a historic building
by the cathedral, this hotel
has simple ensuite rooms.
It features an Italian and a
Polish restaurant.

LESZNO: Akwawit　zł zł
Spa resort　Map B4
ul. Św Józefa 5, 64-100
Tel *65 526 08 11*
W akwawit.pl
This modern business hotel is
also a spa resort. As well as offering treatments, the adjoining
aquacentre features a large pool.

ŁÓDŹ: Grand Hotel　zł zł
Historic　Map D4
ul. Piotrkowska 72, 90-102
Tel *42 633 99 20*
W grand.hotel.com.pl
Boasting the longest history of
any hotel in the city, expect bags
of charm at this hotel in a pre-
World War I building.

ŁÓDŹ: Andel's　zł zł zł
Luxury　Map D4
ul. Ogrodowa 17, 91-065
Tel *42 279 10 00*
W viennahouse.com
Rooms have designer furniture
and exposed brickwork at this
hotel in a former textile factory.

POZNAŃ: Brovaria　zł zł
Boutique　Map C3
Stary Rynek 73, 74 61-772
Tel *61 858 68 68*
W brovaria.pl
An Old Town hotel with its own
microbrewery. Rooms are prim,
with dark woods and soft fabrics.

Twin room with wrought-iron beds at the
Stop Wrocław, Wrocław

POZNAŃ: IBB Andersia　zł zł
Luxury　Map C3
Plac Andersia 3, 61-894
Tel *61 667 80 00*
W andersiahotel.pl
The hotel in the Andersia
Tower, Poznań's tallest build-
ing, offers superb rooms with
great views.

DK Choice

POZNAŃ: Blow Up
Hall 5050　zł zł zł
Luxury　Map C3
ul. Kościuszki 42, 61-891
Tel *61 657 99 80*
W blowuphall5050.com
Named after Michelangelo
Antonioni's 1966 film and
inspired by Lozano-Hemmer's
interactive installation, this
avant-garde, design hotel
is located in the Stary
Browar complex, a reno-
vated brewery. Rooms feature
contemporary gadgets and
original features, such as the
half-moon windows.

Gdańsk

Happy Seven　zł
Hostel　Map D1
ul. Grodzka 7, 80-841
Tel *50 587 70 21*
W happy7hostel.pl
There are big dorms and
private doubles in this comfy
hostel in a medieval building.

Hotel Wolne Miasto　zł zł
Historic　Map D1
ul. św. Ducha 2, 80-834
Tel *58 322 24 42*
W hotelwm.pl
Well-equipped rooms with
photos of the city in its
heyday capture the spirit
of pre-war Gdańsk.

DK Choice

Podewils
Boutique zł zł zł
Map D1
ul. Szafarnia 2, 80-755
Tel *58 300 95 60*
W podewils.pl
This Baroque-style mansion has rooms overlooking the marina, and a lobby filled with antiques and paintings. Amenities include DVD players and Jacuzzi tubs.

Stay Inn
Hostel zł zł zł
Map D1
ul. Piwna 28/31, 80-831
Tel *58 354 15 43*
W stayinngdansk.com
This cross between a design hotel and a backpacker hostel features dorms, doubles and family rooms.

Pomerania

DARŁOWO: Pod Arkadami
B&B zł
Map B1
ul. Admiralska 22–23, 76-153
Tel *604 201 310*
W pod-arkadami.eu
Located near the beach, this quiet hotel has an outdoor pool.

DK Choice

GDYNIA: Villa Lubicz
Historic zł zł
Map D1
ul. Orłowska 43, 81-522
Tel *58 668 47 40*
W willalubicz.pl
Sea views and lots of wood panelling lend an impressive tone to this Modernist hotel near the seafront in Orlowo, south of central Gdynia.

ŁEBA: Neptun
Historic zł zł zł
Map C1
ul. Sosnowa 1, 84-360
Tel *59 866 14 32*
W neptunhotel.pl
The luxurious rooms in this hotel in a 1903 building have sea views.

MALBORK: Stary Malbork zł zł zł
Historic Map D1
ul. 17 Marca 26, 82-200
Tel *55 647 24 00*
W hotelstarymalbork.com.pl
In a 19th-century building, this hotel has simple, comfy rooms.

MIĘDZYZDROJE: Nautilus
Historic zł zł
Map A1
Promenada Gwiazd 8, 72-500
Tel *91 328 09 99*
W hotel-nautilus.pl
Rooms feature wooden beams and a cheerful maritime decor at this seafront hotel.

SOPOT: Hostelino
Hostel zł
Map D1
Krasickiego 11, 81-836
Tel *694 446 663*
W hostelino-sopot.pl
This hostel has several communal areas and a garden.

SOPOT: Villa Baltica
Luxury zł zł zł
Map D1
ul. Emilii Plater 1, 81-777
Tel *58 555 28 00*
W villabaltica.com
A historic building with chic rooms, some with sea views, and a spa.

SZCZECIN: Hotel Atrium
Business zł zł
Map A2
al. Wojska Polskiego 75, 70-481
Tel *91 424 35 32*
W hotel-atrium.pl
A city-centre hotel in a 19th-century building.

TORUŃ: Petite Fleur
Boutique zł zł
Map D2
ul. Piekary 25, 87-100
Tel *56 621 51 00*
W petitefleur.pl
A cosy hotel in the Old Town with smart en suites and great service.

Warmia, Mazuria and Białystok Region

AUGUSTÓW: Warszawa
Spa resort zł zł zł
Map F2
ul. Zdrojowa 1, 16-300
Tel *87 643 85 00*
W hotelwarszawa.pl
This bright, low-rise hotel enjoys a fabulous forest-and-lake setting.

BIAŁYSTOK: Cristal
Business zł zł
Map F2
ul. Lipowa 3/5, 15-424
Tel *85 749 61 00*
W hotelcristal.com.pl
A city-centre hotel with plush rooms and a pub and restaurant.

ELBLĄG: Hotel Żuławy
B&B zł zł
Map D1
ul. Królewiecka 126, 82-300
Tel *55 234 57 11*
W hotel-zulawy.com.pl
A town-centre hotel with en-suite rooms, a sauna and a solarium.

GIŻYCKO: Hotel Cesarski
B&B zł
Map F2
plac Grunwaldzki 8, 11-500
Tel *87 732 76 70*
W cesarski.eu
A 19th-century town house near Lake Niegocin with cosy rooms.

DK Choice

MIKOŁAJKI: Hotel Mikołajki
Spa resort zł zł zł
Map E2
Aleja Spacerowa 11, 11-730
Tel *87 420 60 00*
W hotelmikolajki.pl
This striking glass-and-steel tower rises from an artificial island in Lak Talty, linked to the resort of Mikołajki by causeway. Rooms have wood floors, crisp furnishings and beautiful views. The ideal place for a spot of pampering.

OLSZTYN: Pod Zamkiem
B&B zł zł
Map E2
ul. Nowowiejskiego 10, 10-162
Tel *89 535 12 87*
W hotel-olsztyn.com.pl
A handful of neat en suites, some with balconies, at this restored Art Nouveau house beside the castle.

STARY FOLWARK: Hotel Holiday
Resort zł
Map F1
Stary Folwark 106, 16-402
Tel *87 563 71 20*
W hotel-holiday.pl
This low-rise near Lake Wigry offers rooms with sloped ceilings, a sauna and children's play area.

Floor-to-ceiling windows in a room at the Hotel Wolne Miasto, Gdańsk *(see p304)*

For more information on types of hotels *see pages 298–*

WHERE TO EAT AND DRINK

Polish cuisine is one of the most easily identifiable culinary traditions in Central Europe, with dishes such as borscht (or *barszcz*), *pierogi* and roast duck with apples enjoying iconic status both at home and abroad. Most restaurants serve classic Polish dishes such as these, although there is an increasing range of establishments serving French, Mediterranean or Asian food.

Generally, it is not difficult to find a good restaurant in a large town or city; in smaller towns a little exploration may be required to uncover a restaurant serving good, inexpensive food. The restaurants and bars listed on pages 310–19 have been selected on the basis of the quality of their food and service, but also as a reflection of the sheer variety of culinary styles now on offer.

Exposed brickwork and hanging tapestries at Cyrano de Bergerac, Krakow *(see p312)*

Meals

The classic Polish breakfast has a high calorie content and sets you up for the day. It consists of boiled, fried or scrambled eggs, plus smoked meats and cheese. Traditionally, the evening meal – consisting of soup, a main course (usually a meat dish) and a dessert – is the most important meal of the day. However, many Polish restaurants are gradually adopting a lighter menu suited to midday lunchers, with an increasing range of salads, pasta dishes and soups.

Restaurants

Those who enjoy good food in a pleasant atmosphere will not be disappointed in Poland. Many restaurants in the big cities are housed in historic buildings or medieval cellars, usually painstakingly restored and tastefully furnished. Restaurants in Warsaw, Gdańsk, Krakow and Wrocław frequently

offer contemporary designer interiors or opt instead for a range of retro styles, with candles on the table and antique furniture. An increasing number of restaurants have large areas of outdoor seating, especially on big urban squares. Restaurants in rural areas can be delightful, with wooden beams, rustic knick-knacks and maybe a cottage garden.

In general, there's a good and growing choice of haute cuisine and modern fusion cooking in Poland's main cities, while in the countryside, home cooking and regional gastronomic traditions are nurtured. Wherever you go, restaurants are not too formal, and there is no real dress code.

Canteen Restaurants and Vodka-and-Herring Bars

Much of the best local food is found in a so-called "milk bar" *(bar mleczny)*, a budget

self-service eatery where inexpensive soups, *pierogi*, potato pancakes, pork chops and other Polish staples are served. The decor is often plain in places like these, but prices are rock bottom – diners can enjoy a three-course meal for as little as 20zł. Milk bars often close early (usually late afternoon or early evening, or when the food has sold out).

Another common feature of the cheap-restaurant scene is the *pierogarnia* or *pierogi bar*, often serving imaginative variations on this national staple food.

A popular addition to the Polish dining scene is the so-called vodka-and-herring bar. These establishments serve spirits and traditional bar snacks (marinated herring being one ubiquitous favourite) at very affordable prices. Some vodka-and-herring bars are open around the clock.

The innovative Kitchen at Asian fusion restaurant Thai Me Up, in Warsaw *(see p311)*

Wooden benches at traditional Sielsko Anielsko restaurant, Lublin *(see p311)*

Street Food

Poland's favourite street snack, the *zapiekanka*, is a halved baguette covered in meat, cheese and vegetables, then toasted. *Zapiekankas* are sold from fast-food kiosks all over Poland. Other ubiquitous features of the Polish street-food scene are grilled sausages and, in coastal and lake resorts, fish and chips.

Prices and Tips

The price of food in Polish restaurants is below the European average. Certainly 120zł per person will suffice for a three-course meal without alcohol in all but the more expensive places. If you do wish to drink alcohol with your meal, this will add a substantial amount to the bill. Sometimes, menu prices apply just to the main dish, and an extra charge is made for potatoes, salads and other side dishes. Fish is often priced by weight; ask the server what the likely cost of your meal will be.

Credit cards are becoming ever more popular and should be readily accepted by all the larger restaurants and those located on the main tourist trail. Signs on windows or doors indicate which cards are accepted by the establishment.

All over Poland a customary tip amounts to about ten per cent of the bill.

Vegetarian Food

Most restaurants in Poland serve at least some vegetarian dishes. Italian eateries, which usually have a handful of meat-free pizzas and pasta dishes on their menus, are a good stand-by. Traditional local dishes – such as *pierogi* (dumplings) filled with sauerkraut, wild mushrooms, cheese or fruit, as well as all kinds of savoury pancakes, omelettes and *knedle* (potato dumplings) – are very popular. Colourful salads are available in all restaurants. Beetroot, carrots, cabbage, cauliflower, celeriac and leeks are perennial favourites, but aubergines, broccoli, celery, endives and courgettes have also been introduced to Polish cuisine. Tasty vegetarian food is available not only from most ethnic restaurants, but also from salad bars, which are very popular and also serve freshly pressed fruit and vegetable juices. In some restaurants you can put together your own salad.

Recommended Restaurants

The restaurants listed on pages 310–19 have been chosen to give a cross-section of the most noteworthy places to eat in Poland. Whether located in the bustling centre of Warsaw, the evocative former Jewish quarter of Kazimierz in Krakow or the rustic towns and villages of rural Poland, each restaurant has earned a noteworthy reputation.

The listings cover a range of eateries and cuisine types, from traditional Polish canteens and Central European and Jewish restaurants to pizzerias, Asian eateries, establishments specializing in fish and seafood, characterful cafés and smart, elegant restaurants offering gourmet dining.

Some establishments have been labelled as DK Choice. These stand out from the crowd and offer something particularly special, such as exceptional food, an inventive menu, great value for money, a beautiful setting, particular charm or a combination of these factors. Whatever the reason, it is a guarantee of an especially memorable meal.

The sheltered patio at the Italian restaurant Del Papa, in Krakow *(see p313)*

The Flavours of Poland

Polish cuisine, like that of many Central European countries, makes heavy use of meat, especially pork, which is often served quite plainly with potatoes or rice and cabbage. However, because of the long Baltic coastline in the north of the country, fish is also likely to feature on many menus. Carp, trout and herring are particular favourites. Around Krakow, in the south, the local forests yield a bounty of quality game, with duck being very popular. The legacy of former rule by Austria is also evident in the south, especially in some of the sophisticated cakes and pastries.

Pickled herring

Barbecuing meat at a street celebration on Palm Sunday

Meat

Pork (wieprzowina) is the most popular meat by far in Poland. It usually comes as a steak (kotlet schabowy) or on the bone (golonka wieprzowa) and also appears in soups, sausages and as hams. Polish hams are generally cured and have a rich, sweet flavour. Ham is mainly served cold as an appetizer with cheese and pickles, though it may also be eaten for breakfast. Poland also produces high-quality veal (cielęcina), which is often dished up with a rich mushroom sauce (cielęcina po staropolsku) or with cabbage and raisins.

Poultry and Game

Chicken (kurczak) is a staple food in Poland and drumsticks (podudzie) are especially popular. Chicken livers (wątróbka), served with a fruit sauce, are considered a delicacy.

A wide variety of game roams the forests of southern Poland. Pheasant (bażant), duck (kaczka), goose (gęś), venison (comber), rabbit (królik) and hare (zając) are found on many local menus. Availability varies with the season; autumn is the best time to enjoy game.

Parówka (pork frankfurters)
Gruba krakowska (smoked garlic sausage)
Kabanos (air-cured sausage with caraway seeds)
Wiejska (garlic and herb sausage)
Podwawelska (smoked sausage)
Zagórska (smooth textured, smoked sausage)
Smoked pork loin

Selection of typical Polish sausages and cured meat

Local Dishes and Specialities

Green cabbage

Many classic Polish dishes are offered at restaurants all over the country, but fish also features prominently on northern menus, while those of the south offer a range of game. The most varied and cosmopolitan cuisine is found in large cities, such as Warsaw and Krakow, where top chefs run the kitchens of some of the grand restaurants. The national dish, bigos, comes from eastern Poland. It is hearty and warming for the long, bleak winters found there, as is another dish from this chilly region, pierogi (pasta dumplings, stuffed with meat, cheese or fruit). Both are influenced by the food of neighbouring Russia. Polish cakes and desserts also tend to be heavy and rich, although most originate in the warmer south, once ruled by Austria.

Bigos Chunks of meat and sausage are simmered with sauerkraut, cabbage, onion, potatoes, herbs and spices.

A colourful display of locally grown vegetables at a city market stall

Fish

Fish features strongly on menus in northern Poland, where herring *(śledź)* is a central part of the diet. It comes pickled, in oil, with onions, with soured cream – in fact, with just about everything. *Rolmops po kaszubsku* (marinated herring wrapped around pickled onion, then spiked with cloves and dipped in soured cream) are widely enjoyed. Other popular fish are freshwater trout *(pstrąg)* – served simply grilled with boiled potatoes; carp *(karp)* – often accompanied by horseradish sauce; and salmon *(łosoś)*. A treat in early summer is smoked salmon served with spears of fresh asparagus *(łosoś wędzony ze szparagami)*, which is then in season.

Vegetables

Poland produces many fine quality vegetables. The hardy cabbage *(kapusta)* remains the country's top vegetable. It is used in so many ways, including raw in salads and simply boiled to partner meat or fish. Cabbage soup *(kapuśniak)* and

Polish pretzels on sale in a Krakow bread shop

sauerkraut are on every menu. Potatoes are also a staple. They come boiled, baked and mashed, though rarely roasted. Peppers are popular too, often served stuffed with rice and minced meat or pickled in summer salads. Root vegetables such as carrots, parsnips, swede (rutabaga), turnips and beetroot make their way into a range of dishes. Mushrooms grow wild all over Poland and come both cooked and pickled as a tasty addition to many meals.

SNACKS

Sausages A wide range of smoked and unsmoked varieties are on offer at the profusion of street stalls and snack bars that can be found on most city streets.

Precle (pretzels) Another favourite street snack, these are popular, freshly baked, at train and bus stations first thing in the morning.

Zapiekanki Often referred to as Polish-style pizzas, these are tasty, open-top baguettes, spread with cheese and tomato, then toasted and served piping hot. They are also a common item on street-stall menus.

Smalec This snack consists of fried lard, liberally sprinkled with sea salt, and eaten with chunks of crusty bread. It can be found as a bar snack in most pubs and makes a good accompaniment to beer.

Pierogi These ravioli-style dumplings may be stuffed with meat, sauerkraut, mushrooms, cheese or fruit.

Barszcz This beetroot soup, flavoured with lemon and garlic, may be served clear or with meat and vegetables.

Poppy seed roll A rich yeasted dough is wrapped around a sweet poppy-seed filling and baked until lightly golden.

Where to Eat and Drink

Warsaw

Kafka Café   **zł**
Café   **Map** 2 D5
ul. Obózna 3, 00-001
Tel *694 455 588*
Pastas, quiches, sandwiches and salads are served in this bright, hip café, which offers deckchair seating on the neighbouring lawn in the summer months.

Mleczarnia Jerozolimska   **zł**
Classic Polish   **Map** 3 C2
al. Jerozolimskie 32, 00-024
Tel *602 381 734*
This is the place for good-value dishes, served in a friendly manner in a bright interior. There aren't many tables, so expect a crush at lunchtime.

Palmier   **zł**
International   **Map** 3 C2
ul. Żurawia 6/12, 00-503
Tel *22 622 53 33*
This versatile café-restaurant offers a broad choice of light and main meals, ranging from breakfasts to salads, and plenty of choices for a light lunch.

Zapiecek   **zł**
Classic Polish   **Map** 3 C2
al. Jerozolimskie 28
Tel *22 826 74 84*
The menu here features a broad choice of speciality *pierogi*, including large baked ones. There are also soups and pancakes.

Browarmia   **zł zł**
Brewery Restaurant   **Map** 2 D4
ul. Królewska 1, 00-065
Tel *22 826 54 55*
This busy brewpub has copper brewing vats at the back and a

street-facing terrace at the front. It serves a great range of craft beers. Grilled meats are the speciality dish, best washed down with Browarmia's own brew.

Le Cedre   **zł zł**
Lebanese
al. Solidarności 61, 03-402
Tel *22 618 89 99*
Across the river from the Old Town, Le Cedre cooks up superb Middle Eastern skewered meats and vegetable dishes in an interior that looks like a scene from *One Thousand and One Nights*.

LIF   **zł zł**
Vegetarian
al. Niepodległości 80, 02-626
Tel *22 898 01 55*
This modern restaurant with a hip atmosphere and a sharply dressed clientele serves a wide range of salads, soups and vegetarian mains.

SAM Bakery   **zł zł**
Café   **Map** 2 E5
ul. Lipowa 7A, 00-316
Tel *600 806 084*
A superb range of breakfasts, salads, cakes and light lunches served in an informal style. All breads are home-baked.

Belvedere   **zł zł zł**
Gourmet   **Map** 3 C5
ul. Agrykola 1, 00-460
Tel *22 558 67 01*
Housed in a conservatory in Łazienki Park, Belvedere delivers classic French cuisine of the highest order. Enjoy your meal while watching the peacocks on the lawn outside. Black-tie service.

Price Guide
Prices are based on a three-course meal per person, with a half-bottle of house wine, including tax and service.

zł	up to 80zł
zł zł	80zł to 110zł
zł zł zł	over 110zł

Butchery and Wine   **zł zł zł**
International   **Map** 3 C2
ul. Żurawia 22/20, 00-515
Tel *22 502 31 18*
Quality cuts of fresh meat (particularly steak and ribs) are the highlights of the menu in this carnivore's paradise; although there's always the odd fish dish to even things up. Excellent wine list too.

Dom Polski   **zł zł zł**
Classic Polish
ul. Francuska 11, 03-906
Tel *22 616 24 32*
In the embassy-filled Saska Kepa district, Dom Polski serves some of the classiest fare in Poland. The menu is seasonal and often features fantastic game dishes.

Karma   **zł zł zł**
Indian   **Map** 2 C2
ul. Żurawia 22, 00-515
Tel *501 400 386*
A varied menu of truly spicy, typical dishes, including plenty of vegetarian options, are offered in a tasteful, relaxing interior at Karma.

Kompania Piwna   **zł zł zł**
Classic Polish   **Map** 2 D3
ul. Podwale 25, 00-261
Tel *22 635 63 14*
An Old Town gem, with a courtyard designed to resemble a town square, this restaurant's menu features heaps of meat and potato dishes, all served on wooden boards.

DK Choice

Różana   **zł zł zł**
Classic Polish
ul. Chocimska 7, 00-791
Tel *22 848 12 25*
One of the most attractive restaurants in Warsaw, Różana is located in a villa southwest of Łazienki Park. The dining rooms look like they belong in an English country house, and there is a beautiful garden to boot. Expect traditional food beautifully presented, with liver, tenderloin steaks, roast duck, freshwater fish and game dominating the menu. The meringue desserts are a treat.

Enjoying a quick bite at the trendy Kafka Café, in Warsaw

Sakana Sushi Bar zł zł zł
Asian Map 1 C4
ul. Moliera 4/6, 00-076
Tel 22 826 59 58
There are dozens of sushi joints across Warsaw, and this is one of the best, serving a delectable range of Japanese classics to a fashion-conscious crowd.

San Lorenzo zł zł zł
Italian Map 1 A3
al. Jana Pawla II 36, 01-141
Tel 22 652 16 16
An elegant place with frescoes on the walls, Italian furniture and a refined menu of freshly made pasta and tasty Mediterranean seafood.

DK Choice

Solec 44 zł zł zł
International Map 4 E2
ul. Solec 44
Tel 79 836 39 96
A post-industrial space in the up-and-coming Powiśle district houses this acclaimed restaurant serving traditional meat and fish dishes in an innovative, contemporary style. The seasonally-changing menu runs from burgers to T-bone steaks; vegan and gluten-free options are clearly marked on the menu. Look out for some unusual desserts and puddings. There's a big selection of craft beers and a lot of people come here just to drink and socialize.

Thai Me Up zł zł zł
Asian fusion Map 4 D1
ul. Foksal 16, 00-372
Tel 22 826 11 99
On a popular bar-and-restaurant strip, this chic designer place serves imaginative Oriental meat and seafood dishes. Most dishes are Thai, although there are a few Japanese choices too.

U Fukiera zł zł zł
Classic Polish Map 2 D3
Rynek Starego Miasta 27, 00-275
Tel 22 831 10 13
Set inside a warren of beautiful dining rooms, this restaurant focuses on classic Polish meat and poultry roasts.

Warszawa Wschodnia zł zł zł
Gourmet
ul. Mińska 25, 03-808
Tel 22 870 29 18
Modern Polish-European cuisine is served up in chic surroundings in the red-brick Soho compound. The menu changes daily according to what's fresh and in season.

The ornate entrance of U Fukiera, Warsaw

Mazovia and the Lublin Region

CHEŁM: Gęsie Sprawki zł zł
Eastern European/Italian Map G4
ul. Lubelska 27, 22-100
Tel 82 565 23 21
In an atmospheric cellar, this restaurant serves a mouth-watering combination of Eastern Polish and Lithuanian dishes, plus pizzas and Mediterranean salads.

KAZIMIERZ DOLNY:
Zielona Tawerna zł zł
Classic Polish Map F4
ul. Nadwiślańska 4, 24-120
Tel 81 881 03 08
Traditional dishes – from *pierogi* to roast duck – are served in a light interior or in the enclosed garden. There are good vegetarian options, too.

LUBLIN: Sielsko Anielsko zł
Classic Polish Map F4
Rynek 17, 20-111
Tel 81 532 36 17
Agricultural tools and folksy implements are scattered artfully around the interior of this restaurant serving a huge range of traditional staples.

LUBLIN: Hades Szeroka zł zł
Classic Polish Map F4
ul. Grodzka 21, 20-112
Tel 81 532 87 61
Enjoy elegant, candle-lit dining in the Old Town. The restaurant is famous for its steak tartare, but its freshwater fish and poultry roasts are good too.

LUBLIN: La Traviata zł zł
Italian Map F4
ul. Chopina 16, 22-023
Tel 81 534 20 94 **Closed** *Sun*
Great pizzas from a wood-fired oven are served in a homely,

rustic-themed room. There's also a good choice of pasta dishes, plus meat and poultry mains.

DK Choice

LUBLIN: Kardamon zł zł zł
Gourmet Map F4
Krakowskie Przedmieście 41, 20-007
Tel 81 448 02 57
European haute cuisine is served in an intimate, atmospherically lit interior. Highlights include the steaks, roast duck, freshwater fish and stuffed goose; imaginative salads and pastas provide lighter options. The decor is glitzy without being over the top, the service is impeccable without being over-formal, and there's an impressive wine list too.

NAŁĘCZÓW: Patataj zł zł zł
Classic Polish Map F4
Kolonia Bochotnica 15, 24-150
Tel 81 501 47 01 **Closed** *Mon*
Just east of Nałęczów, on the road to Lublin, this traditional family-run restaurant is housed in a 19th- century manor house boasting fabulous views over the forests.

PUŁAWY:
Willa Cienista zł zł
Classic Polish/
Mediterranean Map F4
ul. Zielona 23, 24-100
Tel 81 887 40 49
Housed in a modern villa built in the style of a Tyrolean chalet, Willa Cienista serves a wide range of dishes – from Italian pasta to the classic Polish roast goose – in an atmosphere of relaxed rural elegance.

For more information on types of restaurants *see pages 306–7*

ZAMOŚĆ: Muzealna zł
Regional Map F5
ul. Ormiańska 30, 22-400
Tel *84 638 73 00*
Big portions of Armenian and
Eastern Polish fare are served in this
restaurant. Menu highlights include
expertly grilled kebabs.

ZAMOŚĆ: Padwa zł zł
Classic Polish Map F5
ul. Staszica 23, 22-400
Tel *84 638 62 56*
Boasting an enviable main-square
location, this brick-walled café-
restaurant offers a selection of
classic Polish fare, including pork
chops and potato pancakes.

ZWIERZYNIEC:
Karczma Młyn zł
Regional Map F5
Wachniewskiej 1a, 22-470
Tel *84 687 25 27*
Occupying a traditional timber
building near the lake, the "Mill
Inn" is a great place to sample
Eastern Polish favourites, such as
pierogi with buckwheat, or game
goulash with forest mushrooms.

Krakow

Camelot zł
Café Map D5
ul. św. Tomasza 17, 31-022
Tel *12 421 01 23*
A relaxing, mildly bohemian café
with a cabaret club downstairs,
Camelot is famous for its coffee,
fine cakes and delicious apple pie.

Chimera zł
Classic Polish Map D5
ul. św. Anny 3, 31-008
Tel *12 292 12 12*
At this buffet restaurant, diners pay
according to plate size, so it is ideal
for trying different dishes. Lots of
vegetarian options, too.

La Petite France zł
Café Map D5
ul. Szpitalna 20, 31-024
Tel *602 466 566*
Combining a deli store and a café,
this cosy, intimate spot serves
some of the finest quiche in
Poland, in addition to some
serious gourmet sandwiches.

Pierożki u Wincenta zł
Classic Polish Map D5
Juliusza Lea 114, 30-133, Polska
Tel *12 636 66 23*
This tiny restaurant offers a wide
range of *pierogi*. The classic
pastry pockets are stuffed here
with all kinds of creative, non-
traditional fillings. There are even
some exotically spicy versions.

Przypiecek zł
Classic Polish Map D5
ul. Sławkowska 32, 31-015
Tel *12 422 74 95*
This spot is a temple to the humble
pierogi. The famous stuffed dumplings are served with a range of
fillings, with savoury, sweet and
baked versions well represented.

U Babci Maliny zł
Classic Polish Map 6 D1
ul. Sławkowska 17
Tel *12 422 76 01*
One of the best budget restaurants
in the city, U Babci Maliny serves
up classic Polish fare in a folksy
bench-filled basement.

Horai zł zł
Asian Map D5
pl. Wolnica 4, 31-000
Tel *12 430 03 58*
Horai has a menu that covers the
entire continent of Asia. The Thai
curries are particularly satisfying.

Klezmer-Hois zł zł
Jewish Map D5
ul. Szeroka 6, 31-053
Tel *12 411 12 45*
Enjoy quality kosher Jewish and
Central European fare in an
atmospheric restaurant filled with
bric-a-brac. Weekend klezmer
music is a an added bonus.

Marmolada zł zł
Classic Polish Map D5
Grodzka 5, 31-044
Tel *12 422 02 33*
Traditional Polish cuisine is on
offer at this smart but soothing
restaurant, where a profusion of
candles and cut flowers provides
the ambience.

DK Choice

Miód Malina zł zł
Classic Polish Map D5
ul. Grodzka 40, 31-044
Tel *12 430 04 11*
Occupying several barrel-vaulted
rooms filled with solid wooden
furniture and decorated in raspberry shades of red, Miód Malina
("Honey Raspberry") is one of the
most welcoming and convivial
places in central Krakow. On the
menu is traditional Polish festive
fare, with generous portions of
meat and poultry followed by
some lovely desserts.

Pietro zł zł
Italian Map D5
Rynek Główny 17, 31-008
Tel *12 422 32 79*
You do pay for the location
at this restaurant on the main
square, but the food is delicious

The rustic but stylish interior of Lublin's
Sielsko Anielsko *(see p311)*

and made with ingredients
imported from Italy.

Szara Gęs zł zł
Classic Polish Map D5
Rynek Główny 17, 31-008
Tel *12 430 63 11*
Feast on goose, venison or
suckling pig in the opulent
dining room of this outstanding
traditional restaurant. The
desserts are not to be missed.

Zazie Bistro zł zł
French Map D5
ul. Józefa 34, 31-056
Tel *500 410 829*
This intimate and popular
French-themed bistro serves
everything from onion soup
to bouillabaisse and mussels
with fries.

Aqua e Vino zł zł zł
Italian Map D5
ul. Wiślna 5/10, 31-007
Tel *12 421 25 67*
At this trendy Italian restaurant,
the dishes appear as carefully
designed as the interior. Expect
imaginative takes on classic
recipes and superb desserts.

Copernicus zł zł zł
Gourmet Map D5
ul. Kanonicza 16, 31-002
Tel *12 424 34 21*
Superlative food and exemplary
service are to be enjoyed in
this atmospheric hotel restaurant
that specializes in classic French
cuisine and in game dishes.

Cyrano de Bergerac zł zł zł
Gourmet Map D5
ul. Sławkowska 26, 31-014
Tel *12 411 72 88*
This is a world-class French
restaurant with impeccable
service, set in two elegant rooms.
Be sure to try the desserts.

Del Papa zł zł zł
Italian **Map** D5
ul. św. Tomasza 6, 31-014
Tel *12 421 83 43*
One of Krakow's best Italians, Del Papa has a menu that offers classic meat dishes as well as Mediterranean seafood. Diners can enjoy their meal in the patio at the back.

Farina zł zł zł
Seafood **Map** D5
ul. św. Marka 16, 31-018
Tel *12 422 16 80*
This Mediterranean-themed restaurant specializes in fish. Fine white fish is served grilled, pan-fried or baked.

Gródek zł zł zł
Gourmet **Map** D5
Na Gródku 4, 31-028
Tel *12 431 20 41*
Polish and international dishes are served in this atmospheric brick-lined basement room beneath the Gródek hotel

DK Choice

Studio Qulinarne zł zł zł
Gourmet **Map** D5
ul. Gazowa 4, 31-060
Tel *12 430 69 14*
One of the most inventive restaurants in town, Studio Qulinarne uses fresh Polish ingredients, Mediterranean flair and a touch of Oriental spice to conjure up an original, seasonally changing menu. The bright interior is filled with bookshelves and wine bottles, while the garden is one of Krakow's loveliest.

Wentzl zł zł zł
Gourmet **Map** D5
Rynek Główny 19, 31-008
Tel *12 429 52 99*
Traditional Polish fare, with a predominance of roast fowl and pork, is on offer at this historic restaurant.

Małopolska (Lesser Poland)

BIESZCZADY MOUNTAINS, WETLINA:
Chata Wędrowca zł
International **Map** F6
Wetlina 113, 38-608
Tel *500 225 533*
Set back slightly from the main road at the western end of Wetlina, the "Wayfarer's Cabin" is renowned for its local-meets-global menu, which features lamb, mountain trout and marinated meats.

BRZESKO: Pawilon zł
Classic Polish **Map** E5
ul. Wesoła 4, 32-800
Tel *14 663 17 61*
Wholesome, good-value Polish fare, including many types of *pierogi*, are served in this inn decorated with floral folk patterns.

CZĘSTOCHOWA:
Café Skrzynka zł
International **Map** D5
ul. Dąbrowskiego 1, 42-200
Tel *34 324 30 98*
A chic, homely café serving a large, inexpensive selection of sweet and savoury pancakes. Freshly made sandwiches and soups of the day make excellent light lunches.

GŁOGOCZÓW-DWOR:
Nowina zł zł zł
Contemporary Polish **Map** D6
Dwór, 32-440
Tel *12 273 77 15*
Enjoy outstanding game dishes and lavish platters of roast meats at this award-winning restaurant serving rustic Polish cooking with a modern urban twist.

KELICE: Magazyn Duza 9 zł
Contemporary Polish **Map** D6
Duza 9, 25-304
Tel *79 445 43 40*
Located near the market square, this place offers fresh, high quality Polish burgers as well as salads and smoothies.

NOWY SĄCZ: Ratuszowa zł
Classic Polish **Map** E6
Rynek 1, 33-300
Tel *18 443 56 15*
Located in the basement of the town hall, Ratuszowa serves a broad range of Polish meat dishes and a famously creative selection of *pierogi*, including buckwheat-, lamb- and lentil-stuffed varieties.

NOWY SĄCZ: Kupiecka zł zł
Classic Polish **Map** E6
ul. Jana Długosza 3, 33-300
Tel *18 442 08 31*
Refined service and quality cuisine, including an excellent *golonka* (roast knuckle of pork) with honey, roast duck with apples, and many other national classics.

OJCÓW: Zajazd Zazamcze zł
Classic Polish **Map** D5
Ojców 1b, 32-047
Tel *12 389 20 83*
A chalet-style building with beautifully tended gardens, this restaurant serves an impressive choice of pork and poultry, plus locally caught trout.

DK Choice

PRZEMYŚL: Café Fiore zł
International **Map** F6
ul. Kazimierza Wielkiego 17b, 37-700
Tel *16 675 12 22*
Przemyśl may not be everybody's idea of a culinary capital, but the pastries, cakes and ice creams on offer at the acclaimed Café Fiore rank with anything that Warsaw, Krakow or even Vienna have to offer. The fruit-and-meringue pies are particularly recommended. The pleasant interior is decorated with Italian-themed murals, and there's a large outdoor terrace at the back.

RĄBKA ZDRÓJ: Siwy Dym zł
Regional **Map** D6
ul. Kilińskiego, 34-700
Tel *18 267 66 74*
A highland-style timber lodge decorated with wooden tables and animal hides, serves local roast lamb dishes and a selection of grilled pork and beef dishes.

Outdoor seating at Camelot café, Krakow *(see p312)*

For more information on types of restaurants *see pages 306–7*

The vaulted, exposed-brick interior of Del Papa, in Krakow *(see p313)*

SANOK: Jadło Karpackie zł
Regional Map F6
Rynek 12, 38-100
Tel *13 464 67 00*
Decked out in wooden benches
and sheepskins, this folksy
restaurant offers Carpathian
treats such as *hreczanyki* (pork-
and-buckwheat patties) and
excellent beer from
nearby Leżajsk.

SIENIAWA: Hotel Pałac zł zł zł
Gourmet Map F5
ul. Kościuszki 32, 37-530
Tel *16 649 17 00*
The Baroque former home of
the Sieniawski family houses
a small hotel and an elegant
restaurant serving classic
European fare, superb desserts
and a big choice of wines.

SUCHA BESKIDZKA:
Karczma Rzym zł zł
Classic Polish Map D6
Rynek 1, 34-200
Tel *33 874 27 97*
All the hearty Polish dishes
available at this traditional inn
have devilish names – a reference
to the legend of Pan Twardowski,
who allegedly crossed the devil
at Karczma Rzym.

TARNÓW: Pasaż zł
Classic Polish Map E5
pl. Kazimierza Wielkiego 2, 33-100
Tel *14 627 82 78*
Plain from the outside but quite
elegant within, Pasaż serves
classic Polish food, including
inexpensive daily specials.

TARNÓW:
Tatrzanska-Kudelski zł
Central European Map E5
ul Krakowska 1, 33-100
Tel *14 622 46 36*
Patrolled by white-shirted
waiting staff and stuffed full
of plants, this genteel café-
restaurant has an international
menu, well-priced specials and
delicious apple pie.

ZAKOPANE: Bąkowo
Zohylina Niżnio zł zł
Regional Map D6
ul. Piłsudskiego 6, 34-500
Tel *18 206 62 16*
Housed in an ornate timber
building in the centre of town,
this folksy restaurant serves such
regional classics as highland
lamb, smoked cheeses and
fresh trout. Dinner is frequently
accompanied by live music.

ZAKOPANE: Czarny Staw zł zł
Regional Map D6
ul. Krupówki 2, 34-500
Tel *18 201 38 56*
Some of the menu highlights at
this popular, timber-beamed restaurant are the sizzling grilled meats
and sausages, the fresh mountain
trout and a renowned fish soup.

ZAKOPANE:
Tuberoza zł zł
Classic Polish Map D6
ul. Piłsudskiego 31, 34-500
Tel *18 201 37 38* **Closed** *Wed*
The bohemian but elegant
atmosphere of Zakopane in
the 1930s is conjured up in this
retro-styled restaurant with a
lavish menu of quality Polish
and international food, including
local lamb and game.

ZAKOPANE:
U Wnuka zł zł
Regional Map D6
ul. Kościeliska 8, 34-500
Tel *18 206 41 67*
Excellent highland dishes –
including *kwaśnica* (sour soup)
and roast lamb with cabbage –
are served in a 150-year-old
timber house. There is live
music at weekends.

ZAKOPANE:
Mała Szwajcaria zł zł zł
Classic Polish/Swiss Map D6
ul. Zamoyskiego 11, 34-500
Tel *18 201 20 76*
This restaurant offers an
intriguing combination of

Polish and Swiss recipes, with
local pork and freshwater fish
vying for attention with the
fondues. Everything is expertly
prepared and stylishly delivered.

Silesia

BRENNA: Skalny Dworek zł
Classic Polish Map D6
ul. Wyzwolenia 45, 43-438
Tel *33 853 61 16*
Large portions of traditional
country-style cooking, with an
accent on roast meat and
poultry, are served in this chalet-
style restaurant with a scenic
summer terrace.

CIESZYN: Kamienica
Konczakowskich zł zł
Classic Polish Map D6
Rynek 19, 43-400
Tel *33 852 18 96*
Located on the main square, this
restaurant has retro furnishings,
lace tablecloths and a varied
menu of classics, from potato
pancakes to roast duck.

GLIWICE: Trattoria
Castello zł zł zł
Italian Map D5
ul. Wiejska 16b, 44-121
Tel *32 333 10 11*
Located inside a converted
granary, this restaurant serves
typical yet modern italian cuisine.

KATOWICE: A Dong zł
Asian Map D5
Wawelska 3, 40-096
Tel *32 258 66 62*
Decorated with the requisite
paper lanterns, this restaurant in
the central pedestrian area offers
an extensive menu of good-value
Vietnamese and Chinese dishes.

KATOWICE: Złoty Osioł zł
Vegetarian Map D5
ul. Mariacka 1, 40-077
Tel *32 253 01 13*
Decked out in Oriental textiles
and comfortable cushions, this
legendary vegetarian café offers
an innovative and filling range
of soups, pasta and tofu dishes,
and pastries.

KUDOWA ZDRÓJ: Czeska
Restauracja Zdrojowa zł
Central European Map B5
Słoneczna 1, 57-350
Tel *74 866 21 33*
This large, popular restaurant
complete with billiard room
serves meat-and-dumplings
staples, plus a range of grilled
meats. Wash them down with
any of the Czech beers on offer.

LWÓWEK ŚLĄSKI:
Pod Czarnym Krukiem zł zł
Classic Polish Map B4
ul. Słowackiego 1, 59-600
Tel *75 782 42 66*
Traditional standards, such as
duck breast and roast pork
knuckle, are served at this
restaurant beside the
picturesque main square.

PSZCZYNA: Frykówka zł zł
Classic Polish/Italian Map D5
ul. Rynek 3, 43-200
Tel *32 449 00 20*
Housed inside an 18th-century
Baroque tenement building,
Frykówka has a menu that
combines traditional Polish
fare, local Silesian dishes and
a number of Italian options. It
has an extensive wine list.

ŚWIDNICA: Rynek 43 zł zł
Central European Map B5
Rynek 43, 58-100
Tel *74 856 84 19* **Closed** *Wed*
Polish, Czech and German
traditions meet in this Silesian
restaurant with a pretty
courtyard. On the menu are
savoury strüdels, goulash
and schnitzels.

WROCŁAW: Grecos zł
Greek Map C4
ul. Rynek 15, 50-101
Tel *71 343 29 12*
Located in the market square,
this Greek tavern is an ideal spot
for lunch and dinner. The menu
offers delicious grilled meat,
Greek salad and chicken gryos.

WROCŁAW: Machina Organika zł
Vegan Map C4
Ruska 19, 50-101
Tel *733 537 210*
Timber ceilings, jellyfish-shaped
lampshades and exotic tiling
make this a fun place to
enjoy vegan soups and mains,
plus a range of fruit cocktails.

WROCŁAW: Pierogarnia
Stary Młyn zł
Classic Polish Map C4
Rynek 26, 50-101
Tel *71 344 14 15*
This small, rustic-styled
room is the place to visit
for a wide range of pierogi,
either boiled in traditional
style, baked in the oven or
deep-fried, and stuffed
with a range of meat or
vegetarian fillings.

WROCŁAW: Mama
Manousch zł zł
Central European Map C4
ul. Świdnicka 4, 50-067
Tel *71 786 62 92*
A contemporary European
food restaurant that serves
dishes with a mixture of
textures, tastes and colours
such as halibut and pumpkin
starter, wild boar dumplings,
goat cheese and duck liver.

WROCŁAW: Art
Restauracja zł zł zł
Central European Map C4
ul. Kiełbaśnicza 20, 50-110
Tel *71 787 71 02*
Stylish meals are served in
the vaulted brick cellar
restaurant of the Art Hotel.
The menu offers a contem-
porary take on the traditional
schnitzel, roast meat and
poultry repertoire, using
regional produce.

WROCŁAW:
Le Bistrot Parisien zł zł zł
French Map C4
ul. Nożownicza 1d, 50-119
Tel *71 341 05 65*
Classic French cuisine, including
a range of outstanding
seafood, is served in a dining
room where the walls are
covered in clippings and
photographs taken from
the French press.

WROCŁAW: Karczma
Lwowska zł zł zł
Central European Map C4
Rynek 4, 50-106
Tel *71 343 98 87*
Themed around the city of L'viv
in western Ukraine, this restaurant
serves borscht, pork with cabbage
and other dishes from the
eastern frontier.

WROCŁAW: Sakana zł zł zł
Japanese Map C4
ul. Odrzańska 17/1a, 50-113
Tel *71 344 64 02*
Sushi and other dishes are skillfully
prepared here, and then sent
floating on paper boats around a
circular bar to be consumed by
a young and fashionable crowd.

DK Choice

WROCŁAW: Spiż zł zł zł
Brewery Restaurant Map C4
Rynek-Ratusz 2, 50-106
Tel *71 344 72 25*
Set in a pair of atmospheric and
evocatively decorated rooms
right beneath the town hall, Spiż
has a superb range of home-
brewed beers. On the menu is
quality Polish fare ranging from
steak to Silesian dumplings,
game goulash and freshwater
fish. Choose between the
beer hall, overlooked by huge
copper vats, or the more formal
wood-panelled dining room.

WROCŁAW: Splendido zł zł zł
Gourmet Map C4
Świdnicka 53, 50-030
Tel *71 344 77 77*
Lamb, duck and seafood are
among the highlights of the
Mediterranean and Central
European menu.

Wielkopolska

GRABOWNO:
Dworek Koper zł zł
Classic Polish/Lithuanian Map C2
Grabowno 36, 89-350
Tel *67 287 41 28*
This rambling manor house on the
road between Pila and Bydgoszcz
serves Polish and Lithuanian
delights in an antique-filled room.

JAROCIN: Gościniec
Walcerek zł
Classic Polish Map C3
ul. Poznańska 73, 63-200
Tel *62 747 28 18*
With an eclectic interior and a
quiet terrace, this chalet-style
guesthouse serves pork-and-
cabbage Polish cuisine at its finest.

Pierogi, traditionally stuffed with sauerkraut, ground meat, pototoes, cheese or fruit

For more information on types of restaurants *see pages 306–7*

ŁÓDŹ: Manekin zł
Pancake House **Map** D4
ul. 6 Sierpna 1, 90-422
Tel *42 671 07 84*
This pancake bar has a huge menu
of inexpensive but filling food and
a sit-down restaurant service. It is a
very popular venue, and both the
service and turnover are quick.

ŁÓDŹ: U Szwajcara zł
Central European **Map** D4
ul. Tymienieckiego 22, 90-422
Tel *42 674 04 40* **Closed** *for dinner*
& Sun
The red-brick former gatehouse
of a once-great textile factory is
now famous for its superb-value
food, with an accent on meat,
poultry and goulash dishes.

ŁÓDŹ: Anatewka zł zł
Jewish **Map** D4
ul. 6 Sierpna 2/4, 90-422
Tel *42 630 36 35*
Diners come here for the fine
selection of Jewish and Central
European dishes, served in a dining
room decorated with menorahs,
prayer shawls and traditional
textiles. There is live violin or
piano music every evening.

DK Choice

ŁÓDŹ: Ciągoty i Tęsknoty zł zł
Gourmet **Map** D4
ul. Wojska Polskiego 144, 91-711
Tel *42 695 991 883*
Something of a culinary cult in
this part of Poland, this café-
restaurant close to the Jewish
cemetery offers an exciting and
inventive menu that combines
rustic French traditions with
contemporary Polish cuisine.
Never too expensive, it's
popular with students and
professors from the Fine Arts
Academy in the park opposite.
Art exhibitions and frequent live
music add to the cultural vibe.

ŁOWICZ: Pizza House zł
Italian **Map** D3
ul. 3-go Maja 8, 99-400
Tel *46 837 83 51*
Located just off Stary Rynek, this
restaurant serves a range of
pizzas. Dine in the attractive
wooden bench-filled back garden
or sit at a snug booth overlooked
by the Łowicz coat of arms.

POZNAŃ: Petit Paris zł
Café/Patisserie **Map** C3
ul. Półwiejska 32, 61-888
Tel *61 667 15 55*
Inside the Stary Browar shopping
mall and arts centre, this bakery
and café serves delicious
sandwiches, soups, salads and
quiches. Pastries, tarts and great
coffee round off the experience.

POZNAŃ: Projekt Kuchnia zł
International **Map** C3
ul. Polwiejska 24, 61-888
Tel *60 699 29 99*
A mix of traditional Polish and
contemporary European cuisine,
with a good balance of meat and
vegetarian dishes. There are also
breakfasts and light bites.

POZNAŃ: Beejays zł zł
Steakhouse **Map** C3
Stary Rynek 88, 61-772
Tel *51 506 53 19*
A popular main-square grill bar
and restaurant serving grill-
steaks, pizzas, fish and chips,
and a range of dishes for children
Wash the food down with something from their big range of
spirits and cocktails.

POZNAŃ: Brovaria zł zł
Brewery Restaurant **Map** C3
Stary Rynek 73/74, 61-772
Tel *61 858 68 68*
Predictably, given its location
in a microbrewery on the main
square, this elegant restaurant
serves excellent beer. The
menu of Central European and

Mediterranean dishes is loaded
with creativity and finesse.

POZNAŃ: Delicja zł zł zł
Gourmet **Map** C3
pl. Wolności 5, 61-738
Tel *61 852 11 28*
A long-standing favourite
among Poznań foodies, Delicja
serves an imaginative mix
of French, Italian and Polish
cuisines in an elegant interior
full of ticking clocks.

POZNAŃ: Ratuszova zł zł zł
Classic Polish **Map** C3
Stary Rynek 55, 61-772
Tel *61 851 05 13*
Traditional Polish fare with a
contemporary twist, including
plenty of meat and poultry
roasts, served in an interior
that mixes warm colours and
exposed brick.

POZNAŃ: Zagroda
Bamberska zł zł zł
Central European **Map** C3
ul. Kościelna 43, 60-534
Tel *61 842 77 90*
Savour traditional regional
dishes, such as roast duck
with cranberry sauce, in this
19th-century farm-style building
with flower baskets hanging
from wooden beams.

Gdańsk

Bar Neptun zł
Classic Polish **Map** D1
ul. Długa 33/34, 80-827
Tel *58 301 49 88*
This traditional *bar mleczny*, or
canteen restaurant, serves filling,
tasty portions of pork, fish, bean
stew and potato pancakes in
sparse but smart surroundings.

Nowa Pierogova zł
Classic Polish **Map** D1
ul. Szafarnia 6
Tel *516 414 200*
Situated on the river, opposite
the Old Town, this good-value,
cheerful *pierogi* joint offers
traditional meat- and cheese-
filled options, as well as some
own-recipe variations featuring
seafood and exotic spices.

Pierogarnia u Dzika zł
Classic Polish **Map** D1
ul. Piwna 59/60, 80-831
Tel *58 305 26 76*
Boar pelts and animal heads add
to the atmosphere at this fast-
food restaurant serving a vast
selection of *pierogi* with all sorts
of fillings, ranging from meat to
cabbage and fresh fruit.

Le Bistrot Parisien, in Wrocław, re-creating a warm Parisian ambience *(see p315)*

The lavish decor at Pod Łososiem, Gdańsk

Pijalnia Wódki i Piwa zł
Classic Polish Map D1
ul. Długi Targ 35/38, 80-830
Tel *530 766 945*
Open 24 hours, this trendy bar serves vodka shots, beer and a spread of good-value traditional snacks, such as marinated herring, *gzik* (cottage cheese, onion and sour cream), as well as steak tartare.

A la Française zł zł
French Map D1
ul. Spichrzowa 24/1, 80-750
Tel *58 765 11 12*
This two-storey café-restaurant with a homely feel offers soups, baguette sandwiches and delicious sweet and savoury pancakes. There are also some hard-to-resist pastries and eclairs.

Tawerna Mestwin zł zł
Classic Polish/Regional Map D1
ul. Straganiarska 20/23, 80-837
Tel *606 745 252*
Crammed with local arts and crafts, this timeless, homely restaurant is a virtual museum. On the menu is traditional Kashubian cuisine, which amounts to tasty offerings of hunks of meat. Welcoming, friendly service.

Fellini zł zł zł
Italian Map D1
Targ Rybny 6, 80-890
Tel *888 010 203*
This smart, cosy Italian restaurant in a riverside area serves home-made pasta with imaginative sauces, veal rolled with pro-sciutto, and some stand-out fish dishes.

Kresowa zł zł zł
Classic Polish Map D1
ul. Ogarna 12, 80-826
Tel *58 301 66 53*
Located near the historic shipyard, this excellent restaurant borrows liberally from the culinary traditions of the Polish-Lithuanian and Polish-Ukrainian borderlands, with waiting staff dressed in traditional Eastern Polish attire.

DK Choice

Kubicki zł zł zł
Classic Polish Map D1
ul. Wartka 5, 80-841
Tel *58 301 00 50*
Founded in 1919, this legendary restaurant remains in the hands of the same family that founded it. The interior is full of vintage furniture, while the high-quality food reflects the traditions of Poland's Baltic cities, with herring, halibut and sole balancing out a menu strong in meaty specialities like *golonka* (roast pork knuckle) or wild boar. Traditional home-made desserts include *sernik* (Polish cheesecake).

Metamorfoza zł zł zł
Contemporary Polish Map D1
ul. Szeroka 22/23, 80-835
Tel *58 320 30 30* Closed *Mon*
Featuring a modern, minimalist decor, this centrally located restaurant offers an exquisitely prepared fusion of local ingre-dients and Mediterranean cuisine, plus a classic French approach to the details.

Pod Łososiem zł zł zł
Gourmet Map D1
ul. Szeroka 52/54, 80-835
Tel *58 301 76 52*
This opulent restaurant with its celebrity-spattered guest list serves classic fine-feasting dishes, including plenty of scrumptious sea-food and game. Grilled salmon is the house speciality.

Targ Rybny zł zł zł
Seafood Map D1
Targ Rybny 6c, 80-838
Tel *58 320 90 11*
Located right beside the fish market, this bright restaurant elevates local fish cuisine to an art form. Highlights include the salmon-stuffed *pierogi* and the sea bass baked with artichokes.

Pomerania

BOROWO: Checz Rybacka zł
Seafood Map D1
ul. Jeziorna 2, 83-332
Tel *58 685 34 04*
This eatery ranks among the best fish restaurants in Poland, with both Baltic sea and freshwater fish served in a variety of ways.

BYTÓW: Zamek zł zł
Central European Map C1
ul. Zamkowa 2, 77-100
Tel *59 822 20 94*
Enjoy hearty meat and goulash dishes inside a 14th-century castle. There is also an attractive garden for alfresco dining.

GDYNIA: Pueblo zł zł
Mexican Map D1
al. Abrahama 56, 80-387
Tel *58 621 60 07*
Pueblo is one of the few authentic Mexican restaurants in northern Poland. Satisfyingly spicy dishes are served in a themed interior filled with ethnic textiles.

HEL: Maszoperia zł zł
Seafood Map D1
ul. Wiejska 110, 84-150
Tel *58 675 02 97*
Serving everything from halibut to salmon, this restaurant is housed in a low-ceilinged fisher-man's cottage stuffed with vintage furnishings and bric-a-brac.

DK Choice

KOŁOBRZEG: Rewiński zł
Seafood Map B1
Jana Szymańskiego 6
Tel *94 354 75 66*
People queue up to eat in this glass-fronted fast-food pavilion near the Kołobrzeg lighthouse. Baltic fish such as turbot, halibut and sole is either simply fried or prepared in batter. You can also opt for platters of marinated herring, stuffed trout or grilled salmon. The fish soup is an ideal warm snack, and the seafront location is simply superb.

For more information on types of restaurants *see pages 306–7*

MALBORK: Gothic   zł zł
International   Map D1
ul. Starościńska 1, 80-200
Tel *55 647 08 89*
Housed in the cellar of the
Teutonic Castle, Gothic serves
an exciting combination of
international and Polish cuisines
with elements of traditional
medieval cooking thrown in for
good measure.

MIĘDZYZDROJE: Marina   zł zł
Classic Polish   Map A1
Gryfa Pomorskiego 1, 72-500
Tel *91 328 04 49*
This small and homely hotel
restaurant serves pork, poultry
roasts and pan-fried freshwater
fish. Be sure to save room for
dessert –the apple pie made
here is delicious.

MIELNO: Meduza   zł zł
European   Map B1
ul. Nadbrzeżna 2, 76-032
Tel *94 348 08 90*
The menu at this beachside
dining room on the main
promenade delivers classic
French and Mediterranean
cuisine, including an assortment of pasta options and
some superbly fresh and
beautifully cooked seafood.

**SASINO: Ewa
Zaprasza**   zł zł
European   Map C1
ul. Morska 49, 84-210
Tel *58 676 33 39*   **Closed** *Dec*
Enjoying a rustic setting in
a village east of Łeba, Ewa
Zaprasza serves some of
the most exciting food in
this part of Poland, with an
eclectic, inspired approach
to locally sourced meat, fowl
and fish.

SOPOT: Bar Przystań   zł
Seafood   Map D1
al. Wojska Polskiego 11, 81-769
Tel *58 550 02 41*
Occupying a conservatory-style
dining room right on the beach,
Bar Przystań is the place for
fish. On the menu are halibut,
sole and a host of other
options, either pan-fried or
cooked in batter.

SOPOT: Image   zł zł
International   Map D1
ul. Grunwaldzka 8/10, 81-759
Tel *58 550 75 76*
A tempting combination of
Mediterranean and Polish
dishes, including some
outstanding fish, is served
in an eccentrically decorated
interior that is in itself a mish-
mash of styles.

Adobe walls, cacti and Mexican decor at Pueblo, in Gdynia *(see p317)*

SOPOT: Rucola   zł zł
International   Map D1
*Bohaterów Monte Cassino 53,
81-777*
Tel *58 555 53 55*
Occupying the basement of the
Sopot Museum, Rucola serves
sophisticated global fusion food,
with an emphasis on Far Eastern
and Mediterranean flavours.

SOPOT: Tropikalna Wyspa   zł zł
International   Map D1
*Sopot beach; end of ul. Traugutta,
81-769*
Tel *58 692 88 33*
Located right on the beach, this
summer-season café-restaurant
serves pork-and-sauerkraut
staples and Baltic fish (either
fried or baked), plus a tempting
menu of alcoholic drinks.

**SOPOT: Cyrano &
Roxane**   zł zł zł
French   Map D1
*Bohaterów Monte Cassino 11,
81-704*
Tel *660 759 594*
An informal, bistro-style
restaurant, Cyrano & Roxane
has a well-chosen menu of
French favourites, ranging from
Provençal fish soup through
confit of duck and assorted
French sausages to crème brûlée.

**SOPOT: Villa
Baltica**   zł zł zł
International   Map D1
ul. Emilii Plater 1, 81-777
Tel *58 555 28 00*
Located right on the beach,
in the hotel of the same
name, Villa baltica, an
outstanding restaurant
serves a classic, predominantly
European mix of steaks, roast
lamb, game and seafood.

**SZCZECIN: Pierogarnia
Kaszubska**   zł
Classic Polish   Map A2
plac Zgody 1, 70-472
Tel *91 485 18 10*   **Closed** *Sun*
Sparsely furnished
but smart fast-food joint,

Plerogarnia Kaszubska
serves boiled, deep-fried
or baked *pierogi* with a
range of fillings. Their
own-recipe borscht is
also worth trying.

SZCZECIN: Bombay   zł zł
Indian   Map A2
ul. Partyzantów 1, 70-222
Tel *91 812 11 71*
This refined restaurant
serves a broad and satisfying
range of subcontinental
fare, including plenty of
vegetarian dishes and a
range of tasty naans.

TORUŃ: Czarna Oberża   zł
Classic Polish   Map D2
Rabiańska 9, 87-100
Tel *606 664 756*
Wooden beams and low-key
lighting set the tone in this
great-value restaurant where
you order at the counter.
Czarna Oberża offers the best
dishes of Polish home cooking,
such as *pierogi* and stuffed
cabbage leaves.

**TORUŃ: Pierogarnia
Stary Toruń**   zł
Classic Polish   Map D2
Most Pauliński 2/10, 87-100
Tel *56 621 10 46*
Rustic knick-knacks decorate
this good-value eatery serving
pierogi stuffed with a variety
of fillings, including huge
oven-baked ones filled with
beef and plums.

TORUŃ: 1231   zł zł
Classic Polish/
Mediterranean   Map D2
Przedzamcze 6, 87-100
Tel *56 619 09 17*
Set in the oldest part of a 13th
century edifice, the lounges of
this restaurant boasts Gothic
style decor. Come here for a
selection of fine Polish and
Italian fare – good steaks
and an excellent range of
freshwater and Mediterranean
fish, as well as fine wines.

For key to prices *see page 310*

TORUŃ: Dom Sushi zł zł zł
Japanese Map D2
Franciszkańska 8, 87-100
Tel *56 652 22 88*
Sushi and sashimi, as well as soups, main dishes and bento boxes are offered in this stylish eatery with paper lanterns and a central kitchen-bar.

Warmia, Mazuria and Białystok Region

AUGUSTÓW: Kaktusik zł zł
Seafood Map F2
ul. 29. Listopada 2, 16-300
Tel *697 720 033*
Enjoy fine dining – freshwater fish, home-made *pierogi* and roast poultry dishes – in this timber house surrounded by a park. There is also a highly respectable wine list.

BIAŁOWIEŻA:
Żubrówka zł zł zł
Gourmet Map G3
ul. O. Gabiec 6, 16-303
Tel *601 800 815*
This hotel restaurant near the entrance to the national park offers a superb selection of local game dishes flavoured with forest fruits, and a handful of freshwater fish options. Breakfast is a smorgasbord.

BIAŁYSTOK: Cristal zł zł zł
International Map F2
ul. Lipowa 3, 15-424
Tel *85 749 61 59*
This popular city-centre eaterie, located inside a hotel, is famous for its well-presented Polish classics, which are served alongside some top-quality French and Mediterranean fare. There is also a bar, café and orangery on site.

IŁAWA: Stary Tartak zł zł
Classic Polish Map D2
ul. Biskupska 5, 14-200
Tel *603 522 588*
In a beautiful setting beside a lake and overlooking an old part of Iława, Stary Tartak specializes in traditional cuisine such as handmade *pierogi* and juicy tenderloins grilled with herbs. In the summer, the chef cooks fish from Lake Jeziorak.

KĘTRZYN: Zajazd pod
Zamkiem zł zł zł
Classical Polish/Grill Map E1
ul. Struga 3a, 11-400
Tel *89 752 31 17*
This atmospheric and ornately decorated restaurant is set beside the castle walls. It specializes in Polish staples and grilled meats. There is a refreshing garden for summer dining. In the warmer months, there is also a fish bar and live music is provided every evening.

KRUTYŃ: Krutynianka zł zł
Seafood Map E2
Krutyń 34, 11-710
Tel *604 630 157*
Located beside a river, this rural restaurant serves some of the best fresh fish in the Warmia, Mazuria and Białystok region. It also excels in long-forgotten rural recipes such as nettle soup.

MIKOŁAJKI: Spiżarnia zł zł
International/Seafood Map E2
Plac Handlowy 14, 11-730
Tel *87 421 52 18*
Decked out in a pleasant country-farmhouse style, Mikołajki, meaning pantry, is a popular restaurant. This eatery serves an impressive array of quality fish, Italian pasta dishes, and tartare made from beef or smoked salmon. The beef cheeks in red wine and the wild boar dishes are highly recommended.

OLSZTYN:
Karczma Jana zł zł
Classic Polish Map F2
Hugona Kołłątaja 11, 10-034
Tel *89 522 29 46*
This delightful restaurant with timber beams and a chalet vibe cooks up a satisfying selection of pork and poultry, plus baked apples with mead for dessert. The eatery boasts an enviable location on the River Łyna in a park in the old town.

DK Choice

OLSZTYN: Przystań zł zł zł
Seafood/Asian Map E2
ul. Żeglarska 3, 10-160
Tel *89 523 77 79*
Boasting a beautiful location on Lake Krzywe, just outside the city centre, this restaurant specializes in freshwater fish – pan-fried, served with an imaginative range of sauces or spices, or sushi. Local mushrooms and vegetarian choices also feature on the menu.

OSTRÓDA: Młyn
pod Mariaszkem zł zł
Classic Polish Map E2
Młyn Idzbarski 2, 14-100
Tel *89 646 03 55*
Just outside Ostróda, this renovated 19th-century mill offers a superb selection of picrogi, as well as home-baked bread and cakes.

RYN: Karczma u
Wallenroda zł
Classic Polish Map E2
pl. Wolności 3a, 11-520
Tel *87 421 86 75*
A plain brick building with a local-pub atmosphere complete with billiard table, this rural inn serves grilled meats, soups and potato-pancake staples.

SUWAŁKI: Karczma
Polska zł
Classic Polish Map F1
Tadeusza Kościuszki 101a, 16-400
Tel *87 566 48 60*
With an interior full of wood panelling and folk craft, Karczma Polska provides the ideal ambience in which to feast on roast pork knuckle, *kartacze* (dumplings stuffed with meat) and other hearty Polish delights.

The front patio at Cyrano & Roxane, in Sopot *(see p318)*

For more information on types of restaurants *see pages 306–7*

SHOPPING IN POLAND

Poland is known first and foremost for its handicraft goods. Polish silver and amber jewellery are especially renowned, but hand-embroidered tablecloths, cut glass from Silesia, porcelain from Ćmielów and ceramics from Bolesławiec are also very popular. Thick, hand-knitted woollen sweaters and ornamented leather slippers are produced by the highlanders of Zakopane and its environs. CDs of Polish classical and contemporary music are available all over the country. Large-format, lavishly illustrated books about Polish landscape and on art, some of which are published in English, French or German, are other tempting souvenirs of a visit to Poland.

Where to Shop

Although there are retail shops everywhere, it often makes more sense to purchase goods from factory and established licensed shops. The most competitively priced handicraft goods can be bought direct from the manufacturers in the markets. Duty-free goods are also available at all international airports.

Shopping in Warsaw

Most shops are located in the city centre. There are many elegant boutiques in the Old Town, along Ulica Krakowskie Przedmieście and Ulica Nowy Świat. There are many clothes shops in Ulica Chmielna, Aleje Jerozolimskie and Ulica Marszałkowska. If you are interested in antiques visit the Sunday morning market in the Koło district on the western side of Warsaw.

Popular department stores are **Galeria Centrum**, **Galeria Mokotów**, **Arkadia**, **Wola Park**, **Klif** and **Złote Tarasy**. Browsing for bargains is an attraction of large markets, for example those held in Hale Mirowskie.

Opening Hours

Shops are open from 10am to 6pm Monday to Friday and, in the main, from 10am to 2pm on Saturdays. In the larger cities, shops usually close at 7pm, with most of the department stores staying open for an extra hour and closing at 8pm.

In the run-up to Christmas, the majority of shops are open much longer hours, and shopping centres open on the

Amber jewellery and other goods displayed in a shop window

last Sunday before Christmas. Normal Sunday opening times are restricted to a few food shops and major shopping centres, although in summer souvenir shops in popular tourist resorts open as well. On public holidays all shops are closed, with the exception of some pharmacies and food shops (those that are open at night). As a last resort, a 24-hour petrol station may fulfil any particularly pressing needs.

Paying

Although cash (in złote, of course) is always welcomed by Polish traders of all kinds, credit cards are nonetheless accepted in most shops in the big cities (this should be indicated by stickers on the door – if not, ask before making a purchase). However, small shops sometimes prefer to give a small discount for payment in cash rather than take a card, so there may be a little margin for haggling. Polish shops do not usually accept travellers' cheques, but it is perfectly easy to change them in banks (see pp340–41). There is VAT on the price of Polish goods, but a range of goods is tax-free to foreign nationals, and on such goods (that have a minimum value of 200 złoty) a VAT refund can be obtained.

The interior of the shopping centre, Złote Tarasy, brimming with people

An antiques market in Krakow's Main Market Square

Books and Records

Well-stocked bookshops can be found in most towns and cities. The **EMPiK** chain of bookshops, with outlets in all big cities, offers the widest choice, and not only of books; there are music sections as well. Guidebooks in foreign languages and glossy coffee-table books aimed at the tourist market are available from tourist information centres. Many second-hand bookshops, to be found in the old parts of big cities, often stock an interesting selection of old books.

Highlanders' sweaters and other local goods at a Zakopane market

Handicrafts

Traditional handicraft products such as hand-woven tapestries, embroidered tablecloths and doilies, leather goods, decorative cut-outs, ceramics and even furniture are sold in **Cepelia** shops, which are to be found in all big cities. In Krakow, most of these shops are located in the Sukiennice in Main Market Square. In Gdańsk, the retail outlet Galeria Sztuki Kaszubskiej specializes in artifacts made by folk artists from Kashubia. Local markets are also worth visiting. For example, one of the best places to buy highlanders' sweaters is

at the market in Zakopane; embroidered tablecloths are on sale at stalls in Święta Lipka and Kashubian ceramics in pottery workshops in Chmielno.

Polish handicraft goods displayed at the Galeria Sztuki Kaszubskiej

Amber Goods

Amber is a fossilized tree resin that ranges in colour from cream through translucent yellow and orange to rich brown. Most Polish amber comes from the Gulf of Gdańsk, and Polish amber goods are largely made in Gdańsk and its environs. Amber jewellery is extremely popular in Poland. It is sold at a range of outlets, but to avoid the risk of buying a fake it is best

to go to an established shop. In Gdańsk there are several such shops, located chiefly in the Old City, particularly in Ulica Mariacka and Ulica Długie Pobrzeże – for example in the **Galeria Wydra**. The town of Mikołajki in the Great Mazurian Lakes region also offers a wide choice of amber artifacts.

Arts and Crafts

Some of the greatest attractions for tourists in Poland are contemporary paintings, prints and posters, which are available at very reasonable prices in galleries. Art galleries also sell original glass, ceramics and designer jewellery. Silver, in the form of sophisticated jewellery and various other artifacts, is relatively cheap.

Painting on glass also has a strong tradition in Poland, and small pieces, with traditional or modern designs, are offered for sale in many galleries around the country.

In Wrocław, the former meat market in Kiełbaśnicza has been taken over by artists. In Krakow, there are many galleries in the historic city centre. Poland is famous for having a strong graphic arts tradition, exemplified by the theatre and cinema posters that emerged in the 1950s and are still being made today. **Galeria Plakatu** in Krakow and **Polish Poster Gallery** in Wrocław are good places to browse for them. A good selection of graphic and other art can be found in Warsaw's **Wawa BlaBla**.

The vibrant Polish Poster Gallery in Wrocław

The modern interior of Warsaw's Złote Tarasy shopping centre

Antiques

In most towns throughout Poland, antiques and collectables are sold in **Desa** shops. Second-hand goods, however, are sold in privately run shops that are to be found in both large and small towns and also in tourist spots. Visitors should bear in mind that there are special provisions pertaining to the export of objects made before 1945; under Polish customs regulations, such objects may not be exported, unless a special permit is obtained.

Pottery and Porcelain

Poland has a long tradition of porcelain manufacture, and there are a few factories that still produce porcelain in both traditional and modern designs. The most renowned type is Ćmielów porcelain, which is available all over Poland. Just as attractive is the porcelain produced by the factory in Wałbrzych, which has its own retail shop situated in **Książ Castle** (see p191). Popular also are traditional ceramics such as those made in Bolesławiec, especially the white and navy-blue crockery decorated with spots, circles and small stylized flowers.

Glass and Crystal

High-quality glass, in both modern and traditional designs, is another Polish speciality, as is traditional cut glass, known as crystal.

Designer glassware is also popular and in great demand. The most beautiful cut glass comes from Silesia, where glass production dates back to the 14th century. The Julia glass factory in Szklarska Poręba, which was established in 1841 as Josephinenhütte, is also renowned.

Clothes and Accessories

Poland has never been synonymous with high-quality clothing, but the quality of clothes made in the country has greatly improved, and many factories can now compete with Western European clothing manufacturers. They are available in department stores and from shops in big cities. Many Polish designers also have their own boutiques, which stock unique collections of suits and dresses.

Warsaw's **Lovley** is a particularly innovative label, whilst **Forum Design** in Krakow stocks garments by many independent designers.

Polish designers producing stylish, witty and affordable T-shirts, bags and other accessories include Łódź-based **Pan tu nie stał** and Katowice's **Gryfnie.**

Food and Drink

Polish liquor is internationally renowned, especially the pure vodkas, which – much like Scotch whisky – are available

in a bewildering range of varieties. The most popular brands are Premium and Chopin, the latter sold in elegant, slender bottles decorated with a picture of the famous composer.

Another popular spirit is *żubrówka*, a vodka with a distinctive, slightly herbal flavour; it is obtained from hierchloe grass, which grows only in the Białowieska Forest. Another alcoholic drink is mead. Made with honey according to traditional recipes, it is the perfect accompaniment to desserts.

Many distilleries have their own retail outlets, where private buyers can taste the different specialities on offer. One such establishment is **Polmos**, in Krakow.

Polish sweets are of a high quality. Chocolates made by the Warsaw firm **Wedel** and the Krakow firm **Wawel** are particularly esteemed.

For a tasty present from Poland you might choose, for instance, a jar of dried ceps (porcini mushrooms, honey, smoked eel or dried sausage). The best places to buy such items are bazaars and markets. There are good markets in Warsaw in Hala Mirowska near Plac Mirowski, in Krakow in Stary Kleparz, in Poznań in Plac Wielkopolski, and in the market halls of Wrocław and Gdańsk.

If travelling to the UK, avoid fish or meat products as they are subject to an import ban.

The front of the Hala Mirowska marketplace

DIRECTORY

Department Stores and Shopping Centres

Arkadia
Warsaw, ul. Jana
Pawła II 82.
Tel 22 323 67 67.

Dom Towarowy Bracia Jabłkowscy
Warsaw, ul. Bracka 25.
Tel 22 826 36 44.

Galeria Centrum
Warsaw, ul.
Marszałkowska 104.
Tel 22 551 45 17.

Galeria Dominikańska
Wrocław,
pl. Dominikański 3.
Tel 71 344 95 17.

Galeria Krakowska
Krakow, ul. Pawia 5.
Tel 12 428 99 00.

Galeria Mokotów
Warsaw, ul. Wołoska 12.
Tel 22 541 41 41.

Klif
Warsaw,
ul. Okopowa 58/72.
Tel 22 531 45 00.

Madison
Gdańsk, ul. Rajska 10.
Tel 58 766 75 30.

Manufaktura
Łódź, Drewnowska 58.
Tel 42 664 92 89.

Stary Browar
Poznań, ul. Półwiejska 42.
Tel 601 348 483.

Wola Park
Warsaw, ul.
Górczewska 124.
Tel 22 533 40 00.

Złote Tarasy
Warsaw, ul. Złota 59.
Tel 22 222 22 00.

Books

American Bookstore
Krakow, Sławkowska 22a.
Tel 795 207 825.

Antykwariat Naukowy
Poznań, Paderewskiego
3/5. **Tel** 61 852 63 12.
W antykwariat.pl

EMPiK

Krakow, ul. Floriańska 14.
Tel 22 451 40 20.

EMPiK Megastore
Warsaw, ul. Złota 59.
Tel 22 462 72 50.
Gdańsk, ul. Podwale
Grodzkie 8.
Tel 22 462 72 50.

Massolit
Krakow, ul. Felizjanek 4.
Tel 12 432 41 50.

Handicrafts

Bołeslawiec Ceramic
Poznań, ul.
Międzyńskiego 16.
Tel 61 853 47 98.

Cepelia
Gdańsk, ul. Długa 47/49.
Tel 58 301 27 08.
W cepelia.pl
Bydgoszcz, ul.
Gdańska 17.
Tel 52 322 17 28.
Częstochowa, ul. NMP 64.
Tel 34 324 43 48.
Warsaw, Marszałkowska
99/101.
Tel 22 628 77 57.
Krakow, Sukiennice.
Tel 12 422 55 04.
Olsztyn, ul. Prosta 1/2.
Tel 89 527 25 97.
Szczecin,
plac Żołnierza 1A.
Tel 91 434 57 87.
Wrocław,
pl. Nankiera 5/6.
Tel 71 343 59 79.

Galeria Sztuk Różnych
Gdańsk,
ul. Ogarna 101.
Tel 58 302 07 02.
W magdabeneda.pl

Galeria Sztuki Kaszubskiej
Gdańsk,
ul. Sw Ducha 48.
Tel 503 005 978.

Vena Pottery
Wrocław, Rynek 4.
Tel 71 344 43 70.
W vena-ceramika.com.pl

Amber Goods

Amber Moda
Sopot,
Grunwaldzka 12-16.
Tel 501 414 900.

Galeria Bursztynek
Warsaw,
ul. Długa 8/14.
Tel 508 511 680.

Galeria Wydra
Gdańsk,
ul. Mariacka 49.
Tel 58 301 77 79.

World of Amber
Krakow,
ul. Grodzka 38.
Tel 12 430 31 14.

Arts and Crafts

Galeria Plakatu
Krakow, ul. Stolarska 8-10.
Tel 12 421 26 40.

Galeria Top-Art
Toruń, ul. Kopernika 21.
Tel 56 621 08 46.

Galeria ZPAP
Krakow, Łobzowska 3.
Tel 12 632 46 22.

Polish Poster Gallery
Wrocław,
ul. Sw Mikołaja 54/55.
Tel 71 780 49 11.
W polishposter.com

Wawa BlaBla
Warsaw, ul. Dobra 15.
Tel 601 635 006.
W wawablabla.pl

ZPAP Gallery
Gdańsk,
ul. Mariacka 46/47.
Tel 58 301 69 14.

Antiques

Desa
Krakow, ul. Floriańska 13.
Tel 12 422 27 06.

Desa Unicum
Warsaw, ul.
Marszałkowska 34/50.
Tel 22 584 95 25.

Ceramics and Glass

Krosno
Krosno,
ul. Tysiąclecia 13.
Tel 13 432 87 55.

Clothes

Forum Design
Krakow, ul. Dołnych
Mlynów 10.
Tel 730 740 025.

Gryfnie
Katowice, ul. Andrzeja 8.
W gryfnie.com

Lovley
Warsaw,
ul. Mickiewicza 24.
Tel 505 998 853.
W lovley.pl

Pan tu nie stał
Krakow,
ul. Nadwiślańska 9.
Tel 667 432 671.
Łódź, Piotrkowska
138/140.
Tel 42 257 28 32.
Warsaw,
ul. Koszykowa 34/50.
Tel 88 / 887 772.
W pantuniestal.com

Vistula
Warsaw,
al. Jana Pawła II 82.
Tel 783 780 084.

Confectionery

E. Wedel
Warsaw, ul. Szpitalna 8.
Tel 22 827 29 16.
Warsaw, ul. Freta 17.
Tel 22 636 04 76.
Wrocław, ul. Rynek 59.
Tel 71 346 06 92.

Polmos
Krakow, Fabryczna 13.
Tel 12 411 48 43.

Wawel
Krakow,
Rynek Główny 33.
Tel 12 423 12 47.
Łódź, ul. A. Struga 5.
Tel 42 632 93 18.
Poznań,
ul. Wrocławska 21.
Tel 61 853 03 67.

What to Buy in Poland

The range of folk art and handicrafts in Poland is truly impressive. Almost every region has its own speciality. The production of Christmas tree ornaments, painted Easter eggs and Christmas crib figures is a distinctive folk industry. The work of Polish artists, in the form of paintings, prints, posters and sculpture, is also highly esteemed and can be found in commercial galleries. Designer jewellery, another high-profile Polish craft, and amber products, which are reasonably priced, are also attractive. Vodka, the national drink, is available in various flavours.

Dolls in Traditional Costume
Small dolls dressed in the traditional costume of the Krakow or Zakopane region make ideal gifts or souvenirs.

Highlanders' Products

The Podhale region is famous for its original folk products. The hand-knitted socks and sweaters and the traditional leather *kierpce* (soft shoes with pointed toes) are very popular.

Oscypek, sheep's milk cheese

Embroidered *serdak*

Woollen socks

Patterned leather *kierpce*

Hand-carved
Christmas crib

Christmas Cribs
Christmas cribs are extremely popular, especially in southern Poland. The finest are hand-carved in wood. As well as a whole crib, it is possible to purchase individual figures.

Hand-painted Christmas decoration

Wooden angel

Easter Decorations

Easter eggs and lambs are essential on the Easter table. Not only are the eggs painted, but patterns are also created by scratching into the shell and applying paper and ribbons.

Christmas Decorations
Traditional Polish Christmas decorations range from painted glass balls to ornaments made of wood, straw, paper or coloured ribbons.

Sugar lamb

Decorated eggs

Jug made out of a
hollow eggshell

Ginger Cake

Ginger cake, a traditional delicacy from Toruń, is made using old moulds and is sometimes decorated with colourful frosting.

Toruń ginger cake

Folk Art

Folk art is deeply rooted in Polish tradition. It takes many forms – from painting, carving and embroidery to other skilled handicrafts. Painting on glass is a particularly vibrant aspect of the genre.

Wicker baskets from Kurpie

Colourful bas-relief

Silver rings

Jewellery

Silver jewellery is a speciality of Polish craftsmen. It is relatively cheap and comes in a variety of sophisticated modern designs.

Nativity scene painted on glass

Paper cut-out

Amber

Amber artifacts epitomize Polish craftsmanship. The translucent material is turned into original jewellery and ornaments and is also used for lampshades and such intricate pieces as model ships.

Amber ship

Art Nouveau-style lamp

Embroidered Doilies

Embroidered tablecloths, doilies and clothes are part of the folk art of many regions of Poland. The finest embroidery is that of Kashubia and Małopolska.

Alcohol

Pure vodka is a Polish speciality. High-grade vodkas, those with a mixture of herbal and other extracts – *żubrówka*, for example – and liqueurs such as Goldwasser are also very popular.

Pure vodkas: Cracovia   Wyborowa   Goldwasser

Cut Glass

Cut glass is made in many Silesian factories. The delicate hand-cut patterns on perfectly transparent glass are appreciated the world over.

ENTERTAINMENT IN POLAND

Poland has a vibrant cultural life. In all the big cities there is an abundance of things to do: nightclubs, jazz clubs, casinos, theatres, opera and cinemas. Modern venues such as the home of the Philharmonia in Wrocław and the NOSPR concert hall in Katowice host some of the finest performances in Europe. In summer, even the smaller tourist resorts have much to offer, and it is possible to chance upon many interesting and unusual events, such as a jousting tournament or a music festival. For those travellers who enjoy taking part in more strenuous pastimes, there is much to satisfy, with trekking, rock climbing, cycling, windsurfing, canoeing, ice sailing and many other sports (see pp330–31) on offer. There are also various spectator sports such as boxing, soccer, speedboat racing and dirt-track motorcycle racing.

Spectators entering the extravagant Tauron Arena, Krakow

Information

Visitors looking for information on Poland's cultural events should consult the local tourist information centres. In larger cities, information bulletins are also issued – in Krakow, for example, there is *Karnet*. The local supplement that is folded into the main copy of Friday's *Gazeta Wyborcza* is another useful source of information. Details of cultural events are also published in the local press and online, although the best way to follow events is to visit the websites of the cultural venues themselves.

Ticket Reservations

Eventim is the biggest ticket agency in the country. They handle internet bookings, have a ticket office in the centre of Warsaw, and also have ticket outlets in EMPiK multimedia stores throughout Poland. In Krakow, tickets can also be bought in advance at the **InfoKrakow** information centre. Theatre, cinema and concert hall box offices will also reserve tickets for their own performances, and these may be collected just before

Oleksandr Usyk warming up for WBO Cruiserweight World Championship

the performance begins. The larger hotels will book tickets for guests on request. Surcharges may be applied for agency bookings.

Venues

Many cultural events, apart from theatrical performances and classical concerts, take place in large public halls. New multipurpose venues such as the **Tauron Arena** in Krakow, the **Krakow Congress Centre** (ICE), and the **Ergo Arena** in Gdańsk host spectacles, from major musicals and ice-skating shows to international rock concerts. In Warsaw, many spectacles are organized in the Sala Kongresowa in the Pałac Kultury. In Katowice, a hall called Spodek (The Flying Saucer) is the venue for both rock concerts and sports events. Wrocław has the Hala Ludowa (People's Hall) and Gdańsk the Hala Olivia. In summer, concerts and festivals are often organized in amphitheatres, for example in the famous **Opera Leśna** (Forest Opera) in Sopot, the amphitheatre in Opole or in Mrągowo in the Great Mazurian Lakes region. In Szczecin and Olsztyn, artistic shows take place in the castle courtyard. Castles, palaces and churches all over Poland also host various cultural events.

Theatres

In Poland, almost all big cities have their own theatres – the country has, in total, over 80. Although theatrical companies move out of town for the summer holiday season, their premises are often used for

A theatrical production at the Teatr Wielki in Warsaw

festivals or theatre reviews. In Warsaw, the most popular theatres include **Ateneum**, Studio, Polski, **Współczesny, Powszechny, Narodowy, Teatr Wielki** (Great Theatre) and Kwadrat, which specializes in comedy shows. The **Teatr Żydowski** (Jewish Theatre) presents spectacles in Yiddish; it is the only such place in Poland and attracts an international audience. In Krakow, the best theatres are considered to be **Teatr Stary** and **Teatr im. J. Słowackiego**. The major theatres in Wrocław are Teatr Polski and Współczesny (Contemporary Theatre).

Poland has enjoyed considerable fame for its avant-garde theatre. The productions of the Krakovian theatre company **Cricot 2** have become world classics; unfortunately, since the death of Tadeusz Kantor, its founder, performances by the company have seldom taken place. The experimental theatre of Jerzy Grotowski and his company, the Laboratorium, was also renowned. The Jerzy Grotowski (Theatrical-Cultural) Research Centre operates in Wrocław. **Wrocławski Teatr Pantomimy**, founded by Henry Tomaszewski and presenting Polish shows, is still active. Poznań has its famous **Teatr Ósmego Dnia**.

Musicals, Opera and Ballet

For those who do not understand the Polish language, musicals, opera and ballet can provide the best form of entertainment, and there is certainly much to choose from in these genres. Poland has many operetta companies. The **Teatr Muzyczny** in Gdynia puts on very popular shows. **Operettas** are performed in Krakow and Gliwice and at **Roma** in Warsaw, which also presents musicals. For opera lovers, the productions of the **Teatr Wielki** in Warsaw are recommended. There are also opera houses in Gdańsk, Wrocław, Łódź, Bydgoszcz, Poznań and Bytom, and operas are staged at the Teatr im. Słowackiego in Krakow. The **Warsaw Chamber Opera**, which specializes in Mozart operas, has won international recognition but performs only a few times a month. Poland's two best ballet companies can be seen in the **Teatr Wielki** in Warsaw and Poznań.

A concert in Warsaw's Concert Studio S1

Classical Music

There are over 20 classical orchestras in Poland and they perform in almost all the country's big cities. Particularly renowned are the **Filharmonia Narodowa** (National Philharmonic Orchestra) in Warsaw, **NOSPR** (Great Symphony Orchestra of Polish Radio) in Katowice and the Poznań Orchestra, which gives concerts in the University Hall. In Poznań there are performances by Poland's most famous choir, Poznańskie Słowiki (The Poznań Nightingales), founded by Stefan Stuligrosz.

Classical music is performed in museums, churches and palaces throughout the year. In the summer, concerts are given in the open air. Concerts of Chopin's music are given on Sundays in Żelazowa Wola and Łazienki Park in Warsaw.

Folk Music

In Poland there are many bands that perform the traditional folk music of individual regions, although it can be difficult to track down their concerts. The most likely occasions are the festivals and reviews that take place mainly in summer *(see p328)*. Regional groups sometimes give concerts on public holidays or harvest festivals. Many singing and dancing groups perform especially for tourists in concerts organized by hotels or tourist agencies, but their shows mostly have little in common with genuine folk traditions. Polish folk music and dance have been popularized outside Poland by such high-profile groups as *Mazowsze* and *Śląsk*. Their shows are professional spectacles based on folk traditions, rather than authentic performances.

The folk dance group *Mazowsze* in Krakovian folk costume

Musical performance at the Dominican Street Market in Gdańsk

Rock, Jazz and Country Music

Student clubs and music pubs are the best places to go to hear rock, jazz and country music in Poland. In most big cities it is quite easy to obtain information on current shows. Polish rock bands are on tour throughout the year, and in summer they usually perform in tourist resorts. There are many festivals for particular kinds of music, so whatever the visitor's taste it will very likely be catered for.

Festivals and Concerts

Poland hosts many festivals, both local and international. Two of the major drama festivals are **Malta International Drama Festival**, held from late June to early July in the streets and theatres of Poznań, and **Kontakt**, which takes place every second year in Toruń from May to June. **Warsaw Theatre Meetings** (Warszawskie Spotkania Teatralne), held in April, present the best productions from across Poland.

Music festivals, such as the **Mozart Festival** in Warsaw, are popular. The most famous classical music festivals are the **Chamber Music Days**, organized in May in Łańcut Palace, the **Chopin Music Festival** in Duszniki Zdrój and the **Moniuszko Music Festival** in Kudowa Zdrój. Events of international renown include **Warsaw Autumn**, and the excellent **Wratislavia Cantans**, a choral festival that takes place in Wrocław in September.

Lovers of church music gather in Hajnówka in June for the **Festival of Orthodox Church Music**. In summer, churches and cathedrals with especially fine organs host festivals of organ music; these take place in Gdańsk-Oliwa, Kamień Pomorski, Koszalin, Słupsk, Święta Lipka, Pasym, Warsaw, Krakow and other towns. Music lovers also enjoy such major international competitions as the Chopin Piano Competition, which takes place every five years in Warsaw in October, and the Wieniawski Violin Competition, which is held in Poznań every four years.

Popular music is celebrated at the **Polish Music Festival** in Opole in June and at the International Festival of Song in Sopot in August. **Country Picnic**, which takes place in Mrągowo in July, is a country music festival. Jazz festivals are also very popular. Major jazz events include **Jazz on the Oder** in Wrocław in May, and **Jazz All Souls'** in Krakow in early November. The **International Festival of Mountain Folklore** in Zakopane and the **Festival of Folk Bands and Singers** in Kazimierz Dolny at the end of June are major showcases for folk music. **Open'er** in Gdynia is the country's premier outdoor rock festival attracting international names

and held in June or July. **Orange Warsaw** and **Kraków Live** take place in June and August respectively, and are also well-attended by locals and visitors. Katowice also hosts the best alternative-rock event, **Off Festival**, in August, as well as the electronica festival, **Tauron New Music**, in July.

Tournaments and Street Markets

Many of the tournaments and street festivals that take place in Poland are colourful events and are popular with tourists. Medieval **jousting tournaments** are organized in medieval castles, some of which – Bytów, Gniew and Golub-Dobrzyń – have witnessed dramatic though bloodless skirmishes. As well as the jousting tournaments and displays of archery, there are often feasts of meat roasted on open-air fires.

Church fairs, festivals, picnics and street markets also take place in towns and villages throughout Poland. The best-known include the **Dominican Street Market** held in Gdańsk at the beginning of August and **St John's Street Market**, held in Poznań. As well as the numerous stalls selling an extraordinary range of goods, there are concerts, games and other events to suit every taste.

A knight at a tournament at the castle in Gniew

DIRECTORY

Information and Ticket Sales

Eventim
Warsaw, al. Jerozolimskie 25.
Tel 59 061 69 15.
W eventim.pl

InfoKrakow
Krakow, ul. św. Jana 2.
Tel 12 429 51 50.
W karnet.krakow.pl

Venues

Ergo Arena
Gdańsk, pl. Dwóch
Miast 1. Tel 58 767 21 01.

Krakow Congress Centre (ICE)
Krakow, ul. Marii
Konopickiej 17.
Tel 12 354 23 00.
W icekrakow.pl

Miasto Ogrodów
Katowice, plac Sejmu
Śląskiego 2.
Tel 32 609 03 00.
W miasto-ogrodow.eu

Opera Leśna
Sopot, ul. Moniuszki 12.
Tel 58 555 84 00.
W operalesna.sopot.pl

Tauron Arena
Krakow, ul. Stanisława
Lema 7. Tel 12 349 11 03.
W tauronarena
krakow.pl

Theatres

Ateneum
Warsaw, ul. Jaracza 2.
Tel 22 502 81 50.
W teatrateneum.pl

Narodowy (National Theatre)
Warsaw, Plac Teatralny.
Tel 22 692 06 04.
W narodowy.pl

Powszechny
Warsaw, ul. Zamoyskiego 20.
Tel 22 818 25 16.
W powszechny.com

Teatr im. J. Słowackiego
Krakow, pl. Świętego
Ducha 1.
Tel 12 424 45 00.
W slowacki.krakow.pl

Teatr Ósmego Dnia
Poznań, ul. Ratajczaka 44.
Tel 61 855 20 86.
W teatrosmiegodnia.pl

Teatr im. St. Witkiewicza
Zakopane, Chramcówki
15. Tel 60 000 15 04.
W witkacy.pl

Teatr Miejski w Gliwicach
Gliwice, ul. Nowy Świat 55.
Tel 32 230 67 18.
W teatr.gliwice.pl

Teatr Stary
Krakow, pl. Szczepański 1.
Tel 12 422 40 40.

Teatr Wielki-Opera Narodowa
Warsaw, pl. Teatralny 1.
Tel 22 692 02 00.
W teatrwielki.pl

Teatr Żydowski
Warsaw, ul. senatorska 35.
Tel 22 620 62 81.
W teatr-zydowski.art.pl

Wrocławski Teatr Pantomimy
Wrocław, al. Dębowa 16.
Tel 71 337 21 03.
W pantomima.wroc.pl

Współczesny (Contemporary Theatre)
Warsaw, ul. Mokotowska
13. Tel 22 825 59 79.
W wspolczesny.pl

Musicals, Opera and Ballet

Opera
Wroclaw, ul. Świdnicka 35.
Tel 71 370 88 80.
W opera.wroclaw.pl

Opera i operetka
Krakow, ul. Lubicz 48.
Tel 12 296 62 60.
W opera.krakow.pl

Opera Śląska
Bytom, ul. Moniuszki 21.
Tel 32 396 68 15.
W opera-slaska.pl

Polski Teatr Tańca
Poznań, ul. Kozia 4.
Tel 61 852 42 42.
W ptt-poznan.pl

Roma (Musical Theatre)
Warsaw, ul. Nowogrodzka
49. Tel 22 628 89 98.
W teatrroma.pl

Śląski Teatr Tańca Rozbak
Bytom, ul. Kilara 29.
Tel 32 428 13 00.

Studio-Buffo
Warsaw, Konopnickiej 6.
Tel 22 625 47 09.
W studiobuffo.com.pl

Teatr Muzyczny
Poznań, ul. Niezłomnych
1a. Tel 61 852 29 27.
W teatr-muzyczny-poznan.pl

Teatr Wielki
Łódź, pl. Dąbrowskiego 1.
Tel 42 633 31 86.
W operalodz.com

Teatr Wielki-Opera Narodowa
Warsaw, pl. Teatralny 1.
Tel 22 692 02 00.
W teatrwielki.pl

Classical Music

Filharmonia
Krakow, ul. Zwierzyniecka
1. Tel 12 619 87 21.
W filharmonia.krakow.pl

Filharmonia Bałtycka
Gdańsk, ul. Ołowianka 1.
Tel 58 320 62 62.
W filharmonia.gda.pl

Filharmonia Częstochowska
Częstochowa, ul. Wilsona
16. Tel 34 324 42 30.
W filharmonia.com.pl

Filharmonia im. M. Karłowicza
Szczecin, ul. Małopolska
48. Tel 91 430 95 10.
W filharmonia.
szczecin.pl

Filharmonia Łódzka im. A. Rubinsteina
Łódź, Narutowicza 20/22.
Tel 42 664 79 79.
W filharmonia.lodz.pl

Filharmonia Narodowa
Warsaw, ul. Jasna 5.
Tel 22 551 71 11.
W filharmonia.pl

Filharmonia Poznańska
Poznań, ul. św. Marcin 81.
Tel 61 852 47 08.
W filharmonia
poznanska.pl

Filharmonia im. Witolda Lutosławskiego
Wrocław, ul. Piłsudskiego
19. Tel 71 342 20 01.
W nfm.wroclaw.pl

NOSPR
Katowice, plac Wojciecha
Kilara 1. Tel 32 732 53 12.
W nospr.org.pl

Opera Bałtycka
Gdańsk, al. Zwycięstwa 15.
Tel 58 763 49 12.
W operabaltycka.pl

Studio Koncertowe PR im. W. Lutosławskiego
Warsaw, ul.
Modzelewskiego 59.
Tel 22 645 99 17.
W studio
nagran.com.pl

Teatr Muzyczny
Gdynia, pl. Grunwaldzki 1.
Tel 58 661 60 00.
W muzyczny.org

Rock, Jazz and Country Music

Blue Note Club
Poznań, C.K. Zamek, ul.
Kościuszki.
Tel 61 657 07 77.
W bluenote.poznan.pl

Harenda
Warsaw, ul. Krakowskie
Przedmieście 4–6. Tel 22
826 29 00.

Hybrydy
Warsaw, ul. Złota 7/9.
Tel 22 822 30 03.
W hybrydy.com.pl

Jazz Club u Muniaka
Krakow, ul. Floriańska 3.
Tel 12 423 12 05.

Kvadrat
Krakow, ul. Skarzynskiego
1. Tel 12 647 50 78.
W klubkvadrat.pl

PiecArt
Krakow, ul. Szewska 12.
Tel 12 429 16 02.
W piecart.pl

Pod Jaszczurami
Krakow, Rynek Główny 8.
Tel 12 429 45 38.
W podjaszczurami.pl

Stodoła
Warsaw, ul. Batorego 10.
Tel 22 825 60 31.
W stodola.pl

Sport and Leisure

Tourists in Poland are fortunate in the enormous range of open-air activities available to them. The possibilities – which range from strenuous rock climbing and exhilarating skiing at one end of the scale to serene sailing or peaceful walks in forests and rolling hills – are almost endless. Horse riding is very popular as Poland has a centuries-old reputation for its excellent stud farms. There are also lakeside fishing and long canoeing trips (*see pp292–3*). Winter attractions include skiing and ice sailing on the frozen Mazurian Lakes.

The caves in the Jurassic rocks of the Krakow-Częstochowa Upland

A tourist scaling a section of the Tatra Mountains

Rock Climbing

The most difficult and dangerous climbing routes are in the Tatra Mountains. Climbing equipment is available in specialist shops. Although a licence is needed for climbing in the Tatra National Park (*see pp170–71*), climbers have free access to the skałki (rocks) of the Karkonosze Mountains and of the Krakow-Częstochowa Upland (*see pp162–3*).

In areas where there are no mountains, climbers can practise on the concrete walls of early 20th-century fortifications.

Horse Riding

Polish studs have long enjoyed high acclaim for the quality of their horses. Even when they were nationalized under Communist rule, they were highly regarded. Horse riding is once again popular, attracting increasing numbers of enthusiasts. In addition to stables with long-standing traditions, more riding stables, both large and small have been established. While some of these are open to all, others are quite exclusive.

Hiking

Hiking is very popular in Poland. The most attractive areas with beautiful landscapes usually have specially marked hiking routes. Hiking maps are available both in specialist bookshops and in local stores and newsagents. Hikers can rest or stay overnight in tourist hostels, which are numerous in the mountains.

When hiking in the mountains, it is forbidden to stray off the marked track. Hiking can be done independently. Alternatively, it is possible to join a hiking camp. Such camps are organized by travel agencies, usually student ones.

Cycling

It is possible to travel the length and breadth of Poland on a bicycle. However, tourist cycling tracks are not marked, so it is definitely advisable to buy one of the guidebooks for cyclists in Poland before setting out. Narrow, busy roads should be avoided. Cycling in the big cities, such as Warsaw, has gained popularity with the locals and they are increasingly well supplied with cycle lanes.

Hang-Gliding

There are numerous hang-gliding schools in Poland. While some operate throughout the year, others are open only in the tourist season. All the schools have up-to-date, officially approved equipment. There are courses for individuals

Hiking in the foothills of the Tatra Mountains

or small groups. Although hang-gliding is associated with mountains, it is also popular in lowland areas, on the coast or around the lakes.

Sailing and Windsurfing

The lakes and rivers of northern Poland offer endless scope for sailing. Yachts and other boats can be hired from lakeside marinas. A stay in a sailing camp is a popular holiday. The longest and most attractive sailing routes are those on the Great Mazurian Lakes (see pp290–91), the estuary of the Vistula and Szczecin Bay. Windsurfing – on the lakes, the coastal bays and the Baltic Sea, especially around the resort of Łeba – is an increasingly popular sport.

Sailing is a popular summer sport

A windsurfing competition in the Gulf of Gdańsk

Canoeing

The most attractive routes for canoeing trips are in the north of Poland, in the region of the Augustów Canal (see pp292–3), and in the Great Mazurian Lakes district. The most beautiful trips are those along the River Krutynia and on the Western Pomeranian Lakes. Most canoeing trips last from a few days to a fortnight, and travellers usually make overnight stops at campsites. Canoes can be hired at riverside hostels. Route maps are available in specialist bookshops or local stores. For the fit, this is a wonderful way to see the country.

Ice Sailing

The best place in all of Poland for ice sailing is Lake Mamry, one of the Great Mazurian Lakes (see pp290–91). Lake Mamry happens to be one of the coldest lakes in Poland, and in winter, when it is frozen over, it is perfect for ice sailing. International ice-sailing competitions have been held here since the inter-war years.

Skiing

Zakopane (see pp170–71), situated at the foot of the Tatra Mountains, is the winter capital of Poland. There are pistes both for beginners and experienced skiers. The longest and most difficult descents are on Mount Kasprowy, and include the Gąsienicowa run, 9.7 km (6 miles) long, and the Goryczkowa run, 5.25 km (3 miles) long. The skiing season runs from November to March. Pistes on Mount Nosal, 590 m (over 1,900 ft) high, are the most popular. Those on Mount Gubałówka, 1,600 m (5,250 ft) high, are less demanding. Beginners will find many easy pistes in the vicinity of Białka and Bukowina Tatrzańska. There are also many long, perfectly prepared ski runs in Szczyrk Brenna, Wisła and Ustroń in the Beskid Mountains of Silesia, and also in Szklarska Poręba in the Karkonosze Mountains and on the slopes of Mount Śnieżnik. The ski routes down Mount Jaworzyna near Krynica Górska are among the longest in Poland.

Golf

Golf did not become popular in Poland until the late 1980s, and is still regarded as a novel and exclusive sport. Most famous politicians, business people and those with a high profile in the arts frequent the 18-hole golf course at Rajszewo, near Warsaw. The best golf courses are in Pomerania and Warmia.

DIRECTORY

Sporting Organizations

Hang-Gliding Association
Warsaw, ul. Nad Wisłą 4a.
w psp.org.pl

Mountaineering and Rock Climbing
Polish Alpine Association,
Warsaw, ul. Corazziego 5/24.
Tel 50 400 26 10.
w pza.org.pl

Polish Horse Riding Association
Warsaw, ul. Karola Miarki 110.
Tel 22 417 67 00.
w pzj.pl

Sailing
Warsaw, all. ks. J. Poniatowskiego
1. Tel 22 541 63 63.
w pya.org.pl

Skiing
Krakow, ul. Mieszczańska 18/3.
Tel 12 260 99 70.
w pzn.pl

Yachting
Warsaw, Wał Miedzeszyński 377.
Tel 22 617 63 11.
w joomla.ykpwarszawa.pl

SURVIVAL
GUIDE

PRACTICAL INFORMATION

Poland's popularity with visitors has been growing steadily since the mid-1990s, and the country's infrastructure has undergone major changes as a result. Tourist information centres are easy to find, and tourist-friendly signs help visitors navigate their way around the major towns and cities. Credit and debit cards are widely accepted, and Wi-Fi Internet is a common feature of hotels, restaurants and bars.

Railway stations in big cities have been modernized, although those in smaller towns offer only limited facilities. Poland's road network has also undergone a significant overhaul, and there are now a number of motorways linking the major cities. Elsewhere, roads are frequently busy with traffic and quite often poorly surfaced, so travelling around the country by road can be time-consuming.

Relaxing at a café in the Cloth Hall, on Krakow's Main Market Square

When to Go

Poland enjoys warm summers; mild springs and autumns; and cold, dry winters. Spring and summer are frequently hit by rain, so it is wise for visitors to pack waterproof clothing regardless of the season.

Spring and summer draw big crowds to much-visited cities such as Warsaw and Krakow, as well as to the country's coastal, lakeside and mountain resorts. Many cultural institutions, such as theatres and concert halls, tend to close in the summer; however, big museums and galleries are at their busiest at this time. The skiing season runs from the end of November until mid-March.

If you are travelling in peak season, it is a good idea to book accommodation in advance. In spring and autumn, many guesthouses, hotels, clubs and restaurants in popular coastal resorts and lakeside spots are closed.

Visas and Passports

Citizens of countries in the European Union, the USA, Australia, Canada and New Zealand can enter Poland without a visa, on production of a valid passport. Visitors from other countries should check the latest visa regulations with their local Polish embassy. Poland is a member of the Schengen group of European Union countries, which means that there are unlikely to be any border controls when entering Poland from another Schengen-zone country.

Foreign embassies are located in Warsaw, although a few countries also maintain consulates outside the capital (the USA has one in Krakow, for example). Be aware that consulates can help

only with minor problems; if you lose your passport, you will be referred to the embassy in Warsaw.

Travel Safety Advice

Visitors can get up-to-date travel safety information from the **Foreign and Commonwealth Office** in the UK, the **State Department** in the US and the **Department of Foreign Affairs and Trade** in Australia.

Customs Information

If you are travelling to or from another EU country, there are few restrictions on items that can be brought into and taken out of Poland, for personal use.

Visitors from outside the EU should check the customs regulations of their home country – there are likely to be limits on the amount of cigarettes, alcoholic beverages, toiletries and gifts that can be taken home. The maximum value of currency that can be brought into or taken out of

The tourist information centre in Zakopane

Strolling on ulica Floriańska by the Florian Gate, Krakow

Poland, if travelling to or from non-EU countries, is €10,000 (or equivalent). Sums in excess of this must be declared to the customs authority.

You will need a licence to export an item that is more than 100 years old, any artwork that is more than 50 years old and exceeding 16,000zł in value, or anything of cultural importance that exceeds 40,000zł in value. For more information contact the Ministry of Culture and National Heritage (www.mkidn.gov.pl).

Tourist Information

Most major towns and cities in Poland have a tourist information centre on or near the main square, although they will vary in size and usefulness. Most tourist centres have well-informed staff who speak English or one other major language and can provide free leaflets about attractions in the area. Very often they will be able to supply a free map or offer a range of local maps for sale. The telephone numbers and addresses of tourist information centres are listed in the relevant parts of this guidebook.

The **Polish National Tourist Office** has a good multilingual website; several regional tourist office websites also have useful content.

Opening Hours and Admission Prices

Generally, Polish museums are open from Tuesday to Sunday, usually from 9 or 10am to 4 or 5pm. Entrance charges for major museums and big art exhibitions are similar to those in Western Europe, although ticket prices in smaller towns are often quite low. In many institutions, admission is free on one day of the week. Churches in big cities are open from dawn till dusk, although visitors are discouraged from sightseeing during religious services. In small towns and villages, churches are frequently closed during the day, so try to arrive just before or just after Mass; Mass times are usually advertised on the church door. Admission to churches tends to be free.

Sign indicating the direction to a church

Language

In terms of nationality, Poland is a very uniform country, and Polish is spoken everywhere. Polish belongs to the same Slavonic family of languages as Czech, Russian, Ukrainian and others; however, these languages are not always mutually intelligible. Younger Poles are likely to understand English and, as a rule, people who work in the tourist industry speak English very well. German is also widely spoken. Older Poles and staff in banks, post offices and railway stations are less likely to speak English.

It is useful – as well as courteous – for visitors to master at least a few basic words and phrases in Polish (see pp374–6).

Etiquette and Smoking

Poland is one of the most devout Roman Catholic countries in Europe, with most citizens trying to attend Mass at least once a week. Religious holidays are solemnly observed, and the cult of the Virgin Mary is particularly strong. Eastern Poland has a large Orthodox minority, and Poland's Tatar population maintains mosques in a handful of eastern villages and in the city of Gdańsk.

Sightseeing is allowed in churches, but visitors should refrain from making noise and use cameras discreetly. In addition, visitors should dress modestly (no bare arms for women; no summer shorts for men).

Before 1939, there was a Polish Jewish population of over 3 million. The vast majority were murdered by Nazi occupiers during the Holocaust. Today, there are working synagogues in a handful of big cities, while many synagogues in small-town Poland are preserved as museums. Some require visitors to wear a black skullcap; these are available at the entrance.

Smoking is banned from most public places. Almost all restaurants and cafés are totally smoke-free indoors, although smoking is still permitted at the outdoor tables in those establishments that have a pavement terrace or garden. Only a handful of bars and clubs have retained a self-contained indoor area where smoking is allowed.

Access to Public Conveniences

Public conveniences are rare in Poland, although most shopping centres, museum attractions and petrol stations have free toilets. Bus and railway stations have pay-to-use toilets in varying states of cleanliness (usually the bigger the station, the better). Facilities in restaurants and bars are free for guests, except in old-fashioned establishments, where everyone must pay.

Crowds celebrating the annual Equality Parade in Warsaw

Warsaw is the most liberal of Poland's cities, with a handful of gay-friendly hotels and plenty of bars and clubs that have a pronounced gay or lesbian clientele. In Krakow, there is a handful of dedicated gay and lesbian nightlife venues and many more bohemian bars and clubs that welcome everyone.

Travellers with Disabilities

Facilities for the disabled in Poland are improving. All renovated and modern public buildings have ramps or lifts for the convenience of disabled people. An increasing number of trams and buses have low-floor entrances for easy wheelchair access, and in Warsaw and Krakow the electronic departure boards at each public transport stop display symbols indicating which of the approaching vehicles is wheelchair-friendly. Special wheelchair-friendly taxis are also available. Some pedestrian crossings have low kerbs, and the number of those equipped with an audio message for the blind is on the rise. However, moving around in a wheelchair is not always easy on account of the cars parked on pavements. Most shops in cities have wheelchair access.

Travelling with Children

The Polish are a family-oriented people, and they quickly warm to travellers with small children. Many public parks feature play areas, and facilities for kids are improving in all of Poland's major tourist attractions.

In Warsaw, the **Copernicus Centre** is largely devoted to children, with hands-on science experiments for all ages and interactive displays for teenagers. Also

in the capital is the **Frederyk Chopin Museum** *(see p84)*, which has a kids' corner with toys and a touch-screen jukebox. In Krakow, the **Stanisław Lem Garden of Experiences** is an outdoor science park involving lots of opportunities for play.

Gay and Lesbian Travellers

Parking sign for disabled people

Poland is a conservative-minded country in which gay and lesbian communities have not yet met with across-the-board public acceptance. There is an Equality March in Warsaw in June, and a Tolerance march in Krakow in April/May; however, both events are sometimes met with counter-demonstrations organized by right-wing groups opposed to gay rights.

Travelling on a Budget

Young visitors and students travelling to Poland can enjoy great benefits by applying for international youth and student cards prior to their trip. The **ISIC** (International Student Identity Card) and the **European Youth Card**, for example, entitle holders to reduced rates in museums, tourist attractions and inter-city buses, as well as to discounts at a wide range of businesses throughout Poland, from hostels and car hire firms to restaurants and entertainment venues. The businesses offering discounts display the logos of the cards in their windows.

An ISIC card is available to anyone who is either a full-time student or under the age of 26. It can be purchased in your home country or through youth tourism specialist **Almatur**, which has offices in most major Polish cities, providing you have documentary evidence of your status. The European Youth Card is available to anyone under the age of 30 and can be bought from numerous outlets throughout Europe or online via the European Youth Card website.

The Copernicus Centre, where the science exhibits will appeal to both children and adults

Time

Poland is in the Central European Time zone, which is 1 hour ahead of Greenwich Mean Time, 6 hours ahead of US Eastern Standard Time and 11 hours behind Australian Eastern Standard Time. Summer time, 2 hours ahead of Greenwich Mean Time, applies from late March to late October.

Electrical Appliances

In Poland, the electric voltage is 220 V. Plugs are of the two-pin type, as is the case in most continental European countries. It is wise to purchase a European travel adaptor in your own country before you leave for Poland.

Responsible Tourism

Green issues have made little impact on Poland as a whole. A handful of hostels advertise themselves as eco-friendly, and there are moves to promote rural B&B tourism under the "ecotourism" banner, but green policies are still in their infancy here.

Travelling responsibly is largely a matter of common sense. Eating in chain restaurants or fast-food outlets increases the likelihood that you will be consuming cheaply supplied products that have not come from ecologically sound sources. When shopping for food, head for an outdoor market. Stall-holders at Krakow's **Stary Kleparz** market (held Mon–Sat) or Warsaw's **Hala Mirowska** market (held daily) are far more likely to sell seasonal produce of local provenance than large supermarkets. **BioBazar** is an organic farmers' market held in Warsaw every Saturday.

Instead of relying on the plastic bags offered by Polish shops, take your own multiple-use bag. When disposing of rubbish, ask locals to direct you to the nearest recycling points. These usually offer bins for paper, glass and plastics.

Fresh produce on sale at the Stary Kleparz market, Krakow

DIRECTORY

Embassies and Consulates

Australia
ul. Nowogrodzka 11, Warsaw. **Tel** 22 521 34 44.
🌐 australia.pl

Canada
ul. Matejki 1/5, Warsaw.
Tel 22 584 31 00.
🌐 canada.pl

Ireland
ul. Mysia 5, Warsaw.
Tel 22 849 66 33.
🌐 dfa.ie/irish-embassy/poland

New Zealand
al. Ujazdowskie 51, Warsaw.
Tel 22 521 05 00.
🌐 mfat.gov.nz

United Kingdom
ul. Kawalerii 12, Warsaw.
Tel 22 311 00 00.
🌐 gov.uk/government/world/poland

United States
al. Ujazdowskie 29/31, Warsaw. **Tel** 22 504 20 00.
🌐 poland.usembassy.gov

Travel Safety Advice

Australia
Department of Foreign Affairs and Trade.
🌐 dfat.gov.au/smartraveller.gov.au/

UK
Foreign and Commonwealth Office.
🌐 gov.uk/foreign-travel-advice

US
US Department of State.
🌐 travel.state.gov

Tourist Information

Polish National Tourist Office
🌐 poland.travel

Gdańsk
Długi Targ 28/29.
Tel 58 301 43 55.
🌐 visitgdansk.pl

Krakow
Pawilon Wyspiańskiego pl. Wszystkich Świętych 2.
Tel 12 354 27 23.
🌐 krakow-info.com

Poznań
Stary Rynek 59/60.
Tel 61 852 61 56.
🌐 cim.poznan.pl

Warsaw
PKiN (Palace of Culture & Science), pl. Defilad 1.
Map 3 A1/B1. **Tel** 22 194 31. 🌐 warsawtour.pl

Wrocław
Rynek 14. **Tel** 71 344 31 11. 🌐 wroclaw-info.pl

Travelling with Children

Copernicus Centre
Wybrzeże Kościuszkowskie 20, Warsaw.
Tel 22 596 41 00.
🌐 kopernik.org.pl

Stanisław Lem Garden of Experiences
Aleja pokoju, Krakow.
Tel 12 346 1285.
🌐 ogroddoswiadczen.pl

Travelling on a Budget

Almatur
Warsaw: ul. Kopernika 23.
Tel 22 826 26 39.

Gdańsk:
al. Grunwaldzka 140.
Tel 58 301 29 31.
Krakow: Rynek Główny 27.
Tel 12 422 46 68.
Poznań: ul. Ratajczaka 8.
Tel 61 855 76 33.
Wrocław: al. Armii Krajowej 12a. **Tel** 71 343 41 35.
🌐 almatur.pl

European Youth Card
🌐 eyca.pl

ISIC
🌐 isic.org

Responsible Travel

BioBazar
ul. Żelazna 51/53, Warsaw.

Hala Mirowska
pl. Mirowski 1, Warsaw.

Stary Kleparz
Rynek Kleparski, Krakow.

Personal Security and Health

Poland is a relatively problem-free country in which to travel, and visitors are unlikely to encounter any trouble providing they take the usual precautions against petty crime. Pharmacies are stocked with well-known remedies, so minor cases of ill health are easily dealt with. Polish hospitals are not as well equipped as their Western European counterparts, but staff are just as highly trained. Basic hospital care is free for citizens of EU countries, although specialized or private treatment can be expensive. Visitors are advised to take out travel insurance before embarking on their trip.

A typical Polish police car, silver with a navy-blue band

Police

Security in Poland is provided by several different forces. The state police are armed and have the right to arrest suspects. Policemen patrol streets on foot or in navy-blue-and-silver cars. In many Polish cities the regular police force is augmented by the Municipal Watch (Straż Miejska), who are unarmed, and have no power of arrest but still perform an important street-patrolling function. There are also private security agencies, which are generally responsible for security in large shops and public buildings, as well as during public events. They are usually uniformed and should always carry identification badges.

Traffic wardens are mainly concerned with the enforcement of parking and traffic regulations. They wear different uniforms from town to town, and their cars carry plates bearing the town emblem.

The highway police are responsible for traffic offences. Anyone found driving a car, motorcycle or bicycle with over 0.02 per cent of alcohol (equivalent to half a glass of wine) in their blood will be subjected to a spot fine or arrested. In the event of a serious road accident, you are required by law to call an ambulance and the fire brigade. You are also required to contact the traffic police.

Police sign

What to Be Aware Of

Poland is generally a law-abiding country, but visitors should exercise a common-sense level of caution when in big cities and busy areas. Crowded bars,

Two policemen patrolling the streets of Krakow

public transport, major railway stations and busy markets are the places where pickpockets are most active. Keep an eye on your bag or rucksack, and carry it in a safe way. Do not put your passport, wallet and other valuables in a back pocket or the external pockets of a rucksack. Pickpockets frequently operate in gangs, and a sudden push or other such tactic intended to distract you is hardly ever accidental. If possible, leave your valuables in the safe of your hotel.

Car break-ins are common, and valuables should never be left unattended in the car. You may save your windows from being smashed by removing the radio and taking it with you. A number of guarded car parks are available in city centres, and it might be wise to use them.

Few Polish cities have no-go areas, although visitors are advised to avoid badly lit neighbourhoods of suburban Warsaw and to take taxis home from outlying nightlife destinations rather than walking. Polish cities that are popular with young weekend tourists (notably Krakow) are prone to over-charging, so avoid the tourist-trap bars and clubs. Male visitors travelling alone or in small groups should be wary of overfriendly young females suggesting a drink in a nearby bar – a hugely inflated bill will probably be the result. Late-night noisy behaviour in Krakow and other party cities is frequent, but outright public disorder is actually very rare.

Football hooliganism is not unknown in Poland. Although violence sometimes flares up at matches, tourists are unlikely to be involved.

In an Emergency

Call 112 for emergencies requiring medical, police or fire services. Ambulance services are on call day and night.

Minor health problems can often be dealt with in

a pharmacy. For more serious injury or illness, when an ambulance is not required, head for the casualty department of one of the big city hospitals.

Lost and Stolen Property

If you lose something in a café, restaurant or museum in Poland, there is a good chance that the staff will keep it for a day or two in the expectation that you will return. It is a good idea to write your phone number inside bags and wallets – in the event of loss, a good citizen or a policeman may well call to inform you that it has been found.

If you lose property on the Warsaw public transport system, call 022 663 32 97 (for trams), 022 655 42 42 (metro) or 022 699 71 95 (suburban trains). Items left on planes, inter-city trains or buses will be kept at lost property offices at the airport, railway station and bus station respectively. There are two lost property offices in Krakow – one for items lost on public transport (MPK Transport Office, ul. Brożka 3, Tel 12 254 11 50), and one for items misplaced elsewhere in the city (Biuro Rzeczy Znalezionych, ul. Wielicka 28, Tel 12 616 57 13). There is one municipal lost property office in Warsaw (ul. Dzielna 15, Tel 22 443 29 61). For any stolen items, contact the police.

Hospitals and Pharmacies

Both state and private health care are available in Poland. Staff are highly trained and professional in both sectors, though private hospitals are more likely to have up-to-date equipment. In the state sector, first aid is provided free of charge, but other treat-

The old-fashioned façade of a pharmacy in Krakow

ment may be subject to a fee, which is often required in advance, along with a passport for identification.

Treatment for minor ailments is available at pharmacies, where helpful trained staff can provide advice on remedies. Polish pharmacies stock all kinds of international over-the-counter medicines.

Travel and Health Insurance

Travel insurance that includes provision for health care is highly recommended. The longer you stay abroad, the more important it is to ensure that you have substantial health cover. Many airlines and travel agents offer insurance when you book your holiday. **World Nomads** is a reputable service that offers travel insurance to citizens of 150 countries.

EU nationals are entitled to state health care in Poland on production of a valid **European Health Insurance Card** (EHIC). In the UK, this can be obtained from a post office or online. A booklet details what health care

you are entitled to, and where and how to claim. You may still have to pay in advance to obtain treatment and claim the money back later. As not all treatments are covered, it is advisable to take out additional health insurance; you must keep official medical reports and receipts in order to recoup the costs of treatment.

Make sure you travel with all relevant insurance documents. Keep a copy in your hotel room or with a reliable family member back home.

DIRECTORY

In an Emergency

Ambulance, Police and Fire
Tel 112.

Hospitals and 24-Hour Pharmacies

Gdańsk
Apteka Dr Max
Podwale Grodzkie.
Tel 58 778 92 13.

Krakow
Szpital im. Gabriela Narutowicza
ul. Prądnicka 35.
Tel 12 416 22 66.

Apteka Pod Opatrznością
Karmelicka 23.
Tel 12 631 19 80.

Warsaw
Apteka Beata
al. Solidarności 149.
Tel 22 620 08 18.
Also: Warszawa Centralna
train station

Medicover
al. Rzeczypospolitej 5.
Tel 500 900 999.
w medicover.pl

Travel and Health Insurance

European Health Insurance Card
For UK residents:
w ehic.org.uk
For Irish residents:
w ehic.ie

World Nomads
w worldnomads.com

An ambulance with flashing blue lights

Banking and Currency

Financial transactions are easy in Poland. ATMs taking all major cards can be found in cities and towns throughout the country. Bureaux de change frequently offer more favourable exchange rates than the banks, and they can be found near railway stations, in city centres and at most tourist destinations. Credit and debit cards are accepted by most shops and restaurants, especially in the main cities. Signs displayed by the entrance to the establishment indicate which cards are accepted.

Automated teller machine (ATM) for cash withdrawal

Banks and Bureaux de Change

Banks are located in most Polish town centres. In the bigger cities, they can also be found in outlying residential areas. Banks generally open at 9 or 10am and close at 5 or 6pm. Banks are busy, and you should expect queues. At some branches, you have to take a numbered ticket at the entrance and wait until the number is displayed on a screen before approaching the counter. Most banks have their own exchange service, but better rates are offered by independent bureaux de change (kantor), which do not charge commission. Most banks cash traveller's cheques, but the process can be time-consuming. Foreign currency can also be changed at hotels (some have a 24-hour service), but rates are usually poor.

Big Polish banks with numerous branches around the country include **PKO Bank** (Bank Polski) and **Bank Pekao**. International banks with branches in Poland include ING, Deutsche Bank and Raiffeisen-Polbank.

ATMs

ATMs (bankomat) can be found outside most banks, as well as in shopping centres, airports, and railway and bus stations. Instructions are usually available in Polish and English plus two or three other major languages. Symbols indicating which cards can be used will be displayed on the machine. Check these carefully – most ATMs accept all cards belonging to the VISA and Maestro/MasterCard families, but a small number do not.

ATM withdrawals will be marginally more expensive than changing cash, the exchange rate is fractionally less advantageous, and a small fee will be added by your bank for each ATM transaction carried out when abroad. The maximum amount of cash you can withdraw in one day will be fixed by your bank at home; check this before you travel.

Be aware of your surroundings when using an ATM. Make sure you shield your PIN and be careful when removing your card.

Credit and Debit Cards

Credit and debit cards are accepted in hotels, car rental outlets, larger railway stations, big museums, most city centre shops, most restaurants and many cafés and bars. Cards are unlikely to be accepted in markets, suburban railway stations and in smaller establishments in suburban areas or country villages so it is a good idea to carry a small amount of Polish cash with you. Owners of rural B&Bs frequently take cash only. Establishments usually indicate which cards they accept by displaying the appropriate stickers in their windows.

It is advisable to notify your bank before you travel so that they expect your card to be used in Poland.

DIRECTORY

Banks

Bank Pekao
Krakow: Rynek Główny 31.
Gdańsk: Garncarska 23.
Poznań: ul. Święty Marcin 52/56.
Warsaw: al. Jerozolimskie 44.

PKO Bank
Krakow: Starowiślna 22.
Krakow: Rynek Główny 21.
Warsaw: Nowogrodzka 35/41.
Wrocław: Wita Stwosza 33/35.

Bureaux de Change

777
al. Jerozolimskie 65/7, Warsaw.
Tel 22 630 51 07.
W 777.com.pl

Euro-Kantor
Szewska 21, Krakow.
Tel 12 421 55 65.

Kantor Dime
Krakowskie Przedmieście 41, Warsaw.
Tel 22 828 44 83.
W dime.com.pl

Kantor Exchange
ul. Pawia 12, Krakow.
Tel 12 430 33 33.

The entrance to a branch of PKO Bank (Bank Polski) in Warsaw

Currency

The Polish unit of currency is the złoty, a term that literally means "golden" and that dates back to the Middle Ages, when gold pieces were used. Złoty is most commonly abbreviated to zł, although you will see the abbreviation PLN in banks and on your credit card statement. One złoty is made up of 100 groszy (gr). Polish coins come in denominations of 1, 2, 5, 10, 20 and 50 gr and 1, 2 and 5 zł. Bank notes come in denominations of 10, 20, 50, 100 and 200 zł. Each bank note bears the portrait of a Polish king.

10 złoty

20 złoty

50 złoty

100 złoty

200 złoty

Banknotes

Polish banknotes are issued in denominations of 10, 20, 50, 100 and 200 zł. All bear the portrait of Polish rulers and are embossed to make them recognizable to blind people. In addition to standard protection against fraud, the 100- and 200-zł notes are also marked with holograms.

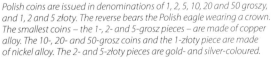

5 złoty 2 złoty 1 złoty 50 groszy

Coins

Polish coins are issued in denominations of 1, 2, 5, 10, 20 and 50 groszy, and 1, 2 and 5 złoty. The reverse bears the Polish eagle wearing a crown. The smallest coins – the 1-, 2- and 5-grosz pieces – are made of copper alloy. The 10-, 20- and 50-grosz coins and the 1-złoty piece are made of nickel alloy. The 2- and 5-złoty pieces are gold- and silver-coloured.

20 groszy

10 groszy 5 groszy 2 groszy 1 grosz

Communications and Media

The main telephone service is provided by Telekomunikacja Polska (TP), although there are several mobile phone operators such as Plus, Orange and T-Mobile. Card-operated public telephones can be found in town centres but are increasingly rare elsewhere. Some phone booths are wheelchair-accessible. Many hotels and cafés offer free Wi-Fi access to their guests. International newspapers and magazines are widely available, and most hotel rooms have cable TV. There is no shortage of post offices, which are run by Poczta Polska.

International and Local Telephone Calls

For EU and UK residents who have a mobile phone it is easy and cheap to make calls in Poland because of the abolishment of international roaming charges. Otherwise, to make a telephone call in Poland, you may choose to use a public telephone or go through the operator service at the post office. Note that calling from your hotel room will work out much more expensive, so it is better to find a public telephone at the hotel or in its vicinity.

The vast majority of public phones are card-operated. Telephone cards (karty telefoniczne) can be bought from newsagents and post offices. It is possible to find 15-, 30- and 60-unit cards. A local call will only use up a few units of a phone card, but for long-distance calls the highest-value card is a much better option.

Mobile Phones

Most European mobile phones will function perfectly well in Poland. However, mobile phones supplied by providers in the US may have only limited global coverage. Contact your service provider prior to your trip for details.

To use your mobile phone abroad, you will need to check with your provider that roaming has been enabled. Remember that you will be charged for the calls you receive as well as for the calls you make, and that you may have to pay a substantial premium for the international leg of the call.

Public telephone

To limit the cost of using a mobile phone while in Poland, you could purchase a SIM card that uses a local mobile network and top it up as you go. You can do this only if your handset is unlocked – ask your network provider for advice.

If you are using a smart phone, be aware that charges for data roaming can be high. If you want to make and receive calls while abroad but do not wish to be charged for use of the Internet or other data, it is possible to switch off the data roaming setting for the duration of your stay and continue using the telephone functions as normal.

Public Telephones

With so many Poles now using mobile phones, public telephones are less commonplace than they used to be. However, they can still be found around town centres and near railway and bus stations.

To make a telephone call, lift the receiver and wait for a continuous dialling tone. Insert a telephone card when the words włóż kartę ("insert card") are displayed. The screen will indicate the amount of credit (kredyt) available. Dial the number you wish to reach, and await connection. Note that a short, rapidly repeating tone indicates that the number is engaged. When you have finished the call, simply replace the receiver and remove the ejected card.

Internet Access

If you are travelling to Poland with a laptop or a smart phone, there are numerous opportunities to log on to the Internet for little or no cost. Most hotels, cafés and bars provide Wi-Fi access for their guests. Some places charge for Wi-Fi use, but in most cases it is free. Establishments that offer Wi-Fi access will display a Wi-Fi sticker in the window. Free Wi-Fi zones can be found in many Polish cities, frequently in the main square.

For those who are travelling without a Wi-Fi-enabled device, most hotels and hostels have a computer terminal in the lobby that can be used by guests. In addition, most Polish towns have at least one Internet café (kafejka Internetowa), offering reasonable rates (around 10zł/hour) for Internet use.

Useful dialling codes and numbers

- For national (Polish) directory enquiries, dial 118 913.
- For international directory enquiries, dial 118 912.
- To call overseas, dial 0 and wait for the tone; dial 0 again, followed by the country code and the area code (omitting the initial 0) and the subscriber's number.
- Country codes: UK 44; Canada and USA 1; Eire 353; Australia 61; South Africa 27; New Zealand 64.

People using the Internet at a Krakow bar

Postal Services

Post offices are usually prominently located in city centres and town squares. In the bigger cities, there are also branches throughout the suburbs. Post office opening hours are usually 8am–6pm Monday to Friday. In major cities there is often a main post office that keeps slightly longer hours (including Saturday mornings). There are also 24-hour branches in Warsaw (see Directory) and Krakow (ul. Lubicz 4).

Post box

At post offices you can buy stamps, send telegrams and parcels, and arrange international money transfers. A poste restante (mail holding) service is also available. Stamps can also be purchased from selected newsagents.

Inland letters are delivered within 2 to 3 days, but international mail takes about a week. Letters and cards sent by express service will arrive sooner. Courier services – available from the larger post office branches, as well as from **DHL** and other courier companies – are the fastest but are very expensive.

Newspapers and Magazines

Foreign newspapers and magazines are available from the larger newsagents and bookshops in Poland's major cities. The biggest choice is available from the **EMPiK**

chain of multimedia stores. Most branches of EMPiK will stock international fashion and lifestyle magazines, as well as a full range of Polish-language publications.

The most important locally produced English-language titles are the travel and lifestyle monthly Warsaw Insider, the news-oriented Warsaw Voice (an internet magazine published as a paper edition four times a year), and the monthly economics and finance-related Warsaw Business Journal. In Krakow, the monthly now internet-only Krakow Post is a good source of local news and views.

Television

Most hotel rooms will have a TV offering a handful of Polish-language stations and a choice of German-, English-, Italian-

A newspaper stand in Gdańsk

and French-language stations. News channels like CNN or BBC are more common than entertainment or film channels. Polish TV stations broadcast a lot of English-language films and drama, although these are usually dubbed into Polish or are narrated by just one person.

DIRECTORY

Internet Cafés

Gdańsk
Jazz 'n' Java
Tkacka 17/18. **Tel** 58 305 36 16.

Krakow
Garinet
ul. Floriańska 18.
Tel 12 423 22 33. **W** garinet.pl
Hetmańska
Bracka 4.
Tel 12 430 01 08.
W hetmanska24.com

Warsaw
N22
Aleje Jerozolimskie 54, lok. 22
(in Warsaw Central train station).
Tel 22 474 10 18.

Wroclaw
N22
Czaterówka, ul. Szewska 75.
Tel 609 578 334.
W czaterowka.za.pl

Postal Services

DHL
Tel 634 53 45.
W dhl.com.pl
Krakow
Main Post Office
Westerplatte 20.

Warsaw
Main Post Office
ul. Świętokrzyska 31/33.

Newspapers and Magazines

EMPiK
Warsaw, ul. Marszałkowska 116/122.
Krakow, ul. Floriańska 14.
W empik.com

Krakow Post
W krakowpost.pl

Warsaw Business Journal
W wbj.pl

Warsaw Insider
W warsawinsider.pl

Warsaw Voice
W warsawvoice.pl

TRAVEL INFORMATION

Most main Polish cities have international airports, and every region in the country can be reached by air. The flexibility offered by budget airlines makes it easy to enter the country at one airport and leave it from another, enabling visitors to travel around more. Coaches from the UK and Western Europe run to virtually every Polish city; car ferries are a good way of approaching from Scandinavia and northern Germany. Poland's rail network is extensive, but station infrastructure and train carriages are in various states of modernization. Polish roads are of mixed quality; modern highways link several cities, but slow, traffic-clogged roads are more common.

Arriving by Air

Poland is well connected with the rest of the world. As well as major airports, such as Warsaw's **Chopin Airport** and Krakow's **John Paul II Airport**, there are international airports at Katowice, Gdańsk, Poznań, Łódź, Wrocław, Szczecin, Bydgoszcz, Olsztyn, Lublin and Rzeszów. Many of these are served by budget airlines from the UK and Western Europe.

The national carrier **LOT** operates direct flights to Warsaw and Krakow from the UK and North America. **British Airways**, **Lufthansa**, **Air France** and **Austrian Airlines** also fly to Warsaw from their home countries, providing useful connections for travellers starting out in South Africa, Australasia or the Far East. Low-cost airlines – **easyJet**, **Wizz Air**, **Ryanair**, **Jet2** and **Eurowings** – offer a wide choice of flights to Poland's international airports from the UK and many Western European cities.

Domestic flights linking Warsaw with provincial Polish cities are operated by LOT; Ryanair and LOT offer internal flights linking the main cities – and without the need to change planes in Warsaw.

Warsaw Airport

Warsaw has two international airports: Warsaw Chopin Airport, at Okęcie, 6 km (4 miles) north of the city centre and **Modlin Airport**, 40km north of Warsaw near Nowy Dwór Mazowiecki. The majority of international flights are handled by Warsaw Chopin, which has just one terminal, Terminal A, which handles both domestic and international flights. Confusingly, the check-in areas within the terminal are also designated by letter: A, B, C, D and E. Terminal A offers ATMs, a restaurant, cafés, car hire desks and a tourist information office.

A railway station beneath Terminal A links the airport to Warsaw city centre. Local trains run by Koleje Mazowieckie travel to Warsaw Central Station (20 minutes). Municipal train

Logo of LOT, the Polish national airline

company SKM operates two services: S2 to Warszawa Zachodnia (Warsaw West) and S3 to Warszawa Śródmieście (next to Warsaw Central Station) and Warszawa Wschodnia (Warsaw East). Both companies accept all public transport tickets, including single fare, short-term and unlimited ride. Tickets can be purchased from newsstands and ticket machines at the station.

There are also bus services between the airport and the city centre. Route 175 runs past Warsaw Central Station and then along Krakowskie Przedmieście to the Old Town, while route 188 goes to Praga Południe, on the eastern side of the Vistula river. Tickets can be bought at newsagents in town and at the airport, or from the bus driver – although in this case the exact fare, plus a handling charge, is required.

Taxi services also run to and from the Warsaw Chopin and cost about 60zł. Shuttle buses run by Modlinbus connects Warsaw Modlin airport to the center. The buses run to and from plac Defilad, in front of the Palace of Culture and Science.

Krakow Airport

Situated 15 km (9 miles) west of the city centre, Krakow-Balice John Paul II Airport is modern and easy to get around. ATMs and car hire desks are in the arrivals hall.

The airport is connected to Krakow's main railway station (Kraków Główny) by train every half-hour between about 5am and 11pm. The journey takes 20 minutes. Tickets (10zł) can be bought from the conductor on

The modern exterior of Chopin Airport, Warsaw

The check-in area at Krakow-Balice John Paul II Airport

board. The airport railway station is 200 m (220 yards) from the international terminal. Follow the signs, or wait for the shuttle bus that departs every 10–15 minutes.

Two daytime bus routes (Nos. 208 and 292) link the airport to the main railway station (a journey time of 40 minutes), running through parts of western Krakow, where several hotels are situated. Between 11pm and 5am, night bus No. 902 makes the same journey.

The taxi journey into town takes 20–30 minutes and costs about 50zł (expect to pay more at night and weekends).

Other Airports

Airports at Bydgoszcz, Gdańsk, Katowice, Łódź, Poznań, Szczecin, Rzeszów, Olsztyn, Lublin and Wrocław all receive flights from the UK and Western Europe, mostly run by budget airlines.

Gdańsk, Łódź, Poznań, Lublin and Wrocław are popular city-break destinations; Bydgoszcz is close to the medieval city of Toruń; and Katowice is a convenient gateway to south-central Poland. Szczecin is a good entry point for the Baltic coast, and Rzeszów is a great springboard to the mountains of the rural southeast.

Gdańsk, Poznań and Wrocław airports are close to their respective cities and have good bus links. Szczecin, Katowice and Rzeszów are a bit further out, and connecting buses are less frequent.

Tickets and Fares

Prices vary greatly depending on the time of year and how far in advance you book. The peak

periods are Easter, June–August, and the winter festive season. Tickets booked direct from the airline's website a month or more in advance are generally cheaper than tickets booked through travel agents or tickets booked near to your date of travel.

Low-cost airlines should be your first port of call if you are looking for inexpensive deals. Be aware, however, that these airlines usually charge extra for each item of hold luggage and add booking fees dependent on what kind of credit or debit card you use, driving up costs considerably.

Most airlines offer reductions for children under 12. Children under 2 years old usually travel free, providing they occupy the same seat as the accompanying parent.

Arriving by Sea

The ports of **Świnoujście** and **Gdynia** have connections with northern Germany and Scandinavia. **Stena Line** operates a service to Gdynia from Karlskrona in Sweden; **Polferries** links **Gdańsk** with Nynäshamn, near Sweden's capital Stockholm and Świnoujście with Ystadt, in southern Sweden.

For information on fares, visit the relevant website.

A POL ferry approaching the port of Gdańsk

Travelling by Train

Poland's rail network is comprehensive and links all major towns and cities. Many big-city railway stations are fully modernized and feature clear, traveller-friendly signage. A lot of stations in provincial Poland, however, lack modern facilities and information displays. Trains are run by a confusing number of different operators, but the process of buying tickets is simple once you know where and when you want to go. Most Polish cities are now linked by stretches of high-speed track served by modern pendolino trains. Be prepared however for slow journey times in provincial areas.

The swift and comfortable InterCity train arriving at the platform

Arriving by Train

Train services run between all major European and Polish cities. It is possible to travel from London to Warsaw with Eurostar (changing at Brussels and Cologne) in 18 hours, and from Paris (changing in Cologne) in about 16. From Berlin there are fast trains to Poznań, Warsaw, Wrocław and Krakow. Vienna offers direct services to Katowice and Warsaw, and Budapest offers one daily train to Warsaw and one overnight train to Krakow. From the east, there are frequent overnight trains from Moscow to Warsaw and from Kiev to Krakow.

Trains

Most express inter-city trains, including InterCity and TLK services, are run by **PKP**. A number of other express and fast trains, such as InterRegio, RegioExpress and RegioPlus, are operated by **Przewozy Regionalne**. This company also runs the Regio trains, slow services that stop every station. Suburban trains in the Warsaw region are run by Koleje Mazowieckie, while fast city trains in Warsaw (SKM) are operated by the municipal transport authority (ZTM). The SKM suburban train is the main link between the coastal settlements of the Tri-City (Gdańsk, Sopot and Gdynia).

PKP's InterCity trains provide the fastest and most comfortable way to travel, with first- and second-class seating. Seat reservations are obligatory and can be made at the time of purchasing the ticket. TLK, InterRegio, RegioExpress and RegioPlus trains are not as fast as the InterCity (and InterRegio only offers second-class seating), but they are cheaper and allow the transport of bicycles.

PKP InterCity services offer a complimentary hot drink and a snack, and they also have a buffet car and trolley service. Other trains do not always provide a buffet car, so you are advised to buy refreshments before boarding.

PKP InterCity trains are modern and comfortable, but carriage quality gets worse the further down the scale you go. Toilets on all but express trains are usually in bad shape.

Tickets

In many big city stations there are separate ticket counters for inter-city trains and regional trains (the PKP Intercity logo, displayed on the ticket window, often means that only Intercity and TLK tickets can be bought there). In smaller stations however ticket windows sell tickets for all trains, regardless of the operator. However, tickets for one operator will not be valid on another operator's train; always state clearly which service you want.

Fares on TLK and Regio trains are reasonable, while the PKP InterCity is much more expensive due to the extra speed and comfort provided. A one-way ticket on the Warsaw–Krakow PKP InterCity (a trip of just under three hours) costs 150zł; the same trip on an InterRegio train takes 3 hours 15 minutes and costs 70zł. Teenagers and students up to the age of 26 who hold valid student cards are entitled to reduced fares (see p336).

Queues for tickets are often long, so arrive early or book your tickets the day before.

Credit and debit cards can be used to pay for tickets in big-city stations but not in small towns and villages. If you are unable to buy a ticket in the station, report to the conductor upon boarding the train and buy one from him. An additional handling fee will be charged.

Sleepers and Couchettes

Couchettes and sleeping cars are provided on trains that travel overnight between the extreme north of Poland and the far south. A sleeping car has two or four beds in each compartment. A couchette usually has six beds that can be folded down during the day to form benches. Tickets for domestic sleepers and couchettes can be bought from all mainline stations. It is wise to book them a few days in advance. Sleepers and couchettes on international trains can be booked from the international ticket counter at railway stations.

Passengers at the ultra modern Wroclaw Train Station

Railway Stations

In the larger cities, stations feature easy-to-read displays with information and train times, and there are lifts for the disabled. Elsewhere in Poland, unmodernized stations can often be disorienting, with confusing signage and electronic display boards that don't work.

Train stations are badly lit at night and signs may be illegible, so be extra careful not to miss your stop.

Train Information

Arrivals (przyjazdy) and departures (odjazdy) are clearly listed in the ticket hall of each station – arrivals on a white background, departures on yellow. The type of train and the train operator are also clearly marked. Trains marked with the letter R require seat reservations. Online timetables provided by **PKP** and **Deutsche Bahn** are excellent sources of information.

Left Luggage

There is a charge for the left luggage service – often a kind of insurance, the price being dependent on the declared value of the luggage. Travellers should, of course, make sure that their luggage is fully insured before travelling to Poland.

The larger stations have a system of coin-operated luggage lockers.

DIRECTORY

Trains

PKP
🆆 intercity.pl

Przewozy Regionalne
🆆 polregio.pl

Train Information

Deutsche Bahn
🆆 bahn.de

PKP
🆆 rozklad-pkp.pl

The Polish Railway Network

Key

— Main route

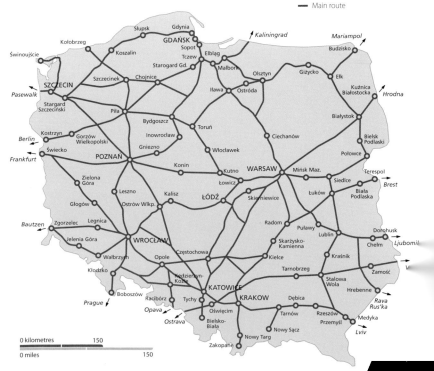

0 kilometres 150

0 miles 150

Travelling by Coach or Bus

Poland's coach and bus network offers comprehensive coverage of the country, and it is particularly useful in rural areas not reached by the railways. Inter-city coaches run between major centres on good roads, and they are a viable alternative to express trains. Comfort in buses varies enormously, with modern, air-conditioned coaches increasingly common on the inter-city routes, and old vehicles with sagging seats operating in rural areas.

The modern interior of the bus station in Krakow

Arriving by Coach

Most European countries have coach connections with Poland's major towns and cities. Often (especially if travelling from the UK or Western Europe), coach travel involves an overnight journey, which can be uncomfortable. Regular stops ensure that you can stretch your legs, but a good night's sleep is probably out of the question. Poland itself is a big country, and if you are aiming for a city in central or eastern Poland, the journey from Western Europe can be gruelling indeed. However, travelling by coach is usually much cheaper than travelling by air or rail.

Eurolines offers routes from all major European cities. International coach tickets can also be bought from Polish agencies **Jordan** and **Sindbad**.

ch Stations

stations in Poland vary
- Krakow, for instance,
dern, well-signposted
vhile many other
old-fashioned, badly
ome have good

websites providing departure information; others have barely decipherable timetable boards that may not even be properly updated.

The central bus station in Warsaw, linked via a pedestrian tunnel to the Warszawa Zachodnia (Warsaw West) railway station, can be difficult to navigate, since the train platforms that take you into central Warsaw are badly signposted. Other bus stations are nearer their respective city centres, which may be only a walk or a short bus or tram ride away. Many are next door to a railway station, allowing easy onward travel. Krakow bus station is linked to the main railway station's platforms by underground tunnel, and it is only a ten-minute walk from the main square.

Most city coach stations have pay-to-use toilets, a left-luggage office, newsagents, simple cafés and an ATM. The smaller the town, the less likely it is that these facilities will be available. The central bus station in Warsaw is poorly equipped with traveller facilities and has limited eating

Buses parked outside Warsaw's coach park

and drinking opportunities, so buy food and drinks before setting out.

Bus timetables are extraordinarily complicated, with a huge array of symbols denoting when the bus runs (such as weekends or holidays). Fast (*pospieszny*) buses, which carry a small supplement, are marked in red; the slow ones are in black.

Tickets should be bought in advance from the ticket counter. Ticket clerks in Krakow and other cities popular with tourists are likely to speak English, but staff outside these areas do not always speak foreign languages; write down your required destination and departure time on a piece of paper to avoid misunderstandings. Bus station ticket counters are unlikely to accept debit or credit cards.

A coach parked outside the bus station at Szczecin

The vibrant livery of PolskiBus

Coaches

Coach travel in Poland used to be run by the state-owned PKS organization. This has now been fragmented into regional companies, many of which still use the initials PKS in their name. There are also many private coach companies running a multitude of both inter-city and rural services. The bigger firms running popular routes are likely to have modern, air-conditioned coaches, although coach quality can be unpredictable whatever route you are travelling on. Some companies (such as PKS Poznań and PKS Białystok) are introducing fast luxury coaches with free Wi-Fi on their much-patronized Warsaw-bound routes. Tickets can be purchased online from the operator's website, at the coach terminal or from a travel agent.

PolskiBus, the coach equivalent of a budget airline, sells inter-city tickets cheaply over the Internet. PolskiBus coaches have free Wi-Fi, but sometimes pick up and drop off in suburban car parks rather than main bus stations. **Dworzec Autobusowy w Krakowie (MDA)** provides coach timetable information in Krakow.

Local Buses

Buses are frequently the only means of travelling to small towns and villages not included on the Polish railway network. Rural bus services are very reliable and punctual, but the buses themselves are often old and uncomfortable. Tickets are available from the driver. Be aware that before 8am and in the afternoon, local buses may be crowded. When planning to visit a small town or village, it is best to check local bus connections in advance, since timetables at more remote bus stops are often vandalized and unreadable. Tourist offices are frequently the best sources of timetable information in small towns.

Minibuses

Minibus services providing both long- and short-distance connections run in many towns and tourist spots in Poland, and provide an extremely cheap and convenient way of getting about locally.

Minibuses are particularly useful in the tourist areas of the Tatra Mountains, where regular services from Zakopane *(see p170)* and Szczawnica *(see p173)* take hikers to beauty spots and trail heads. Minibuses are also well organized in Krakow, where services depart from the main railway station (or nearby) and serve most neighbouring villages, including Wieliczka and Niepołomice *(see pp168–9)*. Tickets, which cost approximately twice the fare of a standard public transport ticket, can be purchased directly from the driver.

Minibuses are also used on long-distance inter-city routes as a faster alternative to coaches. Due to the limited number of seats, minibuses fill up quickly, and it is not always possible to get a seat in the service of your choice. If the minibus is departing from a main bus station, it will be possible to buy tickets in advance – otherwise, it is advisable to arrive early and hope for the best. Minibuses are speedy little vehicles, and they will not suit travellers who are claustrophobic or prone to travel sickness.

DIRECTORY

Arriving by Coach

Eurolines
W eurolines.com

Jordan
Tel 12 421 21 25.
W jordan.pl

Sindbad
Tel 12 429 69 11.
W sindbad.krakow.pl

Coaches

Dworzec Autobusowy w Krakowie (MDA)
Tel 07 03 40 33 40.
W mda.malopolska.pl

PolskiBus
W polskibus.com/en

A typical bus stop in Gdańsk

Travelling by Car

Poland is a big country involving large distances, and roads still vary widely in terms of quality. The number of fast inter-city highways is increasing, and travel times between the major centres are getting shorter. Away from the main highways, however, progress can be slow, with columns of traffic building up on popular routes. Road surfaces in general are improving, although rural routes may be bumpy. Car crime is a worry but can be easily guarded against by parking in secure garages and removing your valuables from the vehicle.

A road leading into the city of Krakow

Arriving by Car

The big cities of western Poland – plus Warsaw and Krakow – are easily reached via Germany thanks to the German Autobahn network and Poland's own stretches of fast motorway. There is also a good fast road from Prague to Katowice and Krakow. If you enter Poland from the south or the east, though, travel is on single-lane roads and progress is slow.

What You Need

Drivers in Poland need to have the following items: a current driving licence, a sticker denoting the country in which the car is registered, an original certificate of insurance, and a red warning triangle in the boot. UK drivers should also affix headlight converters. Drivers from outside the EU are also required to carry

Roads

Poland's main inter-city highways (*autostrady*; denoted by the letter A) provide fast travel along the country's main east–west and north–south corridors, with the city of Łódź at the centre of the network. Not all of the highways are complete, so travel from one major city to another may involve long stretches of highway interspersed with sections of single-lane road. The most complete stretches of highway run from the German border through Wrocław and Katowice to Krakow, and from the German border to Poznań then Warsaw.

Objazd ➡

Signpost indicating traffic diversion

Most other main cross-country routes are classified as expressways (*drogi ekspresowe*; denoted by the letter S); these are largely single-lane affairs. Road surfaces on expressways are good, but traffic can build up. Poland's regional trunk roads (*drogi krajowe*) are numbered from 1 to 94 and labelled red on maps. Regional roads running between major centres can be busy, while those in rural areas are often pleasant and relaxing to drive on. Minor roads are not numbered and are much more unpredictable in terms of quality.

Regulations

The wearing of seat belts is compulsory. Children under the age of 12 are not allowed to travel in the front of the car, and small children must be strapped into special child seats. Headlights must be on, day and night, regardless of the weather conditions.

The national speed limit in built-up areas is 50 km/h (30 mph) between 5am and 11pm, and 60 km/h (35 mph) between 11pm and 5am; on roads it is 90 km/h (55 mph), and on motorways it is 110 km/h (68 mph). Radar speed controls are frequent, and offenders will be given an on-the-spot fine.

The use of mobile phones while driving is banned unless the phone is a hands-free model. The permitted alcohol content in blood is so low in Poland that drinking and driving should be avoided altogether (*see p338*).

Parking

Parking regulations vary from city to city. There is an increasing number of parking garages, especially in or near

Parking meter in Krakow

A breakdown van at a garage in Gdańsk

shopping mall developments just outside city centres.

In central Warsaw there are parking meters in operation, as well as many car parks where you pay a fee to an attendant, although the car park is unguarded.

In the main streets of Gdańsk and Gdynia, coin-operated parking meters have been installed.

Central Wrocław and Poznań have a system of parking cards, which are available from newsagents; the driver circles the date and time of parking and places the card in the windscreen.

In Krakow, most of the Old Town is a no-parking zone for non-residents, although there are usually a limited number of spaces available for hotel guests. Elsewhere in Krakow, a system of parking cards similar to that in place in Wrocław and Poznań applies.

Illegally parked cars are prone to clamping. Details of where to pay the fine and get the clamp removed will be posted on the windscreen.

Petrol

In big cities and on major roads, finding a 24-hour petrol station is not a problem. In addition to selling fuel and car accessories, petrol stations usually have shops. Those outside towns also have bars where travellers can have a coffee or a hot meal.

Drivers planning journeys to rural areas, however, should fill up in advance because most petrol stations in the countryside may close at 6pm or for the weekend.

Breakdown Services

If your car breaks down, the **National Emergency Road Service** will send help to the scene – usually within 1 hour of your call, but quicker if you are near a major urban area. Fees for their services depend on where you are and what the

Warsaw town sign

fault is, so it is recommended that you take out full breakdown insurance. The website www.pomoc-drogowa.pl has contact telephone numbers for car mechanics in each region of the country.

Car Hire

All major international car rental companies – including **Avis**, **Europcar** and **Hertz** – operate in Poland, as well as the Polish firm **Joka**. It is best to book a particular make of car before your arrival. Key conditions are a valid full driving licence and a minimum age of 21 (or 25, depending on the company). Before signing the rental agreement, it is also advisable to check the level of insurance cover provided. Travellers would be wise to take out adequate insurance independently.

Great Drives

Poland is a largely rural country and driving away from the main cities can be a great pleasure. The rolling lake-speckled countryside east of Olsztyn, taking in waterside settlements such as Mikołajki, Giżycko and Węgorzewo, is an ideal introduction to north-eastern Poland *see pp290–91*) – although take note that this area can be busy on summer weekends. A highlight of the southeast of the country is the Bieszczady Mountains Tour *(see pp174–5)*, which takes in bucolic villages and wooded valleys. South of Krakow, the Pieniny mountain trail *(see pp172–3)*, taking in Sczawnica, Krościenko, Czorsztyn and Niedzica, involves castles, subalpine meadows and lakes.

Travelling within Cities

On account of its size, Warsaw is the one city in Poland where exploring everything on foot is not an option. Luckily, the capital has a well-integrated metro, tram, bus and suburban train network. Other Polish cities are compact and easy to walk around, with the occasional tram or bus ride helping you to reach outlying sights. Cycling is a popular way of getting around; facilities for cyclists are improving, and bike hire establishments are more and more widespread. Taxis are widely available and inexpensive.

Green Travel

Polish cities suffer from traffic congestion and a shortage of parking spaces. If possible, refrain from adding to this pressure on the local infrastructure. Electric-powered trams and municipal trains are the cleanest forms of public transport. Krakow, Gdańsk and other Polish cities are increasingly bike-friendly, and local authorities throughout the country are trying to extend the number of cycle lanes in busy areas. In Krakow, the electric-powered *meleks* vehicles available for hire on the Main Market Square provide an emissions-free alternative to hiring a taxi; rickshaw drivers in Łódź provide a similar service.

Walking

Most Polish cities can be easily explored on foot. Warsaw, Krakow, Gdańsk and Poznań boast pedestrianized Old Towns with clearly displayed tourist signage. The streets in most Polish cities are in good order, though visitors might come across the occasional uneven paving stone and crumbling kerb.

Trams and Buses

In most Polish cities, public transport consists of an integrated network of trams and buses. In major conurbations such as Warsaw, Krakow, Katowice and Łódź, trams represent the best way of covering long cross-town distances. The PST in Poznań is a super-fast tram line that speeds its way across the city. Krakow and other cities are investing in similarly fast tram lines. Some of the smaller cities (such as Lublin, Olsztyn and Białystok) do not have trams, and the municipal bus system is much more prominent.

Daytime services usually run from just before 5am until 11pm. Night buses, which run in big cities, operate between 11pm and 5am. Tram and bus stops are clearly marked by signs bearing tram or bus pictograms. Route and timetable information is usually displayed at each stop. Trams always stop at every stop, although you may have to press a button to open the doors. Most municipal buses stop at every stop, although there are some express routes (often marked with a red route number) that stop at key points only.

Metro

The Warsaw metro, the only urban underground rail network in Poland, consists of two lines: Line 1 (north–south) and Line 2 (east–west). The latter is only partially open and will be extended in future. Line 2 is a particularly handy way of getting from the city centre to the Praga district, on the east bank of the river.

The metro is safe, clean and punctual. Entrances are marked by a stylized red M on a yellow background. Stations have lifts for disabled people.

The clean interior of a Warsaw metro station

Tickets

Each city has an integrated ticketing system of its own, in which tickets valid for trams are also valid for buses (and, in the case of Warsaw, the metro too). Although in some cases tickets can be bought from a tram or bus driver, it is far better to buy them in advance. Tickets are available from newspaper kiosks and coin-operated machines placed beside tram stops; in Warsaw, they can also be bought at metro stations. In Warsaw and Krakow, there are ticket machines inside buses and tram cars. The tickets are then validated by punching them in a machine located just inside the entrance of the bus or tram. On the Warsaw metro, tickets should be punched before crossing the yellow line that divides the ticket hall from the platforms. Random checks are carried out by ticket inspectors – plain-clothes officials wearing a conspicuous badge. Passengers travelling without a valid punched ticket are often fined on the spot. Fines are usually

Colourful trams in Krakow

An official taxi waiting for a fare in Gdańsk

several times the price of a normal single fare.

Most cities price their tickets according to a zonal system; tickets for zone one (the city centre) tend to be adequate for most sightseeing visitors. Single-journey tickets cost 4.40zł in Warsaw, less in other cities. In Warsaw, Krakow and some other cities, cheaper single tickets for journeys that only last 15–20 minutes are also available. Most cities offer 24-hour, 2-day and 3-day tickets that offer very good value for money if you plan on using public transport for the majority of your stay. Family tickets, offering a day's travel for two adults and two children, are also available. Children under the age of four and senior citizens over 70 usually travel free of charge.

Taxis

Taxi ranks can be found at railway and bus stations, as well as at the main entrances to pedestrianized zones in city centres. Flagging down taxis on the street is rarely possible, and it's best to go to a rank or order a taxi by phone.

Most taxi journeys are metered, although you may be able to negotiate a fee if you are going a particularly short or long distance.

Private taxis, which do not display a company name and phone number, should be avoided. Similarly, taxi touts in airports or railway stations should be ignored, since their charges may be several times the official rate.

Driving

Driving in city traffic is stressful, and it is wise to use alternative

Veturilo logo

ways of getting around. In addition, it can be difficult to find a parking space in big cities, although hotels sometimes have parking spaces for guests.

Cycling

Polish cities are increasingly bike-friendly, with a growing number of cycle lanes and signed cycle routes in Warsaw, Krakow and many other cities. Green spaces around Krakow and coastal cycle paths near Gdańsk are perfect for easy cycling. In urban zones, cycling on the pavement is permissible in areas where bike lanes do not exist, which means that cyclists don't have to dodge traffic. However, cyclists on pavements should always give way to pedestrians. Bike rental outlets are easy to find in Krakow and are becoming popular in other cities as well. An increasing number of cities have adopted municipal bike rental schemes (including Veturilo in Warsaw and Wawelo in Krakow) in which you pick up and drop off bikes at collection points throughout the city, paying by credit card as you go.

DIRECTORY

Trams and Buses

Krakow
Tel 12 191 50.
W mpk.krakow.pl

Poznań
Tel 61 646 33 44.
W ztm.poznan.pl

Warsaw
Tel 22 19 115.
W ztm.waw.pl

Wrocław
Tel 71 321 72 71.
W komunikacja.iwroclaw.pl

Cycling

Bike Tours and Rental
Wrocław, Rynek 14. Tel 534 100 780. W seewroclaw.pl

Bike Trip
Zwierzyniecka 30, Krakow.
Tel 667 712 054. W biketrip.pl

Kraków Bike Tour
ul. Grodzka 2, Krakow. Tel 12 430 20 34. W krakowbiketour.com

Locoemotion
Pl. Teatralny 5, Wrocław.
Tel 725 762 126.

Maltabike
al. Jana Pawła II, Poznań.
Tel 48 510 316 118.
W maltabike.pl

Rowerownia
ul. Fieldorfa 11/3, Gdańsk.
Tel 58 320 61 69.
W rowerownia.gda.pl

Veturilo
Warsaw.
Tel 22 19 115.
W en.veturilo.waw.pl

Wawelo
Krakow.
Tel 12 290 33 33.
W wawelo.pl

Wygodny Rower
ul. Smolna 10, Warsaw.
Tel 688 498 498.
W wygodnyrower.pl

Visitors on rental bikes in the Old Town, Krakow

General Index